Bruce Russett

The Process of Democratization

A COMPARATIVE STUDY OF 147 STATES, 1980-88

W9-CKJ-316

Tatu Vanhanen

 CRANE RUSSAK

A MEMBER OF THE TAYLOR & FRANCIS GROUP

New York • Bristol, PA. • Washington, D.C. • London

USA	Publishing Office:	Taylor & Francis New York Inc.
		79 Madison Ave., New York, NY 10016-7892
	Sales Office:	Taylor & Francis Inc.
		1900 Frost Road, Bristol, PA 19007-1598
UK		Taylor & Francis Ltd.
		4 John St., London WC1N 2ET

The Process of Democratization:
A Comparative Study of 147 States, 1980–88

First published 1990
Printed in the United States of America

Library of Congress Cataloging in Publication Data

Vanhanen, Tatu.
    The process of democratization: a comparative study of 147
states, 1980–88/Tatu Vanhanen.
        p.   cm.
    Includes bibliographical references.
    ISBN 0-8448-1640-X.—ISBN 0-8448-1641-8 (pbk.)
    1. Democracy—History—20th century.   2. Comparative government.
I. Title.
JC421.V28   1990
321.8′09′048--dc20
                                                          89-71304
                                                              CIP

To Anni,
Rauno and Seija,
Matti and Merja, and
Tuomo and Laura

Contents

v

Pacific
Summary

Preface

This study represents the latest phase in my long quest to find a theoretical explanation for the variation of political systems from the perspective of democratization. I have long wanted to discover why some of the 147 states covered by this comparative study are democracies, and why many others have remained more or less autocratically ruled. The central idea of this study is that we should be able to explain both the existence and the lack of democracy by the same explanatory principles, because human nature is a constant and because similar behavioral predispositions can be assumed to be shared by all human populations. The explanatory principles of my theory of democratization are based on an evolutionary interpretation of politics derived from the Darwinian theory of natural selection. The theory of democratization formulated in this study makes it possible to present research hypotheses on democratization and to test them by empirical evidence, as well as to make predictions on the prospects of democracy in single countries. By this study I have tried to show that the process of democratization follows similar basic rules in all countries of the world and that knowledge of these rules provides a solid basis for formulating political and social strategies of democratization.

I use this opportunity to thank people and institutions that have helped me to carry out this research work during the last five years. My intellectual debts to many scholars can be seen from references, but I want to mention S.M. Lipset in particular, whose study (1960) gave me the idea to relate the level of democratization to the variation of social conditions. My thanks are due to Juan J. Linz, whom I met at Yale University in 1986 and who generously informed me of their research project on *Democracy in Developing Countries,* to Jean Blondel, Dirk Berg-Schlosser, Mattei Dogan, Axel Hadenius, Erik N. Komarov, Claucio Ary Dillon Soares, Karol E. Soltan, and other colleagues who read some drafts of my manuscript or commented on my papers and presentations on this study at the IPSA World Congress in 1985 and in 1988, at the ECPR Joint Sessions of Workshops in 1987, and in seminars at Northern Illinois University (DeKalb) in 1986, at the

European University Institute (Florence) and the University of Florence in 1988, and at the University of Maryland, College Park, in 1989. I am grateful to Edward O. Wilson for the encouragement to apply sociobiological argumentation to the study of politics and to the colleagues of the European Sociobiological Society and the Association for Politics and the Life Sciences, particularly to Vincent S.E. Falger, Heiner Flohr, Roger D. Masters, Albert Somit, and Thomas Wiegele, with whom I have had opportunities to discuss the problems of this study or the use of evolutionary argumentation in the study of politics. I also thank John B. Bruce, Carol Dickerman, and William Thiesenhusen, who commented on my data on Family Farms at the Land Tenure Center, University of Wisconsin, in 1986 and gave me valuable source material, and my students at the universities of Tampere and Helsinki for their responses and comments on my lectures on democratization. Although many people have contributed greatly to this work, I alone am responsible for errors and mistakes.

I also want to express my gratitude to the Academy of Finland for research grants and scholarships in 1985–86 and 1989 and for a travel grant in 1987, the European University Institute (Florence) for a travel grant in 1988, the University of Tampere for a six-month research period in 1989, and the University of Maryland, College Park, for a comfortable reasearch place during the spring term 1989.

My special thanks are due to Dalton A. West (United States Global Strategy Council, Washington, D.C.), who so kindly helped me to find a publisher for this work, editor Ralph H. Salmi of Taylor & Francis for his great help to get this study published, and the copyeditor who copyedited the manuscript. And, finally, I thank Leila Ojanen, University of Tampere, for checking the English of my manuscript.

Tampere, 1989   Tatu Vanhanen

1
INTRODUCTION

> What we need to know is whether and under
> what conditions transformation toward de-
> mocracy is possible today in those countries
> which suffer from authoritarian rule.
>
> *Adam Przeworsky, 1986*

The aim of this comparative study of political systems is to describe and explain the process of democratization in the 1980s. The research questions I try to answer concern the causes of democratization. Why is it so that the level of democratization varies greatly from country to country? Are there any common explanations for democratization, or are the causal factors different and unique in each case? And what are the causes of democratization? Why have some countries democratized and some others not? It is true that political systems differ from each other in many other respects, too, but I focus attention on this aspect of variation because I think that the degree of democratization is a very important feature of political systems. Contemporary political systems vary from autocracies to relatively democratic systems, but the number of democracies has continually increased since the last century. I try to detect causal factors behind this variation of political systems and the trend of democratization.

First, I describe the state of democracy in the 1980s by measuring the variation of political systems from the perspective of democratization. The measurement is based on empirical indicators that are assumed to measure some crucial characteristics of political systems from the aspect of democratization. I do not try to compare all aspects of political systems or even all aspects of democracy. Comparison is limited to particular characteristics that I assume to indicate crucial dimensions of democracy. As Karl R. Popper remarks, it is impossible to study the whole society. We can study only some selected characteristics: "If we wish to study a thing, we are bound to select certain aspects of it. It is not possible for us to observe or to describe a whole piece of the world, or a whole piece of nature; in fact, not even the smallest whole piece may be so described, since all description is necessarily selective" (Popper 1984, 77–79). It is for others to evaluate whether the characteristics of political systems measured in this study represent crucial aspects of democracy or not. I use the same indicators of democratization to all 147 countries of the world covered by this study. This approach is based on the idea that it would not be scientifically justified to use different criteria for different countries because the objects of this study, human beings, belong to the same species and are assumed to be approximately the same everywhere with the same strivings and dreams.

Second, I try to explain why the level of democratization varies so greatly from country to country. The variation of the operationally defined indicators of democratization forms the *explicandum,* the known state of affairs, which is in need of explanation (cf. Popper 1983, 162–70). The problem is: Why do political systems vary so greatly from country to country? Do they vary randomly or systematically, and if they vary systematically, which are the factors related to their variation, and are those relationships causal ones?

Political philosophers and social scientists have discussed these questions for a long time; they have presented various explanatory theories, investigated, empirically, the variation of the forms of government or of political systems, and tried to explain that variation. This study continues the long tradition of comparative study of political systems, which can be traced to Herodotus' *Histories* and particularly to Aristotle, who already compared the constitutions of the Greek city-states and discussed the social conditions favorable or unfavorable for various forms of government. Many of his observations and hypotheses are still relevant. Of the later classical comparative studies of political systems, I would particularly like to mention Machiavelli's *Prince* (1513), James Harrington's *Oceana* (1656), Montesquieu's *De l'Esprit des Lois* (1748), Alexis de Tocqueville's *Democracy in America* (1835–40), and James Bryce's *Modern Democracies* (1921). After World War II the number of comparative studies of political systems increased greatly. Many hypotheses have been formulated to explain the variation of political systems and the conditions of democracy, and some of these hypotheses have been tested by empirical data. I do not try to review the relevant research literature on this field (for reviews, see, for example, Blondel 1969, 43–58; Pennock 1979, 206–259; Dogan and Pelassy 1984; Diamond et al. 1988), but I refer to some contemporary books which I have found especially useful and inspiring in connection with my own work. They include Seymour Martin Lipset, *Political Man* (1960, 1983), Gabriel A. Almond and James S. Coleman, *The Politics of the Developing Areas* (1960), Bruce M. Russett et al. *World Handbook of Political and Social Indicators*

(1964), W. Arthur Lewis, *Politics in West Africa* (1965), Robert A. Dahl, *Polyarchy* (1971), Charles E. Lindblom, *Politics and Markets* (1977), Arend Lijphart, *Democracy in Plural Societies* (1977) and *Democracies* (1984), Larry Diamond, Juan J. Linz, and S.M. Lipset, *Democracy in Developing Countries* (1988–89), and Raymond D. Gastil, *Freedom in the World. Political Rights and Civil Liberties 1987–1988* (1989).

Adam Przeworski (1986) says that studies of regime transformations tend to fall into two types: "Some are macro-oriented, focus on objective conditions, and speak in the language of determination. Others tend to concentrate on political actors and their strategies, to emphasize interests and perceptions, and to formulate problems in terms of possibilities and choices." The studies of the first type "see political transformations as determined, and seek to discover the patterns of determination by inductive generalizations." The studies of the second type "tend to emphasize the strategic behavior of political actors embedded in concrete historical situations." My study on democratization falls into the first type, but with two reservations. First, my method is not based on "inductive generalizations." Second, I discuss the significance of political factors and the role of "the strategic behavior of political actors" at the end of my study, although I assume that the major part of the variation of democratization can be explained by objective environmental factors. The central purpose of this study is to show that it can be done.

My attempt to explain the variation of political systems and democratization is based on the assumption that political structures are mechanisms or organs used in the political struggle for scarce resources and that, consequently, they have evolved in this struggle and become adapted to varying environmental conditions. In other words, I try to apply the principles of the Darwinian theory of evolution by natural selection to the study of political systems. In this point my approach differs from all previous studies of democratization. This theoretical starting point implies that political systems are not assumed to vary at random. It seems more reasonable to assume that they are continually adapted to serve the interests of the most powerful competitors. Human desire to get power can be assumed to be constant (cf. Hobbes 1962), but it depends on changeable environmental conditions that individuals and groups are capable of getting power and using political institutions for their advantage. Therefore, we have to seek explanations for the variation of political systems in environmental conditions. But in what kind of conditions? I assume that when circumstances are such that important power resources are widely distributed among competing groups, it is reasonable to expect the emergence of political structures reflecting the sharing of power among the many, whereas the concentration of those resources can be expected to lead to the concentration of political power. Constant human desire to get power makes this relationship regular and even inevitable. Consequently, my purpose is to detect social and other environmental factors that indicate the distribution of some important power resources and then to investigate whether they are related to the political variables of this study measuring the level of democratization in the hypothesized way. The appearance of hypothesized systematic relationships would provide an explanation for the variation of political systems from the perspective of democratization. It would also help to deliniate social structures and conditions that further or hinder the democratization of political systems. The final aim of my study is to produce this kind of knowledge.

I think that comparison is the best method to get such knowledge. Dogan and Pelassy (1984, 13) say that "in domains where experimentation cannot be applied, comparison is synonymous with an intellectual approach searching to make an inventory of similarities and differences between two or more situations; it is also the only way of collecting information and data in sufficient number to approximate a scientific approach." This argumentation leads to the conclusion that if we want to explain global variation of political systems, we should compare all countries of the world. Only in that way is it possible to differentiate unique and local phenomena and factors from more general relationships. Dogan and Pelassy note, "The observer who studies just one country could interpret as normal what in fact appears to the comparativist as abnormal" (Dogan and Pelassy 1984, 8). The comparison of many countries or all countries, if possible, would help to avoid this danger.

It is true that in many comparative studies the number of cases has been limited, for one reason or other. It has been argued that it would not be sensible to compare all the countries of the world for the reason that they differ too much from each other, or that they do not have enough similarities to make comparison possible. Of course, the validity of these arguments depends on the object of comparison. It is clear that if compared countries differ from each other in all points, it would be impossible to compare them, for comparison presupposes some common characteristics and criteria that apply to all of them. The supporters of limited comparison have particularly referred to social, cultural, developmental, ideological, and historical differences among countries and argued that it might be better to limit comparisons to homogeneous groups of countries. In other words, their approach implies that the variation of political systems could be best explained by different factors in different groups of countries. In the extreme case such an approach would lead to the conclusion that because every country is unique, we cannot find universal explanations and that each political system should be and can be explained only by its own terms (for various strategies of comparative study and the choice of countries, see Bryce 1921, 3–22; Almond 1960, 3–25, 58–64; Macridis 1963, 43–51; Rustow 1963, 57–63;

Holt and Turner 1970, 1–20; Riggs 1970, 73–121; Lijphart 1971, 1975; Dogan and Pelassy 1984; Grawitz and Leca 1985, 20–25).

My argument is that, at the global level, all countries are comparable with each other from the aspect of democratization because human nature cannot be expected to vary much from one country to another. It forms the constant, the similarity between countries, which makes it sensible to compare their differences in some other respects. Racial, cultural, ideological, developmental, and historical dissimilarities among countries may be great, but they cannot eradicate the similarity of human nature on which regular patterns in politics are based. Consequently, it seems to me that the best strategy would be to compare practically all the independent countries of the world.

The study covers 147 contemporary independent countries. Only the smallest states, whose population in 1980 was under 200,000 inhabitants, are excluded. Also, the countries that achieved independence later than in 1980 are excluded. The names of countries are given in the Appendices.

2

DEMOCRATIZATION IN 1980–88

As the term "democracy" is used in many and often contradictory meanings, it is first necessary to review various interpretations of democracy and to make clear what characteristics of political systems the term is used to describe in this study. After that I can formulate operational variables to describe and measure the level of democratization. The results of these measurements provide the basis of classifying the 147 countries of this work into democracies and nondemocracies along the continuum of democracy-autocracy. The same criteria are applied to all countries. In this way we get a panoramic picture on the state of democracy in the world in the 1980s.

WHAT IS DEMOCRACY?

In the Western world, it has been customary to classify forms of government into monarchies, oligarchies, and democracies since the time of Herodotus, who identified democracy with equality, the principle of majority rule, and political responsibility (Pennock 1979, 3; Herodotus 1984, 238–240; Kitromilides 1985, 15). This classical classification of political systems from the rule of the one to the rule of the many (cf. Aristotle 1961, 114–15, 160–162) refers to one crucial aspect of democracy; the sharing of power among the many. The rule of the one and the rule of the many represent the extreme ends of the continuum from autocracy to democracy. Democracy has always been connected with the rule of the people, as Herodotus noted. In fact, the characteristics of democracy, to which Herodotus referred, have ever since been repeated in many definitions of democracy, although the operational interpretations of those characteristics have often differed. For example, in ancient Athens, "the many" included only the free male citizens, not women, slaves, and noncitizens, who together formed the majority of the adult population (see Aristotle 1983, 183–85), whereas in contemporary definitions

6

of democracy "the many" or "the people" usually includes practically the whole adult population (see, for example, Pennock 1979, 7). Interpretations of "equality" and "responsibility" have differed from each other even more, and the contemporary perceptions of democracy differ most sharply from each other in these very points. Although the ideals of democracy have remained more or less similar over centuries, and although even now the Western and Marxist-Leninist ideals of democracy have similarities, the same terms are interpreted quite differently, and procedural definitions of democracy often contradict each other (see, for example, Plamenatz 1978, 34–51, 203–12; Pennock 1979, 3–15). The fact is that the word "democracy" has been used to describe very different and even contradictory states of affairs. Because "democracy" is used as the central concept in this study, it is necessary to define the term operationally.

Let us first examine some previous definitions of democracy. By the term "democracy" Aristotle meant "a constitution in which the free-born and poor control the government—being at the same time a majority" (Aristotle 1961, 164). His point was that democracy is not only the government of the many, but also the government of the poor. The rich and the poor form the opposite classes, and both of them try to form constitutions to suit their own interests. Democracy serves the interest of the poor, and oligarchy the interest of the rich. Aristotle was, however, not fully consistent in his insistence that democracy is only the government of the poor. He differentiated several varieties of democracy, and the first of them is the variety in which "the law declares equality to mean that the poor are to count no more than the rich; neither is to be sovereign, and both are to be on a level" (Aristotle 1961, 167). According to another translation, "the most pure democracy is that which is so called principally from that equality which prevails in it: for this is what the law in that state directs; that the poor shall be in no greater subjection than the rich; nor that the supreme power shall be lodged with either of these, but that both shall share it" (Aristotle 1952, 115). This Aristotle's variety of democracy resembles contemporary Western definitions because it connects democracy with the sharing of power among all important sections of the population.

James Bryce refers to Herodotus and says that he uses the word "in its old and strict sense, as denoting a government in which the will of the majority of qualified citizens rules, taking the qualified citizens to constitute the great bulk of the inhabitants, say, roughly, at least three-fourths, so that the physical force of the citizens coincides (broadly speaking) with their voting power." His definition of democracy is clearly operational. Bryce (1921, 25–26) says that it is the facts that matter, not the name; democracy is used to describe a political system where "the will of the whole people prevails in all important matters."

Karl R. Popper also uses a descriptive or procedural definition of democracy. He distinguishes two main types of government: "The first type consists of governments of which we can get rid without bloodshed—for example, by way of general elections," whereas the second type "consists of governments which the ruled cannot get rid of except by way of a successful revolution—that is to say, in most cases, not at all." Popper reserves the term "democracy"as "a short-hand label for a government of the first type, and the term 'tyranny' or 'dictatorship' for the second." He emphasizes that his argument does not depend on the choice of labels; if somebody would reverse the useage of these terms, he would simply say that "I am in favor of what he calls 'tyranny', and object to what he calls 'democracy'" (Popper 1977 Vol. 1, 124). In another connection Popper stresses that democracy cannot be fully characterized as the rule of the majority because a majority might rule in a tyrannical way. In a democracy, "the powers of the rulers must be limited" (Popper 1977 Vol. 2, 160–61). This resembles Aristotle's remark on the first variety of democracy in which the supreme power is possessed neither by the rich nor the poor alone; it is shared by them.

Robert A. Dahl presents only a minimal definition of democracy, according to which democracy concerns "processes by which ordinary citizens exert a relatively high degree of control over leaders." Then he differentiates three varieties of democratic theory: Madisonian democracy, populist democracy, and polyarchal democracy. The first two are concerned with the ideals of democracy. The Madisonian theory seeks a compromise between the power of majorities and the power of minorities by establishing constitutional restraints upon majority action. The populist theory stresses popular sovereignty and political equality as the ideals of democracy, whereas the polyarchal theory focuses primarily on the social prerequisites for a democratic order (Dahl 1968). In a later study Dahl reformulated his theory of polyarchy. He reserves the term "democracy" for a political system "one of the characteristics of which is the quality of being completely or almost completely responsive to all its citizens." He thinks that in the real world it is impossible for any system to achieve the ideal of democracy, but he defines two dimensions of democratization that can be empirically observed and used as the criteria in evaluating to what degree any particular political system has approached the ideal of democracy. The dimensions are: (1) public contestation, or political competition, which includes the right to oppose, and (2) the right to participate, or inclusiveness. A regime may be located anywhere in the space bounded by the two dimensions. A regime which is characterized by a high degree of public contestation and participation approaches the ideals of democracy. Such systems Dahl calls polyarchies. They are relatively (but incompletely) democratized regimes (Dahl 1971, 1–9; See also Dahl 1982). Dahl's theoretical classification of regimes by the two dimensions of democratization is ingenious, and it offers opportunities to formulate operational measures of democratization.

S.M. Lipset (1960, 45) defines democracy "as a political system which supplies regular constitutional opportunities for changing the governing officials, and a social mechanism which permits the largest possible part of the population to influence major decisions by choosing among contenders for political office." He remarks that his definition is abstracted largely from the works of Joseph Schumpeter and Max Weber. Lipset's definition is basically descriptive, but its criteria are not easily operationalized. Therefore he had to use his own estimates when he classified political systems into democracies and dictatorships. His main criteria refer to free political competition and a high level of participation. These are the two dimensions of democracy that are included in nearly all contemporary Western definitions of democracy. Free elections are presented as the major mechanism of democratic process.

Giovanni Sartori defines democracy by making clear what it is not. Democracy is nonautocracy. It is the opposite of autocracy: "Democracy is a system in which no one can choose himself, no one can invest himself with the power to rule and, therefore, no one can arrogate to himself unconditional and unlimited power" (Sartori 1987, 206; cf. Sartori 1969). This is also a descriptive definition of democracy, but its terms are not easily operationalized.

John Plamenatz uses responsibility as the key idea of democracy. He says: "A political system is democratic if it operates in such a way as to ensure that makers of law and policy are responsible to the people." This presupposes that "citizens are free to criticize their rulers and to come together to make demands on them and to win support for the policies they favour and the beliefs they hold; and where the supreme makers of law and policy are elected to their offices at free and periodic elections." He notes that the criteria for determining whether these conditions hold are not easily defined (Plamenatz 1978, 69–70, 184–188). Surely it is so, but in principle they are empirically measurable characteristics of political systems.

J. Roland Pennock (1979, 3–15) distinguishes ideal and procedural or operational definitions of democracy and prefers a procedural definition, according to which a democracy is rule by the people where "the people" includes all adult citizens and "rule" means that "public policies are determined either directly by vote of the electorate or indirectly by officials freely elected at reasonably frequent intervals and by a process in which each voter who chooses to vote counts equally and in which a plurality is determinative." Jeane J. Kirkpatrick makes the same kind of distinction between the normative and descriptive approaches to define democracy. She prefers the descriptive approach, which uses the word "democracy" as a symbol "for specific patterns of behavior of persons in political context." The patterns of behavior that she connects with democracy concern "electoral systems, legislative processes, interest groups, administrative behavior, voting behavior, political parties, and related institutional practices." She emphasizes the significance of elections as the litmus test of democracy. When power holders "are chosen by democratic elections, the resulting government is termed 'democratic' and the whole is called 'democracy' by political scientists and others employing an empirical approach to defining these terms" (Kirkpatrick 1981; see also Huntington 1984, 99–195).

By democracy Larry Diamond, S.M. Lipset, and Juan J. Linz mean a political system that meets three essential conditions: meaningful and extensive competition among individuals and organized groups, a highly inclusive level of political participation in the selection of leaders and policies, and a level of civil and political liberties sufficient to insure the integrity of political competition and participation (Diamond et al. 1986, 3; see also Diamond et al. 1988a Vol. 2, XVI).

Leonardo Morlino's definition provides a very good summary of the Western concept of democracy. By democracy he means "a set of institutions and rules that allow competition and participation for all citizens considered as equals. Empirically, such a political arrangement is characterized by free, fair, and recurring elections; male and female universal suffrage; multiple organizations of interests; different and alternative sources of information; and elections to fill the most relevant offices" (Morlino 1986, 54).

Jean Baechler (1985, 14–21) defines democracy slightly differently. He says that democracy is characterized by the fact that all power is always rooted in the citizens. He does not demand that citizens should form the majority in all varieties of democracy, although in a proper democracy the group of citizens covers all adult members of the society. His concept of democracy is also intended to apply to primitive societies of the last 40,000 years. (For other definitions of democracy, see Lavau 1985, 29–71).

The Marxist-Leninist concept of democracy differs drastically from Western definitions reviewed above, although by democracy Marxists also mean the rule of the people. Soviet scholars say that democracy implies the rule of the majority over the minority and the equality of all citizens, but the Marxist-Leninist operational definitions of these terms are different, or were before the present movement of democratization. To them, only one majority has been acceptable: the majority formed by the working class and represented by the Communist party. And "the equality of all citizens" has not included, for example, equality to establish political parties and interest organizations that might oppose the Communist party. They claim that "bourgeois democracy has always been inconsistent, imperfect, limited and internally contradictory owing in the last resort to the prevalence of capitalist production relations and the private ownership of the means of production." On the other hand, the "socialist production relations and the public ownership of the means of production are the substance of socialist democracy.

After coming to power, the working class establishes the dictatorship of the proletariat, which is the broadest and truest form of democracy for all the working people" (Topornin and Machulsky 1974, 39–42; see also Sahnazarov 1974; Chekharin, 1977, 28–31; *Marxilais-leniniläinen valtio- ja oikeusoppi* 1980, 108–112).

The Chinese interpretation of Socialist democracy is similar. Wei Jingsheng said about Socialist democracy in 1979: "Socialist democratic rights are only given to the people and not to counterrevolutionaries in our socialist state, people have the freedom to criticize the government, but we definitely will not give counterrevolutionaries freedom to overthrow the government of the dictatorship of the proletariat and the socialist system" (quatation in Bedeski 1985, 4).

Definitions of democracy really vary, and, in the contemporary world, the greatest difference has been between the Western and Marxist-Leninist definitions. But in this study, briefly stated, *by democracy I mean a political system in which ideologically and socially different groups are legally entitled to compete for political power and in which institutional power holders are elected by the people and are responsible to the people.* This kind of descriptive definition is based on the traditional Western perception of democracy.

HOW TO MEASURE DEMOCRATIZATION?

My definition of democracy in the preceeding section, although descriptive, is not enough for the purposes of this study. The comparison of political systems from the aspect of democratization presupposes that we are able to measure the variation of democratization. A more limited operational definition of democracy is needed for this purpose, for it is not possible to measure and compare all relevant aspects of political systems. It is necessary to limit the measurement and comparison to some particular characteristics that are empirically measurable and comparable from one country to another and that can be assumed to indicate some crucial characteristics of political systems from the perspective of democratization. How to measure the level of democratization?

Various Measures of Democracy

Many contemporary researchers have formulated operational indicators of democratization and used them in their comparative studies, but their indicators differ considerably from each other. The measures of democracy used in contemporary empirical studies seem to be much more diversified than the Western definitions of democracy. The fact is that researchers have not yet achieved consensus on measures of democracy. Unfortunately we do not yet have any "meter" as the unit of democracy. Therefore, I first review some measures of democracy used in contemporary studies and evaluate their suitability for this study. Then I formulate and describe the operational indicators that are used to measure the level and variation of democratization in this work.

Let us start with Russell Fitzgibbon, who measured the attainment of democracy in Latin American countries by a technique based on the evaluations of experts. He formulated 15 criteria of democratic achievement and asked experts to rate each country according to these criteria using a five-point scale. The first poll of U.S. observers was carried out in 1945. Since then it has been repeated at five-year intervals (see Fitzgibbon 1951, 1956; Fitzgibbon and Johnson 1961; Johnson 1982). The Fitzgibbon-Johnson Image Index provides interesting rank orderings, and the same criteria are applied to all countries, but their technique is too much based on subjective evaluations. Besides, it would be difficult to find panelists who are experts in all 147 countries of this study.

S.M. Lipset (1959, 1960, 47–49) used a dichotomous classification into democracies and dictatorships, but he thought that it would be plausible to use different criteria of democracy in different political culture areas. He used his own judgment to decide whether a particular country fulfilled the criteria of democracy or not. Lipset's method is not adaptable here because I think that the criteria of democracy should be the same for all countries and it would be better to base measurements on quantitative data than to use subjective evaluations. James S. Coleman (1964, 532–38), following Lipset's example, resorted to his own judgments in classifying 75 developing countries into three categories according to the degree of competitiveness.

Phillips Cutright (1963) improved the measurement technique of democracy significantly by constructing an index of political development, which is a continuous variable. Each country could get from zero to 63 points over the 21-year period of his study on the basis of the characteristics of its legislative and executive branches of government. However, his index seems unnecessarily complicated. Besides, it does not take the level of electoral participation into account.

Several other indexes and indicators of democracy were developed in the 1960s. Deane E. Neubauer (1967) devised an index of democratic development, based on operationally defined variables measuring the percentage of the adult population eligible to vote, "equality of representation," "information equality," and "competition." John D. May (1973, 9–10) complained that Neubauer's index "seems idiosyncratic in conception and results." Martin C. Needler thought it better to use simple noncomposite variables to measure political development in Latin America. He used the years of constitutional government to measure the degree of constitutionality and the percentage of the population voting in general elections around 1960 to measure the degree of participation. Together they were assumed to measure two aspects of political development (Needler 1967). I agree with Needler's way to measure the level of political participation, but his constitutionality index is less appropriate to indicate the level of democratization. Another index of national political development, comprising five dimensions (executive functioning, legislative functioning, party organization, power diversification, and citizen influence) was constructed by Marvin E. Olsen. Each dimension was operationalized with an index based on empirical variables, but in most points he had to resort to subjective judgments (see Olsen 1968). Arthur K. Smith (1969) formulated a very complicated index of the degree of democracy, combining Cutright's index and another interval scale constructed from 19 scales given by Banks and Textor (1963) in their book, *A Cross-Polity Survey*. Each of these 19 ordinal scales was assumed to measure a particular element of democracy (Smith 1969). Smith's index of degree of democracy seems too complicated and too much weighted by subjective evaluations (see also Pride 1970; Winham 1970; Kim 1971; May 1973).

William Flanigan and Edwin Fogelman (1971) formulated an index of democratization based on a combination of four basic characteristics of a democratic political system (electoral or parliamentary succession, political competition, popular electoral participation, and absence of suppression). They devised various measures for each of these characteristics and combined them into a general index of democratization. Arthur S. Banks used eight variables—coups d'etat, major constitutional changes, cabinet changes, changes in effective executive, effective executive (selection), legislature effectiveness, legislative selection, and legislative elections—to measure various aspects of democratic performance and combined them into an index (Banks 1972; see also Banks 1970). These indexes seem to include too many variables, and too many subjective evaluations are needed.

Robert A. Dahl presented the idea that democratization has two important dimensions: public contestation and the right to participate, but he did not devise empirical indicators to measure those dimensions. His associates Richard Norling and Mary Frase Williams (see Dahl 1971, 231–45) attempted to classify 114 countries according to Dahl's two dimensions of democratization, i.e., according to eligibility to participate in elections and degree of opportunities for public contestation, but the result was not fully satisfactory. Their scale of opportunities for oppositions, particularly, is very complicated. Dahl said of their classifications that "many of the variables on which rankings are based necessarily require decisions based on judgments rather than 'hard' data" (Dahl 1971, 1–9, 231–45). Charles S. Perry (1980) following the examples of Dahl, Norling, and Williams, constructed another scale of contestation, but it is also based on judgmental data.

Robert A. Jackman designed another measure of democratic performance. It stresses electoral participartion, political competition, and access to information, and is the sum of four components. The first is the number of adults voting as a proportion of the total voting age population, but the other three components are principally based on judgments (Jackman 1974; cf. Rubinson and Quinlan 1977). Philip Coulter defined the term "liberal democracy" in terms of three separate but related continua—political competitiveness, mass political participation, and public liberties. He measured political competitiveness by Cutright's index. Participation was measured by the percentage of the voting age population that voted in national elections. Public liberties were measured by four criteria developed by Banks and Textor (Coulter 1975). I think that his measurement technique is too much dependent on subjective judgments.

Christopher Hewitt ranked non-Communist industrial societies by the years of full democracy, for which he used three criteria: (1) the executive must be elected, or must be responsible to an elected assembly, (2) there should be universal manhood suffrage, and (3) elections should be "fair," as indicated by the presence of a secret ballot. These three characteristics are good criteria of full democracy, but unfortunately they do not make it possible to measure the variation in the degree of democratization (Hewitt 1977).

Kenneth A. Bollen limited the criteria of democracy to two dimensions: popular sovereignty and political liberties. His index of political democracy includes six components. Three of them (fairness of elections, effective executive selection, and legislative selection) are measures of popular sovereignty, and three others (freedom of the press, freedom of group opposition, and government sanctions) are measures of political liberties. Data on these variables are partly quantitative and partly qualitative. It seems that his index is unnecessarily complex and infested by the necessity to use subjective evaluations. Besides, he left out the dimension of popular participation on the ground that "the percentage of the population voting in an election may reflect factors other than the extent of political democracy" (Bollen 1979; see also Bollen 1980, 1983; Bollen and Grandjean 1981).

Dirk Berg-Schlosser has examined the conditions of democracy in a group of democratic and nearly democratic Third World countries. Following Dahl's definition of polyarchy, Berg-Schlosser selected such Third World countries as seemed basically open and pluralist, including "semi-competitive" and "near-polyarchic" systems (Berg-Schlosser 1985, 1987). Such a dichotomous method, of course, does not make it possible to measure the variation of the level of democratization.

Raymond D. Gastil has rated countries in accordance with political rights and civil liberties in his Comparative Survey of Freedom since 1972. He equalizes democracy with internal political freedom, which, as defined in the Survey of Freedom, requires the existence of both political rights and civil liberties. Consequently, the survey uses separate scales for political rights and civil liberties. Each scale is divided into seven points, with one (1) the highest rating on each scale and seven (7) the lowest. The purpose of Gastil's Comparative Survey has been to give a general picture of the state of political and civil freedoms in the world. On the basis of his ratings, he has classified countries as free, partly free, and not free. Generally, states rated (1) and (2) are "free"; those at (3), (4), and (5) are "partly free"; and those at (6) and (7) "not free." According to his interpretation, the list of democracies is made up of countries given the summary status "free" (Gastil 1985, 1988). Gastil's ratings give a general picture of the level of democracy in the world, but this kind of operationalization was not appropriate for this study, because his ratings are too much based on subjective assessments. However, Gastil's ratings could be used to check my measures of democratization as his are available from the years 1980–87 and because they cover all the 147 states of my study. Gastil's scores have been used in some comparative studies to measure the level of democratization. Jacobus Letterie, and Rob A.G. van Puijenbroek, for example, constructed their democracy scale for 1984 by combining Gastil's scores on political rights and civil liberties (Letterie and Puijenbroek 1987).

Ton Bertrand and Rob A.G. van Puijenbroek attempted to measure two aspects of democracy—freedom and equality. In terms of liberties, they call a political system democratic when there exist: (1) complete freedom of the press, (2) constitutional status of regime, (3) autonomous groups free to enter politics and able to oppose, (4) effective horizontal power distribution, (5) no party ban, no parties excluded, multiparty systems, and (6) competitive and free elections. In terms of power distribution, their criteria of democracy include: (7) significant interest articulation by associational groups, (8) limited articulation by institutional groups, (9) negligible articulation by nonassociational groups, (10) very infrequent articulation by anomic groups, and (11) neutral or apolitical role of the military (Bertrand and Puijenbroek 1987). The disadvantage of this method is that it is difficult to find relevant data on indicators and that most available data are based on judgments. Besides, it seems that their list of criteria is too long and that it is difficult to estimate the relative importance of various indicators (see also Letterie and Bertrand 1982).

Larry Diamond, S.M. Lipset, and Juan J. Linz have not defined any common quantitative measures for the three characteristics of democracy (competition, political participation, and civil and political rights) in their research project on *Democracy in Developing Countries,* but, on the basis of rich descriptive data, they classified the 27 Asian, African, and Latin American countries of their study, by democraticness, into five categories: democratic, semidemocratic, hegemonic party systems, authoritarian situations with strong democratic pressures, and authoritarian situations with weak democratic pressures (Diamond et al. 1986). Such a classification serves the purposes of their comparative study, but the method is not suitable for this study because a continuous variable based on quantitative data is needed.

Michael Coppedge and Wolfgang Reinicke have made a new attempt to operationalize Dahl's two dimensions of democratization. They constructed a scale of polyarchy composed of five variables and 18 categories intended to measure eight "institutional guarantees" of inclusion and public contestation. However, they discarded the variable measuring the "right to vote," because a frequency cross-tabulation of the measurements on the two dimensions led them "to question the usefulness of inclusiveness as a criterion for polyarchy." So their final scale of polyarchy is unidimensional and identical to the scale of public contestation (Coppedge and Reinicke 1988). It appears that this scale of polyarchy is also too much based on subjective evaluations, but it provides another point of comparison for my measures of democratization because it covers all the 147 countries of this study, although only for 1985.

The above review shows that researchers have not achieved any consensus on the operational indicators of democratization. The diversity of measurement methods and operational indicators may be partly due to the fact that perceptions of democracy vary, but probably even more to the fact that the problems of democracy have been studied from different perspectives in these studies. In some studies it has been enough to classify countries into two to five categories (Lipset, Coleman, Hewitt, Berg-Schlosser, and Diamond, Lipset, and Linz) from the perspective of democracy, whereas in some other cases researchers have attempted to measure democracy by interval level variables (Cutright, Neubauer, Needler, Olsen, Smith, Flanigan and Fogelman, Banks, Coulter, Bollen, Letterie, Bertrand, and Puijenbroek) or by a Guttman scale (Coppedge and Reinicke). However, the object of measurement has not always been exactly the degree of democracy or democratization. In some studies the object of measurement was "democratic achievement" (Fitzgibbon and Johnson), "degree of competitiveness" (Coleman), "political development" (Cutright, Needler, Olsen), "democratic development" (Neubauer), "democratic performance" (Banks, Jackman), "scale of contestation" (Perry), "liberal democracy" (Coulter), "freedom" (Gastil), "freedom and equality" (Bertrand and Puijenbroek), or "polyarchy" (Coppedge and Reinicke). This variation has probably affected the selection of operational indicators. Besides, the number of indicators varies greatly from two or three to about 20, and the nature of empirical data varies, too. Some indicators are based on quantitative data, others are wholly or partly judgmental, based on subjective evaluations and ratings. Some indicators are intended only to a particular group of countries, some others are assumed to apply to all countries.

Measures of Democratization in this Study

None of the measures of democracy reviewed above is suitable for the purposes of this comparative study. Some are too complicated, with too many indicators, which makes the gathering of empirical data from all countries of the world extremely difficult and increases the need of estimates. In nearly all of them the most important fault is that they are too much based on subjective evaluations. Besides, it is difficult to agree on the relative importance of various indicators used in these measures. But then again, taken together, they probably include all the aspects of democratization that are measurable and on which a more satisfactory measure of democracy could be constructed. I wanted to construct a measure of democratization based on a few quantitative indicators, which can be applied to all contemporary countries and which takes into account the most important dimensions of democracy. How to construct such a measure of democratization?

It seems that Dahl's (1971) two theoretical dimensions of democratization—public contestation and the right to participate—refer to the most important characteristics of political systems differentiating more democratic systems from less democratic ones. I have called these dimensions competition and participation (see Vanhanen 1971, 1977, 1979, 1984). The existence of legal competition indicates that people and their groups are free to organize themselves and to oppose the government. It also indicates the existence of some equality in the sense that different groups are equally free to compete for power. The degree of participation in crucial decisionmaking through elections or by some other means indicates the extent of "the people" taking part in politics. It seems plausible to regard a political system the more democratized the higher the degrees of competition and participation are. In this study I use the same variables to measure the most important dimensions of democratization.

The problem is how to operationalize these variables. As noted above, Dahl did not devise any satisfactory operational indicators to measure these two dimensions of democratization. I think that satisfactory indicators can be found from electoral data. In my previous comparative studies I used two simple quantitative indicators to measure competition and participation (see Vanhanen 1971, 1977, 1979, 1984). The smaller parties' share of the votes cast in parliamentary or presidential elections, or both, was used to indicate the degree of competition. It was calculated by subtracting the percentage of the votes won by the largest party from 100. If both elections were taken into account, the arithmetic mean of the two percentages was used to represent the smaller parties' share.The percentage of the population who actually voted in these elections was used to measure the degree of electoral participation. The percentage was calculated from the total population, not from the adult population or from the enfranchised population.

Because these two variables are assumed to indicate two different dimensions of democracy, it is reasonable to argue that a combination of the two would probably be a more realistic indicator of democracy than either of them alone. They could be combined in many ways, depending on how we weight the importance of Competition and Participation. Because I am not sure which one of them is more important and how much more important, I have weighted them equally in the construction of an index of democratization. In some of my previous studies (Vanhanen 1977, 1979) I used two ways to combine them. (1) They were combined into an Index of Power Distribution (ID) by multiplying them and dividing the outcome by 100, and (2) they were combined into a Weighted Index of Power Distribution (WI) by the formula $WI = xy/100 + x/4 + y/4$, in which x = the smaller parties' share of the votes cast, and y = the degree of participation. The second formula was based on the argument that power may be somewhat more distributed in a political system where either the smaller parties' share or the degree of participation is higher than zero than in a polity where the values of both variables are zero. In my 1984 study I used only the first index, which was called an Index of Democratization (ID). The first formula may be theoretically slightly better than the second one because it is simpler and includes only two discretionary selections: the decision to weight both variables equally and to combine them by multiplying them. These selections are based on my judgments. It seems plausible to assume that both of them are important for democracy. Therefore, they are weighted equally, and it seems to me more realistic to combine them by multiplying than by adding. A low value of either of the two variables is enough to prevent democratization. A high level of participation cannot compensate the lack of competition, or vice versa. The Index of Democratization gets high values only if the values of both basic variables are high. In this study the Index of Democratization (ID) is used as the sole combination of the two basic indicators.

The selection of the two basic political indicators is based on the fact that in contemporary states the use of political power is constitutionally concentrated in the hands of governmental institutions. On the other hand, in modern constitutional systems, elections have become the standard procedure for selecting persons for the institutions wielding political power. This is so because in nearly all constitutions the highest state authority is said to be vested in the people, who exercise authority through elections. The people elect the highest power holders, the members of parliaments and sometimes also the president. For that reason, the legal competition for power is concentrated in parliamentary or presidential elections, or both. The real importance of elections naturally varies from country to country. In some countries elections play the key role in the struggle for power. In others they are little more than formalities confirming and legitimizing the actual power relations. It is remarkable, however, that elections are held in practically every independent country throughout the world. Therefore I think that in the contemporary world the competition between parties in elections represents the most significant form of legal competition and the sharing of power among people. If only one party is entitled to take part in elections, it means that power is concentrated in the hands of this party, which is able to prevent other potential groups to compete for power positions. The concentration of power in the hands of one group, no matter which this group is, represents the opposite of democracy. The situation is usually the same if power holders are not elected at all, or if no organized groups are allowed to take part in elections.

In elections various groups compete with each other for the support of voters. Since the last century these competing groups have formed more or less permanent political parties. Thus political parties are at the heart of the struggle for power. As I see it, the relative strength of political parties provides the most realistic indicator of the distribution of political power in modern states. But what is "a party" and what is "the largest party"? It is not always obvious which groups should be regarded as "parties." It is also necessary to define how the share of the smaller parties is measured when there is no elected parliament or president and no elections, or when elections are held but parties do not take part in them.

Historically, parties were preceded by factions, political cliques, and groups of notables. Parties as we understand them have emerged since the first half of the last century, along with the process of democratization (see Duverger 1954; LaPalombara and Weiner 1966, 3–21; Sartori 1976). The definitions of political parties emphasize that a party is an organized group and that its principal aim is to win political power (see Friedrich 1950, 419; Michels 1962, 78–80; LaPalombara and Weiner 1966, 5). The most appropriate definition for the purposes of this study is that by Sartori: "A party is any political group identified by an official label that presents at elections, and is capable of placing through elections (free or nonfree), candidates for public office" (Sartori 1976, 63–64). Accordingly, I consider that parties include all political groups that have taken part in elections and have been identified by an official label. In cases of party alliances it may be unclear whether the alliance or its individual member parties should be regarded as "parties." In this study the decisive criterion is a party's behavior in elections. If a party belongs to a larger alliance permanently, it is not regarded as a separate party. In that case the alliance is treated as a separate "party," because my purpose is to measure the relative strength of competing and independent political groups.

In parliamentary elections "the largest party" refers to the party that received the largest single share of the votes. In presidential elections the term refers to the votes of the presidential candidate who won the election, or to his or her party. When the composition of a governmental institution using the highest executive or legislative power is not based on elections, the distribution of power is interpreted in the same way as if one party had taken all the seats and votes. This interpretation applies to military regimes, to other autocratic governments, and to monarchies in which the ruler and/or the government responsible to the ruler dominates and exercises executive and often legislative power as well. In all these cases the share of the smaller parties and the degree of electoral participation is regarded as zero. Sometimes parties have not taken part in elections, although members of parliament have been elected. In such cases election results are usually interpreted as if one party had taken all the votes. This interpretation is based on the assumption that the absence of parties was caused by the ruling group which did not permit organized opposition groups to compete for power. Usually it is easy to check whether this has been the case.

The degree of electoral participation indicates also the sharing of power, because all votes are usually weighted equally and the selection of power holders depends on the distribution of votes. If only a small minority of the adult population takes part in elections, the struggle for power is restricted to the upper stratum of the population, and the bulk of the population remains outside politics. Power distribution is then certainly more superficial than if the majority of the adult population took part in elections. For this reason the degree of participation forms the second crucial dimension of democratization. In this study, Participation represents the percentage of the total population that actually voted. The percentage could have been calculated from the adult population (using some age limit), the voting age population, or the adult population eligible to vote. I selected the total population as the basis of calculation because more statistical data are available on total populations than on age structures of electorates. Besides, data based on total populations are more comparable than data based on different age limits or electorates.

Of course, these two indicators are not faultless for their purposes. In the case of "the smaller parties' share," for example, differences in electoral systems may account for some part of the variation in the smaller parties' share (cf. Duverger 1954, 216–28, 239–55; Rae 1967, 87–103). However, it would not be easy to estimate the independent effect of electoral laws because their existence may be a result of selections made by political forces favoring either two-party or multiparty systems. Further, the difference between two-party and multiparty systems affects the smaller parties' share. In multiparty systems the share of the smaller parties may rise considerably higher than in two-party systems, although both party systems were equally competitive. Party structures also vary. The largest party may be ideologically homogeneous and organizationally disciplined, or it may be a loose organization of ideological, regional, or other interest groups. It is reasonable to assume that power is in fact more dispersed in a loose party than in a disciplined one, but this indicator treats all of them as equals. Furthermore, as noted above, the political importance of elections varies greatly (cf. Nohlen 1978, 18–22). This variable is unable to weigh the importance of elections.

It might be possible to correct at least one of these faults by calculating the degree of electoral competition differently. I have used the combined share of the smaller parties to indicate the level of competition because it effectively differentiates one-party dominated political systems from systems in which several parties share the electoral support of voters. According to this indicator, the level of competition is inversely related to the share of the largest party. As a consequence, the value of Competition is usually higher in multiparty systems than in two-party systems. One could argue, however, that it is a misleading result. Two-party competition in elections may be as real and intense as competition among several parties. Therefore it might be better to use the difference between the two largest parties as the criterion of competition. This could be done by calculating an index of competition: $IC = 100 - (l - s)$, in which IC = the Index of Competition, l = the percentage of the largest party, and s = the percentage of the votes won by the second largest party. This Index of Competition would get a high value when the difference between the two largest parties is small and a low value when the difference is large, or when there is only one party, or no parties. For example, the value of IC would be the same (99) when the two largest parties have received 50 and 49 percent of the votes cast, or when they have received 25 and 24 percent respectively, whereas the value of Competition variable would be 50 in the first case and 75 in the second case. This means that in some cases the results of measurements might vary considerably, although both measures would give systematically higher values for competitive party systems than for one-party dominated systems. It is not easy to say which one of the two measurements would produce more realistic results, but I am inclined to think that for the purposes of this study "the smaller parties' share" may be a slightly better indicator than the Index of Competition because in multiparty systems different social groups may have better chances to participate in politics and further their interests than in two-party systems, in which alternatives are more limited. In other words, in multiparty systems, power is probably shared among more numerous independent groups than in two-party systems, although the competition between the main contenders may be as close and intense in both cases. Therefore I measure the degree of electoral competition with "the smaller parties' share."

In the case of "the percentage of the total population that actually voted" (Participation), one disadvantage is that it does not take into account the variation in the age structures of the populations. The percentage of the adult population is significantly higher in developed countries than in poor developing countries. Another fault is that it does not take into account the variation in the nature and importance of elections. In some systems the competition for power concentrates on elections, whereas in some other systems the position of power holders is not decided by elections. This variable is unable to take into account the variation in the significance of elections; it takes into account only the number of votes. This insensitivity in regard to the significance of electoral participation weakens the validity of this variable, and if it were used alone as the indicator of democratization, the results would be misleading. However, as it is combined with Competition by multiplying the variables, the defects of Participation get corrected to a considerable degree. A country where the degree of electoral participation is high but the degree of competition is low cannot get high ID values, and vice versa. It seems reasonable to assume that if the degree of electoral competition is high, the voting in elections is significant at all levels of participation. So I assume that my Index of Democratization based on both variables is a more valid indicator of democratization than either of the basic variables alone.

As far as I know, no other researcher has used "the smaller parties' share" to indicate the degree of competition, although several reserchers have measured the level of competition or contestation by other means (see Coleman 1964; Cutright 1963; Neubauer 1967; Olsen 1968; Smith 1969; Winham 1970; Flanigan and Fogelman 1971; Jackman 1974; Coulter 1975; Bollen 1979; Perry 1980). At first, I used "the largest party's share of the votes cast in parliamentary elections" to measure the degree of pluralism in the party system (Vanhanen 1968) and then "the share of the smaller parties" to measure the distribution of power (Vanhanen 1971). On the other hand, at least three other researchers have used the second indicator (Participation) in the same form as the one in this study (Needler 1967, "the percentage of the population voting in general elections"; Winham 1970, "the percentage of the total population who voted for the chief executive"; Marquette 1974, "voting in presidential elections as a proportion of the total population"). Several others have measured electoral participation using differently defined indicators (see Neubauer 1967; Lerner 1968; Smith 1969; Banks 1970; Jackman 1974; Coulter 1975). At first I used "the percentage of the adult population that voted in elections" to measure the level of participation (Vanhanen 1971). Later I concluded that "the percentage of the total population which actually voted" might be a more reliable indicator for this purpose (Vanhanen 1975).

The selection of these two indicators is based on the assumption that competition and participation are the most important dimensions of democratization and that these simple quantitative indicators based on electoral data are enough to measure the major differences between political systems in their level of democratization. I have left out other possible dimensions of democracy. For example, I do not try to measure the level of civil and political liberties, which Diamond, Lipset, and Linz (1986) regard as the third important dimension of democratization (see also Coulter 1975; Bollen 1979; Gastil 1985, 1988; Bertrand and Puijenbroek 1987; Letterie and Puijenbroek 1987). It seems that it would be very difficult to find objective quantitative indicators for civil and political liberties. On the other hand, I assume that these liberties would correlate positively with my indicator of competition as legal competition for power would not be possible without civil and political liberties.

My indicators of democratization differ from the measures of democratization discussed above in two important points: (1) I use only two indicators and (2) both of them are based on quantitative electoral data. Most other measures of democracy include more numerous indicators and most of them are based on more or less qualitative data. I think that it is better to use simple quantitative variables with certain faults than more complicated measures loaded with weights and estimations based on subjective judgments. The fact that my Index of Democratization seems to be moderately or strongly correlated with several other measures of democracy (see Bertrand and Puijenbroek 1987, Table 2) supports this approach. As far as I know, Gastil's (1988) survey ratings are the only other available measures of democracy that cover the whole comparison group of 147 states and that can be directly compared with my measures. In fact, as Table 2.1 indicates, the arithmetic means of his two ratings are strongly correlated with my measures of democratization, except with Participation. Correlations are negative because Gastil's ratings rise with the decline of democratization, whereas the values of my measures rise with the increase of democratization. Coppedge and Reinicke's (1988) scale of polyarchy for 1985 is as strongly correlated with my measures of democratization as Gastil's ratings and even more strongly with Gastil's ratings (correlation 0.919 in 1985). The strength of these correlations indicates that different ways to measure democratization may lead to more or less similar results. However, because it is obvious that the use of numerous and complicated variables loaded with subjective evaluations has not produced better measurements of democratization than my two simple quantitative variables, it is reasonable to argue that it is better to use these two simple quantitative variables than to resort to subjective evaluations and estimations. In other words, I think that my method to measure democratization may produce more objective and reliable results than measurements based on subjective evaluations.

Empirical Data on Indicators

Empirical data on Competition and Participation are from the period 1980–88 (Appendix 1). The values of variables for each year are determined on the basis of the situation at the end of the year. After an election, coup d'etat, or other major change, the value of a variable is kept the same until the next election or some other change.

Electoral data on Competition and Participation are based on parliamentary or presidential elections, or both. In each case it was necessary to decide which elections are taken into account. The selection of elections depends on the assumed importance of the two governmental institutions. The relative importance of parliaments and presidents (or other chiefs of state) varies greatly, but usually these two governmental institutions are, at least formally, the most important institutions using political power. Depending on how powers are divided between them, we can speak of parliamentary and presidential forms of government. In the former type the legislature is dominant. The executive branch is dependent on and responsible to the legislature. In the latter type the executive branch is dominant and is not responsible to the legislature. But it is also possible that their powers are so well balanced that neither has a clear dominance. In such cases it seems reasonable to take both of them into account. This can be done in various ways. Previously I combined them by calculating the arithmetic mean of parliamentary and presidential elections. In other words, the weight of both elections was 50 percent. In this study I use a more flexible way to combine them. Depending on the estimated importance of the two branches of government, the weight of parliamentary (or presidential) election can be 25, 50, or 75 percent, and the weight of the other election 75, 50, or 25 percent respectively.

Thus we can distinguish three institutional arrangements of power use at the national level: (1) parliamentary dominance, (2) executive dominance, and (3) concurrent powers. In the first case the values of the two variables are calculated on the basis of parliamentary elections, in the second case on the basis of presidential elections; and in the third, both elections are taken into account. If the support of competing parties is about the same in both elections, it does not make much difference how the governmental system is classified in order to calculate the values of Competition and Participation, but if the electoral systems are significantly different in parliamentary and presidential elections, an incorrect classification of the country's governmental system would distort the results of measurement. The same is true

Table 2.1.

Three Political Indicators of this Study Correlated with the Arithmetic Means of Gastil's Ratings (G) of Political Rights and Civil Liberties and with Coppedge-Reineicke's Scale of Polyarchy in the Comparison Group of 147 States in 1980–87

Political indicators	G80	G81	G82	G83	G84	G85	G86	G87	Scale of polyarchy
C-80	-.831	-.876	-.869	-.847	-.810	-.805	-.806	-.786	-.740
P-80	-.357	-.404	-.403	-.369	-.354	-.325	-.322	-.325	-.309
ID-80	-.811	-.849	-.847	-.840	-.822	-.806	-.799	-.792	-.713
C-81	-.826	-.867	-.873	-.866	-.839	-.836	-.838	-.820	-.776
P-81	-.337	-.389	-.391	-.364	-.360	-.333	-.332	-.341	-.321
ID-81	-.807	-.846	-.856	-.852	-.839	-.825	-.818	-.814	-.732
C-82	-.836	-.857	-.866	-.894	-.867	-.852	-.845	-.828	-.792
P-82	-.346	-.376	-.383	-.378	-.377	-.344	-.343	-.349	-.336
ID-82	-.817	-.842	-.853	-.865	-.852	-.834	-.826	-.820	-.747
C-83	-.823	-.837	-.847	-.893	-.902	-.888	-.884	-.865	-.840
P-83	-.327	-.357	-.364	-.376	-.393	-.360	-.362	-.367	-.360
ID-83	-.800	-.820	-.831	-.861	-.868	-.850	-.846	-.839	-.771
C-84	-.796	-.822	-.830	-.878	-.894	-.894	-.887	-.867	-.870
P-84	-.333	-.375	-.381	-.398	-.414	-.400	-.397	-.406	-.427
ID-84	-.774	-.806	-.816	-.849	-.863	-.867	-.858	-.851	-.807
C-85	-.810	-.819	-.825	-.876	-.893	-.902	-.898	-.879	-.895
P-85	-.340	-.375	-.382	-.399	-.424	-.410	-.403	-.411	-.451
ID-85	-.778	-.806	-.817	-.849	-.863	-.870	-.863	-.856	-.820
C-86	-.797	-.806	-.812	-.859	-.872	-.884	-.894	-.878	-.876
P-86	-.332	-.370	-.377	-.387	-.408	-.395	-.394	-.402	-.446
ID-86	-.778	-.805	-.816	-.847	-.861	-.870	-.869	-.865	-.820
C-87	-.785	-.782	-.788	-.833	-.848	-.862	-.871	-.881	-.856
P-87	-.353	-.354	-.361	-.369	-.394	-.387	-.386	-.428	-.433
ID-87	-.772	-.785	-.795	-.825	-.842	-.853	-.852	-.869	-.807

if the powers of the two institutions differ crucially. For these reasons I have attempted to classify each country's governmental system as realistically as possible. In Appendix 1, which includes electoral data on the two variables, I indicated in each case separately which of the three institutional arrangements of power use is regarded to characterize the country's governmental system and, in the case of concurrent powers, how the two branches of government are weighted for the calculation of ID.

It was relatively easy to find reliable data on nearly all contemporary elections. *Chronicle of Parliamentary Elections and Developments,* published annually by the International Centre for Parliamentary Documentation (Geneva), contains the most extensive compilation of data on parliamentary elections. *Keesing's Contemporary Archives* is another extremely useful source. It informs both of parliamentary and of presidential elections around the world, although less systematically than the *Chronicle.* Besides, it informs on coups d'etat and other major political changes. In addition to these general sources, I used several other international, regional, and national statistical reference works and studies on elections and politics in various countries to complete my data on elections and political systems. Thus it was possible to find nearly complete empirical data on the values of the two political variables from the 147 states of this comparison group.

THE STATE AND TRENDS OF DEMOCRATIZATION IN 1980–88

Empirical data on the operational variables of democratization formulated earlier provide a basis (1) to describe the extent of variation in the degree of democratization, as indicated by the Index of Democratization (ID), in the comparison group of 147 countries in 1980–88 and (2) to classify the 147 countries into the categories of democracies and nondemocracies. These analyses are intended to provide a global picture on the variation of democratization and on the trends of changes in 1980–88.

Variation of Democratization in 147 Countries

Let us start from the rank orders of the 147 countries according to the ID index values given in Table 2.2. The 71 countries for which the value of the Index of Democratization was zero in 1980 are listed in alphabetical order in Table 2.2.

Table 2.2 indicates that the range of democratization extended from zero to 40.1 index points in 1980. It is remarkable that there does not seem to be any natural boderline between more and less democratized countries. The

Table 2.2.

147 Countries Ranked by Index of Democratization in 1980 and with the Values of ID 1980–88

Country	ID-80	ID-81	ID-82	ID-83	ID-84	ID-85	ID-86	ID-87	ID-88
1 Italy	40.1	40.1	40.1	43.7	43.7	43.7	43.7	44.1	44.1
2 Netherlands	39.7	42.2	40.1	40.1	40.1	40.1	40.0	40.0	40.1
3 Denmark	38.2	40.9	40.9	40.9	41.7	41.7	41.7	46.4	45.7
4 Sweden	37.3	37.3	36.3	36.3	36.3	36.9	36.9	36.9	36.4
5 Belgium	35.9	44.2	44.2	44.2	44.2	43.3	43.3	44.7	44.7
6 Germany, W.	35.2	35.2	35.2	39.2	39.2	39.2	39.2	39.1	39.1
7 Iceland	35.0	35.0	35.0	33.7	33.7	33.7	33.7	46.2	46.2
8 Norway	32.8	38.5	38.5	38.5	38.5	37.1	37.1	37.1	37.1
9 New Zealand	32.7	35.1	35.1	35.1	34.0	34.0	34.0	29.3	29.3
10 France	32.5	28.3	28.3	28.3	41.3	41.3	41.3	41.2	27.6
11 Israel	32.2	30.8	30.8	30.8	32.4	32.4	32.4	32.4	35.8
12 Greece	32.2	30.3	30.3	30.3	30.3	34.7	34.7	34.7	34.7
13 Luxemburg	31.7	31.7	31.7	31.7	31.5	31.5	31.5	31.5	31.5
14 United K.	31.4	31.4	31.4	31.3	31.3	31.3	31.3	33.2	33.2
15 Spain	31.3	31.3	28.1	28.1	28.1	28.1	28.9	28.9	28.9
16 Austria	31.2	31.2	31.2	33.5	33.5	33.5	36.5	36.5	36.5
17 Australia	31.0	31.9	31.0	28.5	33.0	33.0	33.0	30.9	30.9
18 Malta	30.2	31.4	31.4	31.4	31.4	31.4	31.4	30.0	30.0
19 Portugal	28.7	28.7	28.7	30.2	30.2	32.0	33.4	27.1	27.1
20 Japan	28.0	28.0	28.0	25.8	25.8	25.8	25.1	25.1	25.1
21 Finland	26.3	26.3	42.2	41.3	41.3	41.3	41.3	41.2	38.6
22 Mauritius	26.2	26.2	18.8	22.7	22.7	22.7	22.7	27.3	27.3
23 Canada	25.6	25.6	25.6	25.6	25.0	25.0	25.0	25.0	28.8
24 Ireland	24.2	27.3	26.6	26.6	26.6	26.6	26.6	28.0	28.0
25 Papua N.G.	21.9	21.9	25.3	25.3	25.3	25.3	25.3	32.8	32.8
26 Switzerland	21.6	21.6	21.6	23.1	23.1	23.1	23.1	22.9	22.9
27 Costa Rica	20.8	20.8	18.2	18.2	18.2	18.2	21.2	21.2	21.2
28 Venezuela	20.1	20.1	20.1	17.3	17.3	17.3	17.3	17.3	18.7
29 Barbados	19.3	22.7	22.7	22.7	22.7	22.7	21.5	21.5	21.5
30 United States	18.7	18.7	18.7	18.7	16.1	16.1	16.1	16.1	16.7
31 India	17.0	17.0	17.0	17.0	16.2	16.2	16.2	16.2	16.2
32 Uganda	16.8	16.8	16.8	16.8	16.8	0	0	0	0
33 Dominican R.	15.5	15.5	17.0	17.0	17.0	17.0	18.7	18.7	18.7
34 Solomon Is.	15.0	15.0	15.0	15.0	19.2	19.2	19.2	19.2	15.7
35 Jamaica	14.6	14.6	14.6	14.6	14.6	14.6	14.6	14.6	14.6
36 Bahamas	14.4	14.4	15.6	15.6	15.6	15.6	15.6	19.3	19.3
37 Nigeria	14.3	14.3	14.3	0	0	0	0	0	0
38 Trin. & Tob.	14.3	16.6	16.6	16.6	16.6	16.6	15.1	15.1	15.1
39 Fiji	14.3	14.3	18.3	18.3	18.3	18.3	18.3	0	0
40 Zimbabwe	14.1	14.1	14.1	14.1	14.1	8.3	8.3	8.3	8.3
41 Peru	12.7	12.7	12.7	12.7	12.7	15.3	15.3	15.3	15.3
42 Guyana	12.3	12.3	12.3	12.3	12.3	7.6	7.6	7.6	7.6
43 Malaysia	11.5	11.5	11.3	11.3	11.3	11.3	12.3	12.3	12.3
44 Cyprus	11.2	30.8	30.8	30.8	30.8	31.9	31.9	31.9	31.9
45 Colombia	9.9	9.9	12.9	12.9	12.9	12.9	10.2	10.2	10.2
46 Gambia	9.7	9.7	10.0	10.0	10.0	10.0	10.0	12.7	12.7
47 Lebanon	9.5	9.5	9.5	9.5	9.5	9.5	9.5	9.5	9.5
48 Iran	8.0	1.3	1.3	1.3	1.3	4.6	4.6	4.6	4.6
49 Ghana	7.7	0	0	0	0	0	0	0	0
50 Ecuador	6.0	5.0	6.0	6.0	12.8	12.8	12.8	12.8	18.3
51 Singapore	5.9	5.9	5.9	5.9	12.2	12.2	12.2	12.2	19.9

Table 2.2. (*continued*)

Country	ID-80	ID-81	ID-82	ID-83	ID-84	ID-85	ID-86	ID-87	ID-88
52 Guatemala	5.6	5.6	0	0	0	6.6	6.6	6.6	6.6
53 Bangladesh	5.4	8.2	0	0	0	0	4.2	4.2	4.2
54 Sri Lanka	5.3	5.3	18.6	18.6	18.6	18.6	18.6	18.6	16.3
55 Botswana	4.1	4.1	4.1	4.1	6.9	6.9	6.9	6.9	6.9
56 Zambia	4.0	4.0	4.0	1.2	1.2	1.2	1.2	1.2	0.9
57 Brazil	3.8	3.8	7.8	7.8	7.8	6.8	7.8	7.8	7.8
58 Paraguay	3.5	3.5	3.5	2.9	2.9	2.9	2.9	2.9	3.5
59 Thailand	3.5	3.5	3.5	4.3	4.3	4.3	5.1	5.1	5.3
60 Senegal	3.3	3.3	3.3	2.9	2.9	2.9	2.9	2.9	4.4
61 Cape Verde	2.4	2.4	2.4	2.4	2.4	1.6	1.6	1.6	1.6
62 Madagascar	2.3	2.3	8.5	8.5	8.5	8.5	8.5	8.5	8.5
63 Tanzania	2.0	2.0	2.0	2.0	2.0	1.0	1.0	1.0	1.0
64 Mexico	1.7	1.7	7.9	7.9	7.9	7.9	7.9	7.9	14.8
65 Korea, South	1.7	2.5	2.5	2.5	2.5	2.8	2.8	22.9	22.9
66 South Africa	1.3	2.0	2.0	2.0	2.0	2.0	2.0	2.8	2.8
67 Romania	1.1	1.1	1.1	1.1	1.1	1.6	1.6	1.6	1.6
68 Indonesia	1.1	1.1	1.1	1.1	1.1	1.1	1.1	0.8	0.8
69 Morocco	1.0	1.0	1.0	1.0	1.0	1.0	1.0	1.0	1.0
70 Rwanda	0.4	0.4	0.4	0	0	0	0	0	0
71 Sudan	0.3	0.3	0.3	0.1	0.1	0	11.7	11.7	11.7
72 Algeria	0.3	0.3	0.3	0.3	2.1	2.1	2.1	2.1	3.3
73 Syria	0.2	0.2	0.2	0.2	0.2	0	0	0	0
74 German, D.R.	0.1	0.1	0.1	0.1	0.1	0.1	0.1	0.1	0.1
75 USSR	0.1	0.1	0.1	0.1	0.1	0.1	0.1	0.1	0.1
76 Gabon	0.1	0.1	0.1	0.1	0.1	0.1	0	0	0
77 Afghanistan	0	0	0	0	0	0	0	0	0
78 Albania	0	0	0	0	0	0	0	0	0
79 Angola	0	0	0	0	0	0	0	0	0
80 Argentina	0	0	0	24.1	24.1	24.1	24.1	24.1	24.1
81 Bahrain	0	0	0	0	0	0	0	0	0
82 Benin	0	0	0	0	0	0	0	0	0
83 Bhutan	0	0	0	0	0	0	0	0	0
84 Bolivia	0	0	16.8	16.8	16.8	14.2	14.2	14.2	14.2
85 Bulgaria	0	0	0	0	0	0	0	0	0
86 Burkina Faso	0	0	0	0	0	0	0	0	0
87 Burma	0	0	0	0	0	0	0	0	0
88 Burundi	0	0	0	0	0	0	0	0	0
89 Cameroon	0	0	0	0	0	0	0	0	0
90 Central Af.R.	0	0	0	0	0	0	2.1	2.1	2.1
91 Chad	0	0	0	0	0	0	0	0	0
92 Chile	0	0	0	0	0	0	0	0	0
93 China	0	0	0	0	0	0	0	0	0
94 Comoros	0	0	0	0	0.3	0.3	0.3	0.3	0.3
95 Congo Republic	0	0	0	0	0	0	0	0	0
96 Cuba	0	0	0	0	0	0	0	0	0
97 Chechoslovakia	0	0	0	0	0	0	0	0	0
98 Djibouti	0	0	0	0	0	0	0	0	0
99 Egypt	0	0.3	0.3	0.3	0.3	0.3	0.3	0.7	0.7
100 El Salvador	0	0	0	0	13.6	13.6	13.6	13.6	13.6

Table 2.2. (*continued*)

Country	ID-80	ID-81	ID-82	ID-83	ID-84	ID-85	ID-86	ID-87	ID-88
101 Eq. Guinea	0	0	1.6	1.6	1.6	1.6	1.6	1.6	1.6
102 Ethiopia	0	0	0	0	0	0	0	0	0
103 Guinea	0	0	0	0	0	0	0	0	0
104 Guinea-Bissau	0	0	0	0	0	0	0	0	0
105 Haiti	0	0	0	0	0	0	0	0	0
106 Honduras	0	14.2	14.2	14.2	14.2	17.3	17.3	17.3	17.3
107 Hungary	0	0	0	0	0	0	0	0	0
108 Iraq	0	0	0	0	0	0	0	0	0
109 Ivory Coast	0	0	0	0	0	0	0	0	0
110 Jordan	0	0	0	0	0	0	0	0	0
111 Kampuchea	0	0	0	0	0	0	0	0	0
112 Kenya	0	0	0	0	0	0	0	0	0
113 Korea, North	0	0	0	0	0	0	0	0	0
114 Kuwait	0	0	0	0	0	0	0	0	0
115 Laos	0	0	0	0	0	0	0	0	0
116 Lesotho	0	0	0	0	0	0	0	0	0
117 Liberia	0	0	0	0	0	8.2	7.7	7.7	7.7
118 Libya	0	0	0	0	0	0	0	0	0
119 Malawi	0	0	0	0	0	0	0	0	0
120 Mali	0	0	0	0	0	0	0	0	0
121 Mauritania	0	0	0	0	0	0	0	0	
122 Mongolia	0	0	0	0	0	0	0	0	
123 Mozambique		0	0	0	0	0	0	0	0
124 Nepal	0	0	0	0	0	0	0	0	0
125 Nicaragua	0	0	0	0	14.8	14.8	14.8	14.8	14.8
126 Niger	0	0	0	0	0	0	0	0	0
127 Oman	0	0	0	0	0	0	0	0	0
128 Pakistan	0	0	0	0	0	0	0	0	12.2
129 Panama	0	0	0	0	14.8	14.8	14.8	14.8	0
130 Philippines	0	5.0	5.0	5.0	5.0	5.0	17.0	17.0	17.0
131 Poland	0	0	0	0	0	0	0	0	0
132 Qatar	0	0	0	0	0	0	0	0	0
133 Saudi Arabia	0	0	0	0	0	0	0	0	0
134 Sierra Leone	0	0	0	0	0	0.1	0.1	0.1	0.1
135 Somalia	0	0	0	0	0	0	0	0	0
136 Suriname	0	0	0	0	0	0	0	7.0	7.0
137 Swaziland	0	0	0	0	0	0	0	0	0
138 Togo	0	0	0	0	0	0	0	0	0
139 Tunisia	0	0	0	0	0	0	0	0	0
140 Turkey	0	0	3.1	11.6	11.6	11.6	11.6	15.0	15.0
141 United Arab E.	0	0	0	0	0	0	0	0	0
142 Uruguay	0	0	0	0	38.2	38.2	38.2	38.2	38.2
143 Vietnam	0	0	0	0	0	0	0	0	0
144 Yemen, North	0	0	0	0	0	0	0	0	0
145 Yemen, South	0	0	0	0	0	0	0	0	0
146 Yugoslavia	0	0	0	0	0	0	0	0	0
147 Zaire	0	0	0	0	0.4	0.4	0.4	0.4	0.4
Arithmetic mean	8.2	8.5	8.9	9.0	9.8	9.8	10.1	10.3	10.4

continuum of ID index points can be interpreted to mean that the countries with the highest ID index points fulfil the criteria of democracy best, whereas the countries with the lowest index points cannot be regarded as democracies.

The political systems of the countries with zero ID index points may considerably differ from each other in many other respects, but what they have in common is that their level of democratization, as measured in this study, is in zero. My indicators are not able, and they are not intended, to discriminate and measure other characteristics of political systems. Besides, I want to emphasize that in the group of countries with the highest ID index points, the differences in index points do not necessarily indicate distinctions in the level of democratization because the variation may be due to such political factors as electoral systems and party systems. My indicators are tended to produce somewhat higher index values for the countries using proportional electoral systems than for the countries using majority and plurality electoral systems (for electoral systems, see Bogdanor and Butler 1983; Grofman and Lijphart 1986). My index is better suited to indicate significant distinctions between the levels of democratization than to measure slight differences at any level of democratization.

The comparison of the ID values of single countries over the years 1980–88 shows that most political systems remained relatively stable from the perspective of democratization. As a consequence, the rank order of 147 countries remained more or less the same over the period 1980–88. The index values of single years are highly intercorrelated. The correlation is 0.981 between the years 1980 and 1981 and 0.872 between the years 1980 and 1988. Correlations have systematically decreased when the distance between the years of comparison has increased. It means that political systems change over time. Table 2.2 illustrates the fact that the political systems of some countries changed drastically in the period 1980–88. It shows the breakdowns of democratic political institutions in Ghana (1981), Bangladesh (1982), Guatemala (1982), Nigeria (1983), Uganda (1985), Fiji (1987), and Panama (1988) and the introduction of popularly elected governmental institutions in Honduras (1981), Bolivia (1982), Argentina (1983), Turkey (1983), El Salvador (1984), Nicaragua (1984), Uruguay (1984), Panama (1984), Guatemala (1985), Liberia (1985), the Philippines (1986), Sudan (1986), South Korea (1987), and Pakistan (1988).

The average level of democratization, as indicated by ID, has continually risen in the comparison group of 147 countries. It has not remained constant over time. In fact, the rise of the arithmetic mean of ID in 1980–88 has continued the historical trend since the 1850s. My previous study covering 37-119 countries of the period 1850–1979 disclosed that the arithmetic mean of the Index of Democratization rose nearly uninterruptedly from the 1850s to the 1970s (Table 2.3). The slight decline in the period 1950–79 was due

to the fact that the number of countries increased sharply and that the level
of democratization was low in most of the new independent countries. Besides, in most cases democratic institutions established at the dawn of independence collapsed soon after independence. These factors caused a slight
decline in the arithmetic mean of ID in the period 1950–79, but they caused
only a temporary halt. The historical trend of democratization has clearly
been rising, and it has continued in the 1980s. However, the fact that the
level of democratization has nearly continually risen in the period 1850–
1988 does not quarantee that the trend will remain the same in future, too.

Democracies and Nondemocracies

The ranking of countries by ID illustrates the continuum of political systems
from autocracies to democracies. The countries with the highest ID values
can be regarded as democracies and the countries with the lowest values as
autocracies. But, as indicated by Table 2.2, the 147 countries of this comparison group are distributed relatively evenly over the continuum. They do
not form two clearly separated clusters of democracies and nondemocracies.
We cannot find any sparsely populated no man's land between the two clusters in the continuum. It means that whatever index value would be selected
to separate democracies from nondemocracies, the democracies with the lowest
index values would be quite near the nondemocracies with the highest index
values.

The variation of the level of democratization can be analyzed without a

Table 2.3.
Decennial Arithmetic Means of ID in the Period 1850–1979 in the Comparison
Group of 37-119 States

Decade	N	ID
1850–59	37	0.467
1860–69	39	0.628
1870–79	41	0.929
1880–89	42	1.169
1890–99	43	1.876
1900–09	47	2.570
1910–19	51	3.741
1920–29	62	6.566
1930–39	63	6.398
1940–49	74	6.950
1950–59	85	8.858
1960–69	117	7.692
1970–79	119	7.033

dichotomous classification of political systems into democracies and non-democracies, but in this study I use a dichotomous classification, too, because the purpose is to describe and explain the democratization of political systems. For this purpose, it is necessary to define democracy operationally and to separate democracies from nondemocracies. It seems that statistical data on political indicators can be used for this purpose by defining the minimum threshold values of democracy for political indicators. The only problem is how to select the threshold values, in other words, at what level of competition and at what level of participation a political system can be regarded to fulfil the minimum criteria of democracy. The selection of minimum criteria is arbitrary to some degree, but not completely so. The descriptive definition of democracy above presupposes both the existence of significant competition and the participation of the people in elections. These demands constrain the selection of threshold values, although they do not determine them exactly. In this connection one could argue that significant competition does not need to follow from the right to compete because people might support one party unanimously. In other words, a high degree of competition cannot be regarded as a necessary characteristic of democracy. Of course, it is possible, in principle, that people unanimously support one party, but in practice it would be highly improbable. All individuals have, to some degree, different and contradictory interests because of genetic differences and because we all have to compete for scarce necessities of life. Therefore, we are bound to conflict in politics, too. The same concerns social and political groups formed by individuals. I assume that individuals and groups are bound to pursue different and contradictory aims whenever they are allowed to act in accordance with their own interests. Consequently political competition for power and for the fruits of power is inevitable. In elections it leads to competition among individuals and groups whenever they are legally allowed to pursue their interests through elections. For that reason it is reasonable to assume that competition is an inseparable part of democracy. The problem is to determine the minimum level of party competition from the perspective of democracy.

If the share of the smaller parties is very low, say, less than 30 percent of the votes cast, the dominance of the largest party is so overpowering that it would not be sensible to regard such a political system as a democracy. Raymond D. Gastil says that "any group or leader that regularly receives 70 percent or more of the vote indicates a weak opposition, and the probable existence of undemocratic barriers in the way of its further success" (Gastil 1988, 15). So it seems to me that a reasonable minimum threshold of democracy might be around 30 percent for Competition, which I use here. The same threshold value was used in my previous comparative study of 119 states (Vanhanen 1984). In the case of Participation it is sensible to use a somewhat lower threshold value for the reason that the percentage of electoral participation is calculated from the total population, not from the adult population. In many developing countries only half or even less than half of the population are over 20 years old. So I shall use 15 percent for Participation as another minimum threshold of democracy. In my previous study I used the threshold of 10 percent for Participation (Vanhanen 1984). These two threshold values are certainly arbitrary to some degree, but I think that they are suitable approximations to separate more or less autocratic systems from political systems that have crossed the minimum threshold of democracy. Because it was assumed that both dimensions of democracy are equally important, it is necessary for a country to reach both threshold values in order to become classified as a democracy. Competition and Participation represent two clearly different dimensions of democratization, for they are only slightly intercorrelated. Correlation between them was only 0.445 in 1980 and 0.443 in 1988.

Besides, because ID will be used as the principal measure of democratization, it is necessary to define the minimum threshold of democracy for it, too. As in my previous study (Vanhanen, 1984), 5.0 index points are used as the minimum threshold of democracy for the Index of Democratization. It is a little higher than the minimum (4.5) produced by the threshold values of Competition and Participation. In the following analysis the countries that have reached all the three minimum thresholds of democracy (30% for Competition, 15% for Participation, and 5.0 index points for the Index of Democratization) are classified as Democracies.

Because the countries only slightly below the threshold of democracy do not differ much from Democracies, it seems sensible to establish a category of Semidemocracies. This can be done by defining the minimum threshold values of political indicators for Semidemocracies. The countries for which the value of Competition is at least 20 percent but less than 30 percent and the value of Participation at least 10 percent but less than 15 percent are classified as Semidemocracies. The rest of the countries are classified as Nondemocracies. The frequency distribution of 147 countries into these three categories in years 1980–88 is given in Table 2.4.

Table 2.4.

Frequency Distribution of 147 Countries into Categories of Democracies, Semidemocracies, and Nondemocracies in Years 1980–88

Category	1980	1981	1982	1983	1984	1985	1986	1987	1988
Democracies	48	49	51	52	58	58	60	60	61
Semidemocracies	7	6	7	7	5	6	6	5	5
Nondemocracies	92	92	89	88	84	83	81	82	81
Total	147	147	147	147	147	147	147	147	147

Table 2.4 shows that 33–42% of the 147 states of this comparison group fulfilled the minimum criteria of democracy and that the number of Democracies increased in nine years from 48 to 61, whereas the number of Semidemocracies decreased from 7 to 5, and the number of Nondemocracies from 92 to 81. However, all changes of governmental systems did not raise the level of democratization. Several countries dropped from the category of Democracies to Nondemocracies. These transformations indicate that political systems are continually tested in the struggle for power. Democratic systems survive only in the countries in which competing groups are strong enough to prevent the usurpation of power by any single group. The extent of changes has varied considerably from gradual modifications within the same constitutional framework to military coups and introductions of democratic institutions through popular pressure and elections. Electoral and other data on the two basic political variables presented in Appendix 1 illustrate the nature of transformations in single cases.

I discuss the changes of political systems in greater detail on the basis of the results of regression analyses in Chapter 4. In this connection I mention only the countries that entered the category of Democracies or dropped to the category of Semidemocracies or Nondemocracies. The group of 48 Democracies in 1980 includes the countries whose ID values were 5.0 or higher (see Table 2.3), except Guyana, Iran, Singapore, Bangladesh, and Sri Lanka, which were Semidemocracies, and Guatemala, which was a Nondemocracy. In the period 1981–88 Argentina, Honduras, Bangladesh, Bolivia, Botswana, Brazil, El Salvador, Guatemala, Liberia, Mexico, Nicaragua, Pakistan, Panama, the Philippines, Singapore, South Korea, Sri Lanka, Sudan, Turkey, and Uruguay entered the category of Democracies, whereas Fiji, Ghana, Nigeria, Uganda, and Zimbabwe dropped from that group, as did Bangladesh, which remained above the threshold of democracy only one year, and Panama, which remained among Democracies for four years. So the net increase of Democracies was 13. The breakdowns of democratic systems were caused by military coups d'etat or usurpations of power in Bangladesh, Ghana, Panama, Nigeria, and Uganda. Zimbabwe fell to the category of Semidemocracies because the share of the votes cast for the ruling party crossed the threshold of 70 percent in the 1985 parliamentary election.

Botswana, Brazil, Mexico, Singapore, and Sri Lanka rose from the category of Semidemocracies to Democracies as a consequence of elections in which the smaller parties' share crossed the threshold of 30 percent and/or the level of electoral participation rose above 15 percent. Sri Lanka was in the category of Semidemocracies only temporarily as a consequence of constitutional changes made in 1978 (see Appendix 1). All these transformations were gradual and relatively small. The introduction of democracy through elections changed the nature of political systems more drastically in the other 15 new Democracies. Military or other authoritarian governments handed over governmental power to popularly elected governments, although, in some cases, power holders remained more or less the same (especially in Liberia and Nicaragua). Popular demands of democratization had preceded the establishment of democratic institutions.

Democracies and Nondemocracies are not geographically evenly distributed in the world. Historical evidence shows that democratization, as defined in this study, started in North America, Europe, and Oceania during last century and spread after World War II to the rest of the world (cf. Vanhanen 1984). The core areas of democracy are still in Western Europe, North America, and Oceania, but the rest of the world is also spotted by Democracies. Latin America has been the major area of democratization and redemocratization in the 1980s. On the other hand, Africa, the Middle East, Eastern Europe, and the major part of Asia form the core areas of Nondemocracies. The problem is: Why are Democracies and Nondemocracies geographically unevenly distributed in the world and why have some countries become democratized and many others remained more or less autocratically ruled? The analysis of purely political factors is not enough to solve this problem. We must take various environmental conditions into account because, according to my theory of democratization, political systems are adapted to their environments and they change with their environments.

3

THEORETICAL EXPLANATIONS OF DEMOCRATIZATION

The variation of political systems from the aspect of democratization, described in Chapter 2, forms the *explicandum* of this study. How to explain the fact that the level of democratization varies so greatly from country to country and between geographical regions? Because this problem has been intensively studied by many philosophers and social scientists since Plato and Aristotle, I first refer to some interpretations and explanations given by others. After that I present the theoretical premises to be used in this study, formulate explanatory variables, and analyze, statistically, the relationships between the indicators of democratization and the explanatory variables of this study.

STUDIES OF AND THEORIES ON THE CONDITIONS OF DEMOCRACY

Since Plato and Aristotle, social scientists have contemplated and investigated what factors might cause the variation of regimes and political systems. Aristotle analyzed, systematically, the variation of political systems and presented empirical data and assumptions on the causes of this variation. He explained, "The reason why there are a number of different constitutions is to be found in the fact that every state has a number of different parts" (Aristotle 1961, 160). By "different parts" he meant that a population is composed of different occupational groups, social classes, and status groups. Each group has its own special interests that it tries to further by modifying the constitution to serve its selfish interests. Consequently, each particular combination of these parts produces a different constitution, which reflects the interests of the most powerful part more than the interests of weaker parts. Aristotle paid particular attention to the class composition of a society and argued: "The real ground of the difference between oligarchy and democracy is poverty and riches. It is inevitable that any constitution should be an oligarchy if the rulers under it are rulers in virtue of riches, whether they are few or many; and it is equally inevitable that a constitution under which the poor rule should be a democracy" (Aristotle 1961, 116). Aristotle differentiated several varieties of democracy and pointed out that each of them is related to particular social conditions and occupational and class compositions. He assumed that the best variety of democracy arises in a society where the farming class and the class possessed of moderate means are in a prevalent position. According to him, "there is thus no difficulty in construction a democracy where the bulk of the people live by arable and pastoral farming" (Aristotle 1961, 163–72, 255–65). It seems that Aristotle traced the causes of democracy and other forms of government particularly to the distribution of wealth and to the relative strength of social classes—the rich, the poor, and the middle class. Implicitly he seemed to think that each group tries to further its own interests by all available means.

Montesquieu was another great comparativist who investigated the variety of political systems and also the conditions of democracy, although briefly. He connected the conditions favoring democracy with the love of equality and frugality. In other words, democracy presupposes a relatively equal distribution of wealth and a simple way of life (see Montesquieu 1961 Vol. I, 46–55, 119–21; Lavau 1985, 51–53). On the other hand, Montesquieu emphasized the influence of geographical and physical environment. One of his main hypotheses is that a cold climate is conducive to freedom and free forms of government, whereas a hot and humid climate produces despotic forms of government and slavery (see Montesquieu 1961 Vol. I, 286–93; Sabine 1966, 551–57). It is, in principle, an empirically testable hypothesis. In a previous comparative study, I tested it by correlating the average annual temperature of each country (capital city) with the smaller parties' share of the votes cast in parliamentary or presidential elections and found that they are negatively correlated, as hypothesized, but only slightly (0.28) (Vanhanen 1971, 105–09, 131–33). However, temperature is not the only important aspect of a tropical climate. Humidity and many diseases connected with a tropical climate may be even more important. Andrew M. Kamarck has argued strongly that certain effects of a tropical climate hinder agriculture and "make the population less vigorous through disease and, possibly, through the direct physiological impact of temperature and humidity." As a consequence, economic development is, under present technological conditions, much more difficult in the tropics than in the temperate zones (Kamarck 1976, 3–21). From the aspect of democratization, this is a relevant hypothesis. It is possible that tropical climate has hindered democratization indirectly by constraining economic development and the distribution of power resources. Unfortunately, it is not possible to test this hypothesis empirically in this connection.

Rousseau thought that, taking the term in its strict sense, there never had existed, and never will exist, any true democracy, because it "is contrary to the natural order that the majority should govern and that the minority should be governed." The best chances for democracy would be in "a very small State, in which the people may be readily assembled, and in which every citizen can easily know all the rest; secondly, great simplicity of manners, which prevents a multiplicity of affairs and thorny discussions; next, considerable equality in rank and fortune, without which equality in rights and authority could not long subsist." Rousseau assumed that these conditions are so difficult to fulfil that democracy is impossible: "If there were a nation of gods, it would be governed democratically. So perfect a government is unsuited to men" (Rousseau 1971, 69–71). He raised the ideal of democracy so high that it became impossible to achieve it.

Alexis de Tocqueville continued the long tradition of relating democracy to the equality of conditions, but he also emphasized the significance of suitable laws and institutions. The opening words of his *Democracy in America*—"Among the novel objects that attracted my attention during my stay in the United States, nothing struck me more forcibly than the general equality of condition among the people"—express the theme of his explanation for democracy in America. He saw equality in the distribution of land and other properties, of knowledge and arms, and found many laws, customs, and institutions that supported the survival of the equality of condition (Tocqueville 1963 Vol. I, 3, 46–54, 288–330; Lavau 1985, 59–60). I think that Tocqueville was right when he traced the origin of this equality of condition to the customs and equality of the first immigrants of New England. He noticed that "great equality existed among the immigrants who settled on the shores of New England." The laws and institutions and social structures they established in America reflected the initial equality among them (see Tocqueville 1963 Vol. I, 46–54). The colonization of America and the establishment of democracy in the United States provide a rare example of the role of people's ideas, knowledge, and capabilities. The immigrants of New England had brought with them democratic ideas and institutions presupposing equality, and they transplanted them in the New World. Comparison with the colonization of Central and South America by Iberian immigrants illustrates the significance of differences in human qualities, ideas, and customs. The Iberian immigrants of Central and South America had brought with them the latifundia system and ideas and institutions presupposing inequalities, and they transplanted them in the New World. It seems reasonable to assume that the difference in the quality of the first immigrants explains, at least in part, the differences in subsequent economic and political developments in the United States and Latin American countries. This assumption is supported by Ingegerd Bauder's findings (1985) that later immigrants from Western Europe have changed social and economic structures in Latin America. The comparison of North and South American different developments highlights the fact that social conditions affecting the nature of political systems are made by people.

James Bryce did not present any general theory or hypothesis on the conditions of democracy, but he gave some interesting remarks on the causes of democracy in particular countries. He distinguished four causes of democratization in the modern world: (1) the influence of religious ideas, (2) discontent with royal or oligarchic misgovernment and consequent efforts at reform, (3) social and political conditions favoring equality, and (4) abstract theory. Of these causes, 1, 2, and 4 seemed to be relevant in the case of England, and abstract theory (4) in France, whereas in the United States, Canada, Australia, and New Zealand social equality (3) seemed to have been the most important factor. Bryce said, reflecting the arguments of Tocqueville, that the North American colonies of England "were settled by persons belonging (except to some extent in Virginia) to the middle and humbler classes, among whom there was at first little difference in wealth, and not very much in rank." Social and economic conditions creating social equality made political equality and democracy ultimately inevitable. The same happened in Australia, New Zealand, and Canada (Bryce 1921 Vol. I, IX, 27–47). However, in spite of these observations, he claimed in another connection that democracy "has nothing to do with Economic Equality, which might exist under any form of government, and might possibly work more smoothly under some other form" (Bryce 1921 Vol. I, 76). So it seems that Bryce was not convinced of the significance of equality as a general prerequisite of democracy, although relative equality was an important explanatory factor in some particular cases.

The explanations given for the variation of political systems and democratization vary in classical studies, although social and economic equality was nearly always connected with democracy. Contemporary social scientists have produced even more varied explanations for the emergence and survival of democracy (for reviews, see Pennock 1979, 206–59; Huntington 1984). Some of them are noted below.

Joseph A. Schumpeter claimed that "historically, the modern democracy rose along with capitalism, and in causal connection with it." He was not sure how democracy is related to socialism, but he assumed that "there is no incompatibility: in appropriate states of the social environment the socialist engine can be run on democratic principles" (Schumpeter 1947, 284, 296–97, 302. cf. Haberler 1981, 89–90; Heilbroner 1981; Hadenius 1987). William Kornhauser (1965, 131, 141) connected the origin of democracy with a pluralist society. He explained that where "the introduction of democratic rule is based on a pluralist society, especially a balance of classes and religious groups, it will tend to be strong and viable." Karl A. Wittfogel (1963) associated democracy with a multicentered society, whereas the origin of Oriental despotism can be traced to the extreme concentration of the control of the strategic means of production, especially cultivable land and hydraulic institutions, in the hands of the Oriental state. Karl de Schweinitz (1964, 3–11, 23–24, 54–58) hypothesized that the emergence of political democracy in the Western world was intimately, even causally, related to industrialization.

Contemporary research on the social requisites of democracy can be traced primarily to the pioneering studies and hypotheses of Daniel Lerner (1958), S.M. Lipset (1959), and Karl W. Deutsch (1961), studies that have been empirically tested, discussed, criticized, and further developed in many later studies (for reviews, see May 1973; Pennock 1979; Vanhanen 1979, 5–13; Lipset 1983, 469–76; Badie 1984; Berg-Schlosser 1985; Soares 1985; Diamond et al. 1986, 29–32).

Daniel Lerner hypothesized that urbanization starts modernization and is followed by increased literacy, media exposure, and economic and political participation. According to him, "democratic governance comes late, historically, and typically appears as a crowning institution of the participant society" (Lerner 1968, 46–64).

S.M. Lipset's hypothesis, "The more well-to-do a nation, the greater the chances that it will sustain democracy," has probably been the most influential contemporary explanation of democracy. He explained that from "Aristotle down to the present, men have argued that only in a wealthy society in which relatively few citizens lived at the level of real poverty could there be a situation, in which the mass of the population intelligently participate in politics and develop the self-restraint necessary to avoid succumbing to the appeals of irresponsible demagogues." On the other hand, he said, "A society divided between a large impoverished mass and a small favored elite results either in oligarchy (dictatorial rule of the small upper stratum) or in tyranny (popular-based dictatorship)" (Lipset 1960, 49–60). Lipset traces his hypothesis to Aristotle, but it seems that he emphasizes the level of economic development and abundance more than Aristotle does, who paid more attention to the distribution of wealth and the balance of forces. Aristotle argued, "The most pure democracy is that which is so called principally from that equality which prevails in it: for this is what the law in that state directs; that the poor shall be in no greater subjection than the rich; nor that the supreme power shall be lodged with either of these, but that both share it" (Aristotle, 1952, 115). It is true that the latter part of Lipset's hypothesis refers to the distribution of wealth, but he did not try to operationalize this part of his hypothesis, and the other users of his hypothesis seem to have forgotten it completely. It seems that Lipset did not realize that the distribution of wealth and the level of economic development are not the same thing. The indicators he himself used to test his hypothesis were intended to measure economic development—wealth, industrialization, urbanization, and education—not the distribution of wealth and other resources. Of these indicators, he paid particular attention to the indicators of education. Lipset hypothesized: "The higher one's education, the more likely one is to believe in democratic values and support democratic practices." On the basis of available evidence he concluded: "If we cannot say that a 'high' level of education is a *sufficient* condition of democracy, the available evidence suggests that it comes close to being a *necessary* one" (Lipset 1960, 56–57). In a revised edition of *Political Man* Lipset repeats his hypothesis and defends it by referring to a number of social scientists who have continued to work in this area and, "using more statistically sophisticated methods, have also found positive relationship between economic development and democracy, although it should be noted that their indicators and definitions of democracy have varied" (Lipset 1983, 469–476).

Karl W. Deutsch assumed that the process of social mobilization produces political side effects, one of which is an increase in voting participation. He did not attempt to explain the emergence of democracy by social mobilization, but voting participation, one of his variables, is an aspect of democratization (Deutsch 1961).

Many researchers have empirically tested these hypotheses, and the results have usually supported them. There is a moderate positive correlation between democracy and economic development or modernization (see Cutright 1963; Neubauer 1967; Olsen 1968; Needler 1967; Smith 1969; Banks 1970; Winham 1970; Kim 1971; Flanigan and Fogelman 1971; Flora 1973; Coulter 1975; Marquette 1974; Bollen 1979, 1980). However, it is not sure that this relationship has been caused by economic development or modernization per se; it may have been caused by something else that economic development indicates. I return to this question in a later connection. In any case, Lipset's thesis has been the most extensively tested hypothesis on the conditions of democratic order. Unfortunately some anomalies, the existence of democracy in several poor countries and the lack of democracy in economically developed Socialist countries in particular, weaken the explanatory power of modernization hypotheses seriously.

Robert A. Dahl (1976, 68) notes that differences in political systems are beyond our capacity to enumerate. His attention is focused on the continuum of political systems from hegemonies to polyarchies, and he traces the democratization of political systems to various explanatory factors, not merely to economic development. Dahl's list comprises seven sets of conditions that are assumed to increase the chances of democratization: historical sequences, the degree of concentration in the socioeconomic order, level of socioeconomic development, inequality, subcultural cleavages, foreign control, and the beliefs of political activists (Dahl 1971). It is interesting to note that Dahl separates the level of socioeconomic development from the degree of concentration or dispersion of resources and that he pays attention to the significance of equalities and inequalities. On the basis of ample evidence he concedes that "there can no longer be any doubt that competitive politics and socioeconomic level do tend to run together," but, on the other hand, he remarks that "the chances for competitive politics and polyarchy by no means depend entirely on socioeconomic levels, for there are too many exceptions and anomalies to be accounted for" (Dahl 1971, 64; 1976, 91). Dahl (1971, 51) emphasizes the significance of resource dispersion for democratization and hypothesizes that the circumstances "most favorable for competitive politics exist when access to violence and socioeconomic sanctions is either dispersed or denied both to oppositions and to government. The least favorable circumstances exist when violence and socioeconomic sanctions are exclusively available to the government and denied to the oppositions." This is a very reasonable hypothesis. Referring to Aristotle, Dahl (1971, 81) assumes that "extreme inequalities help to produce hegemonic regimes and that nonhegemonic systems of a more egalitarian sort must contain a preponderant middling group of citizens more or less equal and therefore must avoid extreme differences (among citizens) in status, income, and wealth." In agricultural societies the distribution of landed property affects the nature of the political system directly. Following James Harrington, who assumed that the distribution of landed property determines "the nature of the empire," Dahl (1976, 93) claims that "a popular government is unlikely to exist in an agricultural society unless landed property is widely distributed with a considerable measure of equality" (Dahl 1976, 93). The problem with Dahl's explanatory model concerns the operationalization of his various explanatory factors. He did not try to operationalize his concepts or to weigh the relative significance of various factors. Therefore it has not been possible to test his theory by empirical data (cf. Dahl 1971, 202–07).

J. Roland Pennock classifies the various factors and propositions about democratic requisites under three headings: (1) history, (2) the socioeconomic order, and (3) political culture. His own assumption is that the elements of political culture may include the best explanation for democracy. He says that none of the items discussed under the headings of "history" or "socioeconomic condition" qualifies as necessary conditions of democracy, whereas most of those discussed under "political culture" at least come close to meriting that designation. He even assumes that "this group may well comprise a sufficient condition for democracy" (Pennock 1979, 206–59). It is difficult to accept Pennock's argumentation because most of the characteristics of political culture to which he refers cannot be regarded as independent factors. They are a part of the *explicandum*, the nature of political systems.

Guillermo O'Donnell challenged Lipset's "optimistic equation" hypothesis, according to which "more socio-economic development = more likelihood of political democracy." He came to the conclusion that, "in contemporary South America, high modernization tends to consolidate new patterns of dependence and to lead to mass praetorianism, which introduces serious distortions in formally democratic political institutions." He hypothesized that "political authoritarianism—not political democracy—is the more likely concomitant of the highest levels of modernization." His thesis is that we cannot explain democratization by the same factors in all parts of the world (O'Donnell 1973; see also Collier 1978a, and b; Badie 1984, 189–92). I think that redemocratizations in South America in the 1980s have contradicted his hypothesis on the positive linkage between modernization and autoritarianism (cf. Muller 1985; Diamond et al. 1986, 26–27).

In a new comparative study *Transitions from Authoritarian Rule,* Guillermo O'Donnell and Philippe C. Schmitter analyze the process of recent redemocratizations descriptively, but they do not have any specific theory on the causes of democratization. They emphasize, however, that transitions from authoritarian rule "should be analysed with distinctly political concepts, however vaguely delineated and difficult to pin down they may be," although it does not mean "a denial of the long-run causal impact of 'structural' (including macroeconomic, world systemic, and social class) factors" (O'Donnell and Schmitter 1986, 4). On the other hand, according to the generalization of Laurence Whitehead (1986, 4), "in all the peacetime cases considered here internal forces were of primary importance in determining the course and outcome of the transition attempt, and international factors played only a secondary role."

The dependency theory formulated by Gunder Frank and others emphasizes the significance of external factors. According to this theory, the economic underdevelopment of the Third World countries is causally related to the development of the core countries of the capitalist world system. Underdevelopment is, as Immanuel Wallerstein (1982, 117) says, "the result of being involved in the world economy as a peripheral, raw material producing area." Underdevelopment is interpreted as the necessary product of capitalism itself (see Frank 1970; Wilson and Woods 1982, 42–51; Badie 1984, 177–200; Zollberg 1985; Muller 1985). Dependency theory does not particularly try to find an explanation for democratization or for its lack, but implicitly it includes an assumption that the lack of democracy in so many Third World countries is due to economic underdevelopment caused by external factors. According to Kenneth Bollen, some dependency theorists "suggest that political inequalities manifested in non-democratic governments in the peripheral and semiperipheral countries is maintained with the economic, political, and, sometimes, military support of the elites in the core countries." Bollen (1983) tested the dependency/democracy hypothesis by empirical data and found that different positions in the world system are associated with different levels of political democracy even after controlling economic development. The level of democracy is the lowest in peripheral countries . This result, however, does not prove that economic dependency has caused the failures of democracy in peripheral countries and it does not solve the causal problem of the origin of economic dependency. Edward N. Muller concludes that breakdowns of democracy in many economically advanced countries of the Third World "ran counter to basic hypothesis of modernization theory," but, on the other hand, he also found that "there is no empirical support for hypotheses that explain breakdowns of democracy in the Third World as a result of dependent economic development." He traced these breakdowns of democracy to a temporary external factor, to the U.S. Cold War support for authoritarian government in the Third World by the Johnson and Nixon administrations (Muller 1985).

Raymond D. Gastil discards socioeconomic explanations of democracy and seems to think that democratization depends principally on the diffusion of democratic ideas. He agrees that favorable economic conditions can help a democratic system to succeed, but these are "the secondary factors in a more general process of the diffusion of democracy." He says that in recent centuries democratic ideas spread from a very few centers, and he comes to the conclusion that the existence or lack of democracy in a particular country can be seen "as primarily the result of the relative effectiveness of the diffusion of democracy and its supporting concepts." Consequently, "the setbacks for democracy that have occurred in recent years, especially on the African continent, can be seen as the inevitable result of insufficient time for the diffusion of the critical ideas to the populations concerned" (Gastil 1985. cf. Fossedal 1989). This seems too easy and superficial an explanation for the failures of democracy in Africa.

Juan J. Linz emphasizes the significance of political variables "that tend to be neglected in many other approaches to the problem of stable democracy." He does not deny the importance of socioeconomic factors, but argues that they leave a lot of room for political actors to make choices "that can increase or decrease the probability of the persistence and stability of a regime." In crisis situations, "leadership, even the presence of an individual with unique qualities and characteristics—a Charles de Gaulle, for instance—can be decisive and cannot be predicted by any model" (Linz 1978, 4–5). However, he did not try to measure or estimate the relative weight of the structural characteristics of societies versus historical political processes, unique personalities, and other political factors. Of political factors, Linz has especially explored the comparative advantages of parliamentarism and presidentialism. He suggests that a shift from presidentialism to parliamentarism "might increase the flexibility and crisis-surviving capability of many Latin American democracies," and he notes that "with the exception of the

United States, a country that is so many ways exceptional, almost all stable democracies in the world have been parliamentary democracies." His thesis is that "political crafting" plays an important role. For example, the economic crisis of the 1930s was for many of the European democracies that survived "period of creative political crafting in which new coalitions and new policies were forged," whereas "in both Germany and Austria there was more active crafting of democratic destruction than there was crafting of democratic consolidation" (Linz 1986; see also 1984). Certainly there is room for political crafting, which depends on the ideas and qualities of political leaders, but the range of alternatives is limited by environmental conditions. For instance, the failures of democracy in Africa may be much more due to unfavorable environmental conditions than to the nature of African political leaders.

Samuel P. Huntington assumes that there are many factors—economic, social, external, and cultural—that appear to be associated with the emergence of democratic regimes. He takes into account both internal and external factors. The emergence of democracy in a society is helped by a number of factors, he explains, "higher levels of economic well-being; the absence of extreme inequalities in wealth and income; greater social pluralism, including particularly a strong and autonomous bourgeoisie; a more market-oriented economy; greater influence vis-a-vis the society of existing democratic states; and a culture that is less monistic and more tolerant of diversity and compromise." Because he thinks that none of these preconditions is sufficient to lead to democratic development and because he does not have any way to estimate their relative importance, he cannot present any testable hypothesis on democratization (Huntington 1984; cf. Pennock 1979, 255–59; Powell 1982, 30–53).

Dirk Berg-Schlosser has investigated conditions conducive to democratic political systems in a comparison group of 22 "semi competitive" and "polyarchal" Third World countries. He took both internal and external conditions into account and concluded that factors involved are highly varied and to a lesser degree economically determined. He found that specific influences of political culture play a clearly important role as demonstrated by factors such as "region" and "former colonial power." He pays particular attention to agrarian structures and remarks "that widespread small-scale farming in predominantly agrarian countries is an important factor in the emergence of democratic social and political structures" (Berg-Schlosser 1985).

Claucio Ary Dillon Soares has attempted to clarify the relationship between economic development and political democracy in Latin America. He is not satisfied with "socioeconomic preconditions theories" that originated in "Core" countries and tend to emphasize internal determinants and to minimize the role of external ones. Researchers "working in developing countries have been far more sensitive both to historical peculiarities of each country and to external factors. Theories of imperialism, colonialism, and of dependency have a far broader public in developing countries than in 'Core' countries." Soares tested his hypothesis that socioeconomic preconditions theories would have a higher predictive value in "Core" countries than in Latin America and found that empirical evidence supported his assumption. Several Latin American countries should be stable democracies by now, if they had followed the same path as the central capitalist countries. He concluded that it would be advantageous to analyze "Core" countries and Latin American countries separately and to "give a greater weight to exogenous variables, which are absent from both the orthodox Marxist and socioeconomic preconditions theories" (Soares 1985).

Huub Spoormans investigated the democratization of 19 mostly European countries on the basis of the proposition "that democratization is the outcome of a rough balance between social forces in struggle." He concludes that from this point of view "democracy is an institutional compromise between conflicting social classes or groups" (Spoormans 1987).

Mitchell A. Seligson studied development and democracy in Central America. He starts from the question: "Why has democracy, which for so long has been orphan in this region, suddenly begun to find a home?" His explanation is based on the hypothesis that minimum levels of wealth and literacy are necessary but not sufficient conditions for the development of democracy. He found the data for Central America to be consistent with the theory. In the 1950s the fundamental prerequisites for democracy were not present in Central America outside Costa Rica, whereas during the past 10 to 15 years these countries have crossed the threshold of necessary prerequisites for democracy. As a consequence, "democracy, however fragile, is beginning to emerge in the region." On the other hand, the social basis of democracy in Central America is still fragile because of great inequalities that produce social unrest and violence (Seligson 1987; see also 1988).

Larry Diamond, S.M. Lipset, and Juan J. Linz aim "to identify which factors have most consistently and powerfully accounted for democratic success and failures in the Third World, and what role is also played by unique and idiosyncratic features of a country's political life" in their project on *Democracy in Developing Countries*. Their comparative research is based on the idea that the same factors are not necessarily equally important in all countries and that the unique peculiarities of a country's political life may have a significant role. Consequently they cannot present any particular hypothesis on the requisites of democracy, which should apply to all countries, whereas they give a long list of tentative propositions on conditions and circumstances that are assumed to develop and sustain democratic government. Their propositions refer to both internal and external factors, as well as to social and political factors. Their method is basically inductive (Diamond et al. 1986).

Many of the theories and interpretations reviewed above have become well known and influential outside the circle of social scientists, too. Thomas A. Sancton (1987), for example, summarized succinctly the most common Western perception of the preconditions of democracy in his essay *Democracy's Fragile Flower Spreads Its Roots:* "Most political scientists agree that certain preconditions are necessary. Among them: a fairly high level of economic development, a strong middle class, a tradition of tolerance and respects for the individual, the presence of independent social groups and institutions, a market-oriented economy and the existence of elites willing to give up power." These are characteristics of industrially developed Western societies. The problem is that it would be very difficult for any poor developing country to establish democratic institutions if "a fairly high level of economic development" were a necessary precondition of democracy.

AN EVOLUTIONARY INTERPRETATION OF DEMOCRATIZATION

The idea that there are a variety of factors sustaining democracy and that we cannot establish any uniform explanation for democratization seems to be common for the theories and studies summarized above. Robert Wesson says, "We do not have anything like a scientific understanding of democracy, although its content is intuitively fairly clear and it is not difficult to give a formal definition" (Wesson 1988, 1). Many kinds of factors, both internal and external, can further or hamper democratization, but, on the other hand, my intention is to argue that there is and there must be a common factor able to account for the major part of the variation of political systems from the aspect of democratization and that a scientific understanding of democracy could be based on this common factor. This argument is based on the idea that, as a consequence of natural selection, all species have species-specific behavioral predispositions that are common to all members of the species in the same sense as common morphological characteristics (see, for example, Wilson 1975, 1978; Lorenz 1977, 223–33, and 1982, 1–11; Alexander 1980, 89–92; Eibl-Eibesfeldt 1984, 35–54). This means, in the case of political behavior, that there must be universal political behavior patterns that have remained more or less the same across all cultural variations.

Thus my attempt to explain the variation and democratization of political systems starts from the assumption that political structures and behavior patterns have evolved in the struggle for existence and reproduction and become adapted to variable environmental conditions. Therefore the Darwinian theory of evolution by natural selection may provide explanatory principles that can be used to explain the necessity and basic rules of politics. I emphasize that there are explanations at different levels of explanation, there are proximate and ultimate explanations (cf. Wind 1984; Mayr 1988, 17). Attention has been concentrated on proximate factors in many previous explanations of democratization, whereas I try to find an ultimate evolutionary explanation for democratization.

Let us first summarize the basic principles of the Darwinian theory of evolution by natural selection. According to this theory, there must be a fierce struggle for existence among the individuals of a population, because more individuals are produced than can be supported by available resources. This inference is based on the facts that (1) all species have great potential fertility, (2) populations normally display stability, and (3) natural resources are limited and, in a stable environment, remain relatively constant. On the basis of these observations Darwin concluded that the survival in the struggle for existence is not completely random but depends in part on the hereditary constitution of the surviving individuals. The individuals in some respects even slightly better adapted to their existing environment have better chances to survive than those whose characteristics are less adaptive in the same environment. As a consequence the survival of individuals and their genes is unequal, and this unequal survival constitutes a process of natural selection. This inference is based on the facts that (1) no two individuals are exactly the same, and (2) that much of this variation is heritable. This means that the characteristics of survived individuals become spread in the population through their offspring, and the less adaptive heritable characteristics become less frequent. Over the generations this process of natural selection will lead to a continuing gradual change in populations, that is, to evolution (Mayr 1982, 479–80; 1988, 215–32; see also Dobzhansky et al. 1977, 96–99; Alexander 1980, 15–22).

My argument is that we can apply these evolutionary principles to politics and to the evolution of political structures. Politics can be interpreted as an expression of the universal struggle for existence in living nature. It is for us a species-specific way to compete for scarce resources and reproduction. And as such it is as necessary and inevitable as the struggle for existence everywhere in nature. It is so because we live in a world of scarce resources where competition and struggle are the major ways to distribute those resources. Thus the evolutionary roots of politics lie in the necessity to solve conflicts over scarce resources by some method. Because everyone seems to have an equal right to those resources, and because they are scarce, we have to compete for them. We should understand that there is no way to avoid this struggle, for it belongs to the nature of all living beings that they do their utmost to preserve their own existence. W.D. Hamilton presented the hypothesis on inclusive fitness, according to which individuals are likely to behave in a manner that maximizes the survival of their genes not only through their own offspring but also through their relatives having the same genes. So inclusive fitness refers to the total reproductive success of an individual, from the gene's point of view, through his/her own offspring and relatives (Hamilton 1978; see also Wilson 1975, 415–16; Alexander 1980, 43–58; Barash 1982, 43, 71–74; Wind 1984, 4–6). This assumption implies that individuals are likely to behave selfishly in the competition for scarce resources. Only those who were successful in this competition were able to survive and reproduce. The selfishness of individuals can be traced to the fact that the genetic interests of individuals are different because of the genetic diversity of sexually reproduced individuals. It is a fact of life that we cannot change. This state of affairs, the scarcity of resources and the genetic diversity of individuals, explains why politics concerns the struggle for scarce resources and why it must be so.

I think that it is legitimate to make analogical inferences from the mechanism of natural selection to political structures and behavior patterns, for they can be regarded as collective organs that have evolved in the struggle for scarce resources (cf. Corning 1971, 303–65; Lorenz 1977, 285; Alexander 1980, 220–33; Meyer 1981, 19, 43). They have evolved to help their users to be more successful in the competition for resources and reproduction. People using different behavior patterns and political structures have competed for survival, and as a consequence of this competition more appropriate patterns and structures with their users have gradually displaced less appropriate ones. This unequal survival of different characteristics of political behavior patterns and structures constitutes the analogical process of natural selection in politics. It is based on the fact that two behavior patterns and structures are rarely exactly the same and that much of their variation is inheritable (through behavioral predispositions and culture). This argumentation leads to the conclusion that existing political behavior patterns and structures, like various political systems, are not entirely random phenomena but results of evolution by natural selection in politics and that they are continually tested in actual politics.

Here we have to separate relatively constant behavioral predispositions, which can be assumed to be genetically inherited and common to our species, and variable political structures and institutions, which are culturally inherited. Both have evolved by natural selection in politics (as defined above), but behavioral predispositions, because of long evolutionary history, are much more stable and constant than political structures and institutions, which vary enormously from one environment to another and become constantly adapted to changing environmental conditions. The variation of political systems and democratization are examples of this kind of adaptive variation. But what characteristics of the environment are responsible for the adaptation of political systems? That is the question. In other words, what are the *explicans* that could provide a satisfactory explanation for the *explicandum*, the variation of political systems from the perspective of democratization?

I am inclined to argue that because politics belongs to the struggle for existence, participants probably resort to all available means in the competition for scarce resources. They struggle for power because power can be used to get scarce resources. Human desire for power and for the fruits of power can be assumed to be constant, but in practice all people and their groups do not have the same chances to get power and the fruits of power because the sources of power, or sanctions, are not equally distributed. Power can be described as the ability to produce intended effects, even against the will of others. This ability is always based on some means that can be used to persuade or compel others (cf. Hobbes 1962, 72; Friedrich 1950, 23–24; Russell 1975, 25; Meyer 1981, 52–54, 83–87; Slack 1981, 3–4). Power is based on sanctions; otherwise it would not be possible to get others to act against their will. W.H. Slack (1981, 3–4) says about this relationship that, without "at least some of the various instruments of power, the would-be power user cannot hope either to influence or to direct the behavior of others." Thus sanctions are used as the principal means in the struggle for power, and this struggle is the mechanism by which political systems become adapted to varying environmental conditions.

In all societies resources used as sources of power are to some degree unequally distributed among individuals and groups, and there are great differences between societies in the way how these resources are distributed among competing groups. As a consequence of this environmental variation, power is distributed differently in different environmental conditions, for all available means are used in the struggle for power. Those having the most effective sanctions at their disposal are able to get more power than those whose power resources are meager. This is a constant that runs through all power structures and makes them regular and to some degree predictable. The adaptation of political systems to environmental conditions means that power structures become adapted to resource structures. The concentration of power resources leads to autocratic political structures, whereas the wide distribution of the same resources makes the sharing of power and democracy possible. On the basis of this argumentation, I hypothesize that

1. The relative distribution of economic, intellectual, and other power resources among various sections of the population is the fundamental factor that accounts for the variation of democratization.
2. Democratization will take place under conditions in which power resources have become so widely distributed that no group is any longer able to suppress its competitors or to maintain its hegemony.

This hypothesis implies that the explicans of democratization are to be found in social structures and conditions reflecting the distribution or concentration of crucial power resources because the distribution of power in a society must be related to the distribution of the most important power resources among competing groups. If relevant power resources are widely distributed among various sections of the population, environmental conditions are favorable for democratization; if they are concentrated in the hands of the few, conditions are unfavorable for democracy and favorable for autocratic political systems. Democracy emerges as a rational compromise between strong competing groups (cf. Spoormans 1987, who presents a similar idea). Thus the relative distribution of economic, intellectual, and other power resources among various sections of the population is the fundamental factor that is assumed to account for the variation of political systems from the aspect of democratization. The problem is to locate these resources and to find some way to measure to what degree they are distributed among the population at the national level. This is certainly much more difficult than to measure the level of democratization by electoral data.

EXPLANATORY VARIABLES

It is extremely difficult to locate crucial power resources for the reason that nearly everything can become a resource in the struggle for power (cf. Friedrich 1950, 23–24). Also, important resources can vary from country to country and from one period to another. Besides, it may be impossible to find reliable and valid empirical indicators to measure the distribution of those resources at the national level and to get such measurements comparable from country to country. These obstacles are formidable, but they do not need to be insurmountable. I think that some aspects of resource distribution can be compared from country to country by using suitable indirect indicators whose meaning remains approximately the same across societies. The dispersion or concentration of economic and intellectual power resources in particular seems to suit this kind of indirect measurement. They do not cover the whole arsenal of power resources, but it seems reasonable to assume that economic and intellectual resources are important means of power in all societies. They can be assumed to be the most important power resources as long as the struggle for power remains more or less peaceful. When competing groups resort to violence, the means of violence and the ability to use them become the most important power resources. Without a satisfactory way of measuring the distribution of the means of violence, the measurement must be restricted to some aspects of economic and intellectual power resources. The problem is how to measure them.

In previous comparative studies I used five social variables to indicate approximate differences among societies in the distribution of these resources. The variables were (1) urban population, (2) nonagricultural population, (3) students in universities and equivalent degree-granting institutions, (4) literate population, and (5) family farms (see Vanhanen 1979, 25–31, 1984, 33–37). The same explanatory variables are used in this study, but, in addition, I use a new variable to indicate the decentralization of the most important nonagricultural economic power resources. Finally, the indicators of these six variables are combined into an Index of Power Resources (IPR), which is used as the principal explanatory variable in statistical analysis.

Urban Population

In all contemporary countries the population is divided into urban and rural populations, although the border between these areas may be unambigious and although the definitions of "urban" and "rural" vary to some degree from country to country. In spite of national variations, "urban areas" denote in all countries densely populated areas, whereas "rural areas" refer to agricultural and other regions outside cities and towns. There are plenty of statistical data on the percentage of urban population; most of my data are from *World Development Reports,* published by The World Bank, and from United Nations' *Demographic Yearbooks,* but several other international and national sources have also been used to complete the data. Empirical data on urban population are given in Appendix 2.

The percentage of urban population has been used in many other comparative studies to indicate economic or socioeconomic development (see Lerner 1958/1968; Lipset 1959; Coleman 1964; Cutright 1963; Russett 1964; Neubauer 1967; Olsen 1968; Smith 1969; Pride 1970; Winham 1970; Flanigan and Fogelman 1971; Marquette 1974; Coulter 1975; Banks 1981). It surely measures one aspect of socioeconomic development, but indirectly it also seems to indicate the dispersion of various economic and organizational power resources. It is reasonable to assume that the higher the percentage of urban population, the more varied economic activities there are and the more widely economic resources are distributed among organized interest groups. Therefore, the level of socioeconomic development usually, although not always, correlates positively with the dispersion of various economic power resources. The variety of economic activities and interest conflicts leads to an easier dispersion of economic resources in highly urbanized societies than in less urbanized societies. On the other hand, because the concept of "urban population" is used approximately in the same meaning in all societies, this indicator is suitable to measure one aspect of the distribution of economic power resources.

Nonagricultural Population (NAP)

The division of labor is a characteristic of all human societies. Occupational classifications describe the division of labor in contemporary societies. From the perspective of this study, the most fundamental division is between agricultural and nonagricultural occupations because it is usually connected with the level of socioeconomic development. It is also easier to separate agricultural population from nonagricultural population than to distinguish various nonagricultural occupations from each other. In the case of agricultural population, the criteria used in national censuses have remained more or less the same, which means that data on the percentage of agricultural population are relatively reliable and comparable. In this study empirical data concern the percentage share of agricultural population, which is usually calculated from the economically active population. The percentage of nonagricultural population (NAP) is calculated by subtracting the share of agricultural population from 100 percent. Nearly all statistical data on agricultural population are from FAO's *Production Yearbooks* (see Appendix 2).

Just like urban population, the percentage of agricultural population has been used to indicate economic and socioeconomic development in many contemporary studies. The assumption has been that the higher the percentage of agricultural population, the lower the level of economic development (see Lipset 1959; Coleman 1960; Deutsch 1961; Cutright 1963; Russett et al. 1964; Neubauer 1967; Olsen 1968; Smith 1969; Pride 1970; Winham 1970; Flanigan and Fogelman 1971; Marquette 1974; Coulter 1975).

I agree that the share of agricultural population indicates the level of economic development, for usually a high percentage of agricultural population means that the country is neither industrialized nor urbanized. In this study, however, I use NAP to indicate indirectly the distribution of economic power resources on the basis of the assumption that the higher the percentage share of nonagricultural population, the more widely those resources are usually distributed. There are more varied economic activities and interest groups in a society with a considerable part of the population working in nonagricultural occupations than in a more agricultural society. Economic resources become distributed among different and competing groups. The argument is the same as in the case of Urban Population. These two variables more or less measure the same phenomenon from two different perspectives. They are imperfect indicators of resource distribution, but, because there are relatively valid and reliable statistical data on these indicators, they can be used to measure some aspects of the distribution of economic and organizational power resources in this study.

Students

Thorkil Kristensen (1974, XIII) has very strongly emphasized the importance of knowledge as the most prominent factor of production and development. He claims that "through the ages the growth of the stock of knowledge has been more important than any other factor leading to change in human societies." I assume that knowledge is also a very important source of power, but it is very difficult to measure the distribution of intellectual power resources quantitatively, because "intellectual resources" are far less concrete things than urban population and nonagricultural population. However, it seems possible to measure some aspects of this phenomenon. In contemporary societies universities and other degree-granting institutions are the most important depositories of higher knowledge, which is needed in the management of modern societies. They reproduce and distribute this knowledge through students. Therefore it seems reasonable to assume that intellectual resources become the more widely distributed the higher the relative number of students in these institutions. Empirical data on the number of students in universities and other degree-granting institutions are available from nearly all countries of the world. In this study statistical data concern the number of students per 100,000 inhabitants. Most data are from Unesco's *Statistical Yearbooks*. The data given in Appendix 2 can be regarded as relatively reliable and comparable, although the definitions of "universities and other degree-granting institutions" and also the definitions of "students" vary considerably. The absolute numbers of students per 100,000 inhabitants, however, are not used in statistical analysis. They are transformed into percentages by using 5,000 students per 100,000 inhabitants to represent the level of 100 percent. The percentages calculated in this way are used in statistical analysis. For example, if the number of students per 100,000 inhabitants is 250, the percentage used in statistical analysis will be 5.

In some form this variable has been used in several previous studies to indicate the level of socioeconomic development, or the level of education (see Lipset 1959; Deutsch 1961; Cutright 1963; Russett et al. 1964; Neubauer 1967; Olsen 1968; Smith 1969; Winham 1970). In this study it is used to indicate the relative distribution of intellectual resources based on higher education, although, of course, it also indicates the level of educational development. In modern societies educated people with special skills and training are needed in politics and in the management of society. If the relative number of students is small, it means that some necessary skills and knowledge are concentrated in the hands of the few, and it is comparatively easy to absorb them into the service of the government or to control them. In contrast, if their number is large, it is more difficult for the government to control them or to employ all of them, and so many of them are available to the service of competing groups and parties. In such a way a wide distribution of intellectual resources represented by educated people creates favorable conditions for competitive politics.

Literate Population

The ability to read and write represents one form of intellectual resources. This ability is, in principle, easily recognizable and comparable from country to country. The number of literates can be counted just like the percentages of urban and agricultural populations. In fact, the number of literates has been counted or estimated in many censuses, and there are empirical data on the percentage of literates from nearly all countries of the world. The statistical data of this study on the percentage of literate population are taken from Unesco's *Statistical Yearbooks,* and from several other global and national data sources (see Appendix 2). Usually the percentage of literates has been calculated from the population 10 or 15 years of age and over. Surely these data include various errors and inaccuracies, but probably not many more than urban population and NAP.

This variable has also been used in many previous comparative studies to indicate the level of socioeconomic development or of educational development (see Lerner 1958; Lipset 1959; Coleman 1960; Deutsch 1961; Cutright 1963; Russett et al. 1964; Neubauer 1967; Olsen 1968; Smith 1969; Winham 1970; Marquette 1974).

In this study literates is principally used to indicate differences between countries in the distribution of basic intellectual resources. It is assumed that the higher the percentage of literate population, the more widely those resources are distributed. Literate persons are assumed to be more capable of taking part in modern politics than illiterates. If only a small minority of the population is able to read and write, the preconditions for democracy are much more unfavorable than in a society in which nearly all adults are literate. In this study Literates measures the distribution of basic intellectual resources, whereas Students is intended to measure the distribution of higher knowledge and skills. Taken together it is hoped that they will be able to describe crucial differences between countries in the distribution of intellectual power resources.

Family Farms

The ownership or control of land constitutes an important power resource, particularly so in agricultural societies where most people are dependent on agriculture. It is easy to use the ownership or control over land as a resource to get social and political power. Therefore, the way in which landownership is distributed among the agricultural population may crucially affect the nature of a country's political system. This relationship was already recognized by Aristotle, who noted that there is no difficulty in constructing a democracy where the bulk of the people live by arable or pastoral farming and where landownership is relatively equally distributed among farmers. On the other hand, oligarchy exists where property has concentrated in the hands of the few (see Aristotle 1961, 115–16, 163–64, 262–63). James Harrington assumed that the type of land tenure determined the nature of the political system, because the social group that owned a sufficient proportion or balance of land was also the governing group in that state (Harrington 1924, 14–15; Blitzer 1960, 114–27). Alexis de Tocqueville thought that the relatively equal distribution of land was one of the causes that tended to maintain democracy in America (see Tocqueville 1963 Vol. I, 46–54, 288–98). André Siegfried said that property is the most solid basis of political liberty. In agrarian societies this means that only the landowners are fully independent. Tenant cultivators and agricultural workers dependent on large landowners are politically less independent than owner-cultivators (Siegfried 1913, 370–80).

Many contemporary reserchers have observed the same relationship between landownership and power structures. Merla Kling (1962, 128, 137) notes, "Traditionally, ownership of land has been regarded as a major economic base for the excercise of power in Latin America." Barraclough and Domike say, "Plainly speaking, ownership or control of land is power in the sense of real or potential ability to make another person do one's will" (Barraclough and Domike 1970, 50.; See also Smith 1968, 15–17; Hung-Chao Thai 1974, 1–5; Kanel 1971, 26–29; Dorner 1972, 69). Robert A. Dahl (1976, 93–94) hypothesizes that "a popular government is unlikely to exist in an agricultural society unless landed property is widely distributed with a considerable measure of equality." He stresses that in agrarian societies "the possession of land is the main source of status, income, and wealth, inequality in land is equivalent to inequality in the distribution of political resources" (Dahl 1971, 53–56).

I agree with these arguments. The ownership or control of land is an economic resource that can be used as a sanction in the struggle for power. Therefore power structures, especially in agrarian societies, can be assumed to reflect the way in which ownership or control of land is distributed among the agricultural population. But how to measure the distribution of landownership?

Bruce M. Russett was, as far as I know, the first to attempt to measure and compare the distribution of agricultural land and to relate it to some characteristics of political systems. He used three separate indicators to indicate the degree of inequality: (1) the percentage of landholders who collectively occupy one-half of all agricultural land, (2) the Gini index of concentration, and (3) farm households that rent all their land as a percentage of the total number of farms. He found that land is everywhere distributed unequally, although the degree of inequality varies from state to state. The correlations between his measures of land equality and measures of political instability were not high, but he found that most of the states with the more equal patterns of land distribution are stable democracies, "whereas only three of twenty-four more unequal countries can be classified stable democracies." On the basis of these results Russett concluded, "Tocqueville's basic observation would therefore appear correct: no state can long maintain a democratic form of government if the major sources of economic gain are divided very unequally among its citizens" (Russett 1968; see also Russett et al. 1964, 237–42; Russett 1965, 117–21). I have not used the same variables in my comparative studies for various reasons. First, from many countries we do not have exact statistical data that are needed for Russett's indicators. Second, the Gini index of concentration, based on the Lorenz curve, may produce highly misleading results in some cases, because it does not take into account the variation in the quality of land and because the results may vary greatly depending on how small holdings were included in the number of holdings. Third, because I think that the concept of family farms provides a more appropriate criterion to measure and compare farm structures from the aspect of distribution of the ownership or control of land (cf. Muller et al. 1989). Therefore, I try to measure the distribution of landownership by the share of family farms.

By "family farms" I mean holdings (1) that are mainly cultivated by the holder family itself and (2) that are owned by the cultivator family or held in ownerlike possession, or, if leased, tenancy does not make the tenant family socially and economically dependent on the landowner (see Vanhanen 1979, 48–54, 1984, 35–36). This definition, however, is not enough for an operational definition of family farms. It is necessary to separate large farms cultivated mainly by hired workers from family-size farms and to separate tenant farms, when tenancy means substantial social and economic dependence on landowners, from family farms. Besides, it is necessary to decide how collective farms and land under traditional communal land tenure systems are classified.

In principle, the number of workers employed is used as the criterion for the upper limit of family farms. The category of family farms is intended to include the farms that provide employment for not more than four people, including family workers (see Barraclough and Domike 1970, 48). The results of several agricultural censuses providing statistical data on employment in agriculture by size-class of holding have facilitated the use of this criterion. The upper hectare limit of family farms was determined on the

basis of data on employment. However, from most countries such statistical
data are not available. In these cases the upper hectare limit of family farms
was estimated. In fact, it has been necessary to determine the upper hectare
limit of family farms separately for every country, because agricultural conditions vary so greatly from country to country that the use of a uniform
hectare limit would be unrealistic and misleading.

Tenanted land is subtracted from the area of family farms, as far as possible, in the case of developing countries, whereas in economically developed countries it is included in the area of family farms on the basis of the
assumption that tenancy does not any longer cause social and economic dependence in these countries. If it was not possible, in the case of developing
countries, to separate tenanted land from owned land, it has been taken into
account by using somewhat lower upper hectare limit for family farms.

The area of state farms and collective farms is excluded from the category
of family farms for the reason that land is not owned by cultivators, but also
for the reason that these holdings are usually much larger than family farms.

It has been very difficult to determine how to classify land holdings under
customary African land tenure systems. Previously they were called communal land tenure systems. It was characteristic for them "that the rights
relating to the land are split between the community and the individuals
belonging to it, in the sense that each individual has an unchallenged right
to use a plot of land, but if he ceases to exercise it, the right to determine
the nature and extent of its use by others is enjoyed not by him but by the
community" (FAO, 1953, 1; see also FAO, 1970a, 3, 38–51; 1970b, 396,
401; Ike 1977, 187–95). Consequently, in previous comparative studies, I
estimated that only a small part of agricultural land (from 5 to 35 percent)
belonged to the category of family farms in Africa (see Vanhanen 1979,
324–30, 1984, 156–59).

John B. Bruce argues that the term "communal" is misleading in the connection of customary African land tenure systems. He calls African land
tenure systems indigenous. There are communal grazing rights in some areas
of Africa, but rights over arable land are "essentially individual—acquired
by the individual, enjoyed by him, and disposed of by him." The stabilization of agriculture and the increasing scarcity of land have strengthened
individual rights over arable land. Bruce estimates that the farmer often has
a more "proprietary" attitude toward his holding than a characterization as
a "mere usufructuary" would imply. In fact, the African landholder is com-
monly quite secure in his holding, although land may not be "sold." African
farmers' rights over land are not as extensive as those of European farmers,
but the rights of the farmers are in most indigeneous tenure systems much
more important than the rights of the group (see Bruce 1985, 1–7). If compared with the concept of "family farms" as used in this study, Bruce would
say that African holdings under customary tenures are 80–90 percent "fam-

ily farms" (discussion with John Bruce, William Thiesenhusen, and Carol Dickerman at Land Tenure Center, University of Wisconsin, February 14, 1986). Dirk Berg-Schlosser expressed the same idea on the individualization of African customary land tenure systems (a letter to the writer, May 21, 1986). I use their interpretation as the starting point in my estimates on the share of family farms in the African countries of customary land tenure systems. However, the category of Family Farms is estimated to comprise less than 80–90 percent of the total agricultural land. Because some holdings are bigger than family farms and because part of land is rented to share-croppers or tenants, I estimate that on an average about 60 percent of the area under indigeneous tenure systems belongs to the category of Family Farms. Besides, estimated areas of de facto "state tenure" and "collective tenure" have been excluded from the category of indigeneous tenure systems. Land under "freehold tenure" is excluded from the category of Family Farms in the cases in which freehold holdings are large farms or plantations.

Statistical data and estimates on the share of family farms as well as the upper hectare limits of family farms or other bases of classifications are given and documented in Appendix 3. Most data are based on the results of agricultural censuses. In the case of African countries, I resorted mainly to the estimates given in the map *De facto agricultural land tenure systems* attached to Riddell and Dickerman's *Country Profiles of Land Tenure: Africa 1986* (1986) and in the *World Atlas of Agriculture, Volume 4* (1976). Otherwise FAO's reports on the results of the agricultural censuses of the world in 1960, 1970, and 1980 and Land Tenure Center's (1979) publication *Land Concentration in the Third World* have been the most useful sources of statistical information.

The Degree of Decentralization of Nonagricultural Economic Resources (DDN)

In modern societies most people work and get their livelihood in nonagricultural sectors of economy. Therefore, it would be useful to know how widely the most important economic power resources are distributed among the nonagricultural population. As in the case of landownership, it seems reasonable to assume that the concentration of important economic power resources would further the concentration of political power, and vice versa. Unfortunately it appears to be very difficult to find empirical variables to measure the relative distribution of the ownership or control of nonagricultural economic power resources and to make such measurements comparable from country to country. I have not found any comparative study on such variables, but some theoretical attempts to define "concentration" and "decentralization" have been made, and there are various studies on the distribution of economic power or resources within single countries.

In his book *Concentration of Economic Power in India*, S.R. Mohnot (1962) argues that the "motivating force of all human reactions in relation to material environment is largely a desire to subjugate it for material welfare, and with the ultimate end in view, for security." He connects this desire with the struggle for survival, for it "is evident also in lesser animals and possibly all biological creatures." Economic power based on economic resources is used as a means in this competition. By "economic power" Mohnot means the ability to control the economic life of other people. This ability is based on the ownership and/or control of productive resources and effective productive capacity. By "effective productive capacity" he means "first, control over material resources expressed in all forms of capital, and secondly, employment of human resources." Mohnot emphasizes that control over employment has to be distinguished from control over material resources (Mohnot 1962, 18–21; see also Vanhanen 1982, 46, 53–56). It is important to note these two aspects of economic power: ownership and control over material resources of production and control over employment, both of which mean power to control the means by which people earn their livelihood.

Richard L. Carson has analyzed the distribution of economic power from the aspect of political centralization or decentralization. He argues that the main difference between economic systems concerns the degree to which economic power is concentrated or decentralized: "We shall call a system in which economic power is highly concentrated, a *power-centralized* economy (which is also an economy with centralized political decision making). In the extreme, only one economic actor, of necessity a dictatorial central planning authority, has power to influence the terms of trade between different goods and services. A completely *de-* centralized system, by the same criterion, would be one in which the influence that any actor might have over *any* terms of trade would be so small that it would not be worth his or her while to take it into account (Carson 1973, 42; cf. Gardner 1988).

Robert A. Dahl (1985, 85–110) also contrasts centralized and decentralized economic orders and assumes that decentralization would be favorable for democracy. He notes that democracy "is and has always been closely associated in practice with private ownership of the means of production," but he argues that "the key question is not whether an order is socialist or nonsocialist, whether enterprises are owned "privately" or "publicly" (though these may be important secondary questions), but how much autonomy is permitted to economic enterprises and the nature of internal and external controls." Dahl assumes that the autonomy permitted to enterprises is theoretically independent of forms of ownership, hence of capitalism and socialism. He explains, "A capitalist order may be, but need not be, highly decentralized. A socialist order may be, but need not be, highly centralized" (Dahl 1982, 108–16).

Charles E. Lindblom has differentiated market-oriented economic systems and centrally planned systems. In the former, production is largely controlled by the market demands of millions of consumers, in the latter, production is directly controlled by authority, usually the central government. Market oriented systems are private enterprise systems in most cases, but they may include also Socialist market systems, of which Lindblom mentions Yugoslavia in particular. Most Socialist systems are centrally planned. Public enterprises play an important role in many market oriented systems, too, but because these "public enterprises are operated under a regime of consumer sovereignty instead of planner sovereignty or direct authoritative control, they are not designed to be especially receptive to state directives" (Lindblom 1977, 112–13). For this reason, the existence of public enterprises in market oriented systems does not necessarily indicate the concentration of economic power resources.

The arguments of Mohnot, Carson, Dahl, and Lindblom lead me to assume that, from the perspective of democracy, the most crucial aspect of economic order concerns the question of whether economic power resources are highly concentrated in the hands of one group, whatever that group is, or whether they are widely distributed among several relatively autonomous groups. Consequently, I attempt to measure to what degree the most important nonagricultural economic power resources are centralized or decentralized at the national level. I mean by "decentralization" that the means of production and through them the means of livelihood are owned or effectively controlled by several relatively independent groups, which may include individuals, corporations, public enterprises, local and regional governments, and the central government. The decentralization of economic power resources does not presuppose an equal distribution of those resources among people or social groups; it is enough that they are distributed among several autonomous and often conflicting groups representing various sections of the population. "Concentration" represents the opposite of "decentralization." By "concentration" I mean that important economic resources are owned or controlled by the few, usually a more or less coherent social or political group. The controlling group may be a group of individuals, one of big corporations (domestic or foreign-owned), one of public enterprises, or a party controlling the state and through it the means of production owned by the state. "Decentralization" and "concentration" are inversely related with each other, which means that either of them can be used to measure the degree of resource distribution.

The problem is how to measure "concentration" or "decentralization." I have not been able to find any single operational indicator like Family Farms to measure these theoretical concepts or at least some important aspects of them, but, in principle, it seems possible to formulate variables that measure, just like Family Farms, to what degree the ownership or control of the most important nonagricultural means of production and through them control over employment is concentrated or decentralized. For this purpose, I use three empirical variables, which measure the degree of concentration:

1. The public sector's share of productive capacity or of employment in nonagricultural sectors of economy, or in the most important sector of it (Public Sector).
2. The share of foreign-owned enterprises of productive capacity or of employment in nonagricultural sectors of economy, or in the most important sector of it (Foreign Sector).
3. The share of a few and big private enterprises (domestic-owned or controlled) of productive capacity or of employment in nonagricultural sectors of economy, or in the most important sector of it (Concentrated Private Sector).

Public Sector is intended to cover all enterprises owned or controlled by public authorities as well as public services that employ people (cf. Short 1984). There may be several public authorities, which are more or less independent from each other, but ultimately the controlling power is, at least potentially, in the hands of the national government. Therefore, public sector represents, actually or potentially, one form of resource concentration. The public sector's share can be calculated by the same criteria in all countries, although the degree of resource concentration represented by the public sector may vary considerably. From the perspective of resource concentration, public enterprises do not form as coherent a group in market-oriented systems as in the centrally planned systems. As Lindblom (1987, 112–13) noted, in the market-oriented systems it has been difficult for the central government to achieve any more significant effective control over public enterprises than over private enterprises.

In principle it is possible to get exact empirical data on Public Sector from every country, but in practice it is not so easy for the reason that systematic empirical data on the public sector's share are available only from a limited number of countries. The most complete data are from Socialist countries. There are partial data and estimations from several other countries, including most of the countries in which the public sector's share is the highest. I estimated the public sector's share for the other countries. But in many cases it has not been taken into account at all because of its relatively low share. I resorted to various information, empirical data, and studies on economic structures in my estimates on the percentage share of the public sector. Statistical data on the percentage share of public enterprises given by R.P. Short (1984) and H. Stephen Gardner (1988) have been particularly useful. Surely my estimates include errors, but it seems sensible to assume that they are not systematically biased.

Foreign Sector is also, in principle, a clearly demarcated variable. It is meant to measure the extent of foreign capital, and through it, economic power concentrated in the hands of foreigners in the nonagricultural sector of economy, or in the most important industries, such as manufacturing, mining, or oil industry. This variable applies uniformally to all countries, but it is difficult to get exact empirical data on the extent of foreign ownership and control. However, there are data and estimations on the share of foreign ownership for most countries in which it plays an important role. I have used such information in estimating the share of foreign sector. However, I have always combined Foreign Sector either with Public Sector or with Concentrated Private Sector because separate data or estimates on the share of foreign sector have been available only from few countries. When it does not seem to play an important role in economy, it has not been taken into account at all. The percentage share of foreign ownership is assumed to indicate one aspect of resource concentration because the ultimate control of these enterprises is not in the hands of the country's own citizens.

In principle, it is easy to define Public Sector and Foreign Sector because they can be separated from the domestic private sector by generally accepted uniform criteria, whereas it is very difficult to give an operational definition for Concentrated Private Sector for the reason that it seems impossible to find any uniform criteria by which we could separate "concentrated" private sector from the group of other private enterprises. The concepts of "big," "medium," and "small" enterprises do not help to solve the problem of demarcation because the meaning of "big" varies from country to country depending on the structure and size of economy. However, one theoretical criterion can be used to define the concept of Concentrated Private Sector. It is meant to include such big enterprises whose owners or controllers can be assumed to form social group or class homogeneous to some degree. This criterion is based on the assumption that any coherent social group has common or similar interests and that, consequently, its members are disposed to have similar political interests, too. This means that I should take into account, not only the size structure of enterprises but also the social coherence of their owners or controllers. Besides, the existence of big corporations does not necessarily imply the concentration of their ownership because the ownership of big corporations may be widely distributed. For these reasons I cannot use uniform criteria, like the number of workers or the value of production, to demarcate the category of big enterprises comprising Concentrated Private Sector. It is uniformly defined only in one respect: public enterprises are excluded from this category. In other respects I have to determine, separately for each country, the criteria by which the enterprises of Concentrated Private Sector are separated from other private enterprises and to estimate their share. My estimations are based on various information on the structure of economy and also on empirical data on some indirect indicators. For example, if a considerable part of the population lives below absolute poverty income level (see Social Indicators of Development 1988), nonagricultural economic resources cannot be widely distributed. As far as possible, I have documented the sources of my estimations in Appendix 4, in which empirical data and estimates on Public Sector, Public and Foreign Sectors, Concentrated Private and Foreign Sectors, and Concentrated Private Sector are given. Raymond D. Gastil's (1988) cross-tabulation of countries by economic and political systems provides an interesting point of comparison for my estimations. Gastil's classification of economic systems from capitalist to Socialist ones corresponds roughly to one dimension of my classification; the share of Public Sector from low to high.

As all of the three variables are assumed to measure the concentration of nonagricultural economic power resources, although from different points of view, and because they are conceptually mutually exclusive, it is reasonable to combine them by adding the percentages. The combined percentage indicates the relative level of resource concentration. In most cases, however, data or estimates are given only for one or two of these variables. Only one variable (often together with Foreign Sector) is taken into account in the cases in which either Public Sector or Concentrated Private Sector dominates economy. The inverse percentage of the combined percentage of resource concentration is assumed to indicate the degree of decentralization of nonagricultural economic resources (DDN). Its value can vary from zero to 100, although, according to my estimations, no country has reached 100 percent. DDN differs from the other explanatory indicators in one respect. Its values are based on my estimations more than empirical statistical data, although two of its components (Public Sector and Foreign Sector) are conceptually clearly demarcated variables. For this reason DDN is a softer indicator than the other five explanatory indicators. However, I assume that the margin of error in my estimations is usually less than 20 percentage points.

Index of Power Resources

Six explanatory indicators defined above are used to measure, from different perspectives, the distribution of economic and intellectual power resources within countries. These explanatory indicators can be and are used separately in statistical analysis, but because they are intended to measure the same basic factor—resource distribution—it is reasonable and even necessary to combine them into an Index of Power Resources (IPR). It would be possible to combine the six variables into an index by many ways, depending on how separate variables are weighted.

It seems that they indicate the distribution of power resources from three different perspectives. Urban Population and NAP indicate the degree of occupational diversification and the level of socioeconomic development. Indirectly they are assumed to measure the decentralization of economic and organizational power resources. It is assumed that usually important economic resources and organizational capabilities are the more widely distributed the higher the level of socioeconomic development and occupational diversification as indicated by Urban Population and NAP. Therefore, these two variables are combined into an Index of Occupational Diversification (IOD) by calculating their arithmetic mean. The combination of these two variables is probably a more reliable indicator of resource decentralization than either of them alone.

Students and Literates indicate the distribution of knowledge and intellectual power resources from two different perspectives. They are combined into an Index of Knowledge Distribution (IKD) by calculating their arithmetic mean. It is assumed that the higher the value of IKD, the more widely intellectual power resources are distributed in a society.

Family Farms and DDN are intended to measure the degree of resource distribution in agricultural and nonagricultural sectors of economy respectively. They are combined into an Index of the Distribution of Economic Power Resources (DER), but not simply by calculating their arithmetic mean. Because the relative importance of these two sectors varies greatly from country to country, it is reasonable to weight the values of Family Farms and DDN by their relative importance. It is done by multiplying the value of Family Farms by the percentage of agricultural population and the value of DDN by the percentage of non-agricultural population (NAP), after which the weighted values of Family Farms and DDN are simply added up. In other words, DER = (Family Farms × AP) + (DDN × NAP). It is assumed that the higher the value of DER the more widely economic power resources are distributed in a society.

In this way the six original explanatory indicators are combined into three new indexes (IOD, IKD, and DER). It is assumed that each of them measures to some degree different and equally important dimension of resource decentralization. Besides, I assume that the concentration of any of these resources might be enough to block democratization. In other words, even high levels of resource distribution in two dimensions cannot compensate the lack of resource distribution in one dimension. Therefore I combine them in the same way as Competition and Participation were combined into the Index of Democratization (ID). The three indexes are combined into an Index of Power Resources (IPR) by multiplying them and by dividing the outcome by 10,000. It is assumed that the higher the value of IPR, the more widely politically relevant power resources are distributed among various sections of the population and the more favorable social conditions are for democratization.

4

EMPIRICAL ANALYSIS OF DEMOCRATIZATION

Previous chapters define, operationally, indicators intended to measure some important aspects of "democratization" and "the distribution of power resources" and refer to the Appendices, which include empirical data on these indicators. Now it is possible to test, empirically, my principal hypotheses on the causes and process of democratization, according to which (1) the relative distribution of economic, intellectual, and other power resources among various sections of the population is the fundamental factor that accounts for the variation of democratization, and (2) democratization takes place under conditions in which power resources have become so widely distributed that no group is any longer able to suppress its competitors or to maintain its hegemony. The results of empirical analysis provide answers to the research questions presented at the beginning of this study and show to what degree evidence supports or fails to support my hypotheses on democratization.

RESEARCH HYPOTHESES AND TECHNIQUES OF ANALYSIS

The above hypotheses on democratization can be tested empirically, at least partially, by replacing the theoretical concepts of "democratization" and "the distribution of power resources" by their operational indicators. In this way the hypotheses can be reformulated into testable research hypotheses:

1. The political indicators of this study, the Index of Democratization in particular, are positively correlated with the explanatory indicators, the Index of Power Resources in particular.

2. All countries tend to cross the threshold of democracy at about the same level of the Index of Power Resources.

These hypotheses are formulated in such a way that it is possible to falsify them by empirical data. The first hypothesis can be regarded as falsified if correlations between explanatory and political indicators are not clearly positive. Negative correlations and correlations near zero would falsify the hypothesis, but also weak positive correlations would weaken it seriously. The higher the correlations are, particularly between the principal indicators, the more confidently we can assume that the distribution of power resources, as measured by our explanatory indicators, is a causal factor accounting for the variation of democratization. If the explained part of variation in the Index of Democratization turns out to be more than 50 percent, it would support the assumption that the distribution of power resources is the fundamental factor behind democratization. The second hypothesis can be regarded as falsified if the changeovers from Nondemocracies to Democracies are not connected with a certain level of IPR. In other words, the second hypothesis presupposes that countries below the transition level of IPR are usually Nondemocracies and that the countries above the transition level of IPR are usually Democracies. Some deviations can be accepted because the relationship between political and explanatory variables cannot be complete. Some indeterminacy belongs to the nature of biological phenomena and therefore also to the nature of politics.

Because all data on empirical indicators are at the level of interval measurement, any techniques of statistical analysis can be used in testing the hypotheses. The first hypothesis is tested by correlation analysis (Pearson's r). The second hypothesis is tested by regression analysis and by comparing the IPR values of single Nondemocracies, Semidemocracies, and Democracies.

CORRELATION ANALYSIS

The first hypothesis on the positive relationship between the political and explanatory indicators of this study was tested by correlation analysis. The principal results are given in Tables 4.1–4.3.

Table 4.1 indicates that the two basic political variables are only slightly intercorrelated. They seem to measure two different dimensions of democratization. Usually, however, in countries with a high level of Competition, the level of Participation is also high, whereas there are many countries in which the level of electoral participation is high, but the level of Competition is low or in zero. Such cases reduce the strength of correlations between

Table 4.1.

Intercorrelations of Political Variables in the Comparison Group of 147 States in 1980 and 1988

Indicator	C-80	P-80	ID-80	C-88	P-88	ID-88
C-80		.445	.900	.752	.344	.753
P-80			.574	.309	.768	.444
ID-80				.740	.487	.872
C-88					.443	.904
P-88						575
ID-88						

Competition and Participation. In Table 4.1 the intercorrelations of the three political variables are limited to years 1980 and 1988, but they remained about the same throughout the period 1980–88.

Five of the six explanatory variables (see Table 4.2) are moderately or strongly intercorrelated (correlations vary 0.485 to 0.852), whereas Family Farms is moderately correlated only with the Degree of Decentralization of Nonagricultural Economic Resources (0.537). Family Farms seems to be completely independent from the other four explanatory variables. Consequently the Index of the Distribution of Economic Power Resources (DER) is also nearly independent from the two other indexes (the Index of Occupational Diversification and the Index of Knowledge Distribution). IPR's correlations with its three components (IOD, IKD, and DER) are about the same (0.710, 0.714, and 0.642). It was assumed that these three components represent three different dimensions of resource distribution, but the strong correlation between IOD and IKD (0.770) indicates that these two dimen-

Table 4.2.

Intercorrelations of the Explanatory Indicators in the Comparison Group of 147 Countries

Indicator	2	3	4	5	6	7	8	9	10
1. Urban	.852	.691	.668	−.062	.485	.957	.705	.058	.667
2. NAP		.687	.782	−.034	.562	.966	.776	.057	.701
3. Students			.687	.075	.553	.715	.844	.213	.746
4. Literates				−.069	.528	.755	.911	.061	.646
5. FF					.537	−.052	−.042	.863	.448
6. DDN						.545	.552	.772	.888
7. IOD							.770	.057	.710
8. IKD								.103	.714
9. DER									.642
10. IPR									

sions differ only partially from each other. However, because one (DER) of the three components of the Index of Power Resources differs substantially from the two others (IOD and IKD) and because they are assumed to measure different dimensions of resource distribution, it is plausible to expect that their combination (IPR) is a more valid indicator of resource distribution than any of IPR's single components.

The correlations between the political and explanatory variables in Table 4.3 test the first hypothesis. All these correlations are positive as hypothesized, but there is considerable variation in the strength of correlations, although not from year to year.

Let us first examine the correlations between the six single explanatory variables and the four political variables. Most correlations are moderate, but the strength of correlations varies from one indicator to another. The first four explanatory variables (Urban Population, NAP, Students, and Literates) are approximately as strongly correlated with the political variables, whereas the correlations of Family Farms are a little weaker and the correlations of DDN are clearly stronger. Besides, there are significant and interesting differences between the three political variables in the strength of correlations. Competition is in all cases more strongly correlated with the explanatory variables than Participation. According to my interpretation, this difference implies that Participation is not as valid an indicator of democratization as Competition. Its considerably weaker correlations with the explanatory indicators are due to the fact that in many countries elections are held without any significant competition between political parties. The weakest correlations are between Participation and Family Farms. The Index of Democratization is more strongly correlated with the explanatory variables than Competition. It means that the combination of Competition and Participation is probably a better indicator for the level of democratization than either of the basic political variables alone. Therefore I use ID as the principal dependent variable in this study.

The three components of IPR (indicators 7–9) are moderately and in many cases more strongly correlated with the political variables than the single explanatory variables. However, DDN clearly differs from this pattern. Its correlations with the political variables are in most cases considerably stronger than the correlations of IOD, IKD, and DER, and in many cases even slightly stronger than the correlations of IPR. In other words, DDN alone seems to explain as much or more of the variation in political variables than the combination of the six explanatory variables (IPR). However, I do not pay particular attention to DDN and its separate explanatory power in causal analysis because the values of this indicator are based more on my own estimates than the values of the other explanatory variables. I use IPR as the principal explanatory variable. DDN is included in IPR but not directly, because IPR is a combination of IOD, IKD, and DER (which combines DDN and FF).

TABLE 4.3.
Correlations Between the Three Political Variables of 1980–88 and the Explanatory Variables (as in Table 4.2) in the Comparison Group of 147 Countries

Political variables	Explanatory variables									
	1	2	3	4	5	6	7	8	9	10
C-80	.392	.500	.458	.506	.331	.800	.466	.498	.559	.710
P-80	.343	.407	.390	.556	.074	.388	.392	.521	.190	.463
ID-80	.478	.578	.510	.558	.397	.858	.550	.557	.623	.841
C-81	.382	.493	.464	.519	.337	.808	.457	.508	.566	.712
P-81	.319	.392	.402	.564	.056	.378	.372	.530	.170	.454
ID-81	.461	.572	.506	.566	.408	.865	.539	.561	.630	.836
C-82	.386	.495	.478	.542	.340	.821	.460	.529	.562	.718
P-82	.329	.389	.397	.578	.049	.382	.376	.536	.163.	.452
ID-82	.459	.568	.514	.579	.420	.871	.535	.572	.632	.836
C-83	.420	.520	.500	.579	.341	.837	.491	.562	.564	.738
P-83	.351	.399	.411	.596	.051	.383	.392	.554	.162	.459
ID-83	.478	.581	.522	.598	.421	.871	.552	.588	.626	.840
C-84	.445	.528	.507	.597	.306	.829	.507	.575	.535	.723
P-84	.403	.446	.449	.654	.029	.413	.443	.620	.154	.490
ID-84	.517	.601	.536	.624	.391	.871	.583	.609	.603	.840
C-85	.465	.540	.517	.588	.302	.839	.524	.574	.530	.730
P-85	.405	.442	.447	.624	.037	.429	.442	.600	.163	.488
ID-85	.533	.607	.543	.619	.390	.876	.593	.609	.600	.843
C-86	.442	.505	.518	.556	.320	.831	.494	.553	.546	.717
P-86	.389	.410	.427	.590	.057	.415	.417	.567	.186	.475
ID-86	.522	.595	.552	.611	.398	.876	.581	.607	.608	.840
C-87	.441	.497	.521	.543	.332	.824	.489	.545	.550	.717
P-87	.414	.438	.444	.607	.058	.420	.444	.570	.177	.485
ID-87	.525	.589	.554	.606	.421	.875	.579	.605	.619	.845
C-88	.436	.492	.504	.509	.311	.817	.484	.541	.536	.707
P-88	.426	.452	.442	.602	.048	.424	.458	.538	.174	.483
ID-88	.534	.595	.556	.597	.400	.872	.587	.599	.612	.842

DER is only moderately correlated with IPR (0.642), but because it is nearly independent from IOD and IKD, it increases the explanatory power of IPR considerably.

The correlations between ID and IPR vary from 0.836 in 1981 to 0.845 in 1987. The explained part of variation in ID varies from 70 to 71 percent. About 30 percent of the variation in the Index of Democratization remained unexplained. Because the empirical indicators used in this study are not complete substitutes for the theoretical concepts of "democratization" and "the distribution of power resources" and because data certainly include some measurement errors, it is possible that the real dependence of the level of democratization on the level of resource distribution is a little higher than the results of this correlation analysis indicate. However, I do not assume that this relationship could be complete. Various random factors always play a role in politics, and there may be some other factors that explain part of the unexplained variation, although the very high correlations between ID and IPR do not leave much room for other explanatory factors. Probably it would not be possible to explain more than 70–80 percent of the variation of democratization by any systematic factors. The remaining unexplained variation represents the range of variation that makes it possible to adapt political systems to varying environmental conditions and experimentations with alternative political systems and institutional and behavioral patterns. It leaves room for political crafting (cf. Linz 1986), accidental factors, historical differences, and cultural variations. People are not determined to behave exactly in the same manner even in similar conditions and to adopt the same political institutions in similar environmental conditions. There is variation in all biological phenomena. The variation of behavior patterns and preferences makes the adaptation and evolution of political structures possible.

The results of correlation analysis did not falsify the first hypothesis because the correlations between the theoretically most important indicators are strongly positive and because only a few of the other correlations are near zero and none of them are negative. Thus the results of empirical analysis support the first hypothesis. The level of democratization seems to be substantially dependent on the relative level of resource distribution. One explanatory factor seems to be able to explain almost all of the variation in the principal dependent variable that can be explained by systematic factors. The ultimate evolutionary explanation of this strong relationship can be traced to the principles of the Darwinian theory of evolution by natural selection, which explains the necessity to struggle for existence and scarce resources by all available means. This constant makes the relationship between the level of democratization and the level of resource distribution regular and predictable. All human populations can be assumed to share the same politically relevant behavioral predispositions evolved in the struggle for scarce resources and reproduction that still maintain regularities in politics.

The results of my previous longitudinal comparative study (Table 4.4) show that this relationship between ID and IPR has remained more or less the same at least since the 1850s (Vanhanen 1984, 46–47).

Most of the decennial correlations between ID and IPR given above are weaker than the correlations of this study, but the direction has always remained the same. The IPR of my previous study did not include DDN as an explanatory variable, but the five other explanatory indicators were approximately the same as in this study. The IPR of my 1984 study was a combination of IOD, IKD, and Family Farms.

Strong positive correlations between ID and IPR provide a solid basis for making predictions on the level of democratization in single countries on the basis of their IPR values. But because correlations between ID and IPR are not complete, such predictions cannot be correct in all cases. Single countries may deviate from the general pattern for some reason or other, although correlation coefficients do not disclose what countries deviate from the general pattern and how much they deviate.

Regression Analysis

The technique of regression analysis is best suited to test the second research hypothesis, which presupposes that all countries tend to cross the threshold of democracy at about the same level of the Index of Power Resources (IPR). The Index of Democratization (ID) is used as the dependent variable, al-

Table 4.4.
ID Correlated With IPR By Decades In 1850–1979

Decade	Correlation	r-squared	N
1850–59	.598	.36	37
1860–69	.743	.55	39
1870–79	.651	.42	41
1880–89	.720	.52	42
1890–99	.779	.64	43
1900–09	.743	.55	47
1910–19	.768	.59	51
1920–29	.847	.72	62
1930–39	.834	.69	63
1940–49	.799	.64	74
1950–59	.781	.61	85
1960–69	.771	.59	117
1970–79	.831	.69	119

though the crossing of 5.0 ID index points does not always mean that a country has crossed the threshold of democracy, as it may still be below the threshold value of Competition (30 percent) or of Participation (15 percent).

The results of regression analysis show how well the general pattern of relationship between IPR and ID (regression line) explains the level of democratization for single countries. In other words, they show how accurately the values of IPR predict the values of ID and at what level of IPR countries have crossed the threshold of democracy. According to the research hypothesis, all countries above a certain level of IPR should be Democracies and below it Nondemocracies. The problem is how to define the transition level of IPR.

If the two indicators were exactly in the same scale, we could assume that a country crosses the threshold of democracy as soon as its IPR rises to 5.0 index points, because 5.0 ID index points was defined as a threshold of democracy and because, according to my hypothesis, the level of democratization depends directly on the level of resource distribution. In other words, the hypothetical regression equation would be ID est. $= 0 + 1.0 \times$ IPR. In fact, the two indicators are almost in the same scale. The arithmetic mean of ID varies from 8.2 in 1980 to 10.4 in 1988, whereas the arithmetic mean of IPR is 10.6. Because the actual scales of the two variables are near each other, we can accept the hypothetical regression equation and assume that 5.0 IPR index points represents the average transition level of IPR. If the correlations between ID and IPR were complete, we could expect that all countries above the IPR level of 5.0 index points are Democracies and below it Nondemocracies, but, actually, correlations are not complete. Therefore it seems reasonable to accept some variation around the average IPR level of transition.

We should define the transition level of IPR in such a way that it includes the major part of variation due to measurement errors and accidental factors but excludes significant deviations. Standard errors of estimate of Y on X can be used to guide the definition of the transition level of IPR. Usually about 68 percent of the cases deviate from the regression line less than one standard error of estimate. Regression analysis, in which ID was used as the dependent variable and IPR as the independent variable, produced the simple regression equations and standard errors of estimate of ID on IPR in Table 4.5.

According to these regression equations, in 1980 the regression line of ID on IPR crossed the ID level of 5.0 index points approximately at the IPR level of 6.2 and in 1988 approximately at the IPR level of 4.0. In other words, the actual crossing points of the regression line were around the hypothesized crossing point of 5.0 IPR index points.

Standard errors of estimate vary from 6.562 to 7.287 ID index points. It would not be sensible to extend the transition level of IPR to one standard

Table 4.5.

Regression Equations of ID on IPR and Standard Errors of Estimate for the Years
1980–88

1980:	Y est. = 0.517 + 0.725X	Std. err.	6.562
1981:	Y est. = 0.62 + 0.75X	Std. err.	6.914
1982:	Y est. = 0.879 + 0.757X	Std. err.	6.980
1983:	Y est. = 0.886 + 0.771X	Std. err.	6.999
1984:	Y est. = 1.461 + 0.793X	Std. err.	7.190
1985:	Y est. = 1.395 + 0.797X	Std. err.	7.138
1986:	Y est. = 1.664 + 0.796X	Std. err.	7.226
1987:	Y est. = 1.676 + 0.819X	Std. err.	7.287
1988:	Y est. = 1.845 + 0.808X	Std. err.	7.272

error of estimate around the average 5.0 index points because it would cover
all countries below the IPR level of 5.0 index points. I use a considerably
narrower range of transition which extends only 1.5 IPR index points around
the average, or from 3.5 to 6.5 IPR index points. Thus "at about the same
level of IPR" means IPR values from 3.5 to 6.5. This is assumed to be the
IPR level of transition at which political systems are expected to cross the
threshold of democracy. Now the second hypothesis can be restated in a
more exact form. It is hypothesized that

2. All countries above the upper limit of the IPR level of transition (6.5)
   are Democracies and all countries below the lower limit of transition
   (3.5) are Nondemocracies or Semidemocracies.

It is easy to test this hypothesis by empirical evidence. All countries above
the IPR level of 6.5 index points should be Democracies and all countries
below the IPR level of 3.5 index points should be Nondemocracies or Semidemocracies. The hypothesis does not predict the nature of political systems
for the countries within the transition level of IPR. They can be Democracies, Nondemocracies, or Semidemocracies. The comparison of IPR values
with the values of the three political variables indicates in what countries
the level of democratization is in harmony with the second hypothesis and
which countries contradict the hypothesis, but the actual values of our variables do not disclose how much particular countries deviate from the average
relationship between IPR and ID. The results of regression analysis disclose
the size of deviations and the most deviating cases. Let us examine the results of regression analyses from year to year over the period 1980–88.
Attention is concentrated on the situations in the first (1980) and the last
years (1988) of the period of comparison.

The Results of Regression Analysis for 1980

The actual values of IPR and of the three political indicators in 1980 as well as the results of regression analysis (residuals and ID estimates) for single countries are given in Table 4.6 The 147 countries are ranked in accordance with their IPR values and divided into three subcategories by the level of IPR. The IPR category above 6.5 index points includes the countries that should be Democracies, the transition level of IPR from 3.5 to 6.5 index points includes the countries that may be Democracies, Semidemocracies, or Nondemocracies, and the countries in the IPR category below 3.5 index points should be Nondemocracies or Semidemocracies. We can see from the actual values of variables what countries contradict these predictions. Besides, the residuals and ID estimates produced by the regression analysis indicate how well the regression equation estimated the ID values for single countries and which countries are the most deviating cases.

Table 4.6 shows that IPR values, just like the ID values of Table 2.2, form a continuum from 0 to 52.2 without any clear breaks, although the cases are clustered at the bottom of the continuum. Consequently the dividing lines between the three IPR categories are more or less arbitrary. The residuals of 1980 indicate how accurately the actual values of ID in 1980 corresponded to the values predicted on the basis of the simple regression equation of ID on IPR. In 36 cases positive or negative residuals are larger than one standard error of estimate (6.6). Large residuals are distributed over the continuum, but most of them are in the upper part of the continuum, which is natural because the predicted values of ID are many times higher for the countries with high IPR values than for those with low IPR values. Figure 4.1 illustrates the results of regression analysis graphically.

Large residuals by IPR categories. In the IPR category above 6.5 index points, 14 out of 28 large residuals are negative and 14 positive. Large positive residuals indicate that the level of democratization is considerably higher than expected on the basis of the average relationship between ID and IPR, and large negative residuals indicate that it is lower than expected. In both cases I have to predict, because of my theory on democratization, that a better balance will be reached in the future. However, all large residuals do not provide an equally valid basis for such predictions for the reason that my indicators are only rough measures of democratization and of the distribution of power resourses. Some deviations may be due to various factors that have not been taken into account in my measures of democratization and resource distribution, but that do not necessarily contradict the hypothesis on the relationship between the level of democratization and the distribution of power resources. Deviating cases should be studied in detail in order to clarify the nature of each deviation.

Table 4.6.

147 Countries Ranked by their IPR Values and Divided into Three Subcategories by the Level of IPR, and the Actual Values of Three Political Variables as well as Residuals and ID Estimates Produced by the Regression Analysis for 1980[1]

Country/IPR level	C-80	P-80	ID-80	IPR	Residual	ID estimate
IPR above 6.5						
1 United States	49.3	38.0	18.7	52.2	−19.7	38.4
2 Iceland	64.4	54.4	35.0	50.9	−2.4	37.4
3 Netherlands	66.2	60.0	39.7	45.3	6.3	33.4
4 Australia	54.9	65.0	31.0	45.1	−2.2	33.2
5 New Zealand	59.6	54.8	32.7	45.0	−0.5	33.2
6 Canada	55.9	45.8	25.6	45.0	−7.6	33.2
7 Germany, West	57.1	61.6	35.2	44.3	2.5	32.7
8 Denmark	61.7	61.9	38.2	44.0	5.8	32.4
9 Sweden	56.8	65.7	37.3	44.0	4.9	32.4
10 United Kingdom	56.1	55.9	31.4	42.2	0.3	31.1
11 Belgium	63.8	56.2	35.9	41.9	5.0	30.9
12 France	63.3	51.3	32.5	41.8	1.7	30.8
13 Finland	46.8	56.2	26.3	41.4	−4.3	30.6
14 Israel	66.6	48.4	32.2	38.7	3.6	28.6
15 Italy	61.7	65.0	40.1	36.7	13.0	27.1
16 Japan	55.4	50.5	28.0	36.3	1.1	26.9
17 Norway	57.7	56.9	32.8	35.8	6.3	26.5
18 Switzerland	75.1	28.8	21.6	34.3	−3.8	25.4
19 Austria	49.0	63.7	31.2	33.9	6.1	25.1
20 Lebanon	54.5	17.4	9.5	33.2	−15.1	24.6
21 Ireland	49.4	49.0	24.2	32.7	−0.0	24.2
22 Spain	65.0	48.2	31.3	32.3	7.3	24.0
23 Luxemburg	65.5	48.4	31.7	31.7	8.2	23.5
24 *Korea, South*	*17.2*	*10.0*	*1.7*	*22.0*	*−14.8*	*16.5*
25 Greece	58.2	55.3	32.2	21.6	16.0	16.2
26 Malta	48.5	62.3	30.2	20.9	14.5	15.7
27 *Uruguay*	*0*	*0*	*0*	*20.7*	*−15.5*	*15.5*
28 Cyprus	30.0	37.5	11.2	18.4	−2.7	13.9
29 *Argentina*	*0*	*0*	*0*	*17.7*	*−13.4*	*13.4*
30 *Chile*	*0*	*0*	*0*	*17.4*	*−13.1*	*13.1*
31 Costa Rica	51.2	40.7	20.8	16.6	8.2	12.6
32 *Yugoslavia*	*0*	*59.7*	*0*	*15.7*	*−11.9*	*11.9*
33 Bahamas	45.0	31.9	14.4	15.6	2.6	11.8
34 *Singapore*	*22.3*	*26.3*	*5.9*	*14.9*	*−5.4*	*11.3*
35 Barbados	47.8	40.4	19.3	14.5	8.3	11.0
36 Venezuela	53.4	37.6	20.1	13.6	9.7	10.4
37 *Philippines*	*0*	*0*	*0*	*13.3*	*−10.2*	*10.2*
38 *Mexico*	*5.6*	*30.2*	*1.7*	*12.1*	*−7.6*	*9.3*
39 Ecuador	31.5	19.0	6.0	11.7	−3.0	9.0

Table 4.6. *continued*

Country/IPR level	C-80	P-80	ID-80	IPR	Residual	ID estimate
40 Portugal	48.8	58.9	28.7	11.1	20.1	8.6
41 Colombia	50.3	19.6	9.9	10.8	1.5	8.4
42 Jamaica	42.4	34.5	14.6	10.1	6.8	7.8
43 *Poland*	*0.5*	*69.7*	*0*	*10.1*	*−7.8*	*7.8*
44 *Jordan*	*0*	*0*	*0*	*10.0*	*−7.8*	*7.8*
45 *Sri Lanka*	*24.2*	*21.9*	*5.3*	*9.8*	*−2.3*	*7.6*
46 Mauritius	59.9	43.7	26.2	9.7	18.6	7.6
47 Peru	54.6	23.3	12.7	9.6	5.2	7.5
48 *Panama*	*10.5*	*0*	*0*	*9.5*	*−7.4*	*7.4*
49 *Turkey*	*0*	*0*	*0*	*9.4*	*−7.3*	*7.3*
50 Trinidad and Tobago	47.0	30.5	14.3	8.7	7.5	6.8
51 *Brazil*	*44.8*	*8.4*	*3.8*	*8.4*	*−2.8*	*6.6*
52 Fiji	47.7	30.0	14.3	7.9	8.1	6.2
53 Dominican Republic	51.4	30.1	15.5	6.9	10.0	5.5

IPR 3.5–6.5

Country/IPR level	C-80	P-80	ID-80	IPR	Residual	ID estimate
54 Malaysia	42.8	26.9	11.5	6.3	6.4	5.1
55 Syria	0.4	49.0	0.2	6.3	−4.9	5.1
56 Thailand	36.4	9.7	3.5	6.2	−1.5	5.0
57 Bolivia	0	0	0	6.1	−4.9	4.9
58 Iran	22.1	36.0	8.0	5.8	3.3	4.7
59 Zambia	20.0	20.0	4.0	5.6	−0.6	4.6
60 Congo Republic	0	0	0	5.6	−4.6	4.6
61 Iraq	0	0	0	5.4	−4.4	4.4
62 Egypt	0.1	24.0	0	5.4	−4.4	4.4
63 Tunisia	0	0	0	5.0	−4.1	4.1
64 Ghana	48.0	16.1	7.7	5.0	3.6	4.1
65 Guyana	26.3	46.6	12.3	5.0	8.2	4.1
66 Honduras	0	0	0	4.9	−4.1	4.1
67 Burma	0	43.5	0	4.8	−4.0	4.0
68 Nicaragua	0	0	0	4.7	−3.9	3.9
69 El Salvador	0	0	0	4.7	−3.9	3.9
70 India	57.3	29.6	17.0	4.5	13.2	3.8
71 Qatar	0	0	0	4.3	−3.6	3.6
72 Indonesia	9.5	11.7	1.1	4.3	−2.5	3.6
73 Bahrain	0	0	0	4.2	−3.6	3.6
74 Kuwait	0	0.6	0	4.1	−3.5	3.5
75 Guatemala	57.7	9.7	5.6	3.8	2.3	3.3
76 Gabon	0.2	54.1	0.1	3.7	−3.1	3.2
77 Algeria	0.7	41.4	0.3	3.7	−2.9	3.2
78 Paraguay	10.4	33.4	3.5	3.7	0.3	3.2
79 Libya	0	0	0	3.5	−3.1	3.1
80 Zaire	0	44.5	0	3.5	−3.1	3.1

Table 4.6. *continued*

Country/IPR level	C-80	P-80	ID-80	IPR	Residual	ID estimate
IPR below 3.4						
81 Morocco	13.8	6.9	1.0	3.4	−2.0	3.0
82 South Africa	33.9	3.9	1.3	3.1	−1.5	2.8
83 Ivory Coast	0	34.2	0	3.0	−2.7	2.7
84 Suriname	0	0	0	2.9	−2.6	2.6
85 *Zimbabwe*	*37.4*	*37.6*	*14.1*	*2.9*	*11.5*	*2.6*
86 Cape Verde	7.6	32.2	2.4	2.8	−0.1	2.5
87 Lesotho	0	0	0	2.7	−2.5	2.5
88 *Nigeria*	*66.2*	*21.6*	*14.3*	*2.6*	*11.9*	*2.4*
89 Cameroon	0	39.0	0	2.5	−2.3	2.3
90 Central African Republic	0	0	0	2.5	−2.3	2.3
91 United Arab Emirates	0	0	0	2.5	−2.3	2.3
92 Madacasgar	5.3	44.2	2.3	2.5	−0.0	2.3
93 Botswana	24.6	16.8	4.1	2.5	1.8	2.3
94 Haiti	0	0	0	2.3	−2.2	2.2
95 Togo	0	52.1	0	2.2	−2.1	2.1
96 *Papua New Guinea*	*64.0*	*33.0*	*21.9*	*2.1*	*19.9*	*2.0*
97 Kenya	0	24.4	0	2.1	−2.0	2.0
98 Djibouti	0	30.0	0	2.0	−2.0	2.0
99 Burundi	0	0	0	2.0	−2.0	2.0
100 Tanzania	7.0	29.2	2.0	2.0	0.0	2.0
101 *Solomon Islands*	*58.2*	*25.8*	*15.0*	*1.9*	*13.1*	*1.9*
102 Cuba	0	0.1	0	1.9	−1.9	1.9
103 Liberia	0	0	0	1.9	−1.9	1.9
104 Pakistan	0	0	0	1.9	−1.9	1.9
105 *Uganda*	*52.8*	*31.9*	*16.8*	*1.9*	*14.9*	*1.9*
106 Swaziland	0	0	0	1.9	−1.9	1.9
107 Sierra Leone	0	0	0	1.8	−1.8	1.8
108 Equatorial Guinea	0	0	0	1.7	−1.8	1.8
109 Senegal	18.2	18.1	3.3	1.6	1.6	1.7
110 Benin	0	0	0	1.5	−1.6	1.6
111 Comoros	0	54.7	0	1.5	−1.6	1.6
112 German Dem. Republic	0.1	67.9	0.1	1.4	−1.4	1.5
113 Bangladesh	22.3	24.0	5.4	1.4	3.9	1.5
114 Angola	0	0	0	1.4	−1.5	1.5
115 Guinea	0	56.4	0	1.3	−1.5	1.5
116 Laos	0	0	0	1.2	−1.4	1.4
117 Sudan	0.9	33.6	0.3	1.2	−1.1	1.4
118 Romania	1.5	70.4	1.1	1.2	−0.3	1.4
119 Rwanda	1.0	42.8	0.4	1.1	−0.9	1.3
120 Chad	0	0	0	1.1	−1.3	1.3
121 Guinea-Bissau	0	0	0	1.0	−1.2	1.2
122 Afghanistan	0	0	0	0.9	−1.2	1.2

Table 4.6. *continued*

Country/IPR level	C-80	P-80	ID-80	IPR	Residual	ID estimate
123 Malawi	0	0	0	0.9	−1.2	1.2
124 *Gambia*	*30.4*	*32.0*	*9.7*	*0.9*	*8.5*	*1.2*
125 Yemen, South	0	32.2	0	0.9	−1.2	1.2
126 Mozambique	0	0	0	0.9	−1.2	1.2
127 Mauritania	0	0	0	0.9	−1.2	1.2
128 Oman	0	0	0	0.8	−1.1	1.1
129 Hungary	0	70.2	0	0.5	−0.9	0.9
130 Vietnam	0	46.5	0	0.5	−0.9	0.9
131 Nepal	0	0	0	0.5	−0.9	0.9
132 Bhutan	0	0	0	0.4	−0.8	0.8
133 Burkina Faso	0	0	0	0.4	−0.8	0.8
134 Kampuchea	0	0	0	0.4	−0.8	0.8
135 Niger	0	0	0	0.4	−0.8	0.8
136 Somalia	0	0	0	0.4	−0.8	0.8
137 Yemen, North	0	0	0	0.4	−0.8	0.8
138 Ethiopia	0	0	0	0.3	−0.7	0.7
139 Saudi Arabia	0	0	0	0.3	−0.7	0.7
140 Chechoslovakia	0	71.1	0	0.2	−0.7	0.7
141 Mali	0	47.8	0	0.1	−0.6	0.6
142 China	0	0	0	0.1	−0.6	0.6
143 Albania	0	0	0	0	−0.5	0.5
144 Mongolia	0	45.9	0	0	−0.5	0.5
145 USSR	0.1	66.4	0.1	0	−0.5	0.5
146 Bulgaria	0	72.8	0	0	−0.5	0.5
147 Korea, North	0	50.0	0	0	−0.5	0.5

[1]Countries contradicting the hypothesis are *italicized*.

Eleven of the 14 countries with large negative residuals were Nondemocracies in 1980. I think that all of these deviations are real ones, and consequently I have to predict the democratization of their political systems. It is remarkable that seven (South Korea, Uruguay, Argentina, Chile, Poland, Panama, and Turkey) of these Nondemocracies were ruled by military or semimilitary governments in 1980 and that in the other four (Yugoslavia, the Philippines, Mexico, and Jordan) cases governments rested on the support of the military. This state of affairs implies, according to my interpretation, that in societies with widely distributed power resources it is possible to establish and uphold nondemocratic governments only by resorting to military power resources. Thus the military government seems to be the last form of nondemocratic government in societies whose social structures are conducive to democracy. In such societies the pressure for democratization can be suppressed only by coercion based on military power resources.

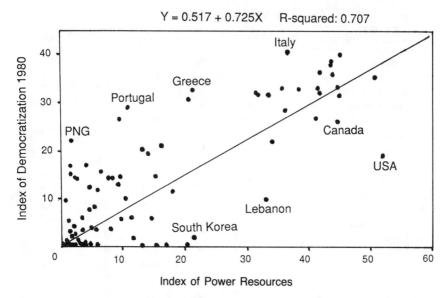

Figure 4.1. The results of regression analysis in which ID-80 is used as the dependent variable and IPR as the independent variable in the comparison group of 147 states.

The three other countries (the United States, Canada, and Lebanon) with high negative residuals are different cases. It seems to me that large negative residuals in the United States and Canada are principally due to their electoral systems. The plurality system discourages party competition and participation because only nationally or at least regionally strong parties have real chances to get their candidates elected. As a consequence, members of many minority groups do not participate in elections. This applies particularly to the United States, which is ethnically a heterogeneous society. Its first-past-the-post electoral system serves the interest of the well-to-do white majority well, but discourages the participation of the poor, blacks, and various other minority groups that have very little chances to get their own representatives elected to governmental institutions. I think that this is the principal reason for the fact that the level of electoral participation is much lower in the United States than in any European democracy. In Canada the persistence of strong regional parties has increased party competition and electoral participation and kept its negative residual relatively small. Lebanon is a special case. Its constitutional political institutions have not been able to function effectively since the breaking out of the civil war in 1975, but the constitutional institutions are still in force, although it has not been possible to hold new parliamentary elections after 1972. It was difficult to decide how to classify Lebanon's political system and how to determine the values of political indicators. Because its constitution remained in force, I decided to keep the values of Competition and Participation the same after the 1972 election. It would not be fair to classify Lebanon as a Nondemocracy because political power is not concentrated in the hands of any hegemonic group. Its democratic process has deteriorated into a violent struggle, but power is still shared by several competing groups. Foreign interventions have contributed to the continuation of civil war between ethnic-religious communities.

It should be emphasized that all large positive residuals do not necessarily indicate the lack of balance in political systems in this IPR category. Some of them seem to be due to proportional electoral systems that are conducive to multipartism. This particularly concerns Italy, Spain, and Portugal. Luxemburg's large positive residual may be a consequence of the fact that its IPR value is about 10 index points lower than in its neighboring countries because the number of students per 100,000 inhabitants is exceptionally low in Luxemburg. Most of its students study abroad. In Mauritius and Fiji, the ethnic heterogeneity of their populations has probably increased multipartism and ID values. I do not have any special explanations for the large positive residuals of Greece, Malta, Costa Rica, Barbados, Venezuela, Jamaica, Trinidad and Tobago, and the Dominican Republic. The level of democratization is clearly higher than expected on the basis of resource distribution in these countries. It makes the survival of democracy less sure in these countries than in those with higher IPR values, but because their IPR values are clearly above the upper limit of the transition level of IPR, there is no reason to predict the breakdowns of democratic institutions.

At the transition level of IPR (from 3.5 to 6.5 index points) only Guyana and India have positive residuals larger than one standard error of estimate. Large negative residuals are not technically possible at this level of IPR because the highest predicted value of ID is not more than 5.1 index points. In Guyana and India the level of democratization is much higher than expected on the basis of their IPR values, but it may be, at least in the case of India, that power resources are more widely distributed than my variables indicate. Therefore the decrease of ID values is not inevitable, although the social basis of democracy is still fragile in these countries. For the rest of the countries in this subgroup, positive and negative residuals vary depending on whether they are Democracies or Nondemocracies. There is no clear relationship between ID and IPR at this level of IPR. The correlation between ID-80 and IPR is only 0.195 in the subgroup of 27 countries of the transition level of IPR, which means that ID and IPR are nearly independent from each other. The correlation was 0.736 in the subgroup of 53 countries above 6.5 IPR index points in 1980 and 0.288 in the subgroup of 67 countries below 3.5 IPR index points. According to my hypothesis, all countries tend to democratize at the transition level of IPR, but it does not seem to happen neatly in small gradual steps. In fact, the transformation of a political system from autocracy to democracy usually presupposes some drastic changes both in political institutions and in the values of Competition and Participation. I cannot predict, on the basis of IPR values, in which countries of the transition level of IPR the process of democratization will succeed first, although I have predicted that the pressure for democratization will increase in all countries that have reached the transition level of IPR. It is quite possible that various historical, local, political, and accidental factors influence the starting, success, and failure of democratization. My theory and explanatory variables explain why the pressure for democracy increases and why it must increase at this level of IPR, but detailed comparative studies of single countries would be needed to explain why the process of democratization has been successful in some of these countries and failed in several others. The variation in the success of democratization may depend on various political, historical, local, and accidental factors that have not been taken into account by my explanatory variables. There is always some variation in political phenomena that cannot be explained by any universal factors. This means that my study, which tries to test a universal explanation of the variation of democratization, does not make detailed studies of particular political systems unnecessary.

There are six positive residuals larger than one standard error of estimate among the 67 countries below 3.5 IPR index points. All these countries— Zimbabwe, Nigeria, Papua New Guinea, Solomon Islands, Uganda, and Gambia— were deviating Democracies in 1980. In fact, the IPR range of deviating Democracies and Nondemocracies extends from 0.9 to 22.0, which means that for many countries of this comparison group it was not possible to predict the nature of their political system with certainty on the basis of their IPR values. Gambia was a Democracy in 1980, although its IPR value is not higher than 0.9, and South Korea was a Nondemocracy, although its IPR value is 22.0. A strong statistical relationship exists between ID and IPR, which means, according to my theoretical interpretation, that the level of democratization depends on the extent of resource distribution indicated by IPR, but several deviating cases weaken the relationship between empirical variables.

Deviating Democracies and Nondemocracies. Table 4.7 summarizes the results of statistical analysis given in Table 4.6. It shows that 20 countries contradict the hypotesis clearly, although 100 (83.3 percent) out of 120 countries in the first and third IPR categories were Democracies or Nondemocracies as hypothesized. The 27 countries (18.4 percent) at the transition level of IPR were excluded from the hypothesis. In other words, 20 countries, including six Democracies, two Semidemocracies, and 12 Nondemocracies, clearly contradicted the hypothesis in 1980. The deviating cases weaken the hypothesis, but they do not need to falsify it. It was assumed in the original hypothesis that all countries tend to cross the threshold of democracy at about the same level of IPR. I could not expect complete relationship because my empirical variables are not perfect substitutes for the theoretical concepts and because there is always some variation in biological phenomena. Besides, it may be that there are not any other theories and empirical variables based on them that could explain as much or more of the variation of democratization than the theory and empirical indicators used in this study. Therefore, I think that it is reasonable to retain the hypothesis and the variables used to test it, although the results do not support the hypothesis uniformly.

According to my interpretation, the relationship between ID and IPR is causal. Democracy emerges in societies in which important power resources have become widely distributed among competing groups. This is a consequence of the continual struggle for power and scarce resources, in which struggle all available means are used. As soon as new groups get enough resources to participate in politics, they begin to demand their share of power and the fruits of power. When resources become so widely distributed that it is not any longer possible for any group to achieve or uphold political hegemony, it becomes rational and necessary to share power with the most important competitors. Democratic political structures have evolved to institutionalize the sharing of power and the rules of the continual competition for power and scarce resources. Democratic institutions are tested in the struggle for power, and, according to my hypothesis, they have the best chances to survive in societies with competing groups strong enough to defend their rights. Democracy emerges from the balance of power. It is based on the ability of various groups to defend their rights even by force, if necessary, and to prevent any single competitor to usurp hegemonic power. Empirical data support this argumentation, although there are exceptions. Democracy has been established below the assumed transition level of IPR in some countries and several other countries have remained Nondemocra-

Table 4.7.

Frequency Distribution of Democracies, Semidemocracies, and Nondemocracies by the Level of IPR in the Comparison Group of 147 Countries in 1980

Political system	IPR above 6.5		IPR 3.5–6.5		IPR below 3.5	
	N	%	N	%	N	%
Democracies	39	73.6	3	11.1	6	9.0
Semidemocracies	2	3.8	3	11.1	2	3.0
Nondemocracies	12	22.6	21	77.8	59	88.1
Total	53	100.0	27	100.0	67	100

cies, or they have experienced a breakdown of democracy, although their IPR values are above the upper limit of the transition level of IPR. How to explain these deviations that contradict my hypothesis? I have not found any satisfactory general explanation for them, although I try to clarify the nature of these deviations.

Let us first examine the six deviating Democracies, which were expected to be Nondemocracies because of their very low IPR values. Several African countries began their independence with constitutions presupposing democratic institutions, competitive elections and multiparty systems. They had inherited these ideas and institutions from the period of self-government before independence. However, democratic institutions collapsed soon after independence in nearly all cases, or they were really not even established. All the deviating African Democracies (Nigeria, Uganda, Gambia, and Zimbabwe) had started their independence with democratic political systems. In Nigeria the first period of democracy ended in 1966 when the military usurped power. Nigeria returned to civilian rule through elections in 1979 and reestablished democratic institutions. The ethnic pluralism of its population has been conducive to multipartism, but it has also made it difficult to share power among regionally based competing parties. They have not yet learned to form coalition governments in which all principal groups would be represented (cf. Beckett 1987; Diamond 1988b). In Uganda the first period of democracy degenerated into one-party hegemony in the latter half of the 1960s, when President Obote attempted to suppress opposition parties and to establish a one-party system. A military coup d'etat removed Obote's civilian government in 1971, and a violent period of military rule followed. Uganda returned to civilian rule through elections in 1980. Its return to democracy was more difficult than in Nigeria, for President Obote was not committed to democratic rule without reservations. The largest opposition party did not fully accept the results of the 1980 elections, and another opposition group continued military struggle against the government. Therefore democracy remained very fragile in Uganda. Ethnic pluralism has supported multipartism and competitive politics there, too, but competing ethnic groups have not been able to form coalition governments (cf. Kokole and Mazrui 1988).

In Gambia, democratic institutions established during the period of self-government have survived without interruptions. Botswana is the only other African country south of the Sahara in which democratic institutions did not collapse after independence, although Botswana was slightly below the threshold criteria of democracy in 1980. It seems to me that some exceptionally favorable political factors have furthered the success of democracy in Gambia and Botswana. Both are small countries without standing armies, and in both the ruling party has been able to win a comfortable majority of 60-80 percent through free elections. The ethnic structure of these countries has also been favorable for the ruling parties. In Gambia the main ethnic group (Mandingo) comprises 40 percent of the population, and in Botswana nearly all tribes belong to the same ethnic stock (Tswana). These factors are important, but they do not suffice to explain the survival of democratic structures in both nations. I assume that the most important political factor has been the will of political leaders to retain democracy (cf. Diamond 1988a, 13). The People's Progressive party, headed by Jawara, has not wanted to establish a one-party system in Gambia. On some occasions President Jawara has expressly rebuffed demands to institute a one-party system. So it seems that the survival of democracy in Gambia has depended on its leading politician's personal ideology. It is a fragile base for a political system. Consequently, the survival of democracy in Gambia is not self-evident after Jawara. Democracy in Gambia has already been under serious stress. Some opposition groups have attempted to overthrow the government by violent means. The most serious insurrection took place in 1981. The government needed Senegalese troops to suppress the uprising in July 1981. Subsequently Gambia established the Confederation of Senegambia with Senegal, which means that since then Senegalese troops have protected Gambia's government and political system (see Diamond and Galvan 1988, 66–67). In Botswana, President Seretse Khama had a crucial role in the establishment of democratic institutions on the basis of tribal loyalties. John D. Holm notes that in Botswana democratic consultation "is consistent with the traditional Tswana consensus style of politics. The resulting distributionist politics also fit in comfortably with the elite's concern to govern through the existing tribal communities" (Holm 1988, 202).

Zimbabwe became independent in 1980 with a constitution presupposing a parliamentary government and competitive elections. The smaller parties' share of the votes cast was 37 percent in the first elections in 1980, and Zimbabwe crossed the threshold criteria of democracy. The ethnic structure of the population is favorable for a hegemonic party system, for 71 percent of the population belong to the Shona tribes, which support the ruling Zimbabwe African National Union (ZANU). However, unlike in Gambia, the leader of the ruling party has not been satisfied with getting a majority through free elections. Prime Minister Mugabe was pledged to transform Zimbabwe into a one- party state (cf. Sithole 1988). Because the level of resource distribution (IPR) is still relatively low, although much higher than in Gambia, the prospects of democracy have been dim since the beginning of independence. Zimbabwe illustrates the fact that when environmental conditions are not favorable enough for democracy, the ideology of crucial political leaders may provide the best explanation for the variation of political systems from the perspective of democracy. An exceptionally strong political will of leaders may be enough to uphold democratic institutions for a while. However, sooner or later the level of democratization surely will become adapted to the level of resource distribution in such societies. It is highly improbable for these deviations to become permanent.

Papua New Guinea and the Solomon Islands are very interesting deviating democracies. It seems that in these two poor Third World countries, in which the percentages of Urban Population and Nonagricultural Population are very low, the distribution of economic power resources, particularly land ownership, and a relatively high level of literacy, have been the most important structural characteristics conducive to democracy. The geographical distribution of the population and resources in these island nations have also supported competitive politics. It is quite possible that important power resources are more widely distributed in PNG and Solomon Islands than IPR indicates. Besides, political leaders seem to have been committed to democratic politics. I think that it has been as important a factor supporting democracy in these countries as that in Gambia and Botswana. However, the stability of democratic institutions in PNG may be partly due to Australia's substantial economic, administrative, and military aid. David Lipset remarks that democracy in PNG has not merely persisted without interruptions, but has thrived in its first 10 years. He seeks an explanation for democracy's success in PNG particularly from its traditional social structures and Australia's colonial rule. He refers to its traditionally egalitarian, factionalized social structures and to Australian colonial rule, which allowed the democratically preadaptive features of traditional Melanesian politics to persist without radical deculturation (Lipset 1989).

On the basis of my second research hypothesis, it was possible to predict in 1980 that democratic institutions would fail in these six countries because of their low IPR values, but, as indicated above, exceptional political and external factors may support the survival of democracy in some of these nations.

The group of deviating Nondemocracies (South Korea, Uruguay, Argentina, Chile, Yugoslavia, the Philippines, Mexico, Poland, Jordan, Panama, Turkey, and Brazil) was heterogeneous in 1980, which implies that it is hardly possible to find any systematic explanation for these deviations. Six of them were Latin American countries, three others were Asian, and two were European countries. Turkey can be regarded as a partly European and partly Asian country. Most of them are developing nations, but they belong to the group of socioeconomically most developed Third World countries. The problem is: Why had democracy not emerged or had failed in spite of high IPR values? I have no satisfactory answer to these questions, but I can present assumptions on some additional factors. It is probable that in some of these countries structural imbalances have impeded the stabilization of democratic politics. In Latin American countries the concentration of land ownership and nonagricultural means of production has hindered the process of democratization, but in this respect these six countries do not significantly differ from other Latin American lands. They differ from most other Latin American nations because of their higher level of socioeconomic variables, which makes them more conspicuously deviating cases. I suspect that various local and temporary political factors made these countries, as well as South Korea, the Philippines, and Turkey, deviating cases. In other words, they were true deviations, and large negative residuals predicted the democratization of their political systems. However, in the case of Mexico, we cannot blame temporary political factors because the same party has already ruled Mexico for more than 50 years. Jordan is a dubious case. Socioeconomic conditions are favorable for a more democratic political system, but it may be that some important power resources, which are not taken into account by my variables, are so much concentrated in the hands of the king and his supporters that they have been able to uphold a hegemonic system. Yugoslavia and Poland are deviating Socialist countries for the reason that the major part of agricultural land is still owned by peasant families. Otherwise economic power resources were nearly completely owned and controlled by the government in 1980, which provides the best explanation for the concentration of political power. This structural factor was significant enough to prevent the process of democratization. In the case of Poland the influence of the Soviet Union formed an additional factor, which impeded the transformation of Poland's political system.

There was popular pressure for democracy in nearly all of these countries, which shows that their political structures were not well adapted to their social environments. On the basis of my hypothesis, it would have been possible to predict in 1980 that all these countries would become democratized, although it would not have been possible to predict the time of democratization.

The Process of Democratization in 1981–88

Let us see how political systems changed from the perspective of democratization in the period 1981–88 and to what degree predictions based on the 1980 regression analysis came true or failed. I review the process of democratization in 1981–88 only briefly by indicating the countries that shifted from one category to another and by pointing out which of the changes took place according to my predictions and contradicted my predictions. This review is based on Table 4.8, which summariezes the results of regression analyses for the years 1981–88.

1981. Five countries changed their category of democratization in 1981; one of the changes (South Korea) supported the hypothesis, another (Bangladesh) contradicted it, and three other changes (Ghana, Iran, and Honduras)

Table 4.8.

Frequency Distribution of Democracies, Semidemocracies, and Nondemocracies
by the Level of IPR in the Comparison Group of 147 Countries in 1981–88

Political system	IPR above 6.5		IPR 3.5–6.5		IPR below 3.5	
	%	N	%	N	%	N
1981						
Democracies	39	73.6	3	11.1	7	10.4
Semidemocracies	3	5.7	2	7.4	1	1.5
Nondemocracies	11	20.7	22	81.5	59	88.1
Total	53	100.0	27	100.0	67	100.0
1982						
Democracies	41	77.4	4	14.8	6	9.0
Semidemocracies	3	5.7	2	7.4	2	3.0
Nondemocracies	9	17.0	21	77.8	59	88.1
Total	53	100.0	27	100.0	67	100.0
1983						
Democracies	43	81.1	4	14.8	5	7.5
Semidemocracies	3	5.7	2	7.4	2	3.0
Nondemocracies	7	13.2	21	77.8	60	89.5
Total	53	100.0	27	100.0	67	100.0
1984						
Democracies	46	86.8	6	22.2	6	9.0
Semidemocracies	2	3.8	2	7.4	1	1.5
Nondemocracies	5	9.4	19	70.4	60	89.5
Total	53	100.0	27	100.0	67	100.0
1985						
Democracies	46	86.8	7	25.9	5	7.5
Semidemocracies	2	3.8	2	7.4	2	3.0
Nondemocracies	5	9.4	18	66.7	60	89.5
Total	53	100.0	27	100.0	67	100.0
1986						
Democracies	47	88.7	7	25.9	6	9.0
Semidemocracies	2	3.8	2	7.4	2	3.0
Nondemocracies	4	7.5	18	66.7	59	88.1
Total	53	100.0	27	100.0	67	100.0
1987						
Democracies	47	88.7	7	25.9	6	9.0
Semidemocracies	1	1.9	2	7.4	2	3.0
Nondemocracies	5	9.4	18	66.7	59	88.1
Total	53	100.0	27	100.0	67	100.0

Table 4.8. *continued*

Political system	IPR above 6.5		IPR 3.5–6.5		IPR below 3.5	
	%	N	%	N	%	N
1988						
Democracies	47	88.7	7	25.9	7	10.4
Semidemocracies	—	—	2	7.4	3	4.5
Nondemocracies	6	11.3	18	66.7	57	85.1
Total	53	100.0	27	100.0	67	100.0

occurred at the transition level of IPR. In the IPR category above 6.5 index points, South Korea rose to the category of Semidemocracies when the share of the smaller parties crossed the threshold of 20 percent, although it still remained below the threshold of Democracy. In the IPR category below 3.5 index points, Bangladesh crossed the threshold of democracy and became a deviating Democracy. At the transition level of IPR, Ghana ceased to be a Democracy as a consequence of a military coup, Iran ceased to be a Semidemocracy and drifted toward autocracy as a consequence of the 1981 presidential election in which the share of the smaller parties decreased to 3.1 percent, and Honduras entered the category of Democracies through the 1981 presidential election. It is remarkable that three of the five changes took place at the transition level of IPR. It implies that many political systems, both Democracies and Nondemocracies, are on shaky ground at this level of IPR. It is difficult to maintain autocratic systems and difficult to stabilize democratic institutions. As a consequence, relatively more drastic changes in political systems seem to take place at this level of IPR than at higher or lower levels of IPR.

1982. Six countries changed their category of democratization in 1982; four of the changes (Sri Lanka, Brazil, Mexico, and Bangladesh) supported the hypothesis, one (Madagascar) was against the prediction, and one change (Bolivia) took place at the transition level of IPR. In the IPR category above 6.5 index points, Sri Lanka reentered the group of Democracies as a consequence of the 1982 direct presidential election, Brazil crossed the threshold of democracy as a consequence of the 1982 parliamentary election, and Mexico rose to the group of Semidemocracies when the share of the smaller parties rose to 25.6 percent in the 1982 presidential election. These were changes toward democracy as predicted by their relatively high IPR values. In the IPR category below 3.5 index points, a short interlude of democratic rule was ended in 1982 by a military coup in Bangladesh, whereas Madagascar, despite its low IPR value, entered the group of Semidemocracies when the share of the smaller parties increased to 20 percent in the 1982 presidential election. This change did not directly contradict the hypothesis because Madagascar still remained below the threshold of democracy. At the transition level of IPR, a transition from military rule to civilian rule and democracy occurred in Bolivia in 1982. The results of the 1980 presidential election had been inconclusive, but the congress elected Siles, who had 36 percent of the votes cast in 1980, as President in 1982. The military government accepted the election and gave up power to the new civilian government.

1983. Five countries changed their category of democratization in 1983; three of the changes (Argentina, Turkey, and Nigeria) supported the hypothesis and two other changes (Thailand and Zambia) took place at the transition level of IPR. In the IPR category above 6.5 index points, Argentina entered the group of Democracies through the presidential and legislative elections in 1983, and Turkey crossed the threshold of democracy as a consequence of the 1983 competitive parliamentary election. These two countries ceased to be deviating Nondemocracies and democratized as predicted by their high IPR values. In the IPR category below 3.5 index points, Nigeria dropped to the group of Nondemocracies as a consequence of a military coup. Its low IPR value had predicted the breakdown of democratic rule. At the transition level of IPR, Thailand entered the group of Semidemocracies, whereas Zambia slided from the category of Semidemocracies to the group of Nondemocracies. These relatively small transformations did not change the nature of Thailand's and Zambia's political systems.

1984. Six countries changed their category of democratization in 1984; three of the changes (Uruguay, Singapore, and Panama) took place according to my predictions, one (Botswana) contradicted the hypothesis, and two other changes took place at the transition level of IPR. In the IPR category above 6.5 index points, Uruguay ceased to be a Nondemocracy and entered the group of Democracies through presidential and legislative elections in 1984, Singapore entered the group of Democracies as a consequence of the 1984 parliamentary election in which the share of the smaller parties crossed the 30 percent threshold, and Panama crossed the threshold of democracy through presidential and legislative elections in 1984. These democratizations were predicted, but it should be noted that Singapore's political system remained the same, dominated by the ruling People's Action party. The quality of democracy remained questionable in Singapore because the ruling party secured nearly all the seats in parliament. In the IPR category below 3.5 index points, an increase in the share of the smaller parties raised Botswana into the category of Democracies. This change contradicted the hypothesis because of Botswana's low IPR value. John D. Holm notes that

"Botswana's democracy is still not institutionalized, so that its future is by no means certain" (Holm 1988, 179). At the transition level of IPR, Nicaragua and El Salvador crossed the threshold of democracy through presidential and legislative elections in 1984, but civil wars continued in both countries.

1985. Four countries changed their category of democratization in 1985; two of the changes (Zimbabwe and Uganda) supported the hypothesis; one (Liberia) contradicted it, and one change (Guatemala) took place at the transition level of IPR. In the IPR category below 3.5 index points, Zimbabwe moved to the group of Semidemocracies as a consequence of the 1985 parliamentary elections in which the share of the smaller parties decreased below the threshold of 30 percent, and a military coup d'etat dropped Uganda to the category of Nondemocracies. These failures of democracy were predicted by Zimbabwe's and Uganda's low IPR values. Zimbabwe is drifting toward one- party dominated autocracy (cf. Sithole 1988), and Uganda is still seeking a democratic way to share power between its clearly distinct ethnic groups (cf. Kokole and Mazrui 1988). Liberia became a new deviating Democracy through the elections of 1985, which legitimized the position of President Doe, who had originally usurped power by a military coup in 1980 (see Ungar 1989, 103–20). Democratic institutions remained fragile in Liberia. At the transition level of IPR, Guatemala entered from military rule to the group of Democracies through the 1985 presidential election.

1986. Only two countries changed their category of democratization in 1986; one change (the Philippines) supported the hypothesis, and another (Sudan) contradicted it. In the IPR category above 6.5 index points, the Philippines ceased to be a Nondemocracy and crossed the threshold of democracy as a consequence of the 1986 presidential election and popular uprising against President Marcos' autocratic rule. This democratization was expected because of the Philippines' high IPR value (cf. Jackson 1989). In the IPR category below 3.5 index points, Sudan contradicted the second research hypothesis by crossing the threshold of democracy in spite of its very low IPR value (see Ungar 1989, 387–88). Its example shows that exceptions are possible and that democratic institutions can be established even at very low levels of IPR, but I predict that democratic institutions will be more fragile the lower the level of IPR.

1987. Only two changes took place in 1987; both in the IPR category above 6.5 index points. South Korea democratized as predicted by its very high IPR value, whereas Fiji, contrary to the hypothesis, dropped to the category of Nondemocracies as a consequence of a military coup in 1987. In South Korea very strong popular pressure and agitation had preceded the democratization that took place through the highly competitive presidential election in 1987 (cf. Sung-Joo Han 1989). For a long time South Korea had been the most deviating Nondemocracy, but in the end the distribution of power resources among large sections of the population made it impossible even for a military government to uphold its hegemony. The breakdown of democracy in Fiji was unexpected because of its relatively high IPR value. Ethnic conflicts contributed to the failure of democratic process in Fiji (cf. West 1988), but its IPR value predicts the reestablishment of democratic rule.

1988. Four countries changed their category of democratization in 1988; one change (Mexico) supported the hypothesis, whereas three other changes (Panama, Pakistan, and Senegal) contradicted it. In the IPR category above 6.5 index points, Mexico finally crossed the threshold of democracy in the 1988 presidential election in which the share of smaller parties rose to 49 percent, whereas Panama dropped to the category of Nondemocracies as a consequence of General Noriega's usurpation of power. In the IPR category below 3.5 index points, Pakistan contradicted the second hypothesis by entering the group of Democracies through the 1988 parliamentary election, and Senegal rose to the group of Semidemocracies, although it remained below the threshold of democracy. This transformation did not change the basic nature of Senegal's political system (cf. Coulon 1988), whereas the change was drastic in Pakistan (cf. Rose 1989).

It was hypothesized that political systems would democratize at the transition level of IPR and that all countries above the upper limit of the IPR level of transition (6.5) would be Democracies and all countries below the lower limit of transition (3.5) would be Nondemocracies. In fact, several countries have contradicted these predictions, but Table 4.8 indicates that most of the countries above 6.5 IPR index points have consistently been Democracies (77–89 percent) and that most of the countries below 3.5 index points have remained Nondemocracies or Semidemocracies (90–92 percent). The number of deviating cases varied from 12 to 21 in the period 1981–88. The review of changes disclosed that the frequency of political changes was the highest, as expected, at the transition level of IPR and around it. Of the 34 changes, 14 took place above 6.5 IPR index points, 9 at the transition level of IPR, and 11 below 3.5 index points. In the first IPR category, changes concerned 26 percent of the total number of countries (53), in the transition category 33 percent of the countries (27), and in the third IPR category 16 percent of the total number of countries (67). However, the 23 countries with the highest IPR values remained in the category of Democracies without any changes and the 23 countries with the lowest IPR values remained in the category of Nondemocracies throughout the period 1981–88.

The Results of Regression Analysis for 1988

In Table 4.9 the results of regression analysis are given for 1988 with the values of the three political variables in 1988. The countries are ranked by their IPR values and divided into three subcategories as in Table 4.6. Deviating cases are *italicized*. All countries above the IPR level of 6.5 were expected to be Democracies and all countries below the IPR level of 3.5 were expected to be Nondemocracies. The residuals and ID estimates produced by the regression analysis indicate how accurately it was possible to estimate the actual values of ID for 1988 on the basis of the simple regression equation Y est. $= 1.845 + 0.808X$. The same results are given graphically in Figure 4.2.

Table 4.9 and Figure 4.2 show that predictions for 1988 were relatively accurate. In most cases, the actual values of ID differ only slightly from the predicted values. In other words, the same explanatory factor, the distribution of power resources, seems to account for both the high and low levels of democratization, although not equally well in all cases. In fact, positive or negative residuals are larger than one standard error of estimate (7.27) for 34 countries. They form the group of the most clearly deviating countries, but it should be noted that only 10 of them contradict the second research hypothesis. Of the 34 countries with large residuals, 22 had large residuals in 1980, too, although a large negative residual had changed into a large positive residual, or vice versa, in three cases. Thus large residuals had remained the same in 19 cases. Let us first examine these 19 countries with persistent large residuals. Are the reasons for deviations more or less unique in each case, or could it be possible to find some common explanations for persistent large residuals?

All the 11 countries with persistent large positive residuals are Democracies; seven of them (Italy, Greece, Malta, Barbados, Portugal, Mauritius, and the Dominican Republic) are in the IPR category above 6.5 index points, India at the transition level of IPR, and Papua New Guinea, the Solomon Islands, and Gambia below 3.5 IPR index points. The last three are deviating Democracies, whereas the other eight countries do not contradict the second research hypothesis. It seems that it is not possible to find any common explanation for the large positive residuals of these countries. A proportional electoral system, for instance, does not provide any coherent explanation for large positive residuals. Italy, Greece, Malta, Portugal, Mauritius, and Papua New Guinea have some variation of proportional representation, but there

Table 4.9.

147 Countries Ranked by IPR Values and Divided into Three Subcategories by the Level of IPR, and the Actual Values of Three Political Variables as well as the Residuals and ID Estimates Produced by the Regression Analysis for 1988[1]

Country/IPR level	C-88	P-88	ID-88	IPR	Residual	ID estimate
IPR above 6.5						
1 United States	46.1	36.2	16.7	52.2	−27.3	44.0
2 Iceland	72.8	63.5	46.2	50.9	3.2	43.0
3 Netherlands	65.4	62.7	41.0	45.3	2.6	38.4
4 Australia	54.2	57.1	30.9	45.1	−7.4	38.3
5 New Zealand	52.0	56.3	29.3	45.0	−8.9	38.2
6 Canada	57.0	50.6	28.8	45.0	−9.4	38.2
7 Germany, West	63.0	62.0	39.1	44.3	1.5	37.6
8 Denmark	70.4	64.9	45.7	44.0	8.3	37.4
9 Sweden	56.8	64.0	36.4	44.0	−1.0	37.4
10 United Kingdom	57.7	57.6	33.2	42.2	−2.7	35.9
11 Belgium	72.5	61.7	44.7	41.9	9.0	35.7
12 France	55.6	49.6	27.6	41.8	−8.0	35.6
13 Finland	64.0	60.3	38.6	41.4	3.3	35.3
14 Israel	68.9	51.9	35.8	38.7	2.7	33.1
15 Italy	65.9	67.0	44.1	36.7	12.6	31.5
16 Japan	50.6	49.7	25.1	36.3	−6.1	31.2
17 Norway	59.2	62.6	37.1	35.8	6.3	30.8
18 Switzerland	77.2	29.6	22.9	34.3	−6.7	29.6
19 Austria	56.9	64.1	36.5	33.9	7.3	29.2
20 Lebanon	54.5	17.4	9.5	33.2	−19.2	28.7
21 Ireland	55.8	50.2	28.0	32.7	−0.3	28.3
22 Spain	55.7	51.9	28.9	32.3	1.0	27.9
23 Luxemburg	65.1	48.4	31.5	31.7	4.0	27.5
24 Korea, South	43.1	53.2	22.9	22.0	3.3	19.6
25 Greece	54.2	64.1	34.7	21.6	15.4	19.3
26 Malta	49.1	61.0	30.0	20.9	11.3	18.7
27 Uruguay	60.5	63.1	38.2	20.7	19.6	18.6
28 Cyprus	66.4	48.0	31.9	18.4	15.2	16.7
29 Argentina	48.2	49.9	24.1	17.7	8.0	16.1
30 *Chile*	*0*	*0*	*0*	*17.4*	*−15.9*	*15.9*
31 Costa Rica	47.7	44.4	21.2	16.6	5.9	15.3
32 *Yugoslavia*	*0*	*59.0*	*0*	*15.7*	*−14.5*	*14.5*
33 Bahamas	46.4	41.7	19.3	15.6	4.8	14.5
34 Singapore	38.2	52.0	19.9	14.9	6.0	13.9
35 Barbados	40.5	53.0	21.5	14.5	7.9	13.6
36 Venezuela	47.1	39.6	18.7	13.6	5.9	12.8
37 Philippines	47.0	36.2	17.0	13.3	4.4	12.6
38 Mexico	49.3	30.0	14.8	12.1	3.2	11.6
39 Ecuador	54.0	33.9	18.3	11.7	7.0	11.3

Table 4.9. *continued*

Country/IPR level	C-88	P-88	ID-88	IPR	Residual	ID estimate
40 Portugal	48.9	55.5	27.1	11.1	16.3	10.8
41 Colombia	41.8	24.3	10.2	10.8	−0.4	10.6
42 Jamaica	42.4	34.5	14.6	10.1	4.6	10.0
43 *Poland*	*0.5*	*55.1*	*0*	*10.1*	*−10.0*	*10.0*
44 *Jordan*	*0*	*0*	*0*	*10.0*	*−9.9*	*9.9*
45 Sri Lanka	47.4	34.3	16.3	9.8	6.5	9.8
46 Mauritius	50.2	54.3	27.3	9.7	17.6	9.7
47 Peru	46.6	32.8	15.3	9.6	5.7	9.6
48 *Panama*	*0*	*0*	*0*	*9.5*	*−9.5*	*9.5*
49 Turkey	36.1	41.6	15.0	9.4	5.6	9.4
50 Trinidad & Tobago	32.7	46.2	15.1	8.7	6.2	8.9
51 Brazil	37.0	21.1	7.8	8.4	−0.8	8.6
52 *Fiji*	*0*	*0*	*0*	*7.9*	*−8.2*	*8.2*
53 Dominican Republic	58.4	32.1	18.7	6.9	11.3	7.4
IPR 3.5–6.5						
54 Malaysia	42.7	28.7	12.3	6.3	5.4	6.9
55 Syria	0	63.5	0	6.3	−6.9	6.9
56 Thailand	37.8	14.0	5.3	6.2	−1.6	6.9
57 Bolivia	65.0	21.9	14.2	6.1	7.4	6.8
58 Iran	14.3	32.2	4.6	5.8	−1.9	6.5
59 Zambia	4.4	20.8	0.9	5.6	−5.5	6.4
60 Congo Republic	0	0	0	5.6	−6.4	6.4
61 Iraq	0	0	0	5.4	−6.2	6.2
62 Egypt	2.9	25.0	0.7	5.4	−5.5	6.2
63 Tunisia	0	0	0	5.0	−5.9	5.9
64 Ghana	0	0	0	5.0	−5.9	5.9
65 Guyana	20.8	36.5	7.6	5.0	1.7	5.9
66 Honduras	48.9	35.3	17.3	4.9	11.5	5.8
67 Burma	0	45.0	0	4.8	−5.7	5.7
68 Nicaragua	33.0	34.7	14.8	4.7	9.2	5.6
69 El Salvador	46.4	29.4	13.6	4.7	8.0	5.6
70 India	50.9	31.9	16.2	4.5	10.7	5.5
71 Qatar	0	0	0	4.3	−5.3	5.3
72 Indonesia	6.7	12.6	0.8	4.3	−4.5	5.3
73 Bahrain	0	0	0	4.2	−5.2	5.2
74 Kuwait	0	0.7	0	4.1	−5.2	5.2
75 Guatemala	31.6	20.8	6.6	3.8	1.7	4.9
76 Gabon	0	58.5	0	3.7	−4.8	4.8
77 Algeria	6.7	48.6	3.3	3.7	−1.5	4.8
78 Paraguay	10.4	33.5	3.5	3.7	−1.3	4.8
79 Libya	0	0	0	3.5	−4.7	4.7
80 Zaire	0.8	50.5	0.4	3.5	−4.3	4.7

Table 4.9. *continued*

Country/IPR level	C-88	P-88	ID-88	IPR	Residual	ID estimate
IPR below 3.5						
81 Morocco	18.8	5.2	1.0	3.4	−3.6	4.6
82 South Africa	47.3	6.0	2.8	3.1	−1.5	4.3
83 Ivory Coast	0	36.5	0	3.0	−4.3	4.3
84 Suriname	15.0	47.0	7.0	2.9	2.8	4.2
85 Zimbabwe	23.7	34.9	8.3	2.9	4.1	4.2
86 Cape Verde	5.5	29.6	1.6	2.8	−2.5	4.1
87 Lesotho	0	0	0	2.7	−4.0	4.0
88 Nigeria	0	0	0	2.6	−3.9	3.9
89 Cameroon	1.3	30.6	0.4	2.5	−3.5	3.9
90 Central African Republic	7.8	27.5	2.1	2.5	−1.8	3.9
91 United Arab Emirates	0	0	0	2.5	−3.9	3.9
92 Madagascar	20.0	42.3	8.5	2.5	4.6	3.9
93 *Botswana*	*32.0*	*21.7*	*6.9*	*2.5*	*3.0*	*3.9*
94 Haiti	0	0	0	2.3	−3.7	3.7
95 Togo	0	56.4	0	2.2	−3.6	3.6
96 *Papua New Guinea*	*85.3*	*38.4*	*32.8*	*2.1*	*29.3*	*3.5*
97 Kenya	0	9.9	0	2.1	−3.5	3.5
98 Djibouti	0	18.1	0	2.0	−3.5	3.5
99 Burundi	0	0	0	2.0	−3.5	3.5
100 Tanzania	4.3	23.0	1.0	2.0	−2.5	3.5
101 *Solomon Islands*	*63.0*	*25.0*	*15.7*	*1.9*	*12.3*	*3.4*
102 *Pakistan*	*61.0*	*20.0*	*12.2*	*1.9*	*8.8*	*3.4*
103 *Liberia*	*32.5*	*23.7*	*7.7*	*1.9*	*4.3*	*3.4*
104 Swaziland	0	0	0	1.9	−3.4	3.4
105 Uganda	0	0	0	1.9	−3.4	3.4
106 Cuba	0	0.1	0	1.9	−3.4	3.4
107 Sierra Leone	0.1	77.4	0.1	1.8	−3.2	3.3
108 Equatorial Guinea	4.2	38.4	1.6	1.7	−1.6	3.2
109 Senegal	26.8	16.6	4.4	1.6	1.3	3.1
110 Benin	0	0	0	1.5	−3.1	3.1
111 Comoros	0.6	57.0	0.3	1.5	−2.8	3.1
112 German Dem. Republic	0.1	74.6	0.1	1.4	−2.9	3.0
113 Bangladesh	16.4	25.9	4.2	1.4	1.2	3.0
114 Angola	0	0	0	1.4	−3.0	3.0
115 Guinea	0	0	0	1.3	−2.9	2.9
116 Laos	0	0	0	1.2	−2.8	2.8
117 *Sudan*	*62.0*	*18.9*	*11.7*	*1.2*	*8.9*	*2.8*
118 Romania	2.3	68.3	1.6	1.2	−1.2	2.8
119 Rwanda	0	40.3	0	1.1	−2.7	2.7
120 Chad	0	0	0	1.1	−2.7	2.7
121 Guinea-Bissau	0	0	0	1.0	−2.7	2.7
122 Afghanistan	0	0	0	0.9	−2.6	2.6
123 Malawi	0	0	0	0.9	−2.6	2.6

Table 4.9. *continued*

Country/IPR level	C-88	P-88	ID-88	IPR	Residual	ID estimate
124 *Gambia*	*40.8*	*31.1*	*12.7*	*0.9*	*10.1*	*2.6*
125 Yemen, South	31.0	0	0	0.9	−2.6	2.6
126 Mozambique	0	0	0	0.9	−2.6	2.6
127 Mauritania	0	0	0	0.9	−2.6	2.6
128 Oman	0	0	0	0.8	−2.5	2.5
129 Hungary	0	63.1	0	0.5	−2.2	2.2
130 Vietnam	0	46.0	0	0.5	−2.2	2.2
131 Nepal	0	7.6	0	0.5	−2.2	2.2
132 Kampuchea	0	49.6	0	0.4	−2.2	2.2
133 Bhutan	0	0	0	0.4	−2.2	2.2
134 Somalia	0.1	40.0	0	0.4	−2.2	2.2
135 Burkina Faso	0	0	0	0.4	−2.2	2.2
136 Niger	0	0	0	0.4	−2.2	2.2
137 Yemen, North	0	0	0	0.4	−2.2	2.2
138 Ethiopia	0	0	0	0.3	−2.1	2.1
139 Saudi Arabia	0	0	0	0.3	−2.1	2.1
140 Czechoslovakia	0	70.1	0	0.2	−2.0	2.0
141 Mali	0	42.6	0	0.1	−1.9	1.9
142 China	0	0	0	0.1	−1.9	1.9
143 Albania	0	59.8	0	0	−1.8	1.8
144 Mongolia	0	47.9	0	0	−1.8	1.8
145 USSR	0.1	66.9	0.1	0	−1.7	1.8
146 Bulgaria	0	74.2	0	0	−1.8	1.8
147 Korea, North	0	50.0	0	0	−1.8	1.8

[1]Countries contradicting the hypothesis are *italicized*.

are many other Democracies with proportional representation for which residuals are smaller than one standard error of estimate. On the other hand, the plurality system is used in Barbados, India, and Gambia. It may be that some unique political or social factors have caused large positive residuals for these countries.

In Italy the extreme ideological pluralism and polarization have increased the number of parties and, together with proportional representation and compulsory voting, decreased the share of the largest party and produced a very high ID value (44.1). For Greece, Malta, and Portugal, the values of ID are not higher than in Western Europe in general, but because of their much lower IPR values residuals are positive and large. I do not have any particular explanations for these deviations. Perhaps their close connections with Western European democracies help them to keep the level of party pluralism much higher than expected on the basis of their IPR values. I do not have any special explanation for the balance of the two major parties in

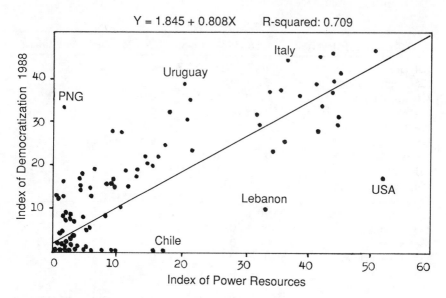

Figure 4.2. The results of regression analysis in which ID-88 is used as the dependent variable and IPR as the independent variable in the comparison group of 147 states.

Barbados, whereas I think that the high level of party competition in Mauritius is at least partly connected with the ethnic pluralism of its population. The same may be true in the case of India, although we should also take into account, as an additional factor, its political leaders' exceptionally strong commitment to democratic values since the days of independence movement (cf. Gupta 1989). The Dominican Republic has attempted to uphold an American pattern of democracy since the civil war in 1965. The vicinity of the United States may have supported the survival of democratic electoral process in the Dominican Republic. Papua New Guinea, the Solomon Islands, and Gambia are deviating Democracies that I have discussed previously.

Three of the eight countries with persistent large negative residuals (the United States, Canada, and Lebanon) are Democracies and the other five (Chile, Yugoslavia, Jordan, Poland, and Panama) deviating Nondemocracies. It seems that the large negative residuals of the United States and Canada can be traced to their electoral system, the plurality system, which decreases the level of participation and the share of the smaller parties. The logic of the plurality system limits the chances of the smaller groups and parties to get their own representatives elected, and, consequently, their willingness to participate in elections decreases, too. In Lebanon the continuation of civil war has prevented the normal process of electoral politics, as explained above. The five deviating Nondemocracies with large negative residuals differ from each other in many respects, but it seems to me that in all these countries the concentration of political power has been crucially based on the support of the military.

The comparison of the results of regression analyses of 1980 and 1988 discloses to what degree the predictions based on the results of the 1980 regression analysis had materialized or failed to materialize in 1988. It was predicted that the 14 deviating Nondemocracies and Semidemocracies in the IPR category above 6.5 index points would cross the threshold of democracy and that we could expect the failure of democracy in the six deviating Democracies below 3.5 index points. What happened in the period 1981–88? Table 4.9 shows that nine (South Korea, Uruguay, Argentina, Singapore, the Philippines, Mexico, Sri Lanka, Turkey, and Brazil) of the deviating Nondemocracies and Semidemocracies of 1980 crossed the threshold of democracy in the period 1981–88. Only five of them (Chile, Yugoslavia, Poland, Jordan, and Panama) remained in the category of Nondemocracies. In all of these five countries popular pressure for democratization is strong. In fact, Poland seems to have crossed the threshold of democracy in 1989 (see, for example, Borrell 1989a, 12-14; b, 24), and it can be expected to take place in the remaining four countries within a few years. In Chile the process of redemocratization started definitively from the referendum of October 1988 (see Heine 1989; Greenwald 1988). Three (Zimbabwe, Nigeria, and Uganda) of the six deviating Democracies dropped from the category of Democracies, as expected, in the period 1981-88, whereas three others (Papua New Guinea, the Solomon Islands, and Gambia) have remained among Democracies. In other words, 60 percent of the predicted changes took place within a short period of eight years. On the other hand, contrary to my predictions, one new deviating Nondemocracy (Fiji) and four new deviating Democracies (Botswana, Pakistan, Liberia, and Sudan) emerged within the same period. These five cases form 5 percent of the 100 correct Democracies and Nondemocracies of the first and third IPR categories in 1980. Besides, Sudan returned back to the category of Nondemocracies as a consequence of a military coup in June 1989 (see Time, July 10, 1989, 134:25). In the case of Liberia, it is not clear whether it should be regarded as a Democracy, for many opposition party leaders have been arrested after the 1985 elections (see Banks 1988, 350–53).

These results indicate that, on the basis of the theory of democratization used in this study, it has been possible to make surprisingly accurate predictions on the chances of various countries to establish democratic institutions or to maintain them, although such predictions and explanations have not been and can never be fully correct because my indicators of theoretical variables are imperfect, because there are errors in the empirical data collected on these indicators, and because random factors always play a role in politics as in all biological phenomena.

5

ALTERNATIVE EXPLANATIONS OF DEMOCRATIZATION

The review of theories and interpretations on the conditions of democracy presented in Chapter 2 indicated that there are several alternative hypotheses on democratization that can be tested empirically. Some of them have been tested since the 1950s. In this chapter we (1) compare the results of some previous studies with the results of my empirical analysis, and (2) retest two particular alternative hypotheses by correlating my measures of democratization with indicators representing the explanatory variables of those hypotheses.

COMPARISON OF RESULTS

Because the hypotheses and empirical variables used, the periods of comparison, and the countries included vary from study to study, the results of empirical analyses are not usually directly comparable, although limited comparisons of some results are possible. It would be particularly interesting to compare how strongly the measures of democracy have correlated with explanatory indicators and what countries have most clearly deviated from the patterns established. From these aspects, the results of empirical analyses given by Lipset (1960), Lerner (1968), Cutright (1963), Neubauer (1967), Olsen (1968), Needler (1968), Smith (1969), and Banks (1970, 1972) are to some degree comparable with the results of this study or with the results of my previous longitudinal studies.

Daniel Lerner's major assumption was that "the Western model of modernization exhibits certain components and sequences whose relevance is global." Urbanization, literacy, media exposure, economic participation, and political participation were assumed to increase together. Lerner argued that urbanization starts the process of modernization and that democratic governance comes late, historically, and appears "as a crowning institution of the participant society." He emphasized that the same basic model reappears in virtually all modernizing societies on all continents of the world, regardless of variations in race, color, and creed. My assumption that explanatory variables are globally relevant is similar. The results of Lerner's empirical analysis, covering 54 countries, indicate that his indices of modernization were moderately correlated with each other. So are they in my study. Urbanization, literacy, and media participation taken together explained 67 percent of the variation in political participation (correlation 0.82). In my study the correlations of Participation with explanatory variables are significantly lower, but it should be noted that I do not have any indicators of media participation and that his "Political participation" was calculated differently (see Lerner 1968 [1958], 43–68).

S.M. Lipset's study, which included 30 European and English-speaking countries and 20 Latin American nations, indicates that in each case the average wealth, degree of industrialization and urbanization, and level of education were much higher for the more democratic countries than for the less democratic ones. On the basis of the evidence presented in his study, he concluded that "all the various aspects of economic development—industrialization, urbanization, wealth, and education—are so closely interrelated as to form one major factor which has the political correlate of democracy." Lipset's hypothesis on a strong causal relationship between economic development and democracy was supported by the evidence presented in his study, but many clearly deviating cases weaken his hypothesis. It does not explain the success of democracy in several poor countries and the lack of it in many economically developed nations (Lipset 1959, 1960, 45–60). In this respect my theory of democratization is crucially different, and the number of deviating cases is smaller. We return to this point in the next section.

Phillips Cutright formulated an index of political development that made it possible to test Lipset's hypothesis by correlation analysis. The correlations between his index of political development and Urbanization (0.69), Education (0.74), and Agriculture (−0.72) were somewhat higher than corresponding correlations in my study (see Table 4.3). The index of political development was even more highly (0.81) correlated with his communications development index. Together the four independent variables explained 67 percent of the observed variation around the mean of the dependent variable, which is only slightly less than in my study (see Table 4.3). The results of Cutright's regression analysis are in many points similar to those produced by my regression analyses (cf. Vanhanen 1984). By this technique he was able to point out which countries seemed to be politically more developed (positive residuals) than expected on the basis of independent variables and which countries seemed to be politically less developed than expected (negative residuals). I have used the same technique of regression analysis to discern deviating cases. In this respect Cutrigt's study has been an example for me (see Cutright 1963).

Deane E. Neubauer tried to show that Lipset's hypothesis is not valid because democratic political development is a threshold phenomenon. He argued that certain levels of "basic" socioeconomic development appeared to be necessary to democracy, but once above this threshold, democratic practice is no longer a function of continued socioeconomic development. The results of his empirical analysis, which covered 23 countries, supported his hypothesis. The correlations between his index of democratic performance and levels of communication, urbanization, education, and agriculture were near zero as hypothesized. However, the results of his analysis do not necessarily falsify Lipset's hypothesis because his sample of countries represents only the group of relatively democratic countries. Low correlations may be due to the fact that there was not enough variation in the assumed dependent variable (see Neubauer 1967). The same might be true in my study if comparison were limited to a section of countries with high ID values.

Marvin E. Olsen tested Lipset's hypothesis by statistical analysis covering 115 independent states. He used five indexes of political modernization and a Combined Index of Political Development as "dependent" variables. He emphasized that "democratization" is only one aspect of national political development. The source of data for all these indexes was Banks and Textor's *A Cross-Polity Survey* (1963), which means that Olsen's data are based on subjective codings made by Banks and Textor. Olsen used 14 variables of socioeconomic development combined into five analytical dimensions of Industrialization, Urbanization, Transportation, Communication, and Education, as "independent" variables. Again, it was found that virtually all measures of socioeconomic development are rather highly intercorrelated. Multiple correlations between his combined dimensions of socioeconomic development and political development indexes were in all cases moderate (from 0.38 to 0.70). Multiple correlations between all 14 socioeconomic variables and political development indexes were very high (from 0.75 to 0.98). The multiple correlation between all 14 socioeconomic variables and the Combined Index of Political Development was 0.83, or about the same as in this study between ID and IPR. Olsen concluded that "Lipset's original emphasis on the importance of economic growth for political modernization is essentially substantiated by these data, with the qualification that transportation facilities seem to be more crucial than industrialization *per se* for some kinds of political development." However, in the end he had to note that each set of factors "provides a powerful regression equation for predicting variation in its index of political development, but the theoretical reasons underlying these particular combinations are not obvious from the data" (Olsen 1968). That is a problem in Olsen's study. He does not have any good theoretical reasons for his explanatory variables, although he thinks that Karl Deutsch's ideas of mass social mobilization provide a tentative explanation of the causal forces linking socioeconomic and political modernization. Another problem, from the perspective of my study, is that his measures of political modernization seem to be too much based on subjective codings and that they are not principally measures of democratization.

Martin C. Needler tested Lipset's hypothesis in the context of 20 Latin American states. He found that per capita GDP correlated moderately (0.72) with his political development score based on the constitutionality index and electoral participation. Thus the results of his study support the hypothesis that political development correlates positively with economic development (Needler 1968).

Arthur K. Smith replicated the Cutright research design with the addition of a new technique for measuring degree of political democracy. The study included 110 countries of the period 1946–65. His Degree of Political Democracy correlated positively with Urbanization (0.597), Education (0.667), and Communication (0.707). These correlations are about the same as the corresponding correlations in this study (see Table 4.3). Besides, Smith subdivided the university of 110 nations into four regional groups (Anglo-European Nations, N = 33, Latin America, N = 20, Sub-Saharan Africa, N = 24, and North African, Middle Eastern, and Asian Nations, N = 33) and found that correlations remained positive in regional subgroups, too, although they became weak in Sub-Saharan Africa (from 0.109 to 0.377) (see Smith 1969).

Arthur S. Banks made a longitudinal study of Latin American and Amer-European countries covering approximately 100 years (1865–66). The results of correlation analysis show that his composite democratic performance indicator correlated positively with his composite index of modernization at all 13 data points in the total group of 36 countries. Correlations (from 0.33 to 0.58) were approximately the same as corresponding correlations in my longitudinal study, or slightly weaker (see Vanhanen 1979, 1984). The results of Banks' study indicate that the relationship between the measures of modernization and democratic performance had remained more or less stable over the period of 100 years (Banks 1970). On the other hand, Banks has attempted to show by the technique of the time-lag analysis that Lerner, Lipset, and others were probably wrong in their assumption that modernization tends to precede democracy in the course of political development. He argued, on the basis of the research reported in his studies, that a contrary assumption would appear to be more tenable. According to his conclusion, "there were no instances of earlier ecological variates correlating systematically with later democratic performance. Thus no evidence suggesting the causal priority of the former emerged" (Banks 1972). In this point I disagree with Banks. I still assume that social factors are more independent and causal than political variables, although I agree that the causal relationship between them may be reciprocal to some degree. Besides, some results of my own cross-lagged panel analysis contradict Banks' conclusions. I found that in several points data clearly support the hypothesis of the temporal priority of social variables, although not universally (see Vanhanen 1979).

The studies reviewed above indicate that different theories, hypotheses, and empirical variables can be used to explain the variation of democratization. In many points the results have been more or less the same as in my study, but because these studies explain less of the variation in the dependent variable than what has been achieved in this study, or because the political variables used in those studies are not intended to measure the variation of democratization merely, they do not help me to increase the power of my explanatory model or to decrease the number of deviating cases.

GNP PER CAPITA AND ETHNIC HOMOGENEITY

Particular attention is paid to alternative hypotheses intended to explain democracy by a high level of socioeconomic development and wealth or by the ethnic homogeneity of the population because it is possible to test these hypotheses by empirical data covering all the 147 states of this study.

Because Lipset's hypothesis claims that the level of democracy depends principally on the level of socioeconomic development, I attempt to retest his hypothesis by correlating GNP per capita with my political variables (Table 5.1) and by calculating a simple regression equation in which the Index of Democratization is used as the dependent variable and GNP per capita as the independent variable (Table 5.2). Of course, GNP per capita is not the only important indicator of socioeconomic development, but it can be regarded as the most central indicator of socioeconomic development. In fact, it has been used as an explanatory variable in several studies that have tested the hypothesized positive relationship between the level of socioeconomic development or modernization and the level of democracy or political development (see Lipset 1959; Coleman 1960; Deutsch 1961; Cutright 1963; Russett et al. 1964; Needler 1968; Olsen 1968; Kim 1971; Hewitt 1977; Banks 1981; Hannan and Carroll 1981; Berg-Schlosser 1985; Muller 1985; Soares 1985; and Letterie and van Puijenbroek 1987). Per capita GNP measures the wealth of nations, but it can also indicate the level of socioeconomic development. Besides, I assume that it, just like Urban Population and Nonagricultural Population, indicates the distribution of economic power

Table 5.1.

GNP per capita in 1983 and the Index of Ethnic Homogeneity correlated with explanatory and political variables in the comparison group of 147 countries

Variable	GNP per capita in 1983	EH
Urban Population	0.670	0.331
Non-Agricultural Population	0.679	0.371
Students	0.505	0.340
Literates	0.455	0.386
Family Farms	0.191	−0.040
Degree of Decentralization of Non-Agricultural Power Resources (DDN)	0.442	0.261
Index of Occupational Diversification (IOD)	0.701	0.367
Index of Knowledge Distribution (IKD)	0.490	0.422
Index of the Distribution of Economic Power Resources (DER)	0.192	0.015
Index of Power Resources (IPR)	0.614	0.332
Competition 1980	0.374	0.127
Competition 1981	0.372	0.166
Competition 1982	0.370	0.158
Competition 1983	0.377	0.215
Competition 1984	0.351	0.235
Competition 1985	0.356	0.247
Competition 1986	0.332	0.250
Competition 1987	0.335	0.262
Competition 1988	0.324	0.253
Participation 1980	0.285	0.201
Participation 1981	0.268	0.239
Participation 1982	0.253	0.242
Participation 1983	0.251	0.270
Participation 1984	0.253	0.324
Participation 1985	0.246	0.311
Participation 1986	0.233	0.308
Participation 1987	0.239	0.307
Participation 1988	0.243	0.299
Index of Democratization 1980	0.498	0.260
Index of Democratization 1981	0.493	0.276
Index of Democratization 1982	0.488	0.265
Index of Democratization 1983	0.483	0.296
Index of Democratization 1984	0.466	0.321
Index of Democratization 1985	0.469	0.335
Index of Democratization 1986	0.458	0.338
Index of Democratization 1987	0.457	0.352
Index of Democratization 1988	0.453	0.341

Table 5.2.

The results of regression analysis in which ID-1988 is used as the dependent variable and GNP per capita (1983) and the Index of Ethnic Homogeneity (EH) as the independent variables in the comparison group of 147 states

Country	ID-88	GNP	Resid.	ID est.	EH	Resid.	ID est.
1 Afghanistan	0	190	−6.2	6.2	50	−6.9	6.9
2 Albania	0	900	−7.2	7.2	93	−14.9	14.9
3 Algeria	3.3	2,320	−5.8	9.1	83	−9.8	13.1
4 Angola	0	470	−6.6	6.6	37	−4.5	4.5
5 Argentina	24.1	2,070	15.4	8.7	97	8.4	15.7
6 Australia	30.9	11,490	9.5	21.4	96	15.4	15.5
7 Austria	36.5	9,250	18.1	18.4	96	21.0	15.5
8 Bahamas	19.3	3,793	8.3	11.0	70	8.7	10.6
9 Bahrain	0	10,360	−19.9	19.9	70	−10.6	10.6
10 Bangladesh	4.2	130	−1.9	6.1	85	−9.2	13.4
11 Barbados	21.5	3,930	10.3	11.2	92	6.8	14.7
12 Belgium	44.7	9,150	26.5	18.2	58	36.3	8.4
13 Benin	0	290	−6.3	6.3	59	−8.6	8.6
14 Bhutan	0	110	−6.1	6.1	61	−9.0	9.0
15 Bolivia	14.2	510	7.6	6.6	45	8.2	6.0
16 Botswana	6.9	920	−0.3	7.2	34	2.9	4.0
17 Brazil	7.8	1,880	−0.7	8.5	53	0.3	7.5
18 Bulgaria	0	4,150	−11.5	11.5	87	−13.8	13.8
19 Burkina Faso	0	180	−6.2	6.2	54	−7.7	7.7
20 Burma	0	180	−6.2	6.2	68	−10.3	10.3
21 Burundi	0	240	−6.3	6.3	83	−13.1	13.1
22 Cameroon	0.4	820	−6.7	7.1	21	−1.2	1.6
23 Canada	28.8	12,310	6.3	22.5	61	19.8	9.0
24 Cape Verde	1.6	360	−4.8	6.4	70	−9.0	10.6
25 Central African Rep.	2.1	280	−4.2	6.3	32	−1.5	3.6
26 Chad	0	80	−6.1	6.1	30	−3.2	3.2
27 Chile	0	1,870	−8.5	8.5	90	−14.4	14.4
28 China	0	300	−6.4	6.4	94	−15.1	15.1
29 Colombia	10.2	1,430	2.3	7.9	50	3.3	6.9
30 Comoros	0.3	340	−6.1	6.4	99	−15.7	16.0
31 Congo	0	1,230	−7.6	7.6	52	−7.3	7.3
32 Costa Rica	21.2	1,020	13.9	7.3	85	7.8	13.4
33 Cuba	0	1,534	−8.0	8.0	70	−11.0	11.0
34 Cyprus	31.9	3,720	20.9	11.0	81	19.2	12.7
35 Czechoslovakia	0	5,820	−13.8	13.8	64	−9.3	9.5
36 Denmark	45.7	11,570	24.2	21.5	99	29.7	16.0
37 Djibouti	0	480	−6.6	6.6	47	−6.4	6.4
38 Dominican Republic	18.7	1,370	10.9	7.8	75	7.1	11.6
39 Ecuador	18.3	1,420	10.4	7.9	50	11.4	6.9
40 Egypt	0.7	700	−6.2	6.9	94	−14.4	15.1
41 El Salvador	13.6	710	6.7	6.9	94	−1.5	15.1
42 Equatorial Guinea	1.6	417	−4.9	6.5	71	−9.2	10.8
43 Ethiopia	0	120	−6.1	6.1	30	−3.2	3.2
44 Fiji	0	1,790	−8.4	8.4	50	−6.9	6.9
45 Finland	38.6	10,740	18.2	20.4	94	23.5	15.1
46 France	27.6	10,500	7.6	20.0	93	12.7	14.9
47 Gabon	0	4,250	−11.7	11.7	34	−4.0	4.0
48 Gambia	12.7	290	6.4	6.4	43	7.1	5.6
49 German Dem. Rep.	0.1	7,180	−15.5	15.6	99	−15.9	16.0
50 Germany, West	39.1	11,430	17.8	21.3	93	24.2	14.9

Table 5.2. *continued*

Country	ID-88	GNP	Resid.	ID est.	EH	Resid.	ID est.
51 Ghana	0	310	−6.4	6.4	44	−5.8	5.8
52 Greece	34.7	3,920	23.5	11.2	95	19.4	15.3
53 Guatemala	6.6	1,120	−0.9	7.5	50	−0.3	6.9
54 Guinea	0	300	−6.4	6.4	41	−5.3	5.3
55 Guinea-Bissau	0	180	−6.2	6.2	27	−2.7	2.7
56 Guyana	7.6	520	0.9	6.7	51	0.5	7.1
57 Haiti	0	300	−6.4	6.4	95	−15.3	15.3
58 Honduras	17.3	670	10.4	6.9	90	2.9	14.4
59 Hungary	0	4,180	−11.6	11.6	99	−16.0	16.0
60 Iceland	46.2	11,083	25.4	20.8	97	30.5	15.7
61 India	16.2	260	9.9	6.3	40	11.1	5.1
62 Indonesia	0.8	560	−5.9	6.7	40	−4.3	5.1
63 Iran	4.6	2,590	−4.8	9.4	45	−1.4	6.0
64 Iraq	0	3,020	−10.0	10.0	77	−11.9	11.9
65 Ireland	28.0	5,000	15.3	12.7	96	12.5	15.5
66 Israel	35.8	5,370	22.6	13.2	83	22.7	13.1
67 Italy	44.1	6,400	29.6	14.5	98	28.3	15.8
68 Ivory Coast	0	710	−6.9	6.9	20	−1.4	1.4
69 Jamaica	14.6	1,300	6.9	7.7	76	2.8	11.8
70 Japan	25.1	10,120	5.6	19.5	99	9.1	16.0
71 Jordan	0	1,640	−8.2	8.2	98	−15.8	15.8
72 Kampuchea	0	100	−6.1	6.1	93	−14.9	14.9
73 Kenya	0	340	−6.4	5.4	21	−1.6	1.6
74 Korea, North	0	1,079	−7.4	7.4	100	−16.2	16.2
75 Korea, South	22.9	2,010	14.2	8.7	100	6.7	16.2
76 Kuwait	0	17,880	−29.9	29.9	42	−5.5	5.5
77 Laos	0	144	−6.2	6.2	56	−8.1	8.1
78 Lebanon	9.5	1,150	2.0	7.5	65	−0.2	9.7
79 Lesotho	0	460	−6.6	6.6	90	−14.4	14.4
80 Liberia	7.7	480	1.1	6.6	27	5.0	2.7
81 Libya	0	8,480	−17.3	17.3	82	−12.9	12.9
82 Luxemburg	31.5	9,838	12.3	19.2	74	20.1	11.4
83 Madagascar	8.5	310	2.1	6.4	26	6.0	2.5
84 Malawi	0	210	−6.2	6.2	59	−8.6	8.6
85 Malaysia	12.3	1,860	3.8	8.5	44	6.5	5.8
86 Mali	0	160	−6.2	6.2	33	−3.8	3.8
87 Malta	30.0	3,710	19.1	10.9	94	14.9	15.1
88 Mauritania	0	480	−6.6	6.6	80	−12.5	12.5
89 Mauritius	27.3	1,150	19.8	7.5	68	17.0	10.3
90 Mexico	14.8	2,240	5.8	9.0	55	6.9	7.9
91 Mongolia	0	830	−7.1	7.1	84	−13.2	13.2
92 Morocco	1.0	760	−6.0	7.0	99	−15.0	16.0
93 Mosambique	0	150	−6.2	6.2	52	−7.3	7.3
94 Nepal	0	160	−6.2	6.2	54	−7.7	7.7
95 Netherlands	40.0	9,890	21.8	19.2	36	36.6	4.4
96 New Zealand	29.3	7,730	13.0	16.3	90	14.9	14.4
97 Nicaragua	14.8	880	7.7	7.1	69	4.3	10.5
98 Niger	0	240	−6.3	6.3	52	−7.3	7.3
99 Nigeria	0	770	−7.0	7.0	29	−3.1	3.1
100 Norway	37.1	14,020	12.3	24.8	98	21.3	15.8
101 Oman	0	6,250	−14.3	14.3	87	−13.8	13.8
102 Pakistan	12.2	390	5.7	6.5	66	2.3	9.9
103 Panama	0	2,120	−8.8	8.8	70	−10.6	10.6
104 Papua New Guinea	32.8	760	25.8	7.0	83	19.7	13.1

Table 5.2. *continued*

Country	ID-88	GNP	Resid.	ID est.	EH	Resid.	ID est.
105 Paraguay	3.5	1,410	−4.3	7.9	90	−10.9	14.4
106 Peru	15.3	1,040	7.9	7.4	54	7.6	7.7
107 Philippines	17.0	760	10.0	7.0	93	2.1	14.9
108 Poland	0	3,900	−11.2	11.2	99	−16.0	16.0
109 Portugal	27.1	2,230	18.1	9.0	99	11.1	16.0
110 Qatar	0	21,060	−34.2	34.2	70	−10.6	10.6
111 Romania	1.6	2,560	−7.8	9.4	89	−12.6	14.2
112 Rwanda	0	270	−6.3	6.3	88	−14.0	14.0
113 Saudi Arabia	0	12,230	−22.4	22.4	90	−14.4	14.4
114 Senegal	4.4	440	−2.2	6.6	35	0.2	4.2
115 Sierra Leone	0.1	330	−6.3	6.4	34	−3.9	4.0
116 Singapore	19.9	6,620	5.1	14.8	77	8.0	11.9
117 Solomon Islands	15.7	640	8.9	6.8	93	0.8	14.9
118 Somalia	0	250	−6.3	6.3	95	−15.3	15.3
119 South Africa	2.8	2,490	−6.5	9.3	72	−8.2	11.0
120 Spain	28.9	5,780	16.5	12.4	73	17.7	11.2
121 Sri Lanka	16.3	330	9.9	6.4	74	4.9	11.4
122 Sudan	11.7	400	5.2	6.5	46	5.5	6.2
123 Suriname	7.0	3,520	−3.7	10.7	35	2.8	4.2
124 Swaziland	0	890	−7.2	7.2	95	−15.3	15.3
125 Sweden	36.4	12,470	13.7	22.7	95	21.1	15.3
126 Switzerland	22.9	16,290	−4.9	27.8	65	13.2	9.7
127 Syria	0	1,760	−8.3	8.3	89	−14.2	14.2
128 Tanzania	1.0	240	−5.3	6.3	21	−0.6	1.6
129 Thailand	5.3	820	−1.8	7.1	54	−2.4	7.7
130 Togo	0	280	−6.3	6.3	46	−6.2	6.2
131 Trinidad & Tobago	15.1	6,850	−0.0	15.1	41	9.8	5.3
132 Tunisia	0	1,290	−7.7	7.7	98	−15.8	15.8
133 Turkey	15.0	1,240	7.4	7.6	87	1.2	13.8
134 Uganda	0	220	−6.3	6.3	18	−1.0	1.0
135 U.S.S.R.	0.1	4,550	−12.0	12.1	52	−7.2	7.3
136 United Arab Emirates	0	22,870	−36.6	36.6	42	−5.5	5.5
137 United Kingdom	33.2	9,200	14.9	18.3	94	18.1	15.1
138 United States	16.7	14,110	−8.2	24.9	83	3.6	13.1
139 Uruguay	38.2	2,490	28.9	9.3	90	23.8	14.4
140 Venezuela	18.7	3,840	7.6	11.1	69	8.2	10.5
141 Vietnam	0	245	−6.3	6.3	88	−14.0	14.0
142 Yemen, North	0	550	−6.7	6.7	98	−15.8	15.8
143 Yemen, South	0	520	−6.7	6.7	93	−14.9	14.9
144 Yugoslavia	0	2,570	−9.4	9.4	36	−4.3	4.3
145 Zaire	0.4	170	−5.8	6.2	18	−0.6	1.0
146 Zambia	0.9	580	−5.8	6.7	34	−3.1	4.0
147 Zimbabwe	8.3	740	1.3	7.0	80	−4.2	12.5

resources indirectly. It can be assumed that the higher the GNP per capita, the more widely economic and intellectual power resources are usually distributed in a society. I did not include it among my explanatory variables because it indicates more or less the same phenomenon as Urban Population and NAP and because data on GNP are probably less reliable and comparable than data on Urban Population and NAP (cf. Bollen 1979, 578). Statistical data on GNP per capita are given and documented in Appendix 5.

Ethnic and linguistic cleavages and conflicts have a great political significance in many countries. Alvin Rabushka and Kenneth Shepsle have strongly argued that "democracy—the free and open competition for the people's vote—is simply not viable in an environment of intense ethnic preferences" and that intense political conflicts based on ethnic cleavages lead to a breakdown of democracy. They conclude: "The fragmented plural society, then, is marked by a plethora of groups, the scarcity or absence of brokerage institutions, the short supply of coalition-building skills necessary to organize political conflict, the eventual anarchy of unstructured conflict as a result of primordial distrust, and, typically, the initiation of rule by the military who possess a monopoly on organizational and other political skills. Democratic practices are foreclosed under such conditions" (Rabushka and Shepsle 1972, 62-92). Donald L. Horowitz (1965, 681–84) remarks that "the claim has repeatedly been advanced that democracy cannot survive in the face of serious ethnic divisions," but he concludes, on the basis of his extensive study: "There is no case to be made for the futility of democracy or the inevitability of uncontrolled conflict. Even in the most severely divided society, ties of blood do not lead ineluctably to rivers of blood."

Larry Diamond, S.M. Lipset, and Juan J. Linz assume in their study that cultural homogeneity is favorable for democracy, but they do not claim that ethnic pluralism is in all circumstances unfavorable for democracy (Diamond et al. 1986, 16-19, 97; see also Linz 1985). As G. Bingham Powell says, "ethnic conflicts involve issues that are difficult to compromise," which is certainly inimical to democracy, but, on the other hand, ethnic cleavages indicate the distribution of some important power resources between separate population groups, which is favorable for democracy (Powell 1982, 43). This means that the effects of ethnic pluralism are not always the same from the perspective of democratization. Besides, this variable is not equally significant in all countries. For these reasons I cannot present any clear hypothesis on the relationship between ethnic and linguistic cleavages and democratization.

Because several researchers have assumed that ethnic heterogeneity impedes democratization and makes it difficult to sustain democratic institutions, I tried to test this assumption by empirical data. For this purpose I needed an index of ethnic pluralism. It is not easy to define indicators of ethnic homogeneity or heterogeneity because there are many types of ethnic groups and cleavages and because researchers have different perceptions on the concept of "ethnic group." As a starting point I used the sociobiological theory of inclusive fitness first formulated by W.D. Hamilton. He looked at evolution from the gene's point of view and realized that natural selection tends to maximize inclusive fitness; the survival of one's genes through one's own offspring and through relatives who have the same genes. It means that the logic of evolution presupposes individual selfishness together with favorism toward relatives. Animals behaving in such a way have the best chances to reproduce their genes (Hamilton 1978). Maynard Smith (1964) coined the term "kin selection" for the same phenomenon. David P. Barash says that it indicates "the evolutionary process whereby individuals maximize their inclusive fitness through their behavior toward kin." Inclusive fitness and kin selection provide "a coherent theory for the biology of nepotism among living beings," he says (Barash 1982, 67–74).

Ethnic groups can be perceived as extended kin groups. The members of an ethnic group tend to favor their group members over nonmembers because they are more related with their group members than with the remainder of the population. Pierre L. van den Berghe notes "that the degree of cooperation between organisms can be expected to be a direct function of the proportion of the genes they share: conversely, the degree of conflict between them is an inverse function of the proportion of shared genes." He continues that nepotism is blindly selected for because nepotistic individuals in social species have higher fitness than nonnepotistic ones." Then he extends kin selection to ethnic groups: "My basic argument is quite simple: ethnic and racial sentiments are extension of kinship sentiments. Ethnocentrism and racism are thus extended form of nepotism—the propensity to favor kin over nonkin. There exsists a general behavioral predisposition, in our species as in many others, to react favorably toward other organisms to the extent that these organisms are biologically related to the actor. The closer the relationship is, the stronger the preferential behavior" (van den Berghe 1981, 7–19). I call this kind of behavior ethnic nepotism.

From the perspective of ethnic nepotism it does not matter what kinds of kin groups are in question. They all can be assumed to practice ethnic nepotism, although the intensity of nepotism may vary depending on how much the group concerned differs from the remainder of the population. Therefore, in my analysis the term "ethnic group" refers equally to racial groups, tribes, national groups, language groups, or old religious communities. It is common for them that their members are genetically more related with each other than with the members of the other sections of the population. Pierre L. van den Berghe emphasizes that ethnicity is defined in the last analysis by common descent. On the other hand, boundaries between ethnic groups or ethnies are not completely closed. There is some migration, principally by women, among groups, but the core of the group is made up of people "who know themselves to be related to each other by a double network of ties of descent and marriage." He continues that ethnic boundaries are "created socially by preferential endogamy and physically by territoriality" (van den Berghe 1981, 15–30).

I attempted to measure the ethnic homogeneity of the national populations by an Index of Ethnic Homogeneity (EH), which is based on the percentage of the largest homogeneous ethnic group (Appendix 6). The problem is that there are two or more types of significant ethnic cleavages in many countries, which often cross each other. It is not always self-evident which one of them should be regarded as the most important one. In such cases it was necessary to estimate the relative significance of different ethnic cleavages and to select the type of cleavage that I assumed to be the most significant one. It means that my Index of Ethnic Homogeneity is based on different types of ethnic cleavages. In some countries racial or tribal cleavages are the most important ones and in some other countries national or language groups or religious communities may be the most important ethnic groups. Because available data collections on ethnic cleavages and groups are usually based on one type of ethnic cleavage (for example, language, religion, tribe, race, nation, or caste), I had to use different data collections and sources in my attempt to find reliable data on the largest homogeneous ethnic group. The correlations of the Index of Ethnic Homogeneity with the explanatory and political variables of this study are given in Table 5.1.

GNP per capita is moderately correlated with most explanatory variables (Table 5.1). The highest correlations are with Urban Population and NAP, which can also be regarded as indicators of the level of socioeconomic development, whereas its correlations with Family Farms and DDN, which are intended to indicate the distribution of economic power resources, are weak. Its correlation 0.614 with IPR means that their covariation is 38 percent.

According to the socioeconomic hypothesis of democratization, GNP per capita should correlate positively with the indicators of democratization and particularly with the Index of Democratization (ID). In fact, all correlations are positive as hypothesized, but they are relatively weak. Correlations vary from 0.233 to 0.498. GNP per capita has the highest correlations with the Index of Democratization as hypothesized, but the explained part of variation in ID is only 21-25 percent. It is nearly 50 percentage points less than in the case of IPR (see Table 4.3). Therefore, I have to conclude that GNP per capita compared with IPR is a poor predictor of democratization. If it were completely independent from the other explanatory variables, its addition to IPR might increase the explained part of variation in ID significantly. It is, however, so closely related with the components of IPR that it increases the variation already explained by IPR only insignificantly. This was tested by multiple regression analysis. IPR alone explains 71 percent of the variation in ID-1988. When GNP per capita and IPR were used together to explain the variation in ID-1988, the explained part of variation (R-squared) increased only to 71.6 percent.

The Index of Ethnic Homogeneity is nearly independent from the other explanatory variables. Its correlations with them vary from -0.040 to 0.422. It is interesting to note that its highest positive correlations are with Literates and IKD. It implies that countries tend to be ethnically more homogeneous at higher levels of socioeconomic development than at lower levels. Its correlations with political variables are positive as hypothesized by Rabuska and Shepsle. The correlations between ID and EH vary from 0.260 to 0.352. This means that the Index of Ethnic Homogeneity explains only about 10 percent of the variation in the Index of Democratization.

Regression analyses in which ID-88 is used as the dependent variable (Y) and GNP per capita and the Index of Ethnic Homogeneity respectively as the independent variable (X) can be used to show how accurately the values of GNP per capita and of the Index of Ethnic Homogeneity predict the values of ID-1988 and at what levels of GNP per capita and EH countries have crossed the minimum threshold of democracy for ID (5.0 index points). The simple regression equations are: ID est. = 5.96 + 0.001GNP per capita and ID est. = −2.319 + 0.185EH. The predicted values of ID-88 and the residuals for single countries are given in Table 5.2.

Table 5.2 and Figure 5.1 show that GNP per capita does not help to make accurate predictions of the level of democratization. Large residuals indicate the inaccuracy of predictions. One standard error of estimate of Y on X is in this case 12.021, or nearly twice as high as in the regression equations based on IPR given above. In fact, the results of regression analysis imply that we cannot say of any country that its GNP per capita is too low for

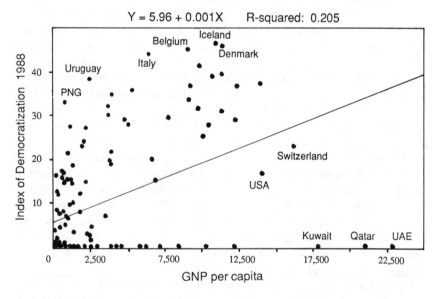

Figure 5.1. The results of regression analysis in which ID-88 is used as the dependent variable and GNP per capita as the independent variable.

democracy. The starting point of the regression line is 5.2 ID index points at the zero level of GNP per capita. This means that there is no threshold of GNP per capita below which democratization is improbable because of too low GNP per capita. Figure 5.1 illustrates the fact that democratizations have started at a very low level of GNP per capita. Thus empirical data contradict the assumption that only relatively wealthy countries could establish and uphold democratic systems. On the other hand, the results support the assumption that the higher the level of GNP per capita the better social conditions are for democracy, although several wealthy Nondemocracies contradict this hypothesis.

Let us compare the most deviating cases of this regression analysis with those of the regression equation of ID-88 on IPR (see Table 4.9). It is interesting to see to what degree the countries with the largest residuals are the same in both lists of the most deviating cases. In the case of the regression equation of ID-88 on IPR (Table 4.9), the countries with residuals larger than 7.3 or −7.3 (one standard error of estimate) were regarded as the most deviating cases. Table 4.9 shows that positive residuals are larger than 7.3 for 22 countries and negative residuals larger than −7.3 for 12 countries. All of the countries with large positive residuals are Democracies, but only four of them (Papua New Guinea, Solomon Islands, Gambia, and Liberia) contradicted the second hypothesis in 1988. In other words, they had crossed the threshold of democracy at a lower level of IPR than expected. Six of the 12 countries with large negative residuals (the United States, Australia, New Zealand, Canada, France, and Lebanon) were Democracies, but they did not contradict the second hypothesis because they were clearly above the minimum threshold of democracy for ID (5.0 index points). The other six countries with large negative residuals (Chile, Yugoslavia, Poland, Jordan, and Panama) contradicted the second hypothesis. Because of their high IPR values they were expected to be Democracies, but they are Nondemocracies (ID below 5.0 index points).

In the case of the regression equation of ID-88 on GNP per capita, the countries with residuals larger than 12.0 or −12.0 can be regarded as the most deviating cases (one standard error of estimate is 12.0). Table 5.2 shows that positive residuals are larger than 12.0 for 26 countries and negative residuals larger than -12.0 for nine countries. The comparison of the lists of countries with the largest positive residuals indicates that 12 countries (Argentina, Belgium, Cyprus, Denmark, Greece, Italy, Malta, Mauritius, New Zealand, Papua New Guinea, Portugal, and Uruguay) are the same in both lists. However, of the four deviating Democracies in 1988, this list includes only Papua New Guinea. This means that democracy in Gambia, Liberia, and the Solomon Islands is not particularly unexpected on the basis of GNP per capita. As noted above, the results of regression analysis indicate that we cannot say of any country that its level of GNP per capita is too low for democracy. This fact, of course, significantly reduces the value of GNP per capita as an explanatory variable. The other countries with large positive residuals are different in the two lists, but all of them are Democracies. On the other hand, the lists of countries with large negative residuals are completely different. The nine countries with large negative residuals of Table 5.2 are: Bahrain, Czechoslovakia, German Democratic Republic, Kuwait, Libya, Oman, Qatar, Saudi Arabia, and the United Arab Emirates. The negative residual of the Soviet Union is exactly -12.0. According to GNP per capita, these Socialist and Middle East oil countries should be Democracies, but they are not. According to my IPR, they should not be Democracies, and they are not. These opposite predictions highlight the differences between GNP per capita and IPR as explanatory variables. I think that GNP per capita is a much poorer predictor of democratization than IPR because it does not take into account the differences in the distribution of wealth and other resources used as sources of power. The most important economic power resources are highly concentrated in the hands of the ruling group in Socialist countries and in the Middle East oil countries. The concentration of power resources has prevented the emergence of democracy in these countries despite their high levels of GNP per capita. IPR takes into account the concentration of power resources in these countries and, consequently, is able to predict the nature of their political systems much more accurately than GNP per capita. Thus it also explains why a high level of GNP per capita has not created favorable conditions for democracy in these countries. S.M. Lipset notes correctly, on the basis of his hypothesis, that there are still "some deviant cases. Most of them, as already indicated, are oil-rich, otherwise less developed, highly inegalitarian, Middle Eastern states, or the more industrialized Communist regimes" (Lipset 1983, 473). He could not explain these deviations on the basis of his socioeconomic hypothesis. These countries are not deviant cases in my study.

Another significant difference between the two lists of large negative residuals concerns the six deviating Nondemocracies of Table 4.9 (Chile, Yugoslavia, Poland, Jordan, and Panama). We can predict the democratization of these countries on the basis of their relatively high IPR values. They are assumed to be the most probable countries to democratize, whereas, on the basis of GNP per capita, their negative residuals are smaller than one standard error of estimate and they are not among the most probable countries to democratize.

I must conclude that GNP per capita predicts the level of democratization less accurately than IPR. First, there does not seem to be any minimum threshold of GNP per capita for democracy, whereas in the case of IPR it was possible to establish such a threshold below which countries are not expected to be Democracies. Second, most residuals produced by the regression equation of ID-88 on GNP per capita are much larger than in Table

4.9, which indicates the greater inaccuracy of predictions. Third, there are several highly deviant Nondemocracies that clearly contradict the hypothesis on the causal relationship between GNP per capita and the level of democracy. The same countries are not deviant cases on the basis of IPR because their IPR values are low.The results of empirical analyses show that we can explain the variation of the level of democratization much more satisfactorily by IPR than by GNP per capita. The evolutionary theory of democratization formulated in this study provides a theoretical explanation for this difference. The level of democratization depends on the level of resource distribution. Therefore democracy is possible even in poor countries if crucial power resources are widely distributed. For the same reason social circumstances are not conducive to democracy in relatively rich countries where crucial power resources are highly concentrated. Thus, according to my interpretation, GNP per capita, or the level of socioeconomic development, can predict the level of democratization only to the extent as it indicates differences in resource distribution.

As Table 5.2 and Figure 5.2 show, the Index of Ethnic Homogeneity is an even poorer predictor of the level of democratization than GNP per capita. The degree of ethnic homogeneity does not seem to be related to the level of democratization in any systematic manner, although its correlations with my measures of democratization are slightly positive. When EH was used together with IPR to explain the variation of democratization (ID-1988),

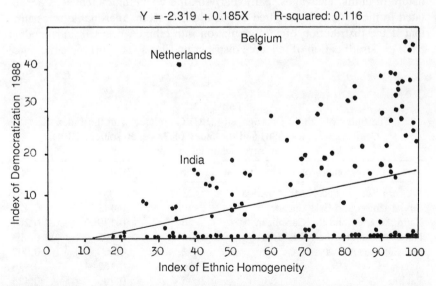

Figure 5.2. The results of regression analysis in which ID-88 is used as the dependent variable and the Index of Ethnic Homogeneity as the independent variable.

the result was the same as in the case of GNP per capita. The explained part of variation (R-squared) increased only from 71 to 71.3 percent. Therefore it would be useless to add the Index of Ethnic Homogeneity to the group of explanatory variables.

I conclude that ethnic homogeneity does not provide a factor related to democratization in the same manner in all circumstances, although it may be an important factor in particular cases. But in what cases and in what way? Let us start from regional (for regional groups, see Chapter 6) correlations of EH with the Index of Democratization (ID) and the Index of Power Resources (IPR). One can assume that if the relative significance of ethnic homogeneity varies regionally or culturally, it should be reflected in regional correlations. Table 5.3 shows, however, that regional correlations vary only slightly and that they are weak. It means that the relative significance of ethnic pluralism does not seem to vary regionally and that it is not able to explain the variation of democratization within regional groups.

The fact that global and regional correlations between the Index of Democratization and the Index of Ethnic Homogeneity are weak and in most points completely insignificant does not exclude the possibility that in particular cases and circumstances ethnic heterogeneity may be a significant positive or negative factor. Now I try to explore in what kind of circumstances ethnic heterogeneity has impeded democratization and in what kind of circumstances it has supported democratization. My starting point is the assumption that the influence of ethnic heterogeneity depends partly on the nature of ethnic cleavages, particularly on the way ethnic cleavages are related to the pattern of resource distribution. It seems reasonable to assume that if the distribution of the population into ethnic groups is independent from the stratification of resource distribution, it may support the emergence

Table 5.3.

The Index of Ethnic Homogeneity (EH) Correlated with the Index of
Democratization (1988) and the Index of Power Resources (IPR)
in seven regional groups

Regional group	N	ID-88	IPR
Western Europe and North America	23	0.057	−0.187
Soviet Union and East Europe	9	0.141	−0.423
Latin America and the Caribbean	26	0.179	0.284
North Africa and the Middle East	22	−0.095	0.003
Sub-Saharan Africa	42	0.060	−0.002
Asia	20	0.162	0.326
Pacific	5	0.796	0.425

of competing parties and competitive politics. In such conditions different and conflicting ethnic groups have more or less equal power resources at their disposal, which means that they are able to defend their rights and support their demands by various sanctions. In such conditions it becomes, sooner or later, necessary to share power among competing ethnic groups and establish democratic institutions to stabilize and maintain the sharing of power. On the other hand, if power resources are concentrated in the hands of one ethnic group and the other ethnic groups are without effective resources, conditions are not favorable for democratic sharing of power. In such conditions the group controlling crucial power resources is able to establish and maintain a hegemonic political system.

Let us look at the six deviating Nondemocracies and the seven deviating Democracies of Table 4.9. Could we explain some of these deviations by ethnic pluralism? Three (Chile, Poland, and Panama) of the deviating Nondemocracies are ethnically relatively homogeneous countries, whereas in the other three cases (Yugoslavia, Jordan, and Fiji) ethnic heterogeneity may be a relevant factor. In Yugoslavia the necessity of one party hegemony has been justified by assuming that it is the only way to maintain the territorial integrity of the state. It is argued that if people were free to organize political parties, they would establish ethnic parties, which would increase conflicts between territorial ethnic groups. Finally political competition on ethnic lines might lead to the disintegration of Yugoslavia (discussion with Professor Blagoje S. Babic in 1983). On the other hand, one could argue that the existence of territorially separate ethnic groups is conducive to the emergence of a multiparty system and democratic sharing of power. In Jordan the ethnic heterogeneity of the population and particularly the hostility between the Bedouins and the non-Bedouins has probably enhanced the hegemonic position of the king. The Bedouins and other native Arabs are unwilling to share political power with economically more successful Palestinian Arabs. In Fiji the conflict between the two major communities of the Fijians and the Indians led to the breakdown of democratic system in 1987, although the same cleavage had previously provided the most important social basis for party competition (see West 1988).

It is remarkable that all seven deviating Democracies (Botswana, Papua New Guinea, the Solomon Islands, Pakistan, Liberia, Sudan, and Gambia) are ethnically more or less heterogeneous countries. In these cases ethnic heterogeneity has not, contrary to Rabuska and Shepsle's hypothesis, prevented democratization. In some of these cases, ethnic heterogeneity may be an additional factor of resource distribution which furthers competitive politics and the sharing of political power (cf. Holm 1988; Lipset 1989; Rose 1989). On the other hand, it is clear that ethnic heterogeneity alone is not enough to provide a favorable social basis for competitive politics.

EXTERNAL FACTORS

Because societies depend on each other in many ways, external factors may affect the nature of political systems. However, it does not seem possible to present any hypothesis on uniform effects of external factors because these factors vary greatly. One can assume that quite often external determinants affect the explanatory variables of this study. For example, they may further or hinder urbanization, literacy, or the diffusion of economic power resources. In such cases it is impossible to separate the effects of external factors from those of internal ones. In some other cases it might be possible to discern particular external factors that have directly influenced the nature of political systems either by furthering democratization or by obstructing democratization.

Dependency theories emphasize the role of external determinants. They argue that the poverty of developing countries is causally related to the wealth of industrially developed countries. Usually they do not include clear hypotheses on the relationship between democracy and economic dependence, but sometimes it is implied that the lack of democracy in poor countries is caused by external factors that maintain economic underdevelopment (see Badie 1984, 178–82; Zollberg 1985). James F. Petras has presented these ideas in an explicit form. In the 1970s he argued that the emergence of homogeneous repressive regimes in Latin America was caused by the North American capitalism and multinationals (Petras 1977, cited in Zollberg 1985). In other words, repressive governments in Latin America were due to external determinants more than to internal factors. On the other hand, some researchers have argued that the emergence of democracy in certain countries, particularly in Japan and Germany after World War II, was due to external factors (see Zollberg 1985, 568–69). It seems that the lack of democracy in many poor countries can be satisfactorily explained by internal factors (the Index of Power Resources), although external factors may have affected the values of eplanatory variables. The same concerns the emergence of democracy in Japan and Germany. When they were democratized in the 1940s, their internal conditions were ripe for democracy. During authoritarian and totalitarian governments they had been clearly deviating cases (see Vanhanen 1984).

There are, however, several more or less deviating Nondemocracies and Democracies. The question is: To what degree could they be explained by external factors. We can detect countries in which external factors have obstructed democratization as well as countries in which they have supported democratization. It seems that external factors explain a considerable part of the low level of democratization in East European countries, except in Yugoslavia and Albania, which are outside the Warsaw Pact. It is true that only one of the Warsaw Pact countries, Poland, is a deviating Nondemocracy, but in the 1940s the breakdowns of incipient democratic institutions in these countries (Bulgaria, Czechoslovakia, German Democratic Republic, Hungary, Poland, and Romania) were due to external factors (the Soviet Union's military presence and ideological influence) (see Seton-Watson 1956; Hammond 1975; Polonsky 1975). Since then the concentration of economic power resources in the hands of the government has drastically decreased IPR values and negative residuals, except in Poland where most of the agricultural land has remained in the hands of private farmers. The concentration of political power seems to be in balance with the concentration of economic power resources, but one could argue that the apparent balance is based on the support of external resources and that the withdrawal of that support would start changes of both economic and political structures in all these countries. In fact, this is a highly actual question now because the Soviet Union has already loosened its ideological control over the East European countries. The process of democratization that has started in Hungary and Poland supports the assumption that one-party hegemony in these countries was based on external power resources. However, we have to note that we cannot use external factors to explain the survival of the Socialist economic system and one-party hegemony in the Soviet Union or in China, which together form the core area of the Socialist bloc.

From the other parts of the world it is difficult to find deviating Nondemocracies supported or maintained by external powers. However, Diamond, Linz, and Lipset refer to the role of the United States in Latin America and South Korea. They note that "the lack of U.S. pressure for democratization was an important 'permissive' factor in the construction and consolidation of authoritarian rule in South Korea" and that it has also helped to perpetuate the Pinochet regime in Chile (Diamond et al. 1988b, 252). Thus I come to the conclusion that external factors may have supported the concentration of political power in Poland and Chile, but it is difficult to find any external explanation for the lack of democracy in Yugoslavia, Jordan, Panama, and Fiji.

It is easier to indicate countries in which external factors have furthered democratization. In Japan and Germany the occupying Western powers initiated the process of democratization. In these two countries the established democratic systems became stabilized because, according to my interpretation, their internal conditions were conducive to democratization. In many other countries attempts to democratize political systems with external support have been less successful. European colonial powers wanted to leave democratic constitutional systems to their former colonies that have achieved independence since World War II, particularly in Africa, but in most cases democratic institutions collapsed soon after independence because, according to my interpretation, internal conditions were not conducive to democracy (see Vanhanen 1979 and 1984; cf. Buchmann 1962; von der Mehden

1969; Lusignan 1970; Keesing's Research Report 6. Africa Independent 1972; Gutterridge 1975; Wesson 1987). Gregory A. Fossedal (1989) argues strongly for the idea that the United States should use interventionist policies in order to further democratization in Asia, Latin America, and elsewhere.

We can hardly say of any of the seven deviating Democracies of the 1980s that they are maintained by external factors, although it is true that Papua New Guinea and the Solomon Islands have inherited their democratic institutions from their colonial powers and that these countries, particularly PNG, are still economically and administratively supported by the former colonial powers (cf. Kurian 1987).

I come to the conclusion that external factors affect the nature of political systems and that they usually affect them through economic and social structures. Therefore, it is not easy to separate possible external determinants from internal factors that affect the values of explanatory variables. Direct external interventions have had the best chances to succeed in circumstances in which internal conditions have been conducive to the desired type of political system. However, the significance of external factors has been, except in some particular cases, marginal compared with the significance of internal factors and social conditions.

6

PROSPECTS OF DEMOCRACY

The results of empirical analysis discussed in previous chapters provide a starting point for examining the prospects of democracy and democratization throughout the world. Is the number of democracies increasing or decreasing? What are the chances for particular countries to maintain democratic institutions or to democratize their political systems?

I assume that the process of democratization is powered by the same causal factors in all parts of the world and that the relative distribution of important power resources is the most important factor affecting the chances to establish and uphold democracy. The results of empirical analysis have supported this assumption because one explanatory indicator, the Index of Power Resources, was able to explain about 70 percent of the variation of democratization as measured by the Index of Democratization. Consequently, it seems plausible to expect that the prospects of democracy in particular countries depend principally on the degree of resource distribution among various sections of the population and on the changes that occur in their distribution. However, because there are great regional differences in the degree of resource distribution as indicated by the Index of Power Resources, it is appropriate to analyze the prospects of democracy in single countries by regional groups. But in what kind of regional groups? It is not self-evident how to divide the 147 states of this comparison group into regional subcategories for the purposes of analyzing them. One way would be to form regional groups simply by continents, but it might not be the best possible classification for the purposes of this study because some continental groups would be very heterogeneous. One way to get more homogeneous subgroups is by taking into account some important cultural characteristics of regions, too. On the basis of these two criteria—geographical coherence and common cultural characteristics—I divided the comparison group of 147 states into seven cultural-geographical regions (cf. Wesson 1987):

121

	N
1. Western Europe and North America	23
2. Soviet Union and Eastern Europe	9
3. Latin America and the Caribbean	26
4. North Africa and the Middle East	22
5. Sub-Saharan Africa	42
6. Asia	20
7. Pacific	5

In most cases it was easy to draw the borders of regional groups on the basis of geographical and cultural criteria, but the classification of some countries may be open to various interpretations. Europe was divided into Eastern and Western parts on the basis of different socioeconomic systems. The United States and Canada were combined with Western Europe because of their European populations and because they would form too small a separate comparison group. Cyprus and Turkey, although they belong to Asia geographically, are combined with Western Europe because of their strong economic, political, and cultural European connections. The region of North Africa and the Middle East was defined principally on the basis of its common ethnic and cultural characteristics. It includes the member states of the Arab League (except Somalia and Djibouti) and, in addition, Afghanistan and Iran because of their geographical vicinity and common religion. Sometimes Mauritania and Sudan are included in the region of Africa south of the Sahara, but I included them in the core region of Arab states because they are members of the League. Somalia and Djibouti were excluded despite their membership in the Arab League because they are geographically separated from the rest of the Arab states and because their populations are not ethnically Arabs. Asia is the most heterogeneous of these regions. In fact, it covers three subregions,—South Asia, Southeast Asia, and East Asia. An alternative would have been to separate the three subregions, but it seemed better to combine them in order to decrease the number of regions. Pacific is treated as a separate region because of its geographical isolation, although it includes only five states, culturally and ethnically quite different.

The comparison of the seven regional groups indicates that there are great differences among them both in the average degree of resource distribution and in the level of democratization. The regional arithmetic means of the Index of Power Resources and the Index of Democratization in 1988 given in Table 6.1 summarize the size of regional differences. The arithmetic means are the highest for Western Europe and North America and the lowest for the Soviet Union and East Europe and Sub-Saharan Africa. The regional correlations between IPR and ID-1988 are also shown in Table 6.1. If subgroups were random samples from the total group, we could expect correlations to be about the same in the total group and in its subgroups. These seven subgroups, however, are not random samples. They are highly biased samples, which can be seen from the arithmetic means of IPR and ID- 88. Therefore it is not plausible to expect as high correlations in regional groups as in the global group of 147 states. High correlations can be expected only in subgroups within which both indicators vary considerably.

Regional correlations vary from -0.157 to 0.841. In the case of Eastern Europe, the correlation is near zero and slightly negative, and is a natural consequence of the fact that nearly all values of ID are in zero. The correlation of Western Europe and North America (0.424) might be much higher because the value of IPR varies from 9.4 to 52.2 and the value of ID from 15.0 to 46.2. The fact that the two indicators do not correlate as strongly as expected may indicate (1) that the level of democratization does not depend on the level of resource distribution as hypothesized or (2) that the accuracy of my indicators diminishes sharply at higher levels of IPR and/or ID. I assume that the latter alternative is more plausible than the former. My indicators may not be able to measure differences in resource distribution and in the degree of democratization at high levels of resource distribution and democratization, although they differentiate satisfactorily less democratic systems from more democratic ones and the concentration of power resources from their wide distribution. They do not take into account all relevant factors. For example, the variation of electoral systems and party systems may affect the values of ID, and the socioeconomic systems of industrially developed societies are simply too complex for my rough indicators. We would need more finely tuned concepts and indicators to show how Western European and North American countries are ranked by level of democratization or by degree of resource distribution. It was not absolutely necessary for the purposes of this study, because my attention is concentrated on the differences between Democracies and Nondemocracies and

Table 6.1.

Arithmetic means of IPR and ID-88 for the Seven Regional Subgroups as well as Correlations Between IPR and ID-88

Region	N	IPR	ID-88	Correlation
Western Europe and North America	23	35.3	33.3	0.424
Soviet Union and East Europe	9	3.2	0.2	-0.157
Latin America and the Caribbean	26	9.4	13.2	0.626
North Africa and the Middle East	22	6.4	3.0	0.804
Sub-Saharan Africa	42	2.2	2.1	0.552
Asia	20	6.4	7.6	0.841
Pacific	5	20.4	21.7	0.472
All 147 countries	147	10.6	10.4	0.842

not on the fine distinctions among Democracies. However, when the group of Western Europe and North America is combined with the nine countries of Eastern Europe, IPR and ID-88 become strongly correlated (0.837). Correlations are positive as hypothesized in the other five regional groups, but, in the case of Sub-Saharan Africa, the moderate positive correlation is mainly due to one outstanding country, Mauritius, which has the highest values of IPR and ID-88, and in the case of North Africa and the Middle East, the strong positive correlation is nearly completely due to two outstanding countries, Israel and Lebanon. The two indicators vary considerably and correlate positively as hypothesized in the regional groups of Latin American, Asian, and Pacific countries.

Claucio Ary Dillon Soares (1987, 1) criticizes Western economic theories of democracy and dictatorship for ethnocentrism and argues that they "have a better empirical fit in advanced industrial societies, both East and West, than in Latin America." He tested his hypothesis by comparing the fit of various explanatory models, including my preliminary study covering the years 1980–83 (Vanhanen 1985), to the Core countries and Latin America. On the basis of his analysis he concluded that "Vanhanen's theory achieves impressive results when applied to the Core countries, in Latin America it fails to explain democracy better than random probability" (Soares 1987, 15; see also Soares 1985, 1988). I would point out that my hypothesis does not presuppose that there should be strong positive correlations in any biased subset of countries. In 1980–83 several Latin American countries were still highly deviating cases, which decreased the relationship between IPR and ID insignificant, but in the context of the global comparison group my explanatory model applied relatively well to the group of 20 Latin American countries. The arithmetic mean of the absolute values of residuals was 6.0 for the 20 Latin American countries and 6.4 for the 30 European and North American Core countries (see Vanhanen 1985). The results of regional analyses in Table 6.1 indicate that my variables are positively correlated in regional subsets, too, although most regional correlations are weaker than those of the global comparison group. Besides, IPR and ID are highly correlated in the subset of Core countries only when the countries of East and West are combined. Soares suggests that Core countries and Latin American countries should be analyzed separately because it is not possible to explain democracy or the lack of it by the same explanatory factors in both groups. I still insist that it is plausible to use the same explanatory factors in all parts of the world because all human populations are assumed to share the same behavioral predispositions.

The application of explanatory variables to regional subsets of countries can be illustrated by calculating the arithmetic means of residuals (Table 4.9) by regional groups and by comparing them with the regional arithmetic means of IPR. The arithmetic means of residuals in Table 6.2 were calcu-

lated in two different ways. First, they were calculated on the basis of absolute values of residuals. The results show how accurately it was possible
to predict the actual values of ID-88 in different regional groups on the basis
of the relationship between ID-88 and IPR in the total group of 147 states.
The predictions are the more accurate the smaller the regional arithmetic
means are. Second, the arithmetic means of residuals were calculated for
regional groups by adding positive and negative residuals and dividing the
sum by the number of countries. A positive arithmetic mean of residuals
indicates that, on the average, the level of democratization is higher than
expected in that regional group, whereas a negative arithmetic mean of residuals shows that the level of democratization is lower than expected. However, because the regional arithmetic means of IPR vary greatly, the absolute
values of arithmetic means of residuals do not indicate the relative accuracy
of predictions. Therefore, each regional arithmetic mean of residuals is also
related to the corresponding regional mean of IPR. "Mean of residuals as a
percentage of IPR" is intended to indicate the relative accuracy of predictions.

The accuracy of predictions seems to have been more or less the same in
all regional subsets. The arithmetic means of absolute values of residuals

Table 6.2.

Regional Arithmetic Means of IPR and of the Residuals Given in Table 4.9 on
the Basis of Regional Absolute Values of Residuals and Regional Sums of
Positive and Negative Residuals

Region	Mean of IPR	Mean of residuals	Mean of residuals as a percentage of IPR	N
(1) Arithmetic means based on the absolute values of residuals				
Western Europe and North America	35.3	7.8	22.1	23
Eastern Europe	3.2	4.2	131.2	9
Latin America and the Caribbean	9.4	6.4	68.1	26
North Africa and the Middle East	6.2	5.1	82.3	22
Sub-Saharan Africa	2.2	3.7	168.2	42
Asia	6.4	4.1	64.1	20
Pacific	20.4	13.2	64.7	5
(2) Arithmetic means based on the sums of positive and negative residuals				
Western Europe and North America	35.3	+2.9	8.2	23
Eastern Europe	3.2	−4.2	131.2	9
Latin America and the Caribbean	9.4	+3.7	39.4	26
North Africa and the Middle East	6.2	−4.0	64.5	22
Sub-Saharan Africa	2.2	−1.6	72.7	42
Asia	6.4	+0.6	9.4	20
Pacific	20.4	3.2	15.7	5

are the highest for the Pacific and Western European subsets and the lowest for Sub-Saharan Africa and Eastern Europe, whereas the relative errors as percentages of the arithmetic means of IPR are the smallest in Western Europe and the largest in Sub-Saharan Africa and Eastern Europe. When positive and negative residuals are added, differences in arithmetic means of residuals decrease, but they are positive for Western Europe, Latin America, and Pacific, and negative for the other regional subgroups. The largest negative means of residuals are for the regional groups of Eastern Europe and North Africa and the Middle East. One could ask whether this difference between regional groups is accidental or whether it implies the existence of some regional factors that have furthered or obstructed the process of democratization. I return to this question in the connection of regional analyses.

The results of regional correlation analyses indicate that IPR and ID tend to correlate positively with each other in regional groups, too, which means that the same explanatory factor is behind the process of democratization in all parts of the world. Consequently the prospects of democracy depend principally on the level of IPR, but because it and its three components vary considerably from one region to another and because there seems to be regional differences in the accuracy of predictions, it is plausible to analyze the prospects of democracy and democratization separately in each regional group, too. It will enable us to pay attention to regional variations and especially to regional environmental conditions and factors that may affect the prospects of democracy.

WESTERN EUROPE AND NORTH AMERICA

Let us start from the geographical and cultural core area of democratization. The first modern democracies emerged in Western Europe and North America in the middle of last century (see Vanhanen 1984). The process of democratization started slowly as a consequence of the industrial revolution and gradually spread across the region. The last Western European countries, Spain and Portugal, crossed the threshold of democracy in the 1970s. Before that they remained for several decades as highly deviating Nondemocracies (see Vanhanen 1984). Now all the 23 countries of this regional group are Democracies (Turkey crossed the threshold of democracy in 1983), and because their IPR values are much higher than 6.5, I predict that they will remain Democracies. It is difficult to imagine any domestic forces that could destroy democratic institutions in these countries and establish any kind of autocratic rule. In principle, of course, it is possible, as indicated by the breakdowns of democracy in Austria and Germany in the 1930s and much more recent military or other autocratic governments in Greece, Portugal, Spain, and Turkey.

Table 6.3 indicates that the values of all explanatory variables are high for the countries of this region. Low values of Students for Cyprus, Luxemburg, Malta, and Turkey are the only exceptions. Consequently the values of IOD, IKD, and DER are also high, and their arithmetic means do not differ much from each other. In other words, nearly all countries are highly urbanized and economically developed. Intellectual resources are also widely distributed in these countries. Economic power resources, as indicated by Family Farms and DDN, are widely distributed. The share of family farms is less than 50 percent only in the United Kingdom, Spain, and Portugal. According to my theory, countries with these kinds of social conditions should be democracies, and so they are without any exception. However, exceptionally large residuals of some countries (see Table 4.9) may imply the existence of imbalances. Large residuals in this regional group are partly, as noted above, due to the inability of my empirical indicators to take into account all significant factors affecting the level of democrati-

Table 6.3.

The Values of Explanatory Variables and Their Arithmetic Means for 23 Countries of Western Europe and North America in 1980[1]

Country	Urban	NAP	Stud	Liter	FF	DDN	IOD	IKD	DER	IPR
1 Austria	54	91	36	99	62	70	72.5	67.5	69.3	33.9
2 Belgium	72	97	42	99	80	70	84.5	70.5	70.3	41.9
3 Canada	80	95	74	99	51	60	87.5	86.5	59.5	45.0
4 Cyprus	42	66	6	89	75	70	54.0	47.5	71.7	18.4
5 Denmark	84	93	41	99	85	70	88.5	70.0	71.0	44.0
6 Finland	62	87	52	100	95	70	74.5	76.0	73.2	41.4
7 France	78	91	40	99	83	70	84.5	69.5	71.2	41.8
8 Germany, West	85	96	40	99	80	70	90.5	69.5	70.4	44.3
9 Greece	62	63	25	92	75	50	62.5	58.5	59.2	21.6
10 Iceland	88	88	46	100	74	80	88.0	73.0	79.3	50.9
11 Ireland	50	79	32	98	87	70	65.0	65.0	73.4	32.7
12 Italy	69	89	39	97	55	70	79.0	68.0	68.3	36.7
13 Luxemburg	78	97	4	100	60	70	87.5	52.0	69.7	31.7
14 Malta	60	95	5	84	75	60	77.5	44.5	60.7	20.9
15 Netherlands	76	95	51	99	84	70	85.5	75.0	70.7	45.3
16 Norway	53	92	39	99	90	70	72.5	69.0	71.6	35.8
17 Portugal	31	74	19	84	44	40	52.5	51.5	41.0	11.1
18 Spain	74	83	36	94	31	70	78.5	65.0	63.4	32.3
19 Sweden	87	95	49	99	71	65	91.0	74.0	65.3	44.0
20 Switzerland	58	95	27	99	94	70	76.5	63.0	71.2	34.3
21 Turkey	47	46	11	69	68	30	46.5	40.0	50.5	9.4
22 United Kingdom	91	98	30	99	37	70	94.5	64.5	69.3	42.2
23 United States	77	98	100	99	55	60	87.5	99.5	60.0	52.2
Mean	68.1	87.1	36.8	95.4	70.0	65.0	77.5	66.1	66.5	35.3

[1]Countries are listed alphabetically.

zation and the degree of resource distribution, but one can assume that the largest residuals also indicate the existence of real imbalances in political systems. The highest negative residual in 1988 was for the United States (−27.3) and the highest positive residuals were for Cyprus (15.2), Greece (15.4), Italy (12.6), Malta (11.3), and Portugal (l6.3). Could we argue, on the basis of these residuals, that the level of democratization in the United States is too low compared to its degree of resource distribution and that the level of democratization is too high in Cyprus, Greece, Italy, Malta, and Portugal? According to my research hypothesis, these large residuals predict, if the degree of resource distribution does not significantly change, the increase of democratization in the United States and the decrease of democratization in the other five countries.

Let us start with the United States whose residuals are the highest in this comparison group of 147 states. How to explain the extremely high negative residuals of the United States in 1980–88, and do they indicate that its political system is in trouble? At first, we have to note that its high negative residuals are partly due to the fact that power resources (IPR) seem to be more widely distributed in the United States than in any other country. Of the six explanatory variables, Students is the most exceptional. Its value (100) is two or three times higher than in most other countries of this region. It may be that the real difference in the distribution of intellectual power resources between the United States and the other countries in this regional group is not as large as Students and IKD indicate because it is possible that the concept of "higher education" is used in a more extensive sense in the United States than in Western European countries. However, the exceptionally low values of Competition and Participation are the principal factors behind its large negative residuals. Of course, one could argue that my political indicators are not valid measures of democratization and that the real degree of democracy is in the United States as high as in the countries of Western Europe, or even higher. Certainly it would be possible to invent other measures of democratization, which might indicate that there is no difference between the United States and Western Europe or that the degree of democratization is higher in the United States than in Western Europe. Probably we cannot solve disagreements about the proper means to measure democracy, and it is not necessary in this connection because we can limit our attention to the values of two operationally defined variables, Competition and Participation. They are applied to all countries in the same way, and my task is to explain why the values of these variables are much lower in the United States than in Western Europe and lower than expected on the basis of explanatory variables.

My argument is that the electoral system of the United States, the plurality system, is the principal institutional factor that keeps the degree of electoral participation low and prevents the emergence of successful third parties.

This kind of electoral system was originally a highly adaptive technical mechanism that helped to create the framework of national politics and compelled different ethnic and regional groups to form two competing national parties for presidential and congressional elections. The unity through electoral "melting pot" was achieved, but at a cost. Various social groups which could not find a common cause with either of the two principal parties became excluded from electoral politics. As a consequence, the level of electoral participation is lower in the United States than in any Western European democracy. I think that the principles of the evolutionary interpretation of politics can be used to explain the low degree of electoral participation in the United States. According to this interpretation, people participate in politics in order to further their interests by political means. If people realize or believe that the available parties do not represent their interests, and the electoral system is such that they cannot get their own representatives elected through their own parties, there are no rational reasons for them to participate in electoral politics. A considerable part of the population in the United States, perhaps about a half, seems to be in this situation. In a homogeneous society a two-party system might satisfactorily represent the interests of most people, but in a very heterogeneous society it is impossible. The United States is in many ways a very heterogeneous society, and consequently many ethnic, ideological, social, and other particular groups cannot secure fair representation through the two major parties, which are near each other and represent, principally, the interests and views of the well-to-do and educated sections of the population. The plurality system qurantees the hegemony of these two parties.

I assume that proportional representation would serve the cause of democracy much better than the present electoral system in the United States. It would lead to the emergence of several new parties representing the interests of the social classes and groups that are now underrepresented or without any political representation and it would inevitably increase electoral participation. It would make voting rational for many new social groups and individuals. From this perspective, I think, the present level of democratization is really lower in the United States than in Western European multiparty countries using proportional representation. I agree that the level and intensity of democratic participation may be as high or higher than in Western Europe in the sections of the American population that are effectively represented through the major parties, but the problem is that a considerable part of the population in the United States does not regard electoral participation in politics rational for them because institutional structures do not make it possible for them to further their particular interests through electoral politics. My point is that the present electoral system of the United States is seriously defective from the perspective of democratization as defined in this study. This defect could be corrected by introducing proportional representation in legislative elections and, of course, even more by introducing a parliamentary system of government. It would increase party competition and electoral participation and produce a better balance between IPR and ID. I think that it would also change the content of politics as new parties and sections of the population getting representation in legislatures would try to use political power to further their own interests. The present electoral system has served the interests of the white middle and upper classes controlling the two major parties, and the content of politics has reflected their interests more than the interests of the lower classes and groups seriously underrepresented. Finally, I present an assumption that the persistence and strong support of the present electoral system in the United States may be based on ethnic nepotism. The white majority is unwilling to create electoral institutions allowing blacks and other ethnic minorities to get proportional representation in political decision-making bodies. For this reason even white lower classes, although they are themselves seriously underrepresented, may regard the present electoral system better than proportional representation, which might open the corridors of power to blacks and other ethnic minorities.

According to my analysis, large negative residuals indicate that the political system of the United States is not in harmony with its social environment and that we can expect popular pressure for changes. Until now the latent dissatisfaction of wide sections of the population has been expressed principally through nonvoting and through various political mass movements and demonstrations. This is a symptom of serious trouble, but it is remarkable that American political scientists have paid hardly any attention to the consequences of their electoral system. Usually they do not see any serious problem in the exceptionally low degree of electoral participation and, even if they recognize the problem, they do not seek its reasons in the plurality system or in ethnic nepotism of the white majority. Many of them have tried to explain nonvoting by personal characteristics. They seem to be unwilling to consider the possibility that their electoral system might be the major villain behind low electoral participation and many other characteristics of their political system (see, for example, Lipset 1960, 179–219; Nie et al. 1976; Milbrath and Goel 1977; Fishel 1978; Pennock 1979, 438–69; Powell 1982, 111–22; Clubb et al., 1981; Wilson 1987; Wattenberg 1987).

Walter Dean Burnham is one of those who have recognized the problem. He admits that by the criterion of electoral participation "the United States is significantly less democratized today than any other polity of consequence holding more or less free elections." He refers to two features of American electoral participation particularly worthy of note. One is that "turnout in contemporary American elections is very much concentrated in the middle and upper classes." Another is the American shift toward functional disfranchisement—especially of the lower classes. Burnham says that "it requires an exceptionally distorted view of democratic procedure to accept with equanimity both the extreme class skewing of participation and its policy implications." In the end he recommends the abolition of personal registration requirements and their replacement by automatic state- enrollment procedures as the first step, but even he does not suggest the change of the whole electoral system (Burnham 1980). My point is that, from the perspective of democratization, proportional representation would be better suited to ethnically heterogeneous societies than the plurality system which tends to stabilize the hegemony of the dominant ethnic group.

Canada has the same problem with its plurality system as the United States, although in a much smaller scale (negative residual −9.4 in 1988). Its largest ethnic minority, the French Canadians, have their own area in which they form the majority. It guarantees them a fair representation even under the plurality system. Consequently, the level of electoral participation in Canada is higher than in the United States, although lower than in Western Europe. Laurence Leduc has traced several political problems of Canada to its British electoral system and has recommended electoral reforms and also proportional representation for Canada and Britain. His conclusion is that the "British electoral system, in both its domestic and exported variations, is today an inadequate tool for the government of complex societies" (Leduc 1987; see also Bogdanor 1983, 1984; Roberts 1987). I agree with his conclusion and think that the introduction of proportional representation would be the best way to further democratization by institutional reforms in these three countries.

The problems of political systems are different in Cyprus, Greece, Italy, Malta, and Portugal, where the level of democratization seems to be much higher than expected on the basis of their IPR values. In Cyprus and Malta, large positive residuals seem to be principally due to their exceptionally low values of Students (6 and 5 percent). These small countries cannot afford to establish all necessary institutions of higher education. Therefore, many of their students study abroad. In other words, the level of democratization may be in a better balance with the degree of resource distribution in these two small countries than my variables indicate. In Cyprus democratic institutions function in the two parts of the country, but the ethnic hostility between the Greek majority (80 percent) and the Turkish minority (18 percent) hindered the proper functioning of the constitutional system established in 1960 and caused the partition of the island into Greek and Turkish sectors in 1974. The problem is political and ethnic. They should find a compromise protecting both Greek Cypriot and Turkish Cypriot interests (see Cyprus Problem, 1977; Tornaritis 1977; Kyle 1984; Perry 1987, 131-33). It may be that the interventions of Greece and Turkey have worsened the ethnic conflict in Cyprus and that it could be solved by an agreement between these two external powers. In the case of Italy, the discrepancy between ID and IPR is real. It seems to be connected with the extreme ideological pluralism of Italy's party system. In Greece and Portugal the real level of democratization may be somewhat lower than their ID values indicate because the military still seems to have more political influence in these countries than what is the case in Western Europe, Spain and Turkey excluded. There was a breakdown of democracy in Greece in 1967 when the military seized power and retained it until its fall in 1974. In Portugal a civilian dictatorship was overthrown by the military in 1974, after which the country was ruled by military governments until 1976. Despite these recent interventions of the military, I expect that democratic civilian rule will continue in these countries as their IPR values are high enough to support democratic competition. Besides, one can assume that the process of socioeconomic development will increase the distribution of power resources and the values of explanatory variables in these southern European and Mediterranean states and decrease their positive residuals. Agrarian reforms intended to transfer more land into the hands of actual cultivators would significantly strengthen the social basis of democracy in Portugal. The same concerns Spain, where the share of family farms is not more than 31 percent.

The prospects of democracy are good for Western European and North American countries. Democracy already has a solid social foundation in these countries, although not as strong in some Mediterranean countries as in the rest of the region. Since the beginning of the Industrial Revolution, technological changes have created new sources of power and furthered the distribution of economic and intellectual power resources within societies. Therefore, I assume that the process of democratization will continue and that it will find new avenues and forms. Political reforms and innovations could be used to promote this process and to remove the remaining institutional obstacles to representative democracy. For example, it seems reasonable to argue that proportional representation is better adapted to serve the needs of representative democracy than the plurality system, which often produces a highly unequal representation of competing parties and interests groups. On the other hand, the sharing of power will probably find new forms. For example, referendums may become a new forum of direct democracy. In these strivings, Switzerland carries the torch of democratization.

SOVIET UNION AND EASTERN EUROPE

The nine Socialist countries of Eastern Europe provide the most challenging group for one to analyse the prospects of democratization. Marxist scholars in the Soviet Union have accustomed to make a sharp distinction between the capitalist or bourgeois state and the Socialist state. They argue that because these two types of state are based on different economic systems, it is not justified to analyze and compare them by the same criteria, but they admit that the same type of state may assume different forms. Thus bourgeois states may be, for example, democratic, parliamentary republics or constitutional monarchies, but it is not justified to compare Socialist democracy and bourgeois democracy by the same criteria. They are on different dimensions. Therefore, Soviet scholars have not tried to measure and compare the degree of democratization in Socialist and bourgeois states, although they sometimes claim that Socialist democracy represents the highest form of democracy (see Chkhikvadze 1969, 11–23; Kelle and Kovalson 1973, 179–91; Burlatski 1978; cf. Topornin and Machulsky 1974; Chekharin 1977; Babiy and Zabigailo 1979; Soviet Political Sciences Association, 1979; Marxilais-leniniläinen valtio- ja oikeusoppi, 1980, 179–83; The Soviet Political Sciences Association 1985).

East European Socialist countries have usually been more or less deviant cases in Western studies that have tested the socioeconomic and modernization theories of democratization. According to these theories, East European Socialist countries should be democracies because they are industrially developed countries, but they are not. Lipset saved his hypothesis in his original study by keeping European and Latin American countries in separate comparison groups, but the results of his analysis indicated that the level of socioeconomic development was considerably higher in the group of European and English-speaking Unstable Democracies and Dictatorships than in the group of Latin-American Democracies and Unstable Dictatorships (Lipset 1959). Lipset included among the deviant cases "the more industrialized Communist countries" in the new edition of his book (Lipset 1983, 473) The results of Cutright's (1963) regression analysis disclosed that Eastern European Socialist countries were negatively deviating cases. Another comparative study of Cutright and Wiley (1970) indicated that the USSR contradicted very clearly their hypothesis on the relationship between social and economic modernization and political development. Robert A. Dahl observed that "the chances for competitive politics and polyarchy by no means depend entirely on socioeconomic levels, for there are too many exceptions and anomalies to be accounted for." He noted that "by 1980, the USSR and most of the other countries of Eastern Europe within the Soviet orbit had become highly industrialized countries with relatively high levels of GNP per capita. Yet they all retained one- party hegemonic regimes" (Dahl 1984, 85–86). That is the problem. Why do they contradict the socioeconomic and modernization theories of democratization so clearly? My answer to this question is simple: the level of resource distribution, not the level of socioeconomic development or modernization, is the causal factor behind the process of democratization. In spite of a relatively high level of socioeconomic development and modernization in Eastern European countries, they have remained Nondemocracies because economic and some other crucial power resources are highly concentrated in the hands of the hegemonic party and state institutions (see Table 6.4). Therefore these countries, except Poland and Yugoslavia, are not deviant cases in my study. Their low values of IPR correspond to the zero values of ID, and residuals are near zero, too (see Table 4.9).

The problem in Eastern Europe is, from the perspective of democratization, in the discrepancy between the first two and the third dimension of resource distribution. The arithmetic means of IOD (the Index of Occupational Diversification) and IKD (the Index of Knowledge Distribution) are nearly as high as in the region of Western Europe and North America, whereas the arithmetic mean of DER (the Index of the Distribution of Economic Power Resources) is only 8.8 (in Western Europe 66.5). The level of socioeconomic development, as indicated by Urban Population and Nonagricultural Population, and the level of education and the distribution of knowledge, as indicated by Students and Literates, provide extremely favorable preconditions for democratization, except in Albania for which the values of these variables are clearly lower. On the other hand, the values of Family Farms are favorable for democratization only in Yugoslavia and Poland and the value of DDN (the degree of decentralization of nonagricultural economic resources) only in Yugoslavia. Because of its system of "social self-management" of enterprises I estimated that the degree of decentralization in industry might be 30 percent (cf. Gardner 1988, 315–33). For the other East European countries the values of Family Farms and DDN are in zero or near zero. On the basis of the first four explanatory variables, East European Socialist countries are highly deviant cases, whereas the concentration of political power has been in harmony with the last two explanatory variables, except in Yugoslavia and, to a lesser degree, in Poland. This

Table 6.4.

The Values of Explanatory Variables and Their Arithmetic Means for the Nine Countries of Eastern Europe in 1980

Country	Urban	NAP	Stud	Lit	FF	DDN	IOD	IKD	DER	IPR
1 Albania	37	40	11	70	0	0	38.5	40.5	0	0
2 Bulgaria	64	67	23	95	0	0	65.5	59.0	0	0
3 Czechoslovakia	63	90	26	99	5	0	76.5	62.5	0.5	0.2
4 German Dem. Rep.	77	90	48	99	5	2	83.5	73.5	2.3	1.4
5 Hungary	54	84	19	99	2	1	69.0	59.0	1.2	0.5
6 Poland	57	70	33	98	76	2	63.5	65.5	24.2	10.1
7 Romania	50	53	17	98	9	0	51.5	57.5	4.2	1.2
8 USSR	62	84	39	100	0	0	73.0	69.5	0	0
9 Yugoslavia	42	63	37	91	75	50	52.5	64.0	46.6	15.7
Mean	56.2	71.2	28.1	94.3	19.1	3.9	63.7	61.2	8.8	3.2

means that the social basis of power concentration in East European societies is not secure, because it is supported only by one structural factor, the concentration of economic power resources, and contradicted by several others, particularly by the fact that intellectual power resources are widely distributed and that the occupational diversification of the population has created inevitable interest cleavages that provide a natural social basis for competing political parties. The discrepancy between the first four and the last two explanatory variables is striking. It seems to prove that a low level of the distribution of any important power resources is enough to block the process of democratization. But an interesting question is: How long can the concentration of power resources in one dimension check the growth and distribution of power resources in other dimensions?

From the perspective of political systems, the consequences of technological changes and socioeconomic development seem to have been quite different in Western Europe from those in Eastern Europe. In Western Europe the trend toward greater decentralization of economic and intellectual power resources has strengthened the social basis of competitive politics, whereas in Eastern Europe the same consequences of socioeconomic development seem to have undermined the social basis of hegemonic politics. This must be so because, according to my theory of democratization, the concentration of political power presupposes the concentration of some crucial power resources. Consequently, the social foundation of socialist political systems would be stronger if the values of the first four explanatory variables were lower than what they are, because high percentages of urban population, nonagricultural population, students, and literacy are assumed to indicate high levels of economic and intellectual resource distribution. The fact is, however, that the governments of East European countries have tried to further socioeconomic development in order to improve the living conditions of their people. The governments have probably assumed that socioeconomic development would strengthen the social foundation of Socialist political systems, but on the basis of my hypothesis we have to come to an opposite conclusion. The distribution of economic and intellectual power resources inevitably undermines the social foundation of the concentration of political power in the hands of one hegemonic party. Historical evidence from the other parts of the world shows that whenever important resources have become widely distributed among various groups, people have begun to challenge existing hegemonic power structures and to demand their share of power. As Alexis de Tocqueville noted on the political consequences of social equality: "It is impossible to believe that equality will not eventually find its way into the political world, as it does everywhere else. To conceive of men remaining forever unequal upon a single point, yet equal on all others, is impossible; they must come in the end to be equal upon all." He remarked, however, that there are "two methods of establishing equality in the political world; rights must be given to every citizen, or none at all to anyone." He concluded that it is "very difficult to discover a medium between the sovereignty of all and the absolute power of one man: and it would be vain to deny that the social condition which I have been describing is just as liable to one of these consequences as to the other" (Tocqueville 1963 Vol. I, 53).

I agree with de Tocqueville's argument that social equality will also increase the pressure to establish political equality, but I do not agree with his conclusion that social equality could as easily lead to the absolute power of one person as to a democratic sharing of power. I do not think that social equality in the sense of equitable resource distribution could as easily produce an autocratic as a democratic political order because, in a true condition of equality, there would not be anyone who could establish the absolute power of one person or to give rights to every citizen or to deprive them of their rights. My assumption is that a true equality of social conditions in the sense of equitable resource distribution will tend to lead toward democratization as all groups would be able to demand a share of power and spoils of power in such social conditions and it would become necessary to share power. All important power resources are not yet widely distributed among various sections of the population in East European societies. Some crucial power resources are still heavily concentrated in the hands of the ruling group, but, as a consequence of socioeconomic development, various intellectual and economic resources have become more and more widely distributed within societies, and the pressure for democratization has increased. The question is how long can the existing power structures withstand this pressure?

The discrepancy between the three dimensions of resource distribution is the same in all East European countries, but there are differences in the significance of domestic factors from the perspective of democratization. One can assume that in the Soviet Union the fate of its political system is completely determined by domestic factors, whereas the political systems of its East European allies are not as fully dependent on domestic factors, or were not before the period of "perestroika." The Soviet Union has formed an external factor that affects the type of economic and political system in its allied states. The political history of these countries supports this assumption. In Hungary a military intervention by the Soviet Union was needed to crush an attempt to change the country's political system in 1956. In Czechoslovakia the same occurred in 1968. In Poland the very strong domestic pressure for democratization in the period 1980–81 led to a military intervention of its own armed forces in December 1981, which made it unnecessary for the Warsaw Bloc to intervene militarily. These historical examples imply that the political systems of East European countries may be fragile and under serious stress. According to my interpretation, the reason of this stress is in the discrepancy between the distribution of some power resources and the concentration of political power. Some power resources, particularly intellectual, are widely distributed, whereas some other resources and political power are heavily concentrated in the hands of the ruling party. Such a situation is bound to lead to conflicts until a better balance is established.

The prospects of democratization in Eastern Europe depend crucially on developments in the Soviet Union because it is, or was until 1987–88, the ultimate guarantor of political systems in the other East European countries. Therefore, it is plausible first to discuss the prospects of democratization in the Soviet Union.

It seems that several social structures of the Soviet Union, particularly the fact that its population is highly educated and that the diversification of its economy has created numerous occupational, regional, and other economic interest clusters, are already favorable for competitive politics. On the other hand, the ownership and control of the means of production are, through the state organs, still highly concentrated in the hands of the ruling party. This discrepancy between the decentralization of some important power resources and the concentration of political power has created increasing popular pressure for democratization in the Soviet Union. The highest leadership of the country has recognized this latent and now more and more open pressure for democratization and the need of reforms, and it has started to experiment with various means to democratize the country's political system and to liberalize its economic system. The terms glasnost and perestroika coined by General Secretary Gorbachev illustrate this strive for structural changes (cf. Powell 1988, 185–218; Gardner 1988, 306–12; Keesing's, 36485–90, 36592–94). It is remarkable that intellectuals have been the forerunners and advocates of democratization in the Soviet Union and that popular pressure for democratization and economic reforms has started from the most developed regions of the country. In other words, the sections of the population with some independent intellectual and/or economic power resources have started to demand democracy. In fact, the Soviet Union has already begun to democratize its political system, and people have expressed their strong desire for reforms, as the results of the 1989 parliamentary elections indicate (see Doerner 1989 *Time,* Special Issue, April 10, 1989; Keesing's, 36512–13). Political reforms have been made side by side with economic reforms that aim to decrease the concentration of economic power resources in the hands of the state and the ruling party.

Thus I come to the conclusion that the striking discrepancy between the first four and the last two explanatory variables predicts the increase of pressure for democratization in the Soviet Union, although the country has not been a deviant case in my study. The concentration of political power has been in complete harmony with the concentration of crucial economic power resources in agriculture and in nonagricultural sectors of economy, but this state of affairs is not stable because some other important power resources indicated by the first four explanatory variables are already widely distributed. As a consequence of technological changes, intellectual and economic power resources tend to become more and more widely distributed, and the process of natural selection in economy seems to favor the dispersion of economic control and to undermine the direction of economy through central authority. I assume that together these factors have predisposed the Soviet Union toward democratization.

In the other East European countries the prospects of democratization differ from each other in some respects, although the basic pattern is the same.

In Poland social conditions are more conducive for democratization than in the other Warsaw Pact states because the concentration of economic power resources is less complete. Agriculture was never collectivized in Poland. Consequently, economic power resources have been more decentralized (DER 24.2) than in the other allied states, and the structural basis of hegemonic political system was more fragile in Poland than in the other East European Socialist countries. Poland has been a clearly deviant Nondemocracy in my study. However, the concentration of nonagricultural economic resources (DDN 2.0) supports the concentration of political power, but it is the only explanatory variable in harmony with the country's political system in the period 1980–88. Public opinion in Poland, or at least the majority of its people, seem to support full democratization of the country's political system. According to a national survey research conducted in 1985, 65.0 percent of the respondents accepted the statement "In elections must exist a competition of various political parties," and only 7.3 percent rejected it (Gebethner 1986). The strong position of the Catholic Church and the formal existence of non-Marxist parties (the United Peasants' party and the Democratic party) and several illegal or semilegal dissident organizations indicated that there was potential for pluralist politics in Poland (cf. Powell 1987, 220–24). Poland's high IPR value predicted the democratization of its political system, which finally took place to a significant extent in 1989 (see, for example, Borrell 1989; Sancton 1989).

In the German Democratic Republic the first four explanatory variables are even more conducive to democratization than in Poland, but its hegemonic system is strongly supported by the concentration of agricultural and nonagricultural economic power resources and the presence of Soviet military forces. The dormant legal existence of other parties, the Christian Democratic Union of Germany, the Democratic Peasants' Party of Germany, the Liberal Democratic Party of Germany, and the National Democratic Party of Germany, indicates the latent readiness and capability of East Germans to competitive politics (cf. Powell 1987, 215–17; Smolowe 1989).

In Romania the values of the first three explanatory variables are not as high as in Poland and GDR but high enough to support competitive politics. On the other hand, the concentration of land ownership and nonagricultural means of production provides a social basis for hegemonic power structures. Because of the concentration of economic power resources, Romania is not a deviant case in my study, but because intellectual power resources are widely distributed and occupational diversification has created many natural interest clusters, I have to predict that the pressure for democratization will increase in Romania, too (cf. Banta 1989). In Hungary and Czechoslovakia the situation is the same. In these two countries the values of the first three variables are clearly higher than in Romania, and the pressure for democratization has also been stronger. This pressure caused a breakdown of the hegemonic political system in Hungary in 1956 and in Czechoslovakia in 1968, as noted above. Later the government responded to latent reform demands in Hungary by starting various economic reform experiments, which are aimed at increasing the share of the private sector both in agriculture and in nonagricultural sectors of economy and to give a greater role to market forces. These reforms have started the process of adaptation to the competitive nature of economy, and, as far as they decentralize the control of economic resources, they transform social conditions more conducive to democratization (cf. Gardner 1988, 342–52). According to one estimate, within three years half of Hungary's economy is expected to be in private hands (Isaacson 1989). The process of democratization has also started in Hungary. Opposition parties will be allowed to participate in the 1990 parliamentary elections (see, for example, Borrell 1989c). The same discrepancy between the first four and the last two explanatory variables exists in Bulgaria, too, and predicts difficulties for the country's hegemonic political system, although there has not been much actual pressure for democratization in Bulgaria. The formal existence of a non-Marxist party, the Bulgarian Agrarian People's Union, implies, however, that there is potential for competitive and pluralist politics (cf. Powell 1987, 1988).

One can assume that the nature of political systems depends entirely on domestic forces in Yugoslavia and Albania because they are not members of the Warsaw Bloc. It is interesting to observe how far the concentration of economic power resources can check the breakthrough of pluralist tendencies in politics emanating from the existence of occupational and economic interest groups and from the distribution of intellectual power resources among various sections of the population. In Albania social conditions may still be more conducive to a hegemonic political system than to democracy because the values of socioeconomic variables are much lower than in the other East European Socialist countries, whereas in Yugoslavia social conditions are already favorable for democratization. Yugoslavia is a clearly deviant case in my study. The persistence of a hegemonic political system seems to be based principally on the control of economic and coercive resources. The government controls the economy but not as completely as in the other East European countries because the greater part of agricultural land is in the hands of private farmers and because the system of "social self-management" has significantly decentralized the control of nonagricultural economic resources. Besides, the ethnic heterogeneity of its population increases the degree of resource distribution. This aspect of interest cleavages has already been taken into account through federalism. Yugoslavia is divided into six federal republics and two autonomous provinces. The adoption of federalism reflects the ethnic pluralism of its population, but until now the hegemonic political group has been able to prevent the emergence of political pluralism based on ideological and other interest cleavages. The League of Communists of Yugoslavia has retained the hegemony which it originally achieved in the resistance against the German and Italian occupation forces and in the civil war against rival resistance movements during the Second World War II. Since then, socioeconomic development has created more and more favorable social conditions for democratization, and the hegemonic position of the ruling party has been challenged by various new groups bound to emerge as a consequence of resource distribution. On the basis of my explanatory variables I conclude that the prospects of democratization in Yugoslavia are good and that we can expect the emergence of pluralist democracy in some way or other (cf. Powell 1987, 1988).

LATIN AMERICA AND THE CARIBBEAN

Latin America used to be an area of autocratic regimes, military coups, and unstable democracies, but in the 1980s there was a decisive turn toward democratization. Military governments made room for civilian governments elected through competitive elections (cf. Tables 4.6 and 4.9).

The number of Democracies was 19 in 1988, and only six countries (Chile, Cuba, Haiti, Panama, Paraguay, and Suriname) were Nondemocracies. Guyana was a Semidemocracy. The number of deviant Nondemocracies had decreased from six in 1980 to two. In other words, nearly all Latin American and the Caribbean political systems seem to be well adapted to their social environments. This balance is also indicated by the fact that the Index of Democratization in 1988 correlated positively with all the explanatory variables. Correlations are 0.233 for Urban Population, 0.287 for NAP, 0.249 for Students, 0.311 for Literates, 0.218 for Family Farms, 0.620 for DDN, and 0.626 for the Index of Power Resources. These correlations are not strong, but the direction is positive, as hypothesized. In 1980 these correlations were much weaker. Many countries with high negative residuals (see Vanhanen 1975, 1979, 1984) were more or less deviating Nondemocracies.

Negative residuals indicated that social conditions were ripe for more democratic systems in Latin America. The democratization predicted by previous negative residuals has taken place. The problem is now whether all these countries are able to maintain their newly established democratic systems. For eight nations (Uruguay, Argentina, Barbados, the Dominican Republic, Bolivia, Honduras, Nicaragua, and El Salvador) positive residuals were higher than one standard error of estimate (6.5) in 1988, whereas negative residuals were higher than one standard error of estimate only for two countries (Chile and Panama).

It is useful to pay attention to the values of single explanatory variables (Table 6.5) in estimating the prospects of democracy in Latin America and the Caribbean . The arithmetic means of Urban Population, NAP, Students, and Literates are slightly lower than for Eastern Europe, whereas the arithmetic means of Family Farms and DDN are much higher than those for Eastern Europe. All these arithmetic means are considerably lower than those for Western Europe and North America. The greatest difference is in the case of the last two explanatory variables. This means that social structures are not as favorable for democracy as in Western Europe and North America, but they are clearly better than in Eastern Europe, for the ownership and control of the means of production seems to be more widely distributed than in Eastern Europe. From the perspective of my explanatory variables, this is the most crucial difference between Latin America and Eastern Europe. Because it was assumed that the concentration of any important power resources might be enough to block the process of democratization, we have to examine the explanatory variables of single countries.

Table 6.5 shows that the values of Urban Population, NAP, and Literates are moderate or high for nearly all countries. The lowest values are for Haiti. The values of Student are very low for some small Caribbean and Central American states, but if the number of students enrolled in institutions of higher learning abroad were taken into account, the value of Students would be significantly higher at least for Bahamas, Jamaica, and Trinidad and Tobago (see Kurian 1987). In the case of Haiti, the value of this variable is the lowest, too. Some economic and intellectual resources as indicated by these variables seem to be distributed widely enough, although great variations within nations may decrease their significance for pluralist politics. For example, a high level of urban population will not necessarily indicate a high degree of resource distribution, if the unemployed and poor people in slums form the major part of the urban population. And a relatively high number of students per 100,000 inhabitants does not necessarily indicate that intellectual power resources are widely distributed among various sections of the population if the major part of students come from the upper social strata.

From the perspective of democratization, however, the concentration of

Table 6.5.

Values of Explanatory Variables and Their Arithmetic Means for 26 Countries of
Latin America and the Caribbean in 1980

Country	Urb	NAP	Stud	Lit	FF	DDN	IOD	IKD	DER	IPR
1 Argentina	82	87	35	95	48	30	84.5	65.0	32.5	17.7
2 Bahamas	54	93	11	93	50	40	73.5	52.0	40.7	15.6
3 Barbados	43	84	32	97	14	40	63.0	64.5	35.8	14.5
4 Bolivia	33	50	29	68	31	30	41.5	48.5	30.5	6.1
5 Brazil	68	62	23	76	20	30	65.0	49.5	26.2	8.4
6 Chile	80	82	26	92	20	40	81.0	59.0	36.4	17.4
7 Colombia	70	73	21	85	25	30	71.5	53.0	28.6	10.8
8 Costa Rica	43	65	49	92	32	50	54.0	70.5	43.7	16.6
9 Cuba	65	77	31	96	21	0	71.0	63.5	4.2	1.9
10 Dominican Rep.	51	44	18	73	30	30	47.5	45.5	31.8	6.9
11 Ecuador	45	55	66	79	35	30	50.0	72.5	32.2	11.7
12 El Salvador	41	50	7	68	25	30	45.5	37.5	27.5	4.7
13 Guatemala	39	45	15	50	35	20	42.0	52.5	28.2	3.8
14 Guyana	38	78	6	94	8	20	58.0	50.0	17.4	5.0
15 Haiti	28	33	2	30	62	20	30.5	16.0	48.1	2.3
16 Honduras	36	37	14	60	40	30	36.5	37.0	36.3	4.9
17 Jamaica	41	79	13	96	35	30	60.0	54.5	31.0	10.1
18 Mexico	67	64	26	83	41	30	65.5	54.5	34.0	12.1
19 Nicaragua	53	57	25	75	13	20	55.0	50.0	17.0	4.7
20 Panama	54	65	41	87	34	20	59.5	64.0	24.9	9.5
21 Paraguay	39	51	17	85	12	20	45.0	51.0	16.1	3.7
22 Peru	67	63	35	80	18	30	65.0	57.5	25.6	9.6
23 Suriname	50	82	13	65	16	10	66.0	39.0	11.1	2.9
24 Trinidad & Tobago	21	84	10	96	38	30	52.5	53.0	31.3	8.7
25 Uruguay	84	88	25	94	43	40	86.0	59.5	40.4	20.7
26 Venezuela	83	82	41	84	10	30	82.5	62.5	26.4	13.6
Mean	52.9	66.5	24.3	80.5	29.1	28.1	59.7	52.4	29.1	9.4

land ownership has traditionally been and still is the most significant unfavorable structural factor in Latin America. The concentration of nonagricultural means of production follows the pattern of agriculture. According
to my data, Haiti is the only country with the share of the family farms
higher than 50 percent, but as agricultural holdings are extremely small and
the values of other explanatory variables are low, this favorable factor alone
has not been enough to provide a sufficient social basis for pluralist politics
in Haiti. The ownership and control of land is still highly concentrated in
nearly all other Latin American and the Caribbean countries, although agrarian reforms have mitigated the situation in several nations. Agrarian structures in Latin America differ radically from the pattern of Western Europe.
The fact is that in nearly all Western European and North American democracies (Spain and Portugal are the major exceptions) family farms have
a dominant role in agriculture. It has been extremely difficult to establish
and maintain democratic political systems in societies where the ownership

or control of agricultural land is highly concentrated. Therefore, it seems that the best way to strengthen the social basis of democracy in Latin America would be to make land reforms that create viable family farms and transform agricultural workers and tenants into independent farmers. The scarcity of land has not been the major obstacle of land reforms in Latin America. There has not been sufficient political will to change land tenure systems.

IPR above 6.5. The prospects of democracy and democratization are not the same in all Latin American and Caribbean countries because their IPR index points vary from 1.9 (Cuba) to 20.7 (Uruguay). It is plausible to assume that democracy has the best chances in the countries of the IPR category above 6.5 index points. In fact, 14 of the 16 countries of this IPR category were Democracies in 1988. Costa Rica has had the longest unbroken tradition of democratic rule (cf. Booth 1985; Martz 1987, 60–61). All the other contemporary Latin American democracies have experienced shorter or longer periods of military rule since the 1950s. In Argentina, Brazil, and Uruguay the latest period of military rule ended in 1983–85. Mexico crossed the threshold of democracy in the 1988 presidential election, although its constitutional system remained the same as during the long decades of one-party dominance. The ruling party had been able to maintain its hegemonic position since the 1920s (cf. Casanova 1972, 1985; Martz 1987). The relatively high value of IPR had predicted democratization in Mexico, and it took place in the 1988 elections in which the support of the opposition parties was nearly 50 percent. Despite the long tradition of military rule in Latin America, I predict the survival of democracy in all these 14 countries on the basis of their high IPR values. Social conditions have become conducive to democracy. Some reservations, however, are needed. Great social inequalities and deep ethnic cleavages in several countries tend to increase the intensity and bitterness of the struggle for power. Therefore political craft is needed to maintain democracy and to strengthen its social basis. Sometimes the necessary political craft is not available, and therefore accidental breakdowns of democracy are still possible although not necessary. The IPR value of the Dominican Republic is the lowest in this group of countries, but it has remained in the category of Democracies since the 1966 presidential election.

The transition period in 1961–66 included the assasination of dictator Trujillo, unstable elected governments, military coups, a short civil war, and a military intervention by the United States. Since the 1960s the standard of living has increased considerably and the middle class has grown. These structural changes have been conducive to democratization, but many other aspects of social conditions are not yet good for democracy. According to Howard J. Wiarda, the social and class structure of the Dominican Republic "does not augur well for democracy." He refers to economic inequalities and class cleavages as well as to the distribution of land, which is inegalitarian, and concludes: "The socioeconomic situation is not auspicious for the building of a democratic system, though it must be said that the growth and affluence of the middle class—and therefore the possibilities for stable democracy—are far greater now than they were a generation ago" (Wiarda 1985). I agree with this evaluation. The best strategy of democratization would be to further social reforms intended to advance the distribution of economic and intellectual power resources and to encourage racial assimilation of its ethnically heterogeneous population.

Chile and Panama are highly deviating Nondemocracies in this IPR category. I predict that both countries will cross the threshold of democracy within the next few years. Chile was the most deviating Nondemocracy in 1988. The persistence of military rule in Chile has been related to its exceptionally violent nature. The fear of revenge has probably hindered the process of redemocratization, as well as the extreme ideological polarization of the civilian opposition, but the military is bound to lose power because social conditions in Chile are much more favorable for democracy than for any type of authoritarian rule (cf. Diamond et al. 1986, 52). The democratization is expected to take place through a direct presidential election.

IPR 3.5–6.5. Five of the seven countries at the transition level of IPR were Democracies in 1988, one (Guyana) was a Semidemocracy, and one (Paraguay) a Nondemocracy. On the basis of their social conditions I cannot predict that democracy will survive in all of them without breakdowns. Large positive residuals of Bolivia, Honduras, Nicaragua, and El Salvador predict the decrease of their level of democratization. At this level of IPR, political systems are often unstable as power resources are so much distributed that it is difficult to maintain autocratic systems, although they are not yet widely enough distributed for the sharing of power to be inevitable. Latin American countries seem to support this interpretation. It is remarkable that most of these countries crossed the threshold of democracy the first time in the 1980s. Democratizations were preceded by political turmoil, popular pressure for democratization, various social and political disturbances, terrorism, repression, and civil wars (cf. Bowdler and Cotter 1982). Popularly elected governments emerged out of political chaos as compromises after periods of undecided violent struggle for power. The competitors realized that it was more rational to share power with their enemies and competitors than to continue the violent struggle for hegemony. In some countries, particularly in Nicaragua and El Salvador, all groups have not yet accepted compromises and they continue to struggle for power by arms.

In Bolivia the long period of unstable civilian governments, military rule, and political turmoil ended formally in 1982 when the congress elected Siles Zuazo as president. The land reform started in the 1950s has decidedly improved the social basis of democratization in Bolivia; before the reform the share of family farms was only about 3 percent(see Vanhanen 1979, 316). However, very great economic and social inequalities, which partly coincide with ethnic cleavages, impede the process of democratic politics. The Indians, who form about 60 percent of the population, have traditionally been excluded from the national politics, and it is still difficult for them to establish their own political organizations. In Honduras the transfer of power from the military to a civilian government took place peacefully within the traditional ruling class, and it was not connected with any structural reforms. Political terrorism has continued after the transfer of power, although it is not as extensive and serious as in El Salvador and Guatemala. The fact that approximately 90 percent of the population is racially mixed makes the sharing of power somewhat easier than in a country like Bolivia where ethnic cleavages are deep. In Nicaragua the Sandinist National Liberation Force, which overthrew the Somoza regime in 1979, started a land reform and other social reforms that may create better social conditions for democracy. The remaining problems are political. Some opponents of the Sandinist regime resorted to civil war supported by the United States, and it is not yet clear how committed that regime is to pluralist democracy (cf. Martz 1987, 65–66). It is possible for democracy in Nicaragua to become stabilized through multiparty elections as in many other Latin American countries. In El Salvador the democratization of its political system was not enough to stop the civil war fostered by great social and economic inequalities and repression and by consequent ideological polarization. President Duarte's government started a land reform program, which may significantly increase the number of family farms and change rural power structures. Therefore, the prospects of democracy may be better in El Salvador than in Honduras where traditional social structures have remained more or less intact (cf. Martz 1987, 62–64). Guatemala crossed the threshold of democracy in 1985. The concentration of all kinds of power resources, very great social and economic inequalities, and deep ethnic cleavages have retarded the process of democratization. Some political groups have continued the armed struggle for power. The probability of new military coups may be greater in Guatemala than in the other Central American states (cf. Martz 1987, 64–65).

In Guyana a partial breakdown of democratic institutions occurred in the 1970s as a consequence of the extremely bitter struggle for power between the two major parties representing the major ethnic groups; the Africans and the East Indians, respectively. The ruling party supported by the Africans has strengthened its dominance through nationalizations. About 80 percent of the country's nonagricultural productive capacity is concentrated in the hands of the government. The ownership of agricultural land is even more concentrated. Guyana shows how difficult it is to achieve compromises and to share power democratically in a society ethnically divided into two equally strong sections of the population. It is possible, of course, that some day a compromise will be found that satisfies the competing groups and makes the sharing of power possible. Paraguay is the only Latin American Nondemocracy at this level of IPR. The extreme concentration of land ownership is the most important structural factor that supports the concentration of political power. The government has not initiated any significant land reform programs. On the other hand, a high level of literacy implies that large sections of the population already have a capacity to organize themselves for political action. Therefore, we can expect popular pressure for democratization and social reforms. The overthrow of President Stroessner in January 1989 opened a way to democratization, which partially took place in the elections of May 1989 (see *Time*, May 15, 1989, 30).

IPR below 3.5. The IPR category below 3.5 index points includes three countries. According to my hypothesis, they should be Nondemocracies as power resources are not sufficiently distributed, and all of them are Nondemocracies (Cuba, Haiti, and Suriname). They differ from each other in many respects, but what they have in common is their autocratic political systems being in harmony with the concentration of power resources. In Cuba the level of socioeconomic development and the distribution of intellectual power resources are as high as those in the most developed Latin American countries, but because of its Socialist system, nonagricultural economic power resources are completely concentrated in the hands of the government, which also controls the major part of agriculture. Democratization in Cuba would surely presuppose a change of its economic system. That is not probable in the near future. The problem is the same as in Eastern Europe; two dimensions of resource distribution are conducive to democracy, but the concentration of economic and coercive power resources has been enough to maintain an autocratic political system. On account of this structural imbalance the social basis of power concentration is not secure in Cuba. In Haiti the share of family farms is exceptionally high (62 percent), but the extreme poverty of its population and a low level of education have made the concentration of political power possible. In 1986, however, popular pressure for democratization caused the downfall of the autocratic Duvalier regime and started the process of democratization. In Suriname the concentration of agricultural and nonagricultural economic power resources also forms an important structural obstacle to democratization. Besides, deep ethnic cleavages have aggravated political polarization. The governmental power has been in the hands of Creoles (31 percent), whereas Hindustanis (38 percent) form the core of the opposition. Democratic institutions collapsed in 1980, but the 1987 parliamentary election won by the opposition Front for Democracy and Development started the process of democratization.

I come to the conclusion that the prospects of democracy and democratization are relatively good in Latin American and the Caribbean countries. The great wave of democratization in the 1980s was not an accidental and temporary phenomenon. It was a consequence of structural changes that had gradually created social conditions conducive to democratization. Democracy is at last thriumphed in Latin America, although it is not yet safe in all countries (cf. Martz 1987). In many countries, there are still groups that hope to achieve hegemony by violent means. The strength of democratic institutions is continually tested in the struggle for power. From the perspective of democratization, even violent uprisings against oppressive regimes may be positive, for they can lead to compromises and the sharing of power. According to my theory, democracy presupposes a certain balance of resources. It emerges when competing groups realize that it is more rational to share power with their opponents than to continue futile attempts to crush them. Democracy survives as long as various groups are able to defend their rights and freedoms, even by force, if necessary. Claucio Soares, however, is less optimistic about the prospects of democracy in Latin America. He notes that "the recent turns in Argentina, Brazil, and Uruguay, among others, in a democratic direction should not be considered as a definite trend towards institutionalized, stable democracy: both democracy and dictatorship are unstable in Latin America" (Soares 1987, 28). My argument for irreversible democratizations in many Latin American countries rests on the fact that IPR has risen above 6.5 index points in 16 countries and is below 3.5 index points only in three countries.

NORTH AFRICA AND THE MIDDLE EAST

Only two of the 22 North African and Middle East countries were Democracies in 1988 (see Table 4.9). In this respect this region differs radically from Latin America, which experienced a major breakthrough of democratization in the 1980s. It is true that the arithmetic mean of IPR is 9.4 for the subgroup of Latin America and the Caribbean and only 6.4 for the subgroup of the North African and Middle East countries. This difference in the relative distribution of power resources explains part of the differences in their political systems but not all of them, for the arithmetic mean of residuals based on the sums of positive and negative residuals (see Table 6.2) is 3.7 for Latin America but −4.0 for North Africa and the Middle East. Residuals are negative for 20 countries in this subgroup and positive only for Israel and Sudan, whereas residuals are positive for most countries of Latin America. In other words, the level of democratization related to IPR values is much higher in Latin America than in the Middle East. How to explain these clear differences between the two regional groups? Are the differences related to cultural differences between these regions? They seem to imply that it is more difficult to start the process of democratization in Muslim countries than in some other cultural areas of the world.

However, if cultural factors like religion could affect the level of democratization independently from the level of resource distribution, we should expect that the level of democratization varies independently from IPR values. This has not been the case in this subset of predominantly Muslim countries. Two (Israel and Lebanon) of the three countries above 6.5 IPR index points were Democracies, as hypothesized in 1988, and one (Jordan), contrary to the hypothesis, was a Nondemocracy. The other 19 countries, except Sudan, were Nondemocracies, but they did not contradict the hypothesis because their IPR values were below 6.5 index points. This means that the nature of political systems correlates with IPR values relatively well. The correlation between ID-88 and IPR is 0.804. The correlations of ID-88 with single explanatory variables are in most cases considerably weaker, although positive. They are 0.284 for Urban Population, 0.260 for NAP, 0.541 for Students, 0.461 for Literates, 0.079 for Family Farms, and 0.718 for DDN. Besides, before accepting a cultural explanation for regional differences in political systems, it is plausible to examine the values of single explanatory variables given in Table 6.6. The imbalances between the three dimensions of resource distribution may provide an alternative explanation for regional differences.

Table 6.6 indicates that there are at least two types of imbalances in the patterns of explanatory variables. It is characteristic of several oil-producing countries that the nonagricultural means of production are highly concentrated in the hands of the government and big oil companies. This group includes at least Qatar, Bahrain, Kuwait, Algeria, Libya, Saudi Arabia, and the United Arab Emirates. In these countries the concentration of economic power resources makes democratization difficult, although, in several of them, occupational structure is diversified and the level of education is at least moderate. In some other countries the concentration of intellectual power resources (low values of Students) seems to be as great a or even greater obstacle to democratization than the concentration of economic power resources. This group includes Sudan, Afghanistan, Mauritania, Oman, South Yemen, and North Yemen. In these countries the percentage of Literates is below 50 and the relative number of students enrolled in institutions of higher learning is very low. Besides, the estimated values of DDN are also very low. I have assumed that the concentration of any important power resources may be enough to prevent democratization. These 13 countries suffer from structural imbalances. In other words, as far as the imbalance of resource distribution inhibits democratization in Muslim countries, we do not need a special cultural explanation based on an idea that Islam is in some way incompatible with democracy. I assume that Islam alone would not be enough to frustrate democratization if other social conditions were favorable for de-

Table 6.6.

Values of Explanatory Variables and Their Arithmetic Means for 22 Countries of North Africa and the Middle East in 1980

Country	Urb	NAP	Stud	Lit	FF	DDN	IOD	IKD	DER	IPR
1 Afghanistan	15	22	2	20	57	5	18.5	11.8	45.6	0.9
2 Algeria	44	50	8	45	50	10	47.0	26.5	30.0	3.7
3 Bahrain	78	97	11	79	33	10	87.5	45.0	10.7	4.2
4 Egypt	45	50	34	42	40	20	47.5	38.0	30.0	5.4
5 Iran	50	61	7	43	44	40	55.5	25.0	41.6	5.8
6 Iraq	72	60	16	47	35	20	66.0	31.5	26.0	5.4
7 Israel	89	93	50	95	40	60	91.0	72.5	58.6	38.7
8 Jordan	56	74	25	65	46	30	65.0	45.0	34.2	10.0
9 Kuwait	88	98	20	68	14	10	93.0	44.0	10.1	4.1
10 Lebanon	76	90	59	77	48	60	83.0	68.0	58.8	33.2
11 Libya	52	84	14	55	40	10	68.0	34.5	14.8	3.5
12 Mauritania	23	17	1	17	60	10	20.0	9.0	51.5	0.9
13 Morocco	41	49	12	29	44	50	45.0	20.5	37.1	3.4
14 Oman	7	38	1	20	50	10	22.5	10.5	34.8	0.8
15 Qatar	88	70	20	51	40	5	79.0	35.5	15.5	4.5
16 Saudi Arabia	67	40	13	25	42	10	53.5	19.0	29.2	0.3
17 Sudan	25	25	3	20	52	20	24.0	11.5	44.6	1.2
18 Syria	50	52	31	53	40	20	51.0	42.0	29.6	6.3
19 Tunisia	52	59	10	47	48	20	55.5	28.5	31.5	5.0
20 United Arab Em.	72	85	6	56	40	5	78.5	31.0	10.2	2.5
21 Yemen, North	10	25	2	9	46	10	17.5	5.5	37.0	0.4
22 Yemen, South	37	41	4	40	10	10	39.0	92.0	10.0	0.9
Mean	51.7	58.1	15.9	45.6	41.8	19.3	54.9	33.9	31.4	6.4

mocracy. Turkey proves that democratization and the establishment of a multiparty system are possible in a Muslim country, too. However, this argument is not intended to exclude the possibility that some features of Islamic culture may hamper the emergence of democracy (cf. Perry 1987). The other Nondemocracies with negative residuals are more problematic than the countries mentioned above.

IPR above 6.5. The three dimensions of resource distribution are sufficiently in balance for the three countries in the IPR category 6.5 index points and above, but the population's ethnic heterogeneity causes troubles for democracy in Lebanon and Israel and has probably been a factor inhibiting the emergence of democracy in Jordan. The problem is that in ethnically heterogeneous societies it is very difficult to invent institutional solutions to satisfy the requirements of democratic competition for power and at the same time safeguard the sharing of power among the major ethnic groups at the level of decision-making institutions. The success of democracy in ethnically segmented societies seems to presuppose that institutional structures make effective participation for all communities possible and that they do not exclude any major group (cf. Lijphart 1977).

Lebanon's constitutional system based on the National Pact of 1943 represents a consociational solution, but the communities have not been able to adapt it to the changed ethnic composition of the population. As a consequence, it no longer satisfies Muslim sects, and in 1975 Lebanon returned to the Hobbesian condition of anarchy and civil war, although its constitutional system remains formally in effect (see Lijphart 1977; McDowall 1984; Perry 1987, 126–28). So the problem is political. They should find a constitutional compromise. The balance of forces based on social conditions and the wide distribution of arms is a factor that makes a compromise, or a partition of the country, necessary. Lebanon illustrates my thesis that democracy presupposes a balance of power, the ability of competing groups to defend their rights even by force, if necessary. No group has been able to establish its hegemony over the others, but, on the other hand, their antagonism is so deep that they have not yet been able to reestablish an inevitable compromise. In this case it is reasonable to assume that external interventions have worsened the situation and caused the present civil war. Lebanon's large negative residual indicates the existence of social potential for democratization.

In Israel democracy has functioned among the numerically dominant (85 percent) Jewish population quite well despite the continual state of war, but they have not yet been able to extend it to Israel's Arab minority, or to find a compromise with the Palestinian population living under Israel's occupation and outside Israel's borders (see Perry 1987, 137–41). This unsolved ethnic problem maintains the state of war between Israel and Arab countries. They are engaged in a desparate struggle for territories that they cannot both enjoy or share. Their conflict reminds one of the dire prediction: "And therefore if any two men desire the same thing, which nevertheless they cannot both enjoy, they become enemies; and in the way to their end, which is principally their own conservation, and sometimes their delectation only, endeavour to destroy, or subdue one another" (Hobbes 1962, 98–99). In the end a compromise in some form or other is the only way to solve the deadlock. The persistence of democracy in Israel illustrates the strength of the democratic system in a society in which intellectual, economic, and military resources are distributed among the many.

In Jordan ethnic differences between the Palestinian Arabs, who make up 60 percent of the country's population, and the original Jordanian population have probably hampered the emergence of elected democratic institutions. Power is concentrated in the hands of the king, who is supported by the original Jordanian population and particularly by Bedouin tribesmen. The minority position of the original population makes it unwilling to establish democratic institutions that would transfer power into the hands of the Palestinian majority. Parliamentary elections were postponed indefinitely in 1976. However, the fact that all Muslims are Arabs has mitigated ethnic antagonism in Jordan. The relatively good balance of our three dimensions of power resources provides a favorable social basis for democratization, and I have to predict democratization in Jordan because of its high IPR value.

In Lebanon, Israel, and Jordan, the problems of democracy and democratization are connected with serious ethnic conflicts. They are formidable, but, in principle, it is possible to find political solutions to them. Political crafting, to use the term of Juan Linz and Alfred Stepan (1986), would be urgently needed in these countries. By constitutional engineering it might be possible to create new political formulas by which competing ethnic groups could share power and establish democratic institutions in these ethnically highly pluralist societies.

IPR 3.5–6.5. The 10 countries at the transition level of IPR form the principal pool of potential new Democracies of this regional group. In principle, democratization could occur in any of these countries, but in practice all of them do not have equal chances because of various local factors decreasing resource distribution. It seems that the chances of democratization are the slightest in Bahrain, Kuwait, and Qatar where the most important nonagricultural power resources (oil) are concentrated in the hands of their ruler families (see Kurian 1987). It would be very difficult for the ruler families to share power with the representatives of the people and still retain their traditional privileges. Revolutions are probable in these countries when intellectual and economic resources become distributed sufficiently and people begin to demand their share of power. Gradual democratizations would presuppose exceptionally capable political leadership. Besides, in the case of Kuwait, the ethnic composition of the population inhibits democratization just like in Jordania. The native-born Kuwaitis are a minority. They have not been willing to share power with new migrants. On the other hand, one can assume that the minority position of the dominant ethnic group makes the foundation of Kuwait's political system shaky.

The seven other countries at the transition level of IPR (Algeria, Egypt, Iran, Iraq, Libya, Syria, and Tunisia) may have significantly better chances of democratization. It is interesting to note that four of them are bordered by the existing Democracies in the Middle East. Socioeconomic and political inventions often tend to spread geographically across borders. In fact, the process of democratization has already started in these countries. There has been popular pressure for democratization particularly in Egypt, Tunisia, and Iran, and they have established some democratic institutions (see Kurian 1987; Perry 1987). Gradual changes from authoritarian systems to democracy seem quite possible in these nations. Iran may have the best chances to democratize, although its IPR is not the highest in this group. Several structural factors are favorable for democracy in Iran, especially the existence of a sizeable urban middle class and the wide distribution of agricultural and nonagricultural economic power resources.

IPR below 3.5. The prospects of democratization seem poor in the nine countries in the IPR category below 3.5 index points because of the concentration of intellectual and nonagricultural economic power resources, but, in fact, significant democratization has occurred in some of them. Morocco is approaching the threshold of democracy. In Morocco economic power resources are distributed relatively widely, although, according to A.A. Belal's study, there is an oligarchy of 300 families controlling the major part of the economy (see Belal 1980). In Sudan massive demonstrations culminated in a coup d'état in April 1986. The transitional military government allowed the establishment of political parties. A parliamentary election was held in April 1986, and Sudan crossed the threshold of democracy (Keesings Contemporary Archives, 34530–31; Perry 1987, 122–24). Sudan became a clearly deviant case, for its IPR is only 1.2, but a military coup in 1989 returned Sudan to the category of Nondemocracies.

SUB-SAHARAN AFRICA

The level of democratization in Sub-Saharan Africa seems to correspond, with some exceptions, to the level of resource distribution quite well (see Table 4.9). Only four of the 42 countries are in the category of Democracies, and three of them are deviant cases. Mauritius is a Democracy as hypothesized on the basis of its IPR value (9.7), whereas Botswana, Gambia, and Liberia are Democracies despite their very low IPR values. These three countries seem to challenge my hypothesis on the causal relationship between democracy and the distribution of power resources. However, it seems that they are democracies only with some qualifications. In Botswana the same dominant party (the Botswana Democratic party) has been in power since independence, and it is not certain whether democracy in Botswana could survive a serious challenge to BDP rule (cf. Diamond 1987, 77–78; Diamond and Galvan 1988, 64–65; Holm 1988). In Gambia the situation is similar. The same party (the People's Progressive party) has ruled uninterruptedly, but it needed the help of Senegalese troops to suppress a bloody coup attempt in 1981, and since then a state of emergency has been in effect (see Diamond 1987, 79–80; Kurian 1987). Elections in Botswana and Gambia have been relatively free, whereas in this respect Liberia is a more dubious case. In the 1985 elections, President Doe was elected with 50.9 percent of the registered vote, and his party secured 44 of the 56 House seats and 22 of the 26 Senate seats, but the election results were described as a "mockery" by the opposition, and since then opposition parties have been repressed. Larry Diamond classifies Doe's rule as a "tyranny" (Diamond 1987, 92–93; see also Diamond and Galvan 1988, 77–79; Keesing's, 366110). Thus Liberia may not be a democracy, although it crossed, according to my indicators, the threshold of democracy in the 1985 elections.

The three Semidemocracies (Madagascar, Senegal, and Zimbabwe) are also slightly deviating cases because their IPR values are below 3.5 index points. In Senegal an attempt has been made to establish a system of "controlled democracy." Elections have been competitive since 1978, but the combined share of opposition parties is still below the 30 percent threshold of democracy (see Coulon 1988). In Zimbabwe democratic institutions were established by the 1980 constitution and confirmed by the 1980 parliamentary elections, but the ruling party (the Zimbabwe African National Union) has repeatedly expressed its intention to establish a one-party state. In the 1985 elections its share of the votes rose to 77 percent and the country slid into the category of Semidemocracies. The establishment of a one-party state would drop Zimbabwe into the category of Nondemocracies (cf. Diamond and Galvan 1988, 68–70; Sithole 1988). Madagascar is a more ambiguous case. Political activity by groups outside the National Front for the Defense of the Revolution is prohibited and dissenting political opinion is limited, but the Front is composed of seven political parties competing intensively in elections. Therefore, Madagascar has risen into the category of Semidemocracies. Larry Diamond and Dennis Galvan classify Madagasclar as an authoritarian regime with limited competition (Diamond and Galvan 1988, 85–86).

Despite the low values of ID and IPR, ID-1988 was moderately correlated with IPR (0.552). Its correlations with single explanatory variables were much lower; with Urban Population 0.214, NAP 0.329, Students 0.016, Literates 0.331 Family Farms −0.140, and DDN 0.552. Because the value of ID- 1988 is zero for 28 out of 42 countries, correlations were bound to be low.

The values of explanatory variables, except FF, are very low for Sub-Saharan African countries, and there are clear imbalances in the patterns of explanatory variables, particularly between Students and Family Farms (see Table 6.7). The values of Students are 10 or below for all Sub-Saharan African countries, whereas the values of Family Farms vary between 40 and 60 percent in most cases. The relatively equal distribution of agricultural land is favorable for democracy, but it alone is not enough to maintain democratic institutions. Because of low educational level peasants and other sectors of common people have not been able to organize themselves and to participate in politics independently. In such conditions only a relatively small urban and educated elite, some wealthy people, bureaucracy and the military, have resources and capabilities sufficient to participate in national politics. The political history of independent African countries provides ample evidence for the thesis that democratic constitutions do not suffice to produce democratic practices and to maintain democratic institutions without the support of a favorable social environment. The democratic institutions established at the dawn of independence collapsed soon after in nearly all

Table 6.7.

Values of Explanatory Variables and Their Arithmetic Means for 42 Countries of Sub-Saharan Africa in 1980

Country	Urban	NAP	Stud	Lit	FF	DDN	IOD	IKD	DER	IPR
1 Angola	21	42	1	30	43	10	31.5	15.5	29.1	1.4
2 Benin	14	54	3	28	52	10	34.0	15.5	29.3	1.5
3 Botswana	16	20	2	60	52	20	18.0	31.0	45.6	2.5
4 Burkina Faso	10	19	1	11	60	10	14.5	6.0	50.5	0.4
5 Burundi	2	17	1	27	60	10	9.0	43.5	51.5	2.0
6 Cameroon	35	19	3	48	43	10	27.0	25.5	36.7	2.5
7 Cape Verde	20	44	3	43	51	20	32.0	23.0	37.4	2.8
8 Central African Rep.	41	13	2	33	60	10	27.0	17.5	53.5	2.5
9 Chad	18	16	1	47	60	10	8.5	42.0	52.0	1.1
10 Comoros	11	36	1	59	27	10	23.5	30.0	20.9	1.5
11 Congo	45	66	10	50	60	20	55.5	30.0	33.6	5.6
12 Djibouti	50	50	0	20	60	20	50.0	10.0	40.0	2.0
13 Equatorial Guinea	51	25	0	37	30	5	38.0	18.5	23.7	1.7
14 Ethiopia	14	21	1	30	13	10	17.5	15.5	12.4	0.3
15 Gabon	36	24	5	50	52	20	30.0	27.5	44.5	5.7
16 Gambia	18	22	1	20	52	20	20.0	10.5	45.0	0.9
17 Ghana	36	49	3	45	67	30	42.5	24.0	48.9	5.0
18 Guinea	19	20	7	25	52	5	19.5	16.0	42.6	1.3
19 Guinea-Bissau	25	18	1	19	52	10	21.5	10.0	44.4	1.0
20 Ivory Coast	40	21	5	35	56	20	30.5	20.0	48.4	3.0
21 Kenya	14	22	2	47	56	20	18.0	24.5	48.1	2.1
22 Lesotho	12	16	3	70	60	10	14.0	36.5	52.0	2.7
23 Liberia	33	30	4	30	43	20	31.5	17.0	36.1	1.9
24 Madagascar	20	17	5	50	56	20	18.5	27.5	49.9	2.5
25 Malawi	10	16	1	35	45	10	13.0	18.0	37.7	0.9
26 Mali	20	13	0	14	60	10	16.5	7.0	53.5	0.1
27 Mauritius	43	72	2	79	46	40	57.5	40.5	41.7	9.7
28 Mosambique	9	36	0	26	43	10	22.5	13.0	31.1	0.9
29 Niger	13	12	1	10	60	10	12.5	5.5	52.9	0.4
30 Nigeria	20	47	4	34	60	20	33.5	19.0	41.2	2.6
31 Rwanda	4	10	0	50	60	20	7.0	25.0	60.2	1.1
32 Senegal	25	26	5	25	52	10	25.5	15.0	41.1	1.6
33 Sierra Leone	22	35	1	25	60	30	28.5	13.0	49.5	1.8
34 Somalia	30	20	1	6	60	10	25.0	3.5	50.0	0.4
35 South Africa	50	71	10	50	10	20	60.5	30.0	17.1	3.1
36 Swaziland	14	27	7	62	34	10	20.5	34.5	27.5	1.9
37 Tanzania	12	19	1	66	43	20	15.5	33.5	38.6	2.0
38 Togo	20	32	4	32	60	20	26.0	18.0	47.2	2.2
39 Uganda	9	19	1	52	60	20	14.0	26.5	52.4	1.9
40 Zaire	34	26	2	55	52	10	30.0	28.5	41.1	3.5
41 Zambia	43	33	3	68	52	20	38.0	35.5	41.4	5.6
42 Zimbabwe	23	41	2	69	30	20	32.0	35.5	25.9	2.9
Mean	23.9	29.4	2.6	39.8	50.0	15.7	26.4	21.9	41.1	2.2

Sub-Saharan African countries and became replaced by various authoritarian and autocratic power structures (see Buchman 1962; Coleman and Rosberg 1964; Mabileau and Meyriat 1967; Merle et al. 1968; Lusignan 1970; Gonidec 1971; Keesing's Research Report. Africa Independent, 1972; Diamond 1987; Hayward 1987, 8–11).

The fact that the populations of nearly all Sub-Saharan African countries are ethnically very heterogeneous may hamper the function of democratic institutions, but we do not need this additional factor to explain the failure of democracy in Africa because the Index of Power Resources provides a satisfactory and more universal explanation for the nature of African political systems. Besides, it is very difficult to get comparable data on the degree of ethnic pluralism in African countries (see Morrison et al. 1972, 415–33). On the other hand, ethnic pluralism might support the survival of democracy in otherwise favorable circumstances because it represents one dimension of resource distribution. W. Arthur Lewis stresses that the weakness of democracy in West Africa does not lie in the nature of the society (the plural society); "on the contrary only democracy can solve its problems, since that is the only framework which makes it possible for men of different tribes, languages and religions to live at peace with each other" (Lewis 1965, 89). It may be so, but resource distribution based on ethnic pluralism does not seem to be enough to produce democratic sharing of power in conditions where some other important power resources are highly concentrated.

IPR above 6.5. The prospects of democracy are still bleak for Sub-Saharan African countries. Mauritius is the only country in the IPR category above 6.5 index points. It is reasonable to expect that democratic institutions will survive in Mauritius because of its sufficiently high IPR value (cf. Diamond 1987, 79). Besides, in this case the ethnic pluralism of its population seems to have been a factor favorable for party competition. To a considerable extent, the major parties have been based on ethnic cleavages. It seems to me that the success of democracy in Mauritius is also partly due to the use of a proportional electoral system which makes it possible for the major ethnic communities to get fair representation through their own parties (see Banks and Overstreet 1983; Kurian 1987; Inter-Parliamentary Union 1983–84).

IPR 3.5–6.5. Five countries (Congo, Gabon, Ghana, Zaire, and Zambia) have reached the transition level of IPR (3.5–6.5), but of them only Ghana has ever crossed the threshold of democracy. In fact, Ghana has three times attempted to establish and maintain democratic institutions, but all attempts failed and ended in military coups (see Apter 1963; Austin 1964; Busia,1967; Card and Callaway 1970; Chazan 1988). The strive for democracy continues in Ghana. In Zambia power is concentrated in the hands of President Kaunda, but the sole legal party (the United National Independence party) allows some competition within the party in parliamentary elections (Diamond 1987, 86–87; see also Mulford 1964; Scott and Molteno 1969). Congo has been a one-party state since 1963. Its relatively high IPR values may be due to errors in my statistical data. In Zaire ethnic pluralism provides a social framework for competitive politics and multipartism, but it was not enough to maintain democratic institutions established at independence. On the basis of IPR values, these five countries have the best chances to democratize, although all of them are now Nondemocracies.

IPR below 3.5. The 36 countries below 3.5 IPR index points are expected to be Nondemocracies, but six of them were Democracies or Semidemocracies in 1988. Deviant Democracies—Botswana, Gambia, and Liberia—clearly contradict my hypothesis, but, as noted above, Liberia may not deserve its place in the category of Democracies, although it crossed that threshold in the 1985 elections. The survival of democratic institutions in Botswana and Gambia may be due to personal factors, to the personal qualities of their first presidents who were willing to maintain democratic institutions (cf. Stevens 1966; Kurian 1987; Holm 1988). Historical and personal random factors always play a role in politics and may cause deviations from usual patterns. Besides, in both these countries the ethnic structure has been favorable for a dominant party representing the largest ethnic groups. Of the three Semidemocracies (Madagascar, Senegal, and Zimbabwe) referred to above, Senegal may have the best chances to stabilize democratic institutions.

The other 30 countries in this IPR category are Nondemocracies as expected, and I cannot predict democratization in any of them because of their low IPR values, but, on the other hand, because several of them have some democratic institutions, or had them in the past, it is reasonable to expect that new attempts to cross the threshold of democracy will be made in the future, too. Some of those attempts may be successful despite low IPR values, as the examples of Botswana, Gambia, and Liberia indicate. The struggle for power leads to the establishment of democratic institutions everywhere when the resources of competing groups are so much in balance that no group is any longer able to achieve or uphold hegemony. The political history of independent African countries tells us about numerous attempts to establish democratic institutions, although most of them failed in the lack of supporting social conditions.

Nigeria, Sierra Leone, and Uganda have experienced the longest periods of democratic rule in the past. In Nigeria the latest period of democratic rule ended in a military coup in 1983 (see Beckett 1987). One can expect that Nigeria attempts to return to democracy in some form or other in the near future. The ethnic heterogeneity of its population and regional differences provide natural bases for competing political parties and make some kind of sharing of power inevitable. In Sierra Leone party competition ended in a short period of military rule in 1967. Since then the country has been a one-party state, but there is some competition in elections between the candidates of the sole party (see Hayward and Kandeh 1987). In Uganda, after a long period of military rule, democracy was reestablished by the 1980 elections, but the system did not work as expected and it ended in a new military coup in 1985. Kenya, Ivory Coast, and Tanzania are other African countries that have institutionalized competition within their one- party systems. Voters are allowed to select between two or three candidates put up by the ruling party (see Diamond 1987; Kurian 1987; Samoff 1987; Barkan 1987). Competition within the sole party may provide a basis for later attempts to introduce competition between separate parties. Some types of elections have been organized in many other Sub-Saharan African countries, too (see Hayward 1987). Senegal provides the most interesting example of an attempt to transform a one-party system into a multiparty system through gradual institutional reforms (see Diamond 1987, 82–83; Hayward and Grovogui 1987; Coulon 1988).

South Africa is a special case. It has remained in the category of Non-democracies because the black majority is excluded from political rights and democratic politics. The concentration of economic, intellectual, and military power resources in the hands of the white minority supports its present system, the limitation of democracy to the white minority. The history of South Africa also shows that deep racial cleavages make it extremely difficult to share power democratically (cf. Diamond 1987, 94–98).

The low level of resource distribution in Sub-Saharan Africa concerns all explanatory variables, except Family Farms. For this reason it is much more difficult to change social conditions favorable for democracy in Africa than in some other regions where only one or two explanatory variables are unfavorable for democratization. In the Soviet Union and East Europe as well as in Latin America and the Caribbean the concentration of economic power resources has been the main social obstacle to democratization, whereas in Africa the level of economic development and that of education seem to have been too low for democratization. Sub-Saharan Africa does not seem to provide any special regional factors that might explain the lack of democracy and failures of democratic experiments, but I refer to its tropical climate, which may have hindered economic and educational development and, indirectly, democratization (cf. Kamarck 1976; see also 1971, 127–33).

ASIA

The level of democratization correlated quite well with the level of resource distribution in the countries of South Asian, South-East Asian, and East Asia in 1980–88. The correlation between IPR and ID-88 was 0.841. The Index of Democratization correlated positively with the single explanatory variables in 1988, too. Correlations are 0.613 for Urban Population, 0.698 for NAP, 0.584 for Students, 0.376 for Literares, 0.481 for Family Farms, and 0.791 for DDN.

All the five countries above 6.5 IPR index points are Democracies as expected. The transition level of IPR includes both Democracies and Nondemocracies, and nine of the 10 countries below 3.5 IPR index points are Nondemocracies as expected (see Table 4.9). Pakistan is the only country that contradicted the second research hypothesis in this regional group in 1988.

Table 6.8 indicates that the three dimensions of resource distribution are balanced extremely well (the arithmetic means of IOD, IKD, and DER vary from 37.1 to 39.3) in this group of Asian countries, although they are more or less imbalanced in many single countries. In Nepal and Bhutan, in particular, the values of Urban Population, NAP, Students, and Literates are extremely low, whereas economic power resources seem to be widely distributed. This lack of balance retards the process of democratization because illiterate and uneducated peasants, who form the majority of the population, are not able to organize themselves for political action. On the other hand, in Socialist countries (Vietnam, Kampuchea, China, Mongolia, and North Korea) economic power resources are highly concentrated in the hands of the ruling party. This structural factor supports the concentration of political power and makes it difficult to establish any independent and competing political organizations. For Singapore the values of Family Farms and DDN are very low compared with values of Urban Population, NAP, and Literates, whereas in the case of India the situation is opposite. Economic power resources seem to be widely distributed in India, but the values of Urban Population, NAP, and Literates are relatively low. These imbalances can be assumed to weaken the social basis of democracy.

IPR above 6.5. The prospects of democracy are quite different for Asian countries depending on the level of resource distribution as indicated by IPR. The IPR values of five countries are above 6.5 index points, and all of them (Japan, South Korea, the Philippines, Singapore, and Sri Lanka) are Democracies. I assume that democracy will survive in these countries, although the quality of democracy is still questionable in Singapore. The share of the smaller parties crossed the threshold of 30 percent in the 1984 parliamentary election, but the ruling Peoples Action Party got 77 of the 79 seats. The party has been supported by an ethnic Chinese majority (cf. Olsen 1987, 190–91). In Sri Lanka the antagonism between the Tamil minority and the Sinhalese majority has threatened the territorial integrity of the country and its democratic institutions, but despite difficulties democratic institutions have survived (cf. Björkman 1987; Makeig 1987, 155–57). South Korea and the

Table 6.8.

Values of Explanatory Variables and Their Arithmetic Means for 20 Asian
Countries in 1980

Country	Urban	NAP	Stud	Liter	FF	DDN	IOD	IKD	DER	IPR
1 Bangladesh	11	16	5	30	68	15	13.5	17.5	59.5	1.4
2 Bhutan	4	7	1	22	70	40	5.5	11.5	67.9	0.4
3 Burma	27	48	4	66	52	20	37.5	35.0	36.6	4.8
4 China	13	40	2	65	1	2	26.5	33.5	1.4	0.1
5 India	22	37	16	36	63	50	29.5	26.0	58.2	4.5
6 Indonesia	20	41	7	67	50	20	30.5	37.0	37.7	4.3
7 Japan	78	89	41	99	79	60	83.5	70.0	62.1	36.3
8 Kampuchea	16	26	0	48	10	0	21.0	24.0	7.4	0.4
9 Korea, North	60	54	36	95	0	0	57.0	65.5	0	0
10 Korea, South	55	61	32	93	93	40	58.0	62.5	60.7	22.0
11 Laos	14	26	1	44	35	5	20.0	22.5	27.2	1.2
12 Malaysia	29	52	8	68	42	40	40.5	38.0	41.0	6.3
13 Mongolia	51	51	14	80	0	0	51.0	47.0	0	0
14 Nepal	5	7	5	23	61	20	6.0	14.0	58.1	0.5
15 Pakistan	28	47	4	26	37	30	37.5	15.0	33.7	1.9
16 Philippines	36	54	53	85	58	30	45.0	69.0	42.9	13.3
17 Singapore	100	98	19	83	7	30	99.0	51.0	29.5	14.9
18 Sri Lanka	27	47	6	86	73	40	37.0	46.0	57.5	9.8
19 Thailand	14	25	26	88	65	30	19.5	57.0	56.2	6.2
20 Vietnam	19	29	4	84	5	5	24.0	44.0	5.0	0.5
Mean	31.4	42.7	14.2	64.4	43.4	23.8	37.1	39.3	37.1	6.4

Philippines contradicted my hypothesis until 1986–87, but they are not any
longer deviant cases. The Philippines crossed the threshold of democracy in
1986 and South Korea in 1987 through elections (cf. Olsen 1987, 176–78,
193–95).

IPR 3.5–6.5. Of the five countries at the transition level of IPR, Malaysia
and India are Democracies, Thailand a Semidemocracy, and Burma and Indonesia Nondemocracies. I assume that Malaysia and India will remain above
the threshold of democracy, although the prospects of democracy in Malaysia are not as good as in India. The Malaysian party system is principally
determined by deep ethnic cleavages of the population. The share of the
smaller parties is about 40 percent of the votes cast in elections, but less
than 20 percent of the seats in parliament (cf. Olsen 1987, 189–190; Khai
Leong Ho 1988). In Thailand the strong political position of the military
has until now prevented the country's rise to the category of Democracies.
Parliamentary elections have been competitive, and no party has a clear majority, but the governments are still quasi-military (see Olsen 1987, 187–
188). In Indonesia the position of the military is even stronger than in Thailand. General Suharto, who crushed a communist uprising in 1965, has since
then ruled the country as president. Parliamentary elections have been held

to legitimize the regime, but they have been dominated by the government-controlled Golkar party. Edward A. Olsen (1987, 193) notes that an attempt "to implement democracy throughout Indonesia would probably be chaotic now and for the foreseeable future." However, on the basis of its IPR, I have to conclude that Indonesia could rise at least to the category of Semidemocracies. Burma also seems to have chances to democratize, but it is still autocratically ruled. It may be that the country's ethnic heterogeneity is a factor that supports the dominance of the military because ethnic minorities have often rebelled against the Burmese government (cf. Olsen 1987, 188–189).

IPR below 3.5. Nine of the 10 countries below 3.5 IPR index points have remained Nondemocracies as expected on the basis of their IPR values, but attempts to democratize have been made in Bangladesh, Nepal, and Pakistan. In Pakistan popular pressure for democratization was strong throughout the period 1980-88, and it led to democratization in the 1988 parliamentary election. The accidental death of President (General) Zia, who had ruled the country since the 1977 military coup, provided an opportunity to return democracy through elections (cf. Rose 1989). In Bangladesh popular pressure for democratization has also been strong, and there is a multiparty system. Until now the government of President (General) Ershad has been able to remain in power, but its position is not strong. In Nepal political power is concentrated in the hands of the king, who has wanted to keep the national parliament on a nonparty basis. The Nepali Congress party has led the campaign to liberalize the political system and to legalize political parties (see Makeig 1988, 153–54). In the six Socialist countries of this group—China, Laos, Kampuchea, Mongolia, North Korea, and Vietnam—the low level of economic and educational development and/or the concentration of economic power resources in the hands of the government have until now frustrated all attempts to democratize the political systems of these countries. Because of their extremely low IPR values, democratization is the least probable in this group of countries. It is true that economic liberalization in China has increased the distribution of agricultural and nonagricultural economic power resources. I do not have any statistical data on the extent of structural changes, but it seems to be evident that reforms have not yet created a sufficient social basis for democratization (cf. Gardner 1988, 374–86). Students were able to organize a surprisingly strong mass movement for democratization in April-June 1989, but eventually it was crushed by the army (see Chua-Eoan 1989; Elson 1989).

It is difficult to find any significant regional factors favoring or hampering democratization in Asian countries. Ethnic heterogeneity may be the most important additional factor affecting the chances of democratization, but it is not easy to interpret the direction of its influence. Six of the eight Democracies of this regional group (India, Malaysia, Pakistan, the Philippines, Singapore, and Sri Lanka) are ethnically heterogeneous societies, but so are also several (Bangladesh, Bhutan, Burma, Indonesia, Laos, and Nepal) of the 11 Nondemocracies. It may depend on various local circumstances and institutional arrangements whether the ethnic pluralism of the population strengthens or weakens the chances of democratization.

PACIFIC

In the small group of five Pacific countries the degree of resource distribution has not predicted the level of democratization well. The correlation between IPR and ID was 0.911 in 1980, but it dropped to 0.472 in 1988, after the 1987 military coup in Fiji. The correlations of ID-88 with the single explanatory variables are: Urban Population 0.331, NAP 0.175, Students 0.507, Literates −0.007, Family Farms 0.709, and DDN 0.424. Three of the five countries contradicted the predictions of the second research hypothesis in 1988. The result is poorer than in any other regional group. Papua New Guinea and the Solomon Islands have remained in the category of Democracies despite their low IPR values, whereas Fiji slid into the group of Nondemocracies, although it should be among Democracies on the basis of its IPR value.

Table 6.9 indicates that the three dimensions of resource distribution are balanced for Australia and New Zealand, whereas there are imbalances in the other three cases. The values of Students are very low for Fiji, Papua New Guinea, and the Solomon Islands. Besides, the values of Urban Population and NAP are very low for PNG and the Solomon Islands. The low IPR values of PNG and the Solomon Islands are due to the low values of the three first explanatory variables. Similar patterns of explanatory variables have been able to prevent democratization in most Sub-Saharan African countries, but not in these two Pacific countries. This implies that there

Table 6.9.
Values of Explanatory Variables and Their Arithmetic Means for Five Pacific Countries in 1980

Country	Urban	NAP	Stud	Liter	FF	DDN	IOD	IKD	DER	IPR
1 Australia	89	94	44	99	51	70	91.5	71.5	68.9	45.1
2 Fiji	42	60	6	82	43	30	51.0	44.0	35.2	7.9
3 New Zealand	85	91	48	99	64	70	88.0	73.5	69.5	45.0
4 Papua New Guinea	18	18	3	40	58	30	18.0	21.5	53.0	2.1
5 Solomon Islands	14	10	2	54	57	60	12.0	28.0	57.3	1.9
Mean	49.6	54.6	20.6	74.8	54.6	52.0	52.1	47.7	56.8	20.4

must be some local explanations for the success of democracy in these countries.

According to my hypothesis, the prospects of democratization depend crucially on the level of resource distribution. Because three of these five countries are above 6.5 IPR index points, they should be Democracies and they have good chances to remain Democracies. However, there was a breakdown of democracy in Fiji in 1987. It was due to ethnic antagonism between Fijians and Indians. According to Dalton West's estimate, each of the two ethnic groups constituted about 48 percent of the population at the time of the coup (West 1988, 220). I have to predict that democratic institutions will be reestablished in Fiji because of its relatively high IPR value.

I should predict breakdowns of democracy for Papua New Guinea and the Solomon Islands on the basis of their IPR values, but it is possible that democracy in those countries is based on some local and external factors not taken into account by my explanatory variables. The most important of those factors may be the dependence of Papua New Guinea and the Solomon Islands on external support. Australia gives significant economic and administrative support to PNG. The small defense force of PNG is still partly officered by Australians, and Australia contributes to the upkeep of the armed forces through annual grants (see Kurian 1987). Olsen (1987, 197–98) notes that "Papua New Guinea enjoys democracy among its elite, but as a country which has moved in a very disjointed fashion from the stone age to the edge of the twenty-first century in about 50 years, its democratic roots are shallow." Lipset (1989) emphasizes the success of democracy in PNG and seeks an explanation from the particular Melanesian ethic, but he also mentions "a benign colonial history that set in train an appropriate parliamentary system, an independent judiciary and media, a committed and astute leadership, vast resources and a relatively healthy economy, an inchoate class structure, and minimal military and international threat." The Solomon Islands has no defense force, and it is under the protection of the United Kingdom military guarantees (see Kurian 1987). In both cases the lack of significant armed forces has until now made military coups d'etat impossible, but as the example of Fiji shows, even a small military unit can carry out a successful coup. I assume that democratic institutions are relatively safe in PNG and the Solomon Islands as long as these countries avoid the establishment of significant defense forces. In many developing countries the military has represented the most significant domestic threat to civilian rule (see Vanhanen 1981).

SUMMARY

The examination of the prospects of democracy and democratization in single countries by cultural-geographical regions has indicated that the process of democratization is powered by the same causal factors in all parts of the world. Regional differences in the patterns of relationship between the Index of Democratization and the explanatory variables of this study are relatively small. The assumption that, because of common behavioral predispositions shared by all human populations, the political struggle for power follows the same rules in all parts of the world, provides a theoretical explanation for the universal application of my explanatory variables. The strive for power seems to be a constant in human societies, and everywhere the sharing of power depends on the way in which crucial power resources are distributed among competing individuals and their groups. Therefore the measurement of the relative distribution or concentration of the most crucial power resources provides a solid basis to predict the nature of a country's political system from the perspective of democratization. The six indicators of resource distribution used in this study seem to be valid in all cultural-geographical regions, but their ability to take into account the most important power resources varies considerably. It is clear that the types of power resources vary from country to country and that my indicators do not take them into account equally well in all cases. Therefore it is necessary to examine the significance of local variation of power resources and the local types of power resources.

In many cases it was noted that the ethnic heterogeneity of the population affects political structures. The problem is how to relate the effects of ethnic pluralism to democratization. Does it favor or impede democratization? I assume that it is not a structural factor that affects the conditions of democratization similarly in all cases. I think that its actual significance and influence depends, to a great extent, on the institutional framework of the political system. Consequently, it is quite possible that ethnic pluralism supports democratization and the survival of democracy in some situations and that in some other circumstances its influence is negative. It would be interesting to study what kinds of institutional arrangements might harness the forces of ethnic pluralism to further democratization and the survival of democratic institutions. In the connection of this study I can only refer to the problem and present some preliminary assumptions.

In some cases it was noted that the nature of a country's political system was affected by external powers and factors. I think that we cannot present any one-way hypothesis on the influence of external factors. In some cases they may further democratization, in some others prevent it, and there are certainly cases in which external factors have not played any significant role in democratization or in the breakdowns of democracy.

Political leadership in the form of exceptional political leaders is a factor that in some countries seems to have affected the nature of the country's political system crucially. Sometimes this factor has made democratization possible even in unfavorable circumstances (low IPR values) and in some other cases it seems to have prevented democratization despite favorable environmental circumstances. It can be regarded as an accidental factor in politics, which is behind some deviations. There is no way to predict the appearance or direction of this factor.

It is also possible that there are particular cultural factors furthering or impeding democratization, but because I do not have any reliable data on them, I have left them out of my analysis. Their possible effects are included in residuals together with other unknown factors.

7

STRATEGIES OF DEMOCRATIZATION

It seems that there are two principal means to affect the process of democratization by conscious political efforts: (1) by changing social conditions affecting the distribution of power resources, and (2) by adapting political institutions to their social environment in such a way that it becomes easier for competing groups to share power and institutionalize the sharing of power. The strategies of democratization based on these principal means presuppose social and political architecture, the shaping of social and political environments to correspond to our visions and aims (cf. Dror 1988; Schlesinger 1988).

Yehezkel Dror complains that the neglect of political leadership by political science is striking and needs rectification. He remarks that a short look at the history of human governance demonstrates the importance of periodic visionary leadership of various types, "as illustrated by Moses, Solon, and Pericles in classical times; Peter the Great, Napoleon Bonaparte, and Mazzini at the beginning of modern history; de Gaulle, Herzel, Hitler, Mussolini, and Lenin, as well as other rulers in France, England, the United States, and the USSR in contemporary Western history; and Bolivar, Gandhi, Nkrumah, Touré, Nyerere, and Mao in contemporary non-Western history" (Dror 1988: 7; see also Keren 1988; MacDougall 1988). Arthur M. Schlesinger notes that "the very concept of leadership implies that individuals make a difference in history." He adds that this proposition has never been universally accepted: "From classical times to the present, eminent thinkers have regarded individuals as no more than pawns of larger forces, whether the gods and goddesses of Mount Olympus or latter-day divinities of Race, Class, Nation, Progress, the Dialectic, the General Will, the Spirit of the Age, History itself." He argues that however much determinists differ, they unite in the conclusion that the individual will is irrelevant as a factor in history, and asks rhetorically: "Suppose, in addition, that Lenin had died of typhus in Siberia in 1895 and Hitler had been killed on the western front in 1916.

What would the 20th century have looked like?" (Schlesinger 1988). I agree that individuals can make a difference, but, on the other hand, I still claim that most part of the variation of democratization can be satisfactorily explained by environmental factors as I have done in this study.

SOCIAL ARCHITECTURE

Let us start from strategies of social architecture. How to create social conditions favorable for democratization in the countries where the existing conditions are in some respects highly unfavorable for democracy? According to my theory and the results of empirical analysis, the strategy of social architecture intended to achieve this aim should further the distribution of economic, intellectual, and other relevant power resources. However, it would not be easy to formulate and carry out such strategies of social architecture because the existing concentration of power resources usually serves the interests of the most powerful groups. Why should they change the social conditions into more unfavorable ones for themselves? Unprivileged groups might be willing to make such reforms because they would be profitable for them, but, because of their very unprivileged position, it would be difficult for them to carry out necessary reforms against the opposition of the more powerful groups. Besides, it is not always easy to know what reforms would be needed to further one's interests or the cause of democratization. Therefore, the emergence of great strategies of social architecture intended to create favorable conditions for democratization is not especially probable and the realization of them would be even less probable. Piecemeal reforms intended to solve actual problems are much more probable. They might form an incremental process of social change, which gradually creates better social conditions for democratization. Such reforms may often be initiated by the government. Robert Wesson says on this strategy that "any relaxation or concession made to people outside the official structures constitutes an edging in the direction of democracy. Conceivably accumulation of such concessions might ultimately lead to a totalitarian ruling party to admit democratic competition for power" (Wesson 1987, 8–9). I do not know how social classes, political parties, or other social groups could formulate great strategies of social architecture intended to create favorable circumstances for democratization and how they could realize such strategies. And it is not the problem of this study. After all each social or political group has to invent its own strategy of struggle that applies to its own situation. My intention is only to indicate, on the basis of my theory and the results of this study, what kind of changes in social conditions might help to create better social circumstances for democratization in different regions of the world and in some particular countries. I am not able to advise how such changes could be implemented in practice.

In this section I discuss the needs of social architecture by the same regional groups as in the previous chapter. In that connection I already made some references to various structural hindrances of democratization and to the need of social reforms in particular countries and regions. Now my intention is to discuss the same problem more systematically. Because there are great regional differences in social conditions reflecting the distribution of power resources, it seems reasonable to explore these problems in regional contexts.

Western Europe and North America

All 23 countries of this regional group are above the threshold of democracy, and in all of them social conditions seem to be sufficiently favorable for democracy. But what social conditions? Dennis A. Kavanagh (1987, 13) refers to Lipset's thesis: "The more well-to-do a nation, the greater the chances that it will sustain democracy," and continues: "His research and later studies showed an association between stable democracy and high levels of national wealth, industrialism, education, urbanization, and communications. Several facts tend to confirm this thesis." I agree that such an association exists at a global level, but, according to my interpretation, this association is principally caused by the fact that in Western Europe and North America a high level of socioeconomic development is connected with the distribution of economic and intellectual power resources among wide sections of the population. I have argued that the distribution of power resources, not a high level of national wealth as such, is the causal factor behind this association. I have repeated this crucial difference between Lipset's and my hypotheses, because they lead to quite different conclusions on the strategies of democratization and on the prospects of democracy in the world. Very few developing countries have realistic chances to achieve the level of national wealth in contemporary Western Europe and North America, whereas it would be much easier to create favorable conditions for democracy by furthering the distribution of intellectual and economic power resources. In fact, many of the countries of this region were relatively poor when democratic institutions were originally established.

It is interesting to note that economic systems in this region are market-oriented (for the term, see Lindblom 1977) in all the countries and have always been. I must emphasize this point. There is an obvious connection between market-oriented economic systems and pluralistic political systems. A good theoretical explanation for their association can be derived from the Darwinian theory of natural selection. The idea of natural selection is simple. Darwin found that all organisms have to compete for survival because there are not resources enough to support all their progeny. Healthy and vigorous individuals have better chances of surviving and leaving progeny than do ailing and frail ones. There is no "selector," or planner, in the process of natural selection (see Dobzhansky et al. 1977, 96–98; Ruse 1987, 16–18). Market-oriented economic systems function in a similar manner. Various enterprises compete for survival. They try to adapt their production and prices to the demands of consumers who form the environment of enterprises. Production and prices are ultimately controlled and guided by the selections made by consumers. There is no planner or central selector. As a consequence of this "natural selection" in economy, the healthy and vigorous enterprises, which are sufficiently adapted to the needs of consumers, survive and grow, and less-adapted enterprises and their products lose ground. Market-oriented systems can be assumed to be superior to planner-oriented systems for the simple reason that millions of independent enterprises are more capable of adapting their production and products to the varying needs of consumers than is any central planner. The same rationale is behind the success of natural selection in nature. From the perspective of democratization, however, the most crucial characteristic of market-oriented systems is that they presuppose the distribution of economic power and resources among many competing and independent groups. It is conducive to the emergence of political competition and pluralistic political systems. On the other hand, pluralistic political systems may support the existence and emergence of market-oriented economic systems because the existence of independent and competing political groups would make the concentration of economic power in the hands of one group very difficult or impossible.

In Western Europe and North America these two systems, which resemble the process of natural selection in nature more closely than planner-oriented economic systems and autocratic political systems, have long coexisted, although, historically, market-oriented economic systems have preceded pluralistic political systems. Charles E. Lindblom (1977, 116) remarks that apparently, "for reasons not wholly understood, political democracy has been unable to exist except when coupled with the market. An extraordinary proposition, it has so far held without exception." I have attempted to explain the reasons of their coexistence (cf. Sartori 1987, 399–490).

The economic systems of this region are compatible with the requirements of pluralistic political systems, and the same concerns social conditions in general. There is no need for extensive social changes in order to strengthen the social basis of democracy. It seems that democratic systems are extremely strong and nearly indestructible in these countries. Some aspects of social conditions change continually in the everyday struggle for scarce resources, and the trend of changes powered by technological innovations seems to be in the direction of greater distribution of intellectual and other important power resources. As long as this trend continues, the prospects of democracy are good. However, some very high negative or positive residuals may imply the existence of structural imbalances, particularly so in the cases of the United States and Portugal, which have the highest positive and negative residuals of this regional group (see Table 4.9).

It seems that in the United States the very low degree of electoral participation and an electoral system that discourages participation are causally connected with the ethnic heterogeneity of its population. Therefore, a strategy of social architecture intended to strengthen democracy should include an extensive program of racial integration through racial intermarriages, especially between whites and blacks, and consistent efforts to uplift the educational and economic position of the poor ethnic groups. These two components of the suggested reform program are closely interrelated. They could support each other. One can assume that, because of ethnic nepotism, biological integration would increase the willingness of the white majority to help their new relatives from poor ethnic groups and to share scarce resources with them, and, on the other hand, the rise of the educational and economic position of the blacks and other poor ethnic groups would make it easier for the members of the white majority to conclude marriages with them.

In Portugal the level of democratization is considerably higher than expected on the basis of its IPR value. Agrarian reforms intended to transfer more land into the hands of actual cultivators would significantly extend the distribution of economic power resources and strengthen the social basis of democracy in Portugal. The same concerns Spain.

Soviet Union and Eastern Europe

In the Soviet Union and the other East European countries, hegemonic political systems are as closely connected with the concentration of economic power resources as democracy is connected with market-oriented economic systems in the West European countries. In Western Europe market-oriented economic systems historically preceded the emergence of democracy, whereas in Eastern Europe political power was first concentrated by revolutionary and military forces and economic systems were transformed by political decisions afterwards. This difference in causal relationships indicates that political systems are not always and everywhere determined by economic or other social factors. In particular circumstances it is possible to change economic systems drastically by political actions and adapt them to desired political structures. In Eastern Europe this was done, but the adaptation of social and economic structures to the requirements of hegemonic political systems has not been complete. As indicated in Chapter 6, there is a serious discrepancy between the first two and the third dimension of resource distribution in the European Socialist countries. The relatively high levels of socioeconomic development and the distribution of knowledge presuppose pluralistic political structures, whereas the concentration of economic power resources corresponds to the concentration of political power. In the course of years this sectoral anomaly has become more and more serious, and the demands of democratization have become more and more vociferous. It is becoming evident both for the people and their rulers that the hegemonic systems of Socialist countries are anomalies in socioeconomically highly developed countries where particularly intellectual power resources have become widespread. The observation that market economies function more effectively than centrally controlled Socialist economies seems to have been the main reason for disillusionment with state direction of the economy and for attempts to reform Socialist systems (cf. Wesson 1987, 233–41). The problem is how to reform these systems.

Because the concentration of economic power resources in agriculture and in nonagricultural industries seems to form the most formidable obstacle to the emergence of democracy in Socialist countries, structural changes should be started in economy. In agriculture the most effective reform would be the establishment of family farms. In fact, some experiments with family farms have already been started, for example, in Estonia (cf. Keesing's, 36594). In the other sectors of economy the concentration of economic power and resources could be decreased by extending the role of private enterprises, relaxing the central direction of the economy, and seeking ways to leave the control of production and prices to market demands of millions of consumers. Some steps toward privatization and market-oriented economy have already been taken in the Soviet Union and even more in Hungary and Poland. It is possible that future developments will depend more on the process of natural selection in economy and politics than on conscious political decisions. It is quite possible that the market-oriented economic system is more effective than a centrally directed economy because market mechanism follows the general rules of natural selection and that it therefore may gradually displace and replace less effective forms of the centrally directed economy. In other words, I assume that the natural trend of change in the Soviet Union will be toward a market-oriented economic system. The process could be furthered or obstructed by political decisions, but it may be that ultimately there is no way to prevent the emergence of market mechanism because the Soviet economy is inevitably connected with the competition of the world economy. A crucial characteristic of market economy is that production and prices are mainly controlled and directed by selections made by millions of consumers. This power of consumers would form a favorable precondition for the selection of power holders through millions of electors. The adoption of a market system does not presuppose that all characteristics of a Socialist economy should be discarded. The term "Socialist" is an extremely flexible one as the use of this term by West European Social Democratic and Labor parties indicates. Besides, all market-oriented economic systems are to some extent mixed systems (cf. Lindblom 1977; Gardner 1988, 6–14).

It seems that the problem of democratization can be solved only by changing the economic systems of Socialist countries together with piecemeal political reforms. Until now the official reform programs in the Soviet Union have been based on the idea that it is not necessary to change the basic characteristics of the Socialist economic system and that market mechanism could be combined with the Socialist concentration of the ownership and control of the means of production. Charles E. Lindblom assumes that market socialism could be established. He mentions Yugoslavia and Hungary as examples of market socialism and says that the system works, though imperfectly, in Yugoslavia (Lindblom 1977, 95–100; cf. Gardner 1988, 325–33). Giovanni Sartori is not fully convinced by Lindblom's arguments. Sartori notes that, first, "we have yet to see a real case of 'social property,' that is, of neither private nor state property." Second, "the Yugoslav experiment does not really dispose of the 'state capitalism' reality. Capital accumulation and its corollary, the allocation of capital resources, are still entirely in the state's hands" (Sartori 1987, 417–25). The idea of "market socialism" seems to include contradictions for which there are no good solutions. First of all, it is probably impossible to create "social property" that is not owned by anybody and that nobody wants to own. And who could share and redistribute "social property" if it is not owned by anybody, neither by the government nor by private persons or corporations? The introduction of a market mechanism would inevitably lead to the strengthening of private property because it presupposes competition between independent economic enterprises. Therefore, the basic characteristics of the Socialist system would not remain intact. It may not be possible to combine market mechanism with central planning. In fact, Hungary and Poland have decided to reintroduce market-oriented economic systems.

My argument is that the best way for the East European Socialist countries to reform their economic and political systems would be to continue the piecemeal privatizations of economic systems and the democratization of political institutions that have already been started. Market-oriented economic systems would gradually emerge as consequences of incremental privatizations and deregulations. The remaining state enterprises would become adapted to a competitive market system. In agriculture the reform strategy should be based on systematic efforts to transfer a considerable part of agricultural land and production to independent farmers. The state should also be prepared to sell agricultural land to private farmers as soon as they are able to buy it. The remaining collective and state farms should compete with private farmers in open markets.

It is plausible to assume that economic reforms would support the democratization of political systems. The emergence of private property and enterprises would create new economic interest groups and provide economic basis for their political actions. They would certainly demand representation in political decisionmaking. As a consequence of new pressures it would become rational to extend political rights of individuals and groups and to extend competition in elections.

Historically, in Western Europe the democratization of political systems took place gradually through incremental changes. I think that the same might happen in the Soviet Union and East European countries, too. Sartori emphasizes that the passage from a competitive to a noncompetitive polity has been, without exception, discontinuous, but he admits that "the rule appears less stringent in the other direction, that is, passing from a noncompetitive to a competitive polity." As an example he mentions the passage of Turkey to democracy in 1945–46 (Sartori 1976, 276–77). Since then the same has happened successfully in several other countries. Therefore, I think that it could occur in Socialist countries, too. After all evolutionary changes may be more natural than revolutionary ones.

Latin America and the Caribbean

The concentration of economic power resources—both in agriculture and in nonagricultural industries—has been, according to my indicators, the greatest structural obstacle to democratization in Latin America and the Caribbean. The highly unequal distribution of economic power resources has traditionally been related to deep ethnic cleavages in many of these countries. Ethnic cleavages have buttressed economic inequalities and frustrated many reform attempts. It is much more difficult to share scarce resources with ethnic strangers than with relatives.

Things have changed, however. Some reforms have been implemented since the 1950s, and the level of educational and economic development has risen. Together these incremental changes have created better environmental circumstances for political democratization, although social conditions in Latin America are not yet secure for democracy. The concentration of economic power resources is still a structural factor unfavorable for democracy in Latin America. The arithmetic mean of Family Farms is only 29.1 percent in the group of 26 Latin American and Caribbean countries, whereas it is 70.0 percent in the group of 23 West European and North American nations. The same difference is in the arithmetic means of DDN. On the other hand, arithmetic means of Urban Population, NAP, and Literates are 70–80 percent of the corresponding arithmetic means of Western Europe and North America.

I assume that the rise of educational level in particular has gradually created better preconditions for other social reforms in Latin America. Experience shows that poor and ignorant people are not able to organize themselves and to pursue their interests through their own leaders and representatives. They are easily manipulated by outsiders trying to further their own interests. For example, a significant reason for many failures and partial failures of land reforms in Latin America may have been in the inability of poor and ignorant peasants and agricultural workers to organize themselves, to defend their interests in land reforms, and to control the implementation of land reform programs. It seems reasonable to assume that when poor and ignorant sections of the population get more education and knowledge, they become able to organize themselves and to pursue their interests much more vigorously than previously. They cease to be "masses" manipulated by outsiders. Thus I assume the diffusion of education and knowledge forms a crucial factor that incubates other reform demands intended to further the distribution of economic and intellectual power resources and to decrease inqualities.

Latin America illustrates the fact that the distribution of the ownership and control of the principal means of production does not depend merely on the type of economic system. Despite the existence of market-oriented economic systems, economic power resources have been highly concentrated in Latin America. They have been concentrated in the hands of the relatively small ruling class in Latin American and Caribbean countries. The poverty and ignorance of large sections of the population and ethnic cleavages have obstructed the diffusion of economic resources in these countries. Consequently, they are still much more highly concentrated than in Western Europe, although economic systems are market-oriented in both regions.

A major problem of social engineering, from the perspective of democratization, concerns the question of how to further the diffusion of economic power resources and to decrease the inequalities based on the ownership and control of the principal means of production. I think that the best strategy would still be to start from land reforms. Latin America needs land reforms intended to create family farms in place of haciendas, large commercial farms, minifarms, and collective farms, which now comprise the major part of agricultural land in Latin America. The implementation of such reforms would presuppose the organized support of peasants and agricultural workers intending to become independent farmers. Until now nearly all land reforms have been inefficient in Latin America because large landowners have dominated governments and legislatures and often also controlled bureaucracies implementing the reform programs and because peasants themselves have been too poor and ignorant to defend their interests. Socialist land reforms have not even intended to create family farms. They have only transferred the control of land from private landowners into the hands of new political power holders. As noted previously, the scarcity of land has not been the major obstacle of land reforms in Latin America. The lack of political will has been the crucial obstacle. The descendants of conquistadors have not been willing to relinquish their land properties and to share them with sharecroppers, tenants, and workers who often differ from landowners ethnically, too. I assume that deep ethnic cleavages have made land reforms much more difficult in Latin America than in Europe. My point is that the rise of the educational level among peasants and agricultural workers will create or has already created more favorable environmental conditions for the implementation of land reforms than previously.

I assume that the emergence of more equal social conditions among the agricultural population would affect the other sectors of economy and society, as was the case in the American colonies in the eighteenth century and in the United States and in many Western European countries in the nineteenth century. The trends of social changes depend, partly, on the will and visions of political leaders.

North Africa and the Middle East

What the Nondemocracies of North Africa and the Middle East have in common is that the values of educational indicators and DDN are relatively low for nearly all of them, although the values of Urban Population, Nonagricultural Population, and Family Farms are moderate in most cases. According to my assumption, the concentration of any important power resources may be enough to prevent democratization. It seems to apply to this region, too. This assumption is supported by the observation that the three components of the Index of Power Resources (IPR) are more or less in balance in the cases of the two Democracies (Israel and Lebanon) of this regional group (see Table 6.6). So the problem is how to raise the level of education and to decrease the concentration of nonagricultural economic power resources.

The problem is not exactly the same for all these countries, for there are significant differences in their social conditions. Jordan, Syria, Egypt, and Tunisia form a group of countries in which democratizations may take place without any special structural changes. Relatively small incremental changes may be enough to create social conditions in which the sharing of power becomes a rational alternative to their present hegemonic political systems. These countries have already achieved a level of resource distribution at which the visions of political leaders can play a crucial role in democratization.

Social conditions are much less favorable for democratization in several oil-exporting countries (Iraq, Qatar, Iran, Bahrain, Kuwait, Algeria, Libya, Saudi Arabia, and the United Arab Emirates) where the ownership and control of oil resources and production is highly concentrated in the hands of the ruling groups. Political domination exercised by the ruling groups in these countries is crucially dependent on the control of oil resources. It seems that the strategy of democratization should be based on education. In fact, conditions may change into more favorable ones for democratization without any conscious strategy. The governments of these countries already use a significant part of their oil incomes for education. They need educated people for new industries established by oil money. If and when people achieve relative equality in education, they may begin to demand equality in other areas of social life and politics, too.

Morocco is also a country where the rise of educational level might be enough to produce favorable conditions for democracy. In the rest of the countries of this region (Sudan, Mauritania, Afghanistan, North Yemen, and South Yemen), nearly all social conditions are still very unfavorable for democracy, and I cannot see any strategy of social engineering that could create favorable conditions in the near future.

In some of these countries the population is ethnically divided into clearly separate groups, which means that many important power resources are distributed, at least to some extent, between the same groups. Ethnic cleavages and the distribution of power resources based on them provide a foundation for competitive politics, but this kind of resource distribution can lead to democratization only under appropriate institutional arrangements. I return to this question in the next section when the strategies of democratization based on political architecture are discussed.

Sub-Saharan Africa

According to my indicators, social conditions are less favorable for democracy in Sub-Saharan Africa than in any other major region of the world. Only one structural factor seems to be conducive to democratization. The ownership or control of agricultural land, as indicated by Family Farms, is widely distributed among the agricultural population. This is an important factor, for the majority of the population is occupied in agriculture in most Sub-Saharan African countries, but it alone is not enough. We cannot expect democratization as long as all the other important dimensions of resource distribution are unfavorable for democratization. The fact that most farmers are still illiterate and uneducated makes them an inefficient group in national politics. Poor and illiterate farmers, without their own national organizations and leaders, are unable to participate efficiently in national politics. Despite their numbers, they have been unable to control modern politics pursued in cities. The most important economic, intellectual, and military power resources are in the hands of the military, the bureaucracy, and economic elite groups, mostly in cities. Until now it has been possible for any determined elite group, particularly for the military, to usurp power and to control unorganized farmers as well as traders and workers in cities. The problem of democratization concerns the inability of poor and uneducated farmers, traders, and workers to organize themselves and to use power based on their numbers to control the modern elite groups of cities that now dominate national politics and control crucial power resources.

I think that the strategies of social architecture could be used to improve the social preconditions of democracy in Sub-Saharan Africa, but inevitably it would be a long process. Social engineering should be directed to raise the level of popular education and to promote the development of market-oriented economic systems. The rise of popular education would make it possible for farmers and other social groups to organize themselves into economic and political interest groups and parties and to get leaders from their own ranks. The promotion of market-oriented economic systems would create independent economic resources and power centers, which are necessary in pluralist politics. Together these two strategies of social architecture could strengthen social structures conducive to democratization. As noted, this would be a long process, but it is possible that there is not any shorter way to democracy.

The political history of Sub-Saharan African countries indicates that until now ethnic cleavages and the distribution of power resources between competing ethnic groups have played an important role in the experiments of democray. It is significant that in Mauritius, which is the most stable democracy in Africa, party competition has traditionally reflected the ethnic heterogeneity of its population, although ethnic interest conflicts have not provided the only social foundation for party formation (see Kurian 1987). In Nigeria the party systems were based on the major ethnic cleavages during the periods of democratic rule in 1960–66 and 1979–83 (see, for example, Sklar and Whitaker 1964; Schwartz 1965; Keesing's Contemporary Archives, 30621–27). In the same manner multiparty systems have reflected ethnic cleavages in several other African countries in the periods when it was possible to establish competing parties. This was so in Ghana during the periods of constitutional civilian rule in 1957–64, 1969–72, and 1979–81 (see Chazan 1988), in Uganda in 1962–71 and 1980–85, in Zaire (Congo) in 1960–65, in Sierra Leone in 1961–78, in Somalia in 1960–69, and in Zambia in 1964–72 (see Coleman and Rosberg 1964). In contemporary Sub-Saharan Africa, there are multiparty systems in Botswana, Gambia, Liberia, Madagascar, Senegal, and Zimbabwe. At least in Botswana, Gambia, and Zimbabwe the existing multiparty systems reflect tribal cleavages and interest conflicts (see Kurian 1987). It seems that, in the conditions of contemporary Sub-Saharan Africa, the distribution of power resources between the major ethnic groups provides the most viable basis for democratic sharing of power, but it is a fragile basis because ethnic cleavages can easily lead to violent conflicts and to the struggle for hegemony, as has happened in several countries, and because the government-versus-opposition model of democracy is not well suited to the needs of plural societies (see Lijphart 1977). I return to this problem in the next section. Therefore, it would be useful to strengthen other social structures favorable for democratization.

The Republic of South Africa is a special case. Its political system has long been democratic at the level of the white minority, but its system is not democratic at the national level because the majority of the population is without political rights and freedoms and excluded from elections and governmental institutions. The concentration of economic and military resources in the hands of the white minority has supported the existing hegemonic systems, but the black majority has already acquired sufficient intellectual and organizational resources to challenge the white hegemony. From the perspective of democratization, the problem is how to transform the existing racial hegemonic rule into a democratic system under which the major racial groups could share power. This problem is principally a political one. Many social reforms and structural changes are also needed, but they are hardly possible before a political formula has been found that makes it possible for the majority to get its share of power.

Asia and Pacific

Because the group of 20 Asian countries is very heterogeneous, I discuss the strategies of democratization at the level of subgroups and individual countries. Let us start from the existing Democracies.

In six Democracies (Japan, South Korea, the Philippines, Singapore, Sri Lanka, and Malaysia), the three components of the Index of Power Resources are more or less in balance and social conditions are favorable for democracy (see Table 6.8), although, particularly in Singapore, economic power resources should be more widely distributed. The hegemony of the ruling party may reflect the concentration of economic power resources. India is a special case, for two components (IOD and IKD) of the Index of Power Resources (IPR) are at the level of Nondemocracies (see Table 6.8) and only one component, the Index of the Distribution of Economic Power Resources (DER), is at the normal level of Democracies. Because of this structural imbalance, the social foundation of competitive politics is still fragile in India. It could be strengthened by raising the level of popular education and by removing regulations restraining market forces in economy. I assume that, to a certain extent, the survival of competitive politics in India has been due to the ethnic pluralism of its population. Because of ethnic cleavages, all significant power resources are distributed among many competing groups. This kind of resource distribution has effectively pre-vented the concentration of crucial resources and political power in the hands of any single group. In the case of India I am ready to argue that the ethnic heterogeneity of its population has been favorable to the emergence and survival of democracy (cf. Vanhanen 1982). Pakistan has been a deviating Democracy since 1988 because of its low IPR value. The social basis of democracy could be strengthened in Pakistan by raising the level of edu-cation and by land reforms aimed at increasing the share of family farms. In Thailand intellectual and economic power resources seem to be widely distributed, whereas the low level of urban and nonagricultural population has probably hindered the stabilization of competitive politics. The lack of significant ethnic cleavages may have decreased the need of competitive political parties. Urban elite groups have struggled for power without close ties with the rural majority, which has not been able to organize its own national interest groups and parties. I assume that, in the case of Thailand, socioeconomic development will improve the social foundation of compet-itive politics without any special social reforms, particularly, if the growth of population starts to decrease.

According to my indicators, power resources are as widely distributed in Burma and Indonesia as they are in India, but these two countries have remained below the threshold of democracy. There may be particular local factors to explain the failures of democratization in these countries. In Burma the insurgencies of ethnic minority groups have provided a rationale to the continuation of the military rule, but the need to struggle against insurgen-cies does not make a centrally planned economy necessary. I would like to argue that the reintroduction of a market-oriented economic system would change environmental conditions into more conducive ones for the emer-gence of a competitive party system. Federalism might provide a political solution to the problem of ethnic insurgencies. In Indonesia the principal obstacles to democratization seem to be even more political than in Burma. Social conditions are ripe for the emergence of democratic institutions, but the military, controlling the most important economic resources through the government, has so far been strong enough to maintain its hegemony and to prevent the emergence of independent political parties (see Kurian 1987). I assume that socioeconomic development will gradually create more and more independent economic and political interest groups and weaken the hegemony of the military. Thus I think that Indonesia is bound to democ-ratize even without any drastic social reforms.

Bangladesh, Bhutan, and Nepal form a subgroup of poor South Asian countries in which economic and intellectual power resources are too much concentrated in the hands of small elite groups. There are no easy ways to remove the basic obstacles to democratization, like the poverty and igno-rance of the large sections of the population, but, particularly in Nepal, the utilization of significant ethnic cleavages might consolidate the development of a multiparty system.

China, Kampuchea, Laos, Mongolia, North Korea, and Vietnam form a subgroup of poor Socialist countries in which the concentration of economic and military power resources in the hands of hegemonic parties makes the emergence of democracy extremely difficult and improbable. It seems to me that the best strategy of democratization would be to start from the introduction of a market-oriented economy and from the extension of the sphere of private enterprises. Market-oriented economies would generate the formation and consolidation of various interest groups and organizations and thus provide a social foundation for later development of political interest groups. China seems to have adopted some parts of this strategy of development in the hope of modernizing its economy and accelerating its socioeconomic development. However, I emphasize that, because of their poverty, the prospects of democratization are much worse in the Asian Socialist countries than they are in the European Socialist countries, in which a high level of socioeconomic development provides a favorable social environment for democratization.

Four of the the five Pacific countries are Democracies, and Fiji was until 1987, but in two of them the social basis of democratic institutions is still fragile. Democratic institutions are on a fragile basis in Papua New Guinea and the Solomon Islands because of their poverty and a low level of education, which means that politics is dominated by narrow elite groups. One strategy for the governments to strengthen the social basis of democracy would be to increase investments in education.

POLITICAL ARCHITECTURE

The chances of democratization in a country depend not only on the existence of favorable social conditions but also on the appropriateness of its political institutions and on political leadership. Any institutional framework of democracy, which is appropriate in particular environmental circumstances, does not necessarily apply to different constellation of political forces equally well. The problem of political architecture, from the perspective of democratization, is to formulate and construct political institutions that in particular social circumstances provide channels for meaningful political participation and make democratic sharing of power among competing groups possible. Many failures and maladies of democratic institutions imply that this is not an easy problem to solve. Besides, even if an optimal solution is found, it will not guarantee that it will be implemented. In practice it might be very difficult to change less optimal institutions into more optimal ones, because a less optimal institutional framework may serve the interests of some powerful groups better than a suggested more optimal framework. It is reasonable to assume that each group attempts to mold political institutions to serve its particular interests. In this connection, however, I am not concerned with practical difficulties in implementing political reforms. I only argue and try to show that in particular circumstances certain institutional arrangements might serve the cause of democratization better than some other institutions do.

Arend Lijphart has studied the problem of applying democratic institutions to divided societies. First he examined the problem and its solution in the Netherlands (Lijphart 1968). Later he extended his exploration to all plural societies. On the basis of his studies, Lijphart presented a model of consociational democracy to plural societies. The basic idea behind this model is that in a plural society institutional arrangements should be such that all sections of the population can participate in political decisionmaking. He defined consociational democracy in terms of four characteristics: (1) government by a grand coalition of the political leaders of all significant segments of the plural society, (2) the mutual veto, which serves as an additional protection of vital minority interests, (3) proportionality as the principal standard of political representation, and (4) a high degree of autonomy for each segment to run its own internal affairs. He notes that a special form of segmental autonomy is federalism. Lijphart's message is that if the political leaders of plural societies wish to establish or strengthen democratic institutions, they must become consociational engineers (Lijphart 1977). In a later study Lijphart discerned two diametrically opposite models of democracy: the majoritarian model (or the Westminster model) and the consensus model. According to him, majoritarian democracy is appropriate for homogeneous societies, whereas consensus democracy is more suitable for plural societies (Lijphart 1984). I think that he is right. In plural societies democracy should be consensus democracy based on Lijphart's four characteristics of consociational democracy. But I must add, on the basis of my own analysis, that no matter how perfect institutional arrangements have been made, democratic institutions will probably fail, if crucial power resources are not sufficiently distributed among competing groups.

Juan J. Linz emphasizes the significance of creative political crafting in the process of democratization, the ability of political leaders to perceive alternatives and to make selections supporting democratization or consolidating the existing democracy. He also stresses the importance of institutional arrangements: "Does it make any difference for the success of the transition to democracy that the new regime will be presidential or parliamentary, unitary or federal, unicameral or bicameral, etc.?" (Linz 1982, 42). He pays particular attention to the comparison of parliamentarism and presidentialism and complains that the differences between them have not attracted the attention of political science. Besides, most of the discussion of presidential government in classic works on democratic politics is limited to the United States with practically no reference to long experience with presidential regimes in Latin America. Linz says, "It might not be an accident that with the exception of the United States, a country that is many ways exceptional, almost all stable democracies in the world have been parliamentary democracies." But, unfortunately, "the presidential example of the United States has had always a great attraction for Latin Americans, although in many respects their politics and social structure has had more similarities with Europe" (Linz 1986, 33). He comes to the conclusion that parliamentary democracy would suit the conditions of the developing countries better than presidential democracy, and he argues that parliamentary democracies "provide a greater flexibility in the process of transition to an consolidation of democracy" (Linz 1984, 35). Therefore, he suggests that "Latin Americans who, for so many problems look to Europe, and who so often reject the American model, might look at European political institutions whether of the classic parliamentary or the semi-presidential formula such as the French Fifth Republic as alternatives" (Linz 1986, 33). I agree with his arguments. Institutional arrangements certainly matter. Differences in institutions may account for part of the unexplained variation in the Index of Democratization. For example, it is quite possible that in some cases democratic experiments have failed because of inappropriate institutions. In some other cases the values of political variables (Competition and Participation) may have risen much higher than expected because of particular institutional arrangements like proportional representation. Unfortunately, I do not know any way to measure the relative significance of institutional differences.

Guillermo O'Donnell and Philippe C. Schmitter pay attention to the crucial role of political factors in the process of redemocratization, although they do not want to deny the causal impact of "structural" (including macroeconomic, world systemic, and social class) factors. On the basis of case studies they generalize that successful transitions have started from "providing more secure guarantees for the rights of individuals and groups," and "once some individual and collective rights have been granted, it becomes increasingly difficult to justify withholding others." On the basis of guaranteed political rights people and groups begin to demand democratization. They found that in all cases "crucial individual and collective rights were made effective before the convocation of competitive elections, the organization of effective interest representation, and the submission of executive authority to popular accountability" (O'Donnell and Schmitter 1986; cf. Kaufman 1986; Stepan 1986).

The contemporary studies mentioned above indicate that many kinds of political and institutional factors may affect the process of democratization.

I do not try to list all of them or to estimate their relative significance, but I discuss two of them—federalism and proportional representation—in greater detail. They might facilitate democratization and the survival of democracy in particular circumstances better than some alternative institutional arrangements do. Both of these techniques can be used to institutionalize the sharing of power especially in territorially and/or ethnically heterogeneous societies.

Federalism

Let us first examine possibilities of using federalism to stabilize territorial distribution of political power. The exploration of the 147 political systems of this study has disclosed several countries in which federalism has helped the cause of democratization or in which the establishment of federal structures might be helpful.

The success of democracy in the United States has probably been facilitated by its truly federal structures. Federalism has strengthened the territorial distribution of power and made it impossible to concentrate all power in the hands of a national government or of any single group. Federalism is a technique of territorial pluralism. Spain is a contemporary example of a country attempting to satisfy the demands of territorial and ethnic groups by extending regional autonomy.

Yugoslavia has also successfully decentralized political power through federal institutions, and it is even possible that a democratic order emerges in Yugoslavia on the basis of territorial and ethnic sharing of power. The Soviet Union is constitutionally a federal state, but the autonomy of its federal units is rather limited because power is heavily concentrated in the hands of the central government and the central organs of the Communist party. Therefore, the Soviet Union is a centralized state in practice (cf. Banks 1988, 608–17). I think that it might start democratization by decentralizing power to federal units, several of which are inhabited by ethnic minorities. I argue that it is as true in the Soviet Union as in all other parts of the world that each ethnic group wants to manage its own affairs and to defend its interests. In ethnically divided societies ethnic cleavages provide a very important basis for political competion and conflicts. Because of ethnic nepotism, it is not possible to eradicate these conflicts, but truly federal structures would mitigate them and provide a basis for democratic sharing of power (cf. Grigulevich and Kozlov 1979).

In Latin America there are at least two countries in which the establishment of federal structures would further democratization. In Bolivia and Peru most of the whites and the Indians live in different regions. In both of these countries governmental institutions are dominated by the white minority.

Federal structures would make it possible for Indians to control the state governments of their own regions, which would certainly extend the scope of democracy in these countries. Until now the Indians, who form nearly half of the population in Peru and more than half in Bolivia, have played only a minor part in national governmental institutions (see Kurian 1987). Besides, the territorial decentralization of political power would make it more difficult to carry out military coups in the future.

Cyprus and Lebanon are also countries in which federal systems are urgently needed. In Cyprus a federal system or a confederation is probably the only way to solve the ethnic conflict between the Greeks and the Turks (see Kyle 1984; Kurian 1987). In a country where the population is clearly divided into two ethnic-religious communities and where both communities have their own majority areas, a federal system provides the best way to mitigate inevitable ethnic conflicts. Lebanon, despite its small size, should be divided into so many federal units that each important ethnic- religious community could manage its own affairs. They could use Switzerland as an example. The creation of a confederation of cantons, each based upon traditional confessional hertlands, might be an ideal solution in Lebanon. Because of extremely strong ethnic nepotism in this ethnically deeply divided society, the secularization of politics within a unitarian state is not a realistic alternative (see McDowall 1984; Kurian 1987).

In North Africa, Sudan is an ethnically severely divided country. The two major ethnic groups live in different parts of the country: the Arabs in the north and the black Africans in the south (see Kurian 1987). The establishment of a federal system would institutionalize a territorial division of power and decrease the need for civil war between the major ethnic groups. It would also further the stabilization of democratic institutions and guarantee a fair representation for the black Africans in the national governmental institutions, which until now have been dominated by the Arabs.

Sub-Saharan African countries provide a challenging ground for political architecture. The constitutional systems inherited from the colonial powers were not well suited to social conditions in Africa. Nearly all constitutions of newly independent African countries presupposed unitary states, although the populations of these countries are ethnically very heterogeneous. Ethnic (mostly tribal) cleavages and their political significance were not taken into account in constitutions. It seems that in most Sub-Saharan African countries constitutional systems should be restructured by establishing federal systems. Tribal areas would provide the most natural social basis for the territorial units of federal states. Political institutions should be adapted to the reality of ethnic nepotism. Because the members of a tribe are usually more related to each other than to outsiders, tribal communities are the most significant interest groups in many African countries. Therefore, a federal system based on tribal units would be more coherent and satisfactory to people than a unitary state. Territorial sharing of power within the framework of federal institutions might also provide a starting point for democratization of political systems. Of course, the success of federalism presupposes that federal units are able to defend their autonomy and interests. It may be that, because of their poverty and lack of modern education, many territorial tribal units would not yet be ripe for self-government. In principle, however, it seems that federal systems would be appropriate to many African countries and that their establishment would further democratization, although federalism alone is not enough to produce or maintain democracy if other social conditions are unfavorable to democratization.

Nigeria is the only significant federal state in Sub-Saharan Africa. Its political history shows that it has been difficult to agree on the number and borders of federal units and that a federal system is not enough to maintain democracy and to prevent military coups in a poor country where crucial power resources are still in the hands of small elite groups. But its political history also shows that its federal system has supported the distribution of power among several competing groups and strengthened a multiparty system. In fact, so far it has been impossible to establish a one-party system in Nigeria, although it is common in many other countries of Africa.

In other African states, which are smaller than Nigeria, federal systems should be adapted to local conditions. Federal systems are not needed in all Sub-Saharan African countries, but a federal system might be more appropriate than a unitary state at least for Angola, Benin, Cameroon, Chad, Ethiopia, Ghana, Kenya, Togo, Uganda, and Zaire. There are several relatively large and clearly different ethnic groups in all these countries, and ethnic conflicts have played a prominent role in politics. In some of these countries ethnic conflicts have led to civil wars (see Kurian 1987). My argument is that territorial sharing of power within a federal state would mitigate ethnic conflicts and provide a foundation for the growth of democratic institutions. The creation of federal institutions would, however, be problematic in practice. It might not be in the interests of a unitary government, dominated by one group, to establish federal structures as long as it is able to maintain its hegemony. In fact, true federalism presupposes a kind of democracy, the sharing of power between equal territorial units.

Malaysia and India are the only federal states in Asia, and India of these two is less than a fully federal state. As G.T. Kurian says, its "constitution is federal in structure with unitary features" (Kurian 1987, 874). Historical traditions and linguistic and other ethnic cleavages made it natural for India to adopt a federal system, and it seems that the territorial distribution of power connected with federalism has consolidated political pluralism and democracy in India. However, federalism has not yet found its final form in India. Ethnic conflicts in various parts of India imply that there might be a need for more federal units. On the other hand, many people and groups have demanded greater autonomy for the states within the existing constitutional framework (cf. Sukhwal 1985; Rajasekharaiah 1987). I agree with these arguments. Democracy in India could be strengthened by extending federal distribution of power.

The rest of the governmental systems of Asia are unitary, but it seems that a federal system would be more appropriate for many of them, particularly for Burma, China, Indonesia, Pakistan, the Philippines, and Sri Lanka. Burma has been infested by ethnic insurgencies throughout the period of its independence. The establishment of a federal state might satisfy the demands of minority ethnic groups and provide a solid basis for reestablishing a democratic order. In a big country like China the establishment of a federal system would support the process of democratization by diffusing power territorially and by creating new autonomous centers of power. Indonesia is the largest archipelago nation in the world, and it is ethnically a plural society. In such conditions democratization might succeed better if combined with some kind of territorial distribution of power. For the same reason a federal system would be natural for the Philippines, too, although it is ethnically more homogeneous than Indonesia. Pakistan is religiously homogeneous, but otherwise it is ethnically divided into four major groups: Punjabis, Sindhis, Baluchis, and Pushtuns, each of them being dominant in its own region. As Uma Singh claims, "Islam has failed to nationally integrate such ethnic groups. The Pakistani society is still polarized along ethnic lines" (Singh 1986, 151). From the perspective of democratization, a federal system might be better than a unitary system that is dominated by the largest ethnic group. In Sri Lanka a federal system would decrease the ethnic conflict between the Tamils and the Sinhalese and strengthen the institutional framework of democracy (see Suryanarayan 1986; Björkman 1987).

Proportional Representation

The electoral system of a country is an institutional factor that can facilitate or hamper the function of democratic institutions especially in plural societies, although the major reasons for the failures of democracy in most Third World countries have been in the social structures, as I have tried to show in my comparative studies (see Vanhanen 1979, 1984). Because it is much easier to change a country's electoral system than to transform social and economic structures, it is worthwhile to take this institutional factor into account. It is clear that all electoral systems are not equally suited to all societies. My argument is that proportional representation would serve the cause of democratization much better in plural societies than the majority/plurality systems (for electoral systems, see Bogdanor 1983, 1984; Taagepera and Shugart 1989). Dieter Nohlen says that the political objective of majority/plurality systems is to obtain a parliamentary majority for one party or for a party alliance, even though it may be based on a minority of votes (Nohlen 1984, 20). Such a system may be suitable for homogeneous societies, but not for plural societies. Proportional representation is more suitable for them because proportionality as an electoral system translates voting strength into parliamentary seats as faithfully as possible (see Lijphart 1977, 40; Nohlen 1984, 20). This is very important in plural societies where people are segmented into more or less permanent ethnic and other social groups with their own interests. The plurality system is poorly suited to such societies because it may secure a permanent parliamentary majority for the largest group and because it leaves the other segments of the population permanently underrepresented and excluded from government. Such a situation aggravates disunity, intensifies adversary politics, and causes dissatisfaction and frustration among the underrepresented sectors of the population. Arend Lijphart says that especially in plural societies "majority rule is not only undemocratic but also dangerous, because minorities that are continually denied access to power will feel excluded and discriminated against and will loose their allegiance to the regime. In plural societies, therefore, majority rule spells majority dictatorship and civil strife rather than democracy" (Lijphart 1984, 22–23).

W. Arthur Lewis has dealt with this question extremely succinctly in his book Politics in West Africa (1965). He claims, "The surest way to kill the idea of democracy in a plural society is to adopt the Anglo-American electoral system of first-past-the-post." He emphasizes the importance of electoral systems: "The plural society goes back to the primary meaning of democracy, according to which all those who are affected by a decision should have a chance to participate in making a decision. This leads to proportional representation, with all parties offered seats in all decision making bodies, including the cabinet itself" (Lewis 1965, 64–74). Arend Lijphart comes to the same conclusion. Proportional representation is one of the four characteristics of his model of consociational democracy. He notes that several plural societies in Europe have achieved stable democracy by consociational methods and he thinks that the same pattern would be appropriate for a number of plural societies in the Third World, too (Lijphart 1977). I agree with the arguments of Lewis and Lijphart. From the perspective of democracy, proportional representation would probably be better than the majority/plurality systems in all countries, but in this connection I concentrate my attention on plural societies because they highlight the different political consequences of electoral systems.

Let us see what are the ethnically plural societies in which proportional representation might help the process of democratization. Appendix 7 indicates that in 63 out of 147 states the percentage of the largest ethnic group is 60 percent or less, and in 25 other states from 61 to 80 percent. All these

88 states can be regarded as ethnically severely dividied societies. Proportional representation would suit all of them, but in the following discussion I focus on some critical cases in which the role of an electoral system has been or could be significant.

In the subgroup of the Western European and North American countries the percentage of the largest ethnic group is 80 percent or less in Belgium, Canada, the Netherlands, Spain, Switzerland, and the United Kingdom. In Belgium, the Netherlands, Spain, and Switzerland the electoral system is proportional, whereas Canada and the United Kingdom use the plurality system. These two countries have long suffered from the serious disproportionality of representation produced by their electoral system. Laurence Leduc has traced several political problems of Canada to its British electoral system and has recommended electoral reforms and also proportional representation for Canada and Britain. His conclusion is that the "British electoral system, in both its domestic and exported variations, is today an inadequate tool for the government of complex societies" (Leduc 1987; see also Bogdanor 1983; 1984; Roberts 1987). It seems to me that the introduction of proportional representation would be the best way to further democratization by institutional reforms in these countries. In a previous chapter I argued that a proportional electoral system would suit the United States, because of its population's heterogeneity, better than its present plurality system, which limits the number of political alternatives and excludes many significant segments of the population from electoral politics.

Czechoslovakia, the Soviet Union, and Yugoslavia are the ethnically most divided societies in the subgroup of the Soviet Union and East Europe. I assume that a proportional electoral system would help the process of democratization in these countries, too.

All the Latin American and Caribbean countries are ethnically heterogeneous to some degree, although in some of them the percentage of the largest ethnic group is higher than 80 percent. Besides, social heterogeneity based on occupational, educational, and class differences is great in all of them. Therefore, proportional representation would suit them better than majority/plurality systems. Proportional electoral systems are used in parliamentary elections in many Latin American countries, but because their governmental systems are presidential, presidential elections are usually more important than parliamentary elections, and presidents are elected by majority/plurality systems. Presidential elections have often caused political troubles and polarized political conflicts with unfortunate consequences. It might be better for Latin American countries to change their governmental systems into parliamentary ones, as Juan J. Linz (1986) has suggested, and to retain a system of proportional representation in parliamentary elections. The Caribbean states, which were previously British colonies, adopted the British parliamentary system and the first-past-the- post electoral system, except Guyana, whose electoral system was changed into a proportional one in 1964, two years before independence (see Nohlen 1978, 152–53, 244–46). I think that a proportional electoral system would suit their conditions better than the British plurality system, which has seriously discriminated smaller parties and sharpened polarization. However, the example of the Bahamas, Barbados, Jamaica, and Trinidad and Tobago shows that the plurality system is not incompatible with democratization. In Guyana the ethnic conflict between the two major racial groups, the East Indians and the Afro Guyanese, has been very serious, and the country's party system reflects its ethnic cleavage. In Guyana, because of its very deep ethnic cleavage, proportional representation has not been enough to consolidate democratic institutions, but it may be that, without proportionality in parliamentary elections, its situation, from the perspective of democratization, would be even worse. The 1980 constitution made the country's governmental system semipresidential, which has reduced the political significance of proportionality in parliamentary elections (see Kurian 1987).

In nearly all Sub-Saharan African countries the percentage of the largest ethnic group is 80 percent or less. Therefore, proportional representation would be natural for them. One can argue that the adoption of a proportional electoral system would improve the chances of democratization (cf. Lewis 1965). In some cases, however, the plurality system and the overrepresentation of the ruling party produced by it may have supported the survival of democratic institutions. The fact that the plurality system has increased the parliamentary majorities of the ruling parties in Botswana and Gambia has probably diminished the temptation to introduce one-party systems. However, in Mauritius, in which ethnic cleavages are much deeper than in Botswana and Gambia, a modified plurality system is used. Deputies are chosen on the basis of a party-list system by simple majority vote from three-member constituencies, the three candidates receiving the largest number of votes being declared elected. In other words, the electoral system has some characteristics of proportional representation. I would argue that in the case of Mauritius the proportional features of its electoral system have facilitated the survival of democratic institutions and diminished ethnic conflicts (see Nohlen 1978, 151–52; Inter-Parliamentary Union, 1982–83).

Nigeria provides an opposite example. The plurality system probably contributed to the breakdowns of democracy in Nigeria by exaggerating the tribal and regional cleavages between political parties and by creating regional one party hegemonies (cf. Nohlen 1978: 149–51). It is surprising how poorly the effects of electoral systems have been understood in Nigeria. They wanted to support the emergence of all-Nigeria parties by constitutional arrangements and to weaken tribal and regional characteristics of political parties, but they selected an electoral system (the plurality system) that maximizes the regional dominance of one party and discriminates against all regional minority parties. The change of the governmental system from parliamentarism to presidentialism in 1979 only furthered the polarization of political forces and weakened national integration. Alternative electoral systems seem to have been completely unknown to Nigerian politicians. The same concerns, unfortunately, Anglo-American political scientists, too. In their studies on politics in Nigeria the role of the country's electoral system has hardly been mentioned. They have not seen any connection between the plurality system and the regional polarization of political forces (see, for example, Post 1964; Sklar and Whitaker 1964; Schwartz 1965; Hayward 1987; Diamond 1988b). Ghana and Uganda provide similar examples. In both countries the plurality system manufactured overrepresentation of the largest party and exaggerated the regional cleavages between the major parties. These developments contributed to the emergence of one-party hegemonies and the breakdowns of democracy. My argument is that in both of these countries proportional representation might have improved the survival chances of democratic institutions. I agree with W. Arthur Lewis' general argument for proportional representation: "In a plural society, proportional representation with a few large several-member constituencies is better than electoral systems with many single-member constituencies not only because it gives more satisfaction to the minorities, but also because it reduces the geographical conflict, and the racial, religious, and other differences which go with geography" (Lewis 1965, 72). In South Africa whenever they start to democratize their political system, they should adopt a proportional electoral system because it would facilitate the success of cross-racial and minority parties.

In the subgroup of Asian countries, Bhutan, Burma, India, Indonesia, Laos, Malaysia, Nepal, Pakistan, Singapore, and Sri Lanka are ethnically the most plural societies. Democracy has more or less succeeded in India, Malaysia, Pakistan, Singapore, and Sri Lanka despite the use of the British plurality system. This seems to contradict my assumption that proportional representation would provide a better institutional framework for democratization than the plurality system does, but, in fact, they have never tried a proportional electoral system, except Sri Lanka, which has already changed its electoral system into a proportional one. One could argue that democratic institutions would function better in these countries if they were based on proportional representation. In Singapore, for example, opposition parties, as a consequence of the plurality system, have hardly any representation in the parliament despite their significant percentage share of the votes. The adoption of proportional representation would make Singapore's political system more democratic. In India as a consequence of the very disproportional distribution of seats in the Lok Sabha and State assemblies, the party system has been more unstable and volatile than in any Western democracy. Most opposition parties in India have already recognized that these and some other malfunctions of the country's political system are causally related to their electoral system and they have begun to demand electoral reforms and a proportional electoral system (see Nohlen 1978, 137–39; Vanhanen 1987). In Malaysia, the disproportionality of party representation has also caused dissatisfaction and troubles and magnified the dominance of the largest party. It has been impossible for the smaller parties to get a fair representation in the parliament despite their significant electoral support (cf. Nohlen 1978, 144–47). I assume that the introduction of a proportional electoral system would consolidate democratic institutions in Malaysia. In Sri Lanka the extreme disproportionality of representation in the parliament aggravated political conflicts (cf. Nohlen 1978, 139–141). The country's electoral system was made proportional in 1978 (see Warnapala 1980). Consequently, opposition parties got a fair representation in the 1989 parliamentary election (see Keesing's Contemporary Archives, 36467–68).

In the subgroup of five Pacific countries, Fiji, Papua New Guinea, and Solomon Islands are ethnically plural societies. In Papua New Guinea and the Solomon Islands the members of parliaments are chosen by simple majority vote from single-member constituencies. In Fiji the plurality system was modified by establishing separate communal Rolls for the Fijian and Indian communities and the National Roll (see Inter-Parliamentary Union, 1982–83 and 1984–85). So far the plurality system seems to have worked satisfactorily in Papua New Guinea and Solomon Islands. In these two countries the smallness of ethnic groups makes it necessary for them to cooperate in politics. In Fiji the modified plurality system secured fair representation to the two major ethnic groups, but in the end the system was too fair to Indians. A military coup followed the electoral victory of an opposition alliance in 1987 (see Keesing's Contemporary Archives, 35251–54; West 1988).

I come to the conclusion that there is room for social and political architecture in many countries trying to establish or consolidate democratic institutions. At critical stages the survival or failure of democratic institutions may depend on how well they are adapted to their social environment. Therefore, political leadership matters. It is possible, by political decisions, to make social conditions more favorable to democratization. There is always a margin of alternative strategies and the need to make selections. The research on the strategies of democratization should provide data and knowledge on the nature of available alternatives.

CONCLUSION

In this study I argue that political structures and behavior patterns have evolved in the continual struggle for existence and reproduction and become adapted to variable environmental conditions. Different behavior patterns and political structures have competed for survival, and more appropriate patterns and structures have gradually displaced less appropriate ones. This process of natural selection in politics still continues. Consequently, I assumed that political structures would also become more or less similar in similar environmental conditions. So we can use environmental differences to explain the variation of political systems and also the variation of the degree of democratization. But it is not self-evident what kind of social conditions would further or hinder democratization. I attempt to answer this crucial question on the basis of evolutionary argumentation.

My argument is based on an evolutionary interpretation of politics, according to which politics can be conceived as a struggle for scarce resources. We are bound to the struggle for survival for the same reason as all other forms of life, and there is no way to avoid this struggle. Politics is for us a species-specific form of the struggle for survival. The evolutionary meaning of politics is in its ability to distribute scarce resources among individuals and groups. Because all available means are used in this struggle, it is plausible to assume that the distribution of relevant power resources among competitors inevitably affects the results of this struggle and the nature of political systems. When relevant power resources are widely distributed among competing groups, social conditions are favorable for democratization; when they are concentrated in the hands of the few, conditions are unfavorable for democracy and favorable for autocratic political systems. On the basis of this argumentation, I hypothesized that *democratization will take place under conditions in which power resources are so widely distributed that no group is any longer able to suppress its competitors or to maintain its hegemony*. Democracy was assumed to emerge as a more or less unintended consequence of resource distribution. Democratic institutions take shape when a political system adapts to circumstances that are characterized by a balance of forces between competing groups. The process of adaptation is often difficult, but in the end the competing groups will have to accept the sharing of power and to institutionalize it because none of them is any longer able to establish a hegemony and to suppress its competitors. I assumed that the pattern of democratization must be more or less similar in all human societies, despite their cultural differences and different historical experiences, because all human beings and populations can be assumed to share approximately the same behavioral predispositions that have evolved and become selected in the struggle for scarce resources and power during millions of years. They have become engraved in our genome and they still determine some basic behavior patterns and structures and make politics to some degree similar and predictable in all human societies.

On the basis of this argumentation I formulated a theory of democratization that is based on the idea that the relative distribution of economic, intellectual, and other power resources among various sections of the population is the fundamental factor that accounts for the variation of democratization. Democracy emerges from the necessity of circumstances when important power resources have become widespread. This theory was made empirically testable by formulating operationally defined indicators to measure the degree of democratization and the degree of the distribution of some important power resources. It was assumed that the same indicators can be applied to all countries because all human populations share the same behavioral predispositions, and, consequently, the struggle for power can be assumed to follow the same rules in all societies. This does not mean that the significance of my universal indicators should necessarily be the same in all countries. Local and cultural variations are possible. Besides, I did not assume that my indicators would cover all important aspects of democratization and resource distribution. They are inevitably insufficient to measure all aspects of the theoretical concepts they are intended to operationalize, but I assumed that they could indicate the major differences between countries on the levels of democratization and resource distribution. I still think that they are valid for this purpose. However, because my operational indicators are inevitably imperfect, I could not expect complete correlations between dependent and explanatory variables. Besides, there is another source of variation that my indicators do not even attempt to cover. There is always some randomness in politics as in all biological phenomena. It represents an unpredictable source of variation and it may account for part of the unexplained variation of democratization. However, it was hypothesized that correlations between the measures of democratization and the measures of resource distribution should be positive and relatively strong. Weak correlations would falsify my research hypothesis and theory on democratization.

The hypotheses were tested by empirical data on political and explanatory variables covering 147 countries of the period 1980–88. The results show that the combined indicator of resource distribution, the index of Power Resources (IPR), was able to explain, statistically, about 70 percent of the variation in the Index of Democratization (ID). It can be regarded as a very high percentage of explanation by taking into account the fact that my indicators are inevitably imperfect and that there are always random factors in politics. The examination of individual countries on the basis of regression analyses disclosed several deviating cases; countries that had crossed the threshold of democracy at a lower level of resource distribution (IPR) than expected, or countries that had not crossed the threshold of democracy, although it was expected on the basis of their high IPR values. These deviating cases contradict my second major research hypothesis, which predicts that all countries tend to cross the threshold of democracy at about the same level of the Index of Power Resources. However, because most countries (80–90 percent) were Democracies or Nondemocracies as predicted on the basis of IPR values and because some deviating cases may be due to local factors of resource distribution, measuring errors, or random factors in politics, I concluded that the observed deviating countries were not enough to falsify the research hypothesis. High negative residuals were interpreted to predict tha the level of democratization should rise and high positive residuals to predict that the level of democratization should decrease. In fact, several of the 1980 deviating cases had ceased to be deviating cases in 1988. Argentina, Brazil, South Korea, Mexico, the Philippines, Singapore, Sri Lanka, Turkey, and Uruguay, which were deviating Nondemocracies or Semidemocracies in 1980, crossed the threshold of democracy in 1981–88 as predicted on the basis of their high IPR values, whereas Nigeria, Uganda, and Zimbabwe, which in 1980 were deviating Democracies, dropped below the threshold of democracy as predicted on the basis of their low IPR values. This indicates that many of the deviating cases have contradicted the hypothesis only temporarily and that we can really make relatively reliable predictions on democratization on the basis of IPR values. However, because the correlations between my measures of democratization and the Index of Power Resources are not complete, such predictions cannot come true in all cases. Chile, Jordan, Panama, Poland, and Yugoslavia, which were deviating Nondemocracies in 1980, remained deviating Nondemocracies in 1988, and Papua New Guinea, the Solomon Islands, and Gambia remained deviating Democracies in 1988.

The results of empirical analyses support the theory of democratization used in this study and provide a theoretically satisfactory and universal explanation for the process of democratization in the world. We do not need a different theoretical explanation for every country and cultural region, although some cultural differences matter and although there are local factors of democratization that are not taken into account by my global indicators. The explained part of variation is so high that it does not leave much room for particular local and cultural explanations, but I agree that they could complete and enrich the explanation provided by this study. The fact that it has been possible to explain and predict the existence or lack of democracy in most countries of the world by six global variables can be regarded as the major empirical and theoretical result of this study. The process of democratization seems to follow the same basic rules in all countries. Political systems tend to democratize when important power resources become widespread and they tend to remain nondemocratic as long as important power resources are concentrated in the hands of the few. The explanation of democratization provided by this study is not only an empirical explanation based on observed relationships between variables but also a theoretical explanation because it explains why the variables must be related as they are and why their relationship must be the same in all societies.

The prospects of democratization depend on whether the distribution of crucial power resources increases or decreases. Since last century power resources have become more and more widespread as indicated by IPR values and, consequently, the number of democracies has continually increased (see Vanhanen 1984). According to my interpretation, technological inventions and developments have been the principal causal factors behind these trends of change. Technological developments have facilitated and made the distribution of various economic and intellectual power resources necessary among large sections of the population in technologically and economically developed countries. The distribution of various resources has been an unintended consequence of technological changes. If the same trend continues, it is plausible to expect that the number of democracies will increase in the world, but we cannot be sure of the future course of technological developments. However, as long as important power resources become more and more widespread within societies, it is plausible to predict that democratization will also continue in the world. The pressure for democratization will increase in all countries where power resources become widespread, and it becomes more and more difficult for the power holders of autocratic systems to maintain their hegemony and to keep the gates of democratization closed.

From theoretical and practical points of view, one of the most interesting results of this study has been the observation that successful democratizations have taken place not only in rich and socioeconomically highly developed countries but also in several poor countries at a relatively low level of socioeconomic development. It seems difficult to establish any lower limit of GNP per capita that could be regarded as a necessary condition for democratization (see Figure 5.1). For example, in India GNP per capita was only $260 in 1983. The existence of democracy in several poor countries and the lack of democracy in several rich and socioeconomically relatively highly developed countries contradict clearly socioeconomic hypotheses of demoralization given by Lipset and others. Many deviating countries are anomalies that cannot be explained by their theories, whereas most of the same countries have not been deviating cases in my study. This is a crucial difference between my theory of democratization and various socioeconomic theories of democratization. According to my theoretical explanation, the level of socioeconomic development is not the ultimate causal factor behind democratization It is only an intervening variable that correlates positively with democratization because various power resources are usually more widely distributed at higher levels than at lower levels of socioeconomic development. However, a positive relationship between the level of democratization and the level of wealth or socioeconomic development does not need to concern all countries. It is possible that important power resources become widespread in some poor countries and that they remain highly concentrated in some rich and economically developed countries. Therefore, in some cases, the prospects of democratization may look quite different depending on whether they are estimated on the basis of socioeconomic theories of democratization or on the basis of my theory. Socioeconomic theories of democratization presuppose a relatively high level of socioeconomic development and wealth, which leads to the prediction that poor countries have hardly any chances to establish and maintain democratic institutions. Democracy is considered possible only in rich societies. On the basis of my theory the prospects of democracy are not so bleak for poor countries. It is possible even for relatively poor countries, as empirical evidence shows, to establish and maintain democratic institutions, if relevant power resources are distributed widely enough. The crucial precondition of democray is not a certain level of wealth or economic development but a certain balance of forces between competing groups, which prevents any competitor of achieving hegemony and makes the sharing of power necessary for them. The problem is how to achieve or create this kind of favorable social environment for democratization.

Are favorable social conditions produced by environmental changes not under conscious human control, or could it be possible, at least to some degree, to shape social conditions favorable for democracy by conscious political choices? The question is of the relative weights of environmental determinism versus free human choices. I am not able to solve this eternal controversy, but I have to clarify my position because it depends on the answer given to this question whether it is worthwhile to formulate conscious strategies of democratization or not. If we assume that political structures and social conditions are completely determined by environmental forces outside our conscious control, it would not be worthwhile to attempt to guide social and political developments by conscious political choices and efforts. On the other hand, if we assume that they are, at least partly, products of conscious human choices, it would be worthwhile to formulate strategies of social and political reforms intended to further democratization. I think that the level of democratization mainly depends on environmental conditions defined in this study. This assumption is supported by empirical results of this study. The analysis of 147 countries by seven cultural-geographic regions indicated that there are great differences between the seven regions both in the average degree of resource distribution and in the degree of democratization, but the predictions of ID values (the level of democratization) based on IPR values (resource distribution) were approximately equally accurate for all regions (see Tables 6.1, 6.2). It implies that apart from differences in political leadership, cultures, and ideologies, the explanatory factor of democratization (IPR) has been equally important in all parts of the world. In other words, the level of democratization has been principally determined by similar environmental factors everywhere. However, the unexplained part of the variation of the Index of Democratization (about 30 percent) leaves room for other factors and various political choices.

It is much more difficult to estimate to what extent the social conditions affecting the level of democratization have been produced by uncontrollable environmental forces or by conscious human choices and efforts intended to create such conditions. Of course, all social conditions are directly or indirectly created by human choices and actions, but, on the other hand, it seems that they have mostly been produced without any conscious plan to affect political structures. Usually they have been combined results of individual and group efforts to further their own interests in the struggle for scarce resources, but sometimes social conditions have been reformed on purpose to further certain political or other ends. Some of these reforms may have produced intended consequences, but quite often they have also had unintended and uncontrollable consequences. Besides, scientific inventions and new technologies based on them may have caused more profound changes in human societies than any conscious political choices and reforms. They constitute an important uncontrollable factor that affects social and political structures indirectly. So I come to the conclusion that changes in social conditions affecting the prospects of democratization have mostly been unintended consequences of various environmental forces and human choices, but it does not exclude the possibility of making social conditions favorable for democracy by conscious political choices and efforts. I cannot define the extent to which it is possible to shape social conditions and, through them, political structures by conscious strategies, but I am sure that the formulation of such strategies is worthwhile. Human choices certainly matter, although I have argued that political and social structures have evolved by natural selection in politics. Our various choices provide the necessary material for natural selection in politics. We cannot change the basic rules of political struggle for scarce resources, but a better understanding of those rules might help people to select more rational means to further their aims than what they previously did. In this study I have attempted to explore the process of democratization and the factors affecting it. The strategies of democratization that are based on the knowledge of the factors of democratization can be assumed to be more successful than randomly selected strategies or strategies that contradict some basic rules of democratization.

APPENDIX 1

Percentage of the Largest Party and Percentage of Electoral Participation in the Parliamentary and/or Presidential Elections of 147 countries in 1980–88

Symbols:
—— data not available
( ) data in brackets are the writer's estimates

Notes by country:
Only the name of the writer or the editor(s) or alternatively the name of the publication and usually also the year of publication are given in these notes, as well as relevant page numbers. More complete bibliographic data appear in the Bibliography. The degree of electoral participation was calculated, if not otherwise noted, on the basis of the population data given in United Nations, Demographic Yearbook 1985 and Demographic Yearbook 1986.

State/Election year/Largest party or elected presidential candidate	Votes for the largest party		Total votes	
	Number	% of total votes	Number	% of total population

1. Afghanistan
Executive dominance, 1980–88; revolutionary government 1979–85.
| 1986 Najibullah (PDPA) | — | 100.0 | — | 0.0 |

See Delury 1987; Kurian 1987; Banks 1988; *Keesing's Contemporary Archives (Keesing's)*, 35782.

2. Albania
Parliamentary dominance, 1980–88
1978 Democratic Front	1,436,285	100.0	1,436,285	56.0
1982 Democratic Front	1,627,959	100.0	1,627,959	58.5
1987 Democratic Front	1,830,652	100.0	1,830,652	59.8

1978: Inter-Parliamentary Union (IPU) 1978–79; *1982:* IPU 1982–83. *1987:* IPU 1986–87.

3. Algeria
Executive dominance, 1980–88
1979 Col. B. Chadli (FLN)	7,434,118	99.3	7,489,700	41.4
1984 Col. B. Chadli (FLN)	8,729,000	95.4	9,150,000	45.4
1988 Col. B. Chadli (FLN)	10,603,057	93.3	11,369,304	48.6

1979: Keesing's, 29778. *1984: Africa Research Bulletin,* Jan. 1–31, 1984. *1988: Africa Research Bulletin,* Jan. 15, 1989.

198

APPENDIX 1 (*continued*)

State/Election year/Largest party or elected presidential candidate	Votes for the largest party		Total votes	
	Number	% of total votes	Number	% of total population

4. Angola
Parliamentary dominance, 1980–88

1980	MPLA-PT	—	100.0	—	0.0
1986	MPLA-PT	—	100.0	—	0.0

1980: IPU 1980–81; Delury 1987. Members of the People's Assembly were elected indirectly by electoral colleges set up in each province. *1986:* IPU 1986–87.

5. Argentina
Executive dominance, 1980–88; military coup d'etat in 1976, and military governments 1976–82.

1983	Raul Alfonsin (UCR)	7,659,530	51.8	14,779,239	49.9

See Delury 1987. *1983: Keesing's,* 32553–55; cf. IPU 1983–84.

6. Australia
Parliamentary dominance, 1980–88

1980	Australian Labor party	3,749,605	45.1	8,305,633	56.5
1983	Australian Labor party	4,297,521	49.5	8,684,862	56.4
1984	Australian Labor party	3,748,776	42.2	8,885,506	57.1
1987	Australian Labor party	4,231,183	45.8	9,232,189	57.1

1980: IPU 1980–81; *1983:* Mackie and Rose 1984, 335. *1984:* IPU 1984–85. *1987:* IPU 1987–88.

7. Austria
Parliamentary dominance, 1980–88

1979	Socialist party	2,413,226	51.0	4,784,173	63.7
1983	Socialist party	2,312,529	47.6	4,853,417	63.9
1986	Socialist party	2,092,024	43.1	4,852,188	64.1

1979: Mackie and Rose 1980. *1983:* IPU 1982–83. *1986:* IPU 1986–87.

8. Bahamas
Parliamentary dominance, 1980–88

1977	Progressive Liberal party	—	55.0	62,818	31.9
1982	Progressive Liberal party	—	55.2	76,098	34.9
1987	Progressive Liberal party	53,508	53.6	99,874	41.7

1977: IPU 1977–78; Keesing's, 28531. *1982:* IPU 1981–82; Keesing's, 32009. *1987:* IPU 1986–87.

APPENDIX 1 (*continued*)

State/Election year/Largest party or elected presidential candidate	Votes for the largest party		Total votes	
	Number	% of total votes	Number	% of total population

9. Bahrain

Executive dominance, 1980–88

Bahrain is ruled by the emir and other members of the royal family without an
  elected legislative body, although the 1973 constitution presupposes a national
  assembly. See Delury 1987; Kurian 1987; Banks 1988.

10. Bangladesh

Executive dominance, 1980–88

1978	Ziaur Rahman	15,765,740	77.7	20,287,000	24.0
1981	Abdus Sattar	14,217,601	65.8	21,600,000	23.9

A military coup on March 24, 1982, and General Ershad's military government
  in 1982–85.

1986	Gen. H.M. Ershad (Jatiya party)	21,795,337	83.6	26,070,900	25.9

1978: Keesing's, 29197; cf. Khan and Zafarullah 1979. *1981: Keesing's,* 31385.
  1982: Delury 1987. *1986:* Keesing's, 34812–13.

11. Barbados

Parliamentary dominance, 1980–88

1976	Barbados Labour party	51,958	52.2	99,463	40.4
1981	Barbados Labour party	61,845	52.2	118,467	47.4
1986	Democratic Labour party	80,147	59.5	134,730	53.0

1976, 1981: Keesing's, 31092; cf. IPU 1980–81. *1986:* IPU 1985–86.

12. Belgium

Parliamentary dominance, 1980–88

1978	CSP/CPP	2,006,621	36.2	5,533,206	56.2
1981	CSP/CPP	1,563,581	26.4	5,919,250	60.1
1985	CSP/CPP	1,774,154	29.3	6,064,415	61.2
1987	CVP/PSC	1,686,526	27.5	6,141,212	61.7

1978: Mackie and Rose 1979, 305. *1981:* IPU 1981–82. *1985:* IPU 1985–86.
  1987: IPU 1987–88.

13. Benin

Executive dominance, 1980–88

1980	Ahmed Kerekou	—	100.0	—	0.0
1984	Ahmed Kerekou	—	100.0	—	0.0

1980, 1984: Africa Research Bulletin, Feb. 1–29, 1980, and Aug. 15, 1984;
  Europa Year Book 1988. The president was elected by the National
  Revolutionary Assembly.

APPENDIX 1 (*continued*)

State/Election year/Largest party or elected presidential candidate	Votes for the largest party		Total votes	
	Number	% of total votes	Number	% of total population

14. Bhutan
Executive dominance, 1980–88
Bhutan is a limited monarchy ruled by the king. Legislative authority is
  nominally vested in the National Assembly (Tsongdu). See Kurian 1987; *World
  Elections on File* 1987; Banks 1988.

15. Bolivia
Executive dominance, 1980–88
Military governments in 1980–81.

1982 Siles Zuazo (UDP)	528,696	36.0	1,469,377	26.2
1985 Banzer Suarez (ADN)	493,735	35.0	1,410,845	21.9

See Delury 1987. *1982: Keesing's,* 29853, 31942–45; Facts on File 1982, 766.
  The data refer to the results of the inconclusive presidential election in 1980.
  On October 5, 1982, the Congress elected Siles president. *1985: Keesing's,*
  33905. As no candidate attained the required outright majority, the Congress
  chose out of the three leading contenders. Paz Estenssoro was elected
  president.

16. Botswana
Parliamentary dominance, 1980–88

1979 Botswana Democratic party	100,398	75.4	133,196	16.8
1984 Botswana Democratic party	154,863	68.0	227,756	21.7

1979: IPU 1979–80. *1984:* IPU 1984–85.

17. Brazil
Concurrent powers, 1980–88 (50–50%)
Parliamentary elections:

1978 ARENA	15,053,387	50.4	29,856,913	26.4
1982 PDS	17,775,738	43.2	41,125,008	32.4
1986 PMDP	—	(53.3)	58,650,000	42.3

Presidential elections:

1978 Gen. Figueiredo	355	60.0	592	0.0
1985 Tancredo Neves (PMDP)	480	72.7	660	0.0

1978: IPU 1978–79; *Keesing's,* 29546. *1982:* IPU 1982–83. *1985:* Bruneau
  1985, 7:974. Tancredo Neves was hospitalized before he was to take office as
  president on March 15, 1985. Vice-president José Sarney assumed the
  presidency. See also *World Elections on File* 1987. *1986:* IPU 1986–87.
  PMDP's share of the seats in the Chamber of Deputies was 53.3%.

APPENDIX 1 (*continued*)

State/Election year/Largest party or elected presidential candidate	Votes for the largest party		Total votes	
	Number	% of total votes	Number	% of total population

18. Bulgaria
Parliamentary dominance, 1980–88

1976 Fatherland Front	6,369,762	100.0	6,375,092	72.8
1981 Fatherland Front	6,519,674	100.0	6,519,674	73.3
1986 Fatherland Front	—	100.0	6,645,645	74.2

1976: Keesing's, 27868. 1981: IPU 1980–81. *1986:* IPU 1985–86.

19. Burkina Faso
Executive dominance, 1980–88
Military governments 1980–88.
See Delury 1987; Banks 1988; *Keesing's,* 32056, 32482, 36196–97.

20. Burma
Parliamentary dominance, 1980–88

1978 Burma Socialist Program party	—	100.0	14,000,000	43.5
1981 Burma Socialist Program party	—	100.0	15,800,000	45.0
1985 Burma Socialist Program party	—	100.0	—	(45.0)

A military coup on September 18, 1988.
1978: IPU 1977–78. *1981:* IPU 1981–82. *1985:* IPU 1985–86; *Keesing's,*
   33954, 36221–25. *1988:* See *The Far East and Australasia* 1989.

21. Burundi
Executive dominance, 1980–88
A military government 1980–83.

1984 Col. Jean-Baptiste Bagaza (Uprona)	—	99.6	1,700,000	37.5

A military coup in 1987, and a military government 1987–88.
See Banks 1988. *1984: Africa Research Bulletin,* Aug. 15, 1984; *Africa
   Contemporary Record* 1984–85, B 186. *1987: Africa Contemporary Record*
   1986–87, B 247; *Keesing's,* 35631–32.

22. Cameroon
Executive dominance, 1980–88

1980 A.B. Ahidjo (CNU)	—	100.0	—	(39.0)
1984 Paul Biya (CNU)	—	100.0	3,881,300	39.3
1988 Paul Biya (CNU)	3,321,872	98.7	3,364,090	30.6

1980: Africa Research Bulletin, Apr. 1–30, 1980; *Africa Contemporary Record*
   1980–81, B 395. *1984, 1988: Africa Research Bulletin,* June 15, 1988.

APPENDIX 1 (*continued*)

State/Election year/Largest party or elected presidential candidate	Votes for the largest party		Total votes	
	Number	% of total votes	Number	% of total population
23. Canada				
Parliamentary dominance, 1980–88				
1980 Liberals	4,853,914	44.1	11,015,514	45.8
1984 Conservative party	6,276,530	50.0	12,545,973	49.9
1988 Conservative party	5,625,288	43.0	13,075,042	50.6

1980: Mackie and Rose 1981, 320. *1984:* IPU 1984–85. *1988:* Canadian News Facts, Vol. 22, No. 21, Dec. 4, 1988.

24. Cape Verde				
Parliamentary dominance, 1980–88				
1980 PAICV	88,309	92.4	95,486	32.2
1985 PAICY	93,252	94.5	98,692	29.6

1980: IPU 1980–81. *1985:* IPU 1985–86; *Africa Research Bulletin,* Febr. 15, 1986.

25. Central African Republic				
Executive dominance, 1980–88				

President David Dacko's regime in 1979–81. A military coup on September 1, 1981, and a military government 1981–85.

1986 General A.-D. Kolingba	696,055	92.2	754,807	27.5

See Delury 1987; *World Elections on File* 1987; Banks 1988. *1986: Africa Contemporary Record* 1986–87, B 180.

26. Chad				
Executive dominance, 1980–88				

Military governments 1980–88.
See Delury 1987; Kurian 1987; Banks 1988.

27. Chile				
Executive dominance, 1980–88				

General Pinochet's military government 1980–88.
See Garreton 1986; Delury 1987; Banks 1988.

28. China				
Parliamentary dominance, 1980–88				
1978 Communists and their allies	—	100.0	—	0.0
1983 Communists and their allies	—	100.0	—	0.0

APPENDIX 1 (*continued*)

State/Election year/Largest party or elected presidential candidate	Votes for the largest party		Total votes	
	Number	% of total votes	Number	% of total population
1988 Chinese Communist party	—	100.0	—	0.0

1978: IPU 1977–78. Indirect elections. *1983:* IPU 1982–83. Indirect elections. *1988:* IPU 1987–88. Indirect elections.

29. *Colombia*
Executive dominance, 1980–88

1978 Turbay Ayala (Liberal party)	2,506,228	49.7	5,037,865	19.6
1982 Belisario Betancur (Cons. p.)	3,189,278	46.8	6,815,700	24.2
1986 Bargo Vargas (Liberal party)	4,123,716	58.2	7,085,400	24.3

1978: Keesing's, 29204; *Europa Year Book* 1982 Vol. II, 163. *1982:* Keesing's, 31720. *1986: Keesing's,* 34801–02.

30. *Comoros*
Executive dominance, 1980–88

1978 Ahmed Abdallah	195,186	100.0	195,290	54.7
1984 Ahmed Abdallah	244,130	99.4	245,510	57.0

1978: Keesing's, 29334. *1984: Keesing's,* 33201.

31. *Congo, People's Republic of*
Executive dominance, 1980–88

1979 Col. Sassou-Nguesso (PCT)	—	100.0	—	0.0
1984 Col. Sassou-Nguesso (PCT)	—	100.0	—	0.0

1979: Delury 1987; Banks 1988; *Keesing's,* 30059. *1984: Keesing's,* 33201.

32. *Costa Rica*
Executive dominance, 1980–88

1978 Carazo Odio (Unity)	419,824	48.8	860,206	40.7
1982 Monge Alvarez (PLN)	—	57.3	991,679	42.7
1986 Arias Sanchez (PLN)	620,314	52.3	1,185,222	44.4

1978: Keesing's, 28975. *1982:* Cerdas 1986. *1986: Keesing's,* 34350; see also *World Elections on File* 1987.

APPENDIX 1 (*continued*)

State/Election year/Largest party or elected presidential candidate	Votes for the largest party		Total votes	
	Number	% of total votes	Number	% of total population
33. Cuba				
Parliamentary dominance, 1980–88				
1976 Communist party	—	100.0	—	0.1
1981 Communist party	—	100.0	—	0.1
1986 Communist party	—	100.0	(13,256)	0.1

1976: IPU 1976–77. Indirect elections. The deputies of the National Assembly were elected by the country's Municipal Assemblies of People's Power. *1981:* IPU 1981–82. *1986:* IPU 1986–87. Indirect elections. The deputies to the National Assembly were elected by 13,256 delegates of the municipal assemblies.

34. Cyprus				
Parliamentary dominance, 1980–88				
1976 Pro-Makarios parties	—	70.0	229,223	37.5
1981 AKEL	95,364	32.8	291,021	45.9
1985 Democratic Rally	107,223	33.6	319,467	48.0

1976: Facts on File 1976, 772; IPU 1976–77. *1981:* IPU 1980–81. *1985:* IPU 1985–86.

35. Czechoslovakia				
Parliamentary dominance, 1980–88				
1976 National Front	10,605,672	100.0	10,609,255	71.1
1981 National Front	10,725,609	100.0	10,730,205	70.0
1986 National Front	—	99.9	10,884,947	70.1

1976: IPU 1976–77. *1981:* IPU 1980–81. *1986:* IPU 1985–86; *Keesing's*, 34434.

36. Denmark				
Parliamentary dominance, 1980–88				
1979 Social Democratic Party	1,213,456	38.3	3,171,002	61.9
1981 Social Democratic Party	1,026,726	32.9	3,123,563	61.0
1984 Social Democratic Party	1,062,561	36.6	3,362,010	65.8
1987 Social Democratic Party	985,906	29.3	3,362,557	65.6
1988 Social Democratic Party	992,682	29.6	3,329,129	64.9

APPENDIX 1 (continued)

State/Election year/Largest party or elected presidential candidate	Votes for the largest party		Total votes	
	Number	% of total votes	Number	% of total population

1979: IPU 1979–80. *1981:* IPU 1981–82. *1984:* IPU 1983–84. *1987; 1988:* IPU 1987–88.

37. Djibouti
Parliamentary dominance, 1980–88

1977	Popular Independence Rally	75,621	100.0	75,621	30.0
1982	Popular Rally for Progress	78,031	100.0	78,031	23.6
1987	Popular Rally for Progress	88,193	100.0	88,193	18.1

1977: IPU 1976–77. *1982:* IPU 1981–82; *Keesing's,* 31747–48. *1987:* IPU 1986– 87; *Europa Year Book* 1988.

38. Dominican Republic
Executive dominance, 1980–88

1978	Antonio Guzman (PRD)	756,084	48.6	1,554,357	30.1
1982	Jorge Blanco (PRD)	854,868	46.6	1,834,000	31.9
1986	Joaquin Balaguer (PRSC)	857,942	41.6	2,062,000	32.1

1978: Europa Year Book 1982 Vol. II, 242. *1982: Keesing's,* 31794; cf. IPU 1981–82. *1986: Keesing's,* 35057.

39. Ecuador
Executive dominance, 1980–88

1979	Roldos Aguilera (CFP)	1,025,148	68.5	1,496,000	19.0
1984	Febres Cordero (PSC)	1,268,564	52.2	2,430,213	26.7
1988	Rodrigo Borja (ID)	1,762,417	46.0	3,335,068	33.9

1979: Keesing's, 29729, 29916. The second round of the presidential election. *1984: World Elections on File* 1987; *Keesing's,* 32974. The second round of the presidential election. *1988: Keesing's,* 36097. The second round of the presidential election.

40. Egypt
Executive dominance, 1980–88

1976	Anwar Sadat (NDP)	9,151,288	99.9	9,156,893	24.0

APPENDIX 1 (*continued*)

State/Election year/Largest party or elected presidential candidate	Votes for the largest party		Total votes	
	Number	% of total votes	Number	% of total population
1981 M. Husni Mubarak (NDP)	9,567,904	98.5	9,717,554	22.4
1987 M. Husni Mubarak (NDP)	12,304,000	97.1	12,672,000	25.0

1976: Die Wahl der Parlamente. Afrika, 1978, 295. *1981: Keesing's,* 31253–54.
   1987: Keesing's, 35673.

41. El Salvador
Executive dominance, 1980–88
A coup d'état in 1979, and a military-civilian junta 1980–81.

1982 Alvaro Magana	36	68.0	53	0.0
1984 J. Napoleon Duarte (PDC)	752,625	53.6	1,404,366	29.4

See Delury 1987; Banks 1988; Keesing's, 30045, 31613–18. *1982: Keesing's,*
   31613–14. Magana was elected interim president by the Constituent Assembly
   on Apr. 29, 1982. *1984:* Chitnis 1984, 6:980. The second round of the
   presidential election; cf. *Keesing's,* 32853–55, 33205.

42. Equatorial Guinea
Executive dominance, 1980–88
A military coup in 1979, and a military government 1979–81.

1982 Col. Obiang Nguema	—	95.8	140,877	38.4

See Kurian 1987; Banks 1988. *1982: Africa Contemporary Record* 1982–83, B
   391. The results of a referendum on the new constitution, which designated
   Col. Obiang Nguema president for the first seven years.

43. Ethiopia
Executive dominance, 1980–88
A Provisional Military Administrative Council ruled the country 1974–86.

1987 Lt. Col. Mengistu	—	100.0	—	0.0

See Delury 1987; Kurian 1987; Banks 1988. *1987: Keesing's,* 35367–68; IPU
   1986–87. Mengistu was elected by the National *Shengo*.

44. Fiji
Parliamentary dominance, 1980–88

1977 Alliance party	378,349	52.3	(180,000)	(30.0)
1982 Alliance party	507,207	51.8	(251,700)	(38.0)

A military coup in 1987, and a civilian-military government 1987–88.
1977: Keesing's, 28681. Each voter was entitled to cast four votes. Therefore,
   the number of votes cast is much higher than the number of voters. *1982:* IPU
   1982–83; *Keesing's,* 32259–60. *1987:* Banks 1988; IPU 1986–87; West 1988.

APPENDIX 1 (*continued*)

State/Election year/Largest party or elected presidential candidate	Votes for the largest party		Total votes	
	Number	% of total votes	Number	% of total population
45. Finland				
Concurrent powers, 1980–88 (50–50%)				
Parliamentary elections:				
1979 SDP	691,512	23.9	2,906,066	61.0
1983 SDP	795,813	26.7	2,975,866	61.2
1987 SDP	694,666	24.1	2,877,520	58.2
Presidential elections:				
1978 Urho Kekkonen	2,017,631	82.4	2,448,384	51.5
1982 Mauno Koivisto (SDP)	1,370,314	43.1	3,177,525	65.8
1988 Mauno Koivisto	1,513,234	47.9	3,094,449	62.4

1978: Mackie and Rose 1979, 306. *1979:* Mackie and Rose 1980, 351. *1982:* Mackie and Rose 1983, 345. *1983:* IPU 1982–83. *1987:* IPU 1986–87. *1988:* Central Statistical Office of Finland, *Presidential election 1988.*

State/Election year/Largest party or elected presidential candidate	Votes for the largest party		Total votes	
	Number	% of total votes	Number	% of total population
46. France				
Concurrent powers, 1980–88 (50–50%)				
Parliamentary elections:				
1978 Rally for the Republic	6,462,462	22.6	28,560,243	53.5
1981 Socialists and allies	9,432,362	37.5	25,141,190	46.4
1986 Socialist party	8,705,163	31.0	28,037,180	51.3
1988 Socialist party	8,493,702	34.8	24,432,095	43.8
Presidential elections:				
1974 Giscard d'Estaing	13,396,203	50.8	26,367,807	49.1
1981 Francois Mitterand	15,708,262	51.8	30,350,568	56.0
1988 Francois Mitterand	16,704,279	54.0	30,923,349	55.4

1974: Mackie and Rose 1975, 323. The second round of the presidential election. *1978:* Mackie and Rose 1979, 307. The results of the first ballot including the overseas departments and territories. *1981:* IPU 1981–82; Mackie and Rose 1982, 334–335. The results of the first ballot (National Assembly). The second round of the presidential election. *1986:* IPU 1985–86; cf. *Keesing's,* 34305. The results of the first ballot. *1988: Keesing's,* 35979–81, 36228; IPU 1987–88. The second round of the presidential election. The results of the first ballot (National Assembly).

State/Election year/Largest party or elected presidential candidate	Votes for the largest party		Total votes	
	Number	% of total votes	Number	% of total population
47. Gabon				
Executive dominance, 1980–88				
1979 Bongo (GDP)	725,818	99.8	727,270	54.1
1986 Bongo (GDP)	903,779	100.0	904,039	58.5

APPENDIX 1 (*continued*)

State/Election year/Largest party or elected presidential candidate	Votes for the largest party		Total votes	
	Number	% of total votes	Number	% of total population

1979: Keesing's, 30276; *Bulletin de l'Afrique noire,* 1980, 19923. According to Africa Today, 1981, 551, the population of Gabon was 1,343,000 in 1981. *1986: Keesing's,* 35047. According to Banks 1988, the population was 1,545,000 in 1986.

48. Gambia
Parliamentary dominance, 1980–88

1977	People's Progressive party	123,297	69.6	177,181	32.0
1982	People's Progressive party	102,545	61.7	166,102	26.1
1987	People's Progressive party	123,385	59.2	208,479	31.1

1977: Keesing's, 28339. *1982:* IPU 1981–82; *Keesing's,* 31684. *1987:* IPU 1986–87; *Keesing's,* 35109–10.

49. German Democratic Republic
Parliamentary dominance, 1980–88

1976	National Front	11,245,023	99.9	11,262,946	67.9
1981	National Front	12,235,515	99.9	12,252,128	73.2
1986	National Front	12,392,094	99.9	12,399,606	74.6

1976: Keesing's, 28115. *1981:* IPU 1980–81. *1986:* IPU 1985–86.

50. Germany, Federal Republic of
Parliamentary dominance, 1980–88

1980	Social Democratic Party	16,260,677	42.9	37,938,981	61.6
1983	Social Democratic Party	14,865,807	38.2	38,940,687	63.4
1987	Social Democratic Party	14,025,763	37.0	37,867,319	62.0

1980: IPU 1980–81. The data concern "second votes." *1983:* IPU 1982–83. The data concern "second votes." *1987:* IPU 1986–87; *Keesing's,* 35014. Second votes.

51. Ghana
Executive dominance, 1980–88

1979	Hilla Limann (PNP)	1,118,405	62.0	1,804,537	16.1

APPENDIX 1 (*continued*)

State/Election year/Largest party or elected presidential candidate	Votes for the largest party		Total votes	
	Number	% of total votes	Number	% of total population

A military coup on December 31, 1981, and Jerry Rawlings' military government 1981–88.
1979: Keesing's, 30444–47. The second round of the presidential election. *1981:* See Delury 1987; *Keesing's,* 31477–86; Chazan 1988.

52. Greece
Parliamentary dominance, 1980–88

1977	New Democracy	2,146,365	41.8	5,129,771	55.3
1981	PASOK	2,726,309	48.0	5,671,057	58.3
1985	PASOK	2,916,735	45.8	6,365,094	64.1

1977: IPU 1977–78. *1981:* IPU 1981–82. *1985:* IPU 1984–85.

53. Guatemala
Executive dominance, 1980–88

1978	Gen. Laugerud Garcia	269,979	42.3	638,405	9.7

A military coup on March 23, 1982, and military governments 1982–84.

1985	Cerezo Arévalo (PDCG)	1,133,517	68.4	1,657,000	20.8

1978: Keesing's, 29021. *1982:* See Banks 1988; Delury 1987. *1985:* Keesing's, 34285. The second round of the presidential election; cf. IPU 1985–86; Delury 1987.

54. Guinea
Executive dominance, 1980–88

1974	Sekou Touré (PDG)	2,432,129	100.0	2,432,129	56.4
1982	Sekou Touré (PDG)	3,630,700	100.0	3,630,708	64.1

A military coup on April 3, 1984, and military governments 1984–88.
1974: Africa Contemporary Record 1974–75, B 660; IPU 1974–75. *1982: Africa Research Bulletin,* 1982, 6458; cf. *Keesing's,* 31785. *1984:* Delury 1987; Banks 1988.

55. Guinea-Bissau
Executive dominance, 1980–88
A coup d'état on November 14, 1980, after which Guinea-Bissau was ruled by a predominantly military revolutionary council 1980–83.

1984	Gen. J.B. Vieira (PAIGC)	—	100.0	—	0.0

See Delury 1987; Banks 1988; *Keesing's,* 30785–86, 34162. General Vieira was elected by the National Assembly.

APPENDIX 1 (*continued*)

State/Election year/Largest party or elected presidential candidate	Votes for the largest party		Total votes	
	Number	% of total votes	Number	% of total population
56. Guyana				
Parliamentary dominance, 1980–88				
1980 People's National Congress	312,988	77.7	403,014	46.6
1985 People's National Congress	228,718	79.2	288,630	36.5
1980: IPU 1980–81. *1985:* IPU 1985–86.				
57. Haiti				
Executive dominance, 1980–88				
1971 Jean-Claude Duvalier	—	100.0	—	0.0
Military-civilian governments ruled the country 1986–88.				

1971: See Banks and Overstreet 1983; Delury 1987. J-C. Duvalier took the office of president for life on Apr. 22, 1971, after the death of his father. His designation as successor to his father had been confirmed by a national referendum of Jan. 31, 1971. *1986:* IPU 1985–86; Banks 1988. After Duvalier's flight from the country on Feb. 7, 1986, a military-civilian council took power. See also *Keesing's,* 35695–99, 36281–82; IPU 1987–88.

58. Honduras				
Executive dominance, 1980–88				
Coup d'état in 1972, and military governments 1971–80.				
1981 Suazo Cordova (PL)	636,392	53.9	1,180,060	30.9
1985 J.S. Azcona (PLH groups)	—	51.1	1,541,878	35.3

See Banks and Overstreet 1983. *1981: Statistical Abstract of Latin America* 1984, 731; cf. *Keesing's,* 31407. *1985:* IPU 1985–86; *Keesing's,* 34288–34289.

59. Hungary				
Parliamentary dominance, 1980–88				
1980 Patriotic People's Front	—	100.0	7,516,663	70.2
1985 Patriotic People's Front	—	100.0	6,716,387	63.1
1980: IPU 1979–80. *1985:* IPU 1984–85.				
60. Iceland				
Parliamentary dominance, 1980–88				
1979 Independence party	43,841	35.6	123,021	54.4
1983 Independence party	50,251	38.5	130,422	54.8
1987 Independence party	—	27.2	155,500	63.5

APPENDIX 1 (*continued*)

State/Election year/Largest party or elected presidential candidate	Votes for the largest party		Total votes	
	Number	% of total votes	Number	% of total population

1979: IPU 1979–80. *1983:* Mackie and Rose 1984, 338; cf. IPU 1982–83. *1987:* IPU 1986–87; *Electoral Studies* 1987, 6:300.

61. India
Parliamentary dominance, 1980–88

1980	Congress (I)	83,938,634	42.7	196,384,705	29.6
1984	Congress (I)	115,221,078	49.1	234,792,840	31.9

1980: IPU 1979–80; Weiner 1983, 150. *1984:* IPU 1984–85.

62. Indonesia
Concurrent powers, 1980–88 (25–75%)
Parliamentary elections:

1977	Golkar	39,750,096	62.1	63,988,344	46.8
1982	Golkar	48,334,724	64.3	75,126,306	49.1
1987	Golkar	62,783,680	73.1	85,885,000	50.5

Presidential elections:

1978	Gen. Suharto	920	100.0	920	0.0
1983	Gen. Suharto	920	100.0	920	0.0
1988	Gen. Suharto	—	100.0	—	0.0

1977: Keesing's, 28474. *1978: Keesing's,* 29072–73. *1982:* IPU 1981–82; *Keesing's,* 32255. *1983: Keesing's,* 32253. *1987:* IPU 1986–87. *1988: Keesing's,* 36024–25; Banks 1988.

63. Iran
Executive dominance, 1980–88

1980	Abol Hasan Bani-Sadr	10,747,345	77.9	13,797,757	36.0
1981	Hojatolislam Khamenei	16,007,972	97.0	16,490,627	41.7
1985	Hojatolislam Khamenei	12,203,870	85.7	14,244,630	32.2

1980: Keesing's, 30214. *1981: Keesing's,* 31510. *1985: Keesing's,* 33948.

64. Iraq
Executive dominance, 1980–88
General Saddam Hussein's military government in 1979–88.
See Delury 1987; Banks 1988. The Revolutionary Command Council designated Hussein president on July 12, 1979, for an indefinite period.

APPENDIX 1 (*continued*)

State/Election year/Largest party or elected presidential candidate	Votes for the largest party		Total votes	
	Number	% of total votes	Number	% of total population
65. Ireland				
Parliamentary dominance, 1980–88				
1977 Fianna Fail	811,615	50.6	1,603,027	49.0
1981 Fianna Fail	777,616	45.3	1,718,211	49.9
1982 Fianna Fail	763,313	45.2	1,688,720	48.5
1987 Fianna Fail	784,606	44.2	1,777,242	50.2

1977: Mackie and Rose 1978, 322. *1981:* IPU 1980–81. *1982:* IPU 1982–83. *1987:* IPU 1986–87; see also Farrell 1987.

66. Israel				
Parliamentary dominance, 1980–88				
1977 Unity (Likud)	583,968	33.4	1,747,820	48.4
1981 Likud Front	718,941	37.1	1,937,366	49.0
1984 Alignment	724,074	34.9	2,073,321	49.8
1988 Likud	709,305	31.1	2,283,123	51.9

1977: Mackie and Rose 1978, 323. *1981:* IPU 1980–81. *1984:* IPU 1984–85. *1988:* Diskin 1989.

67. Italy				
Parliamentary dominance, 1980–88				
1979 Christian Democratic party	14,007,594	38.3	36,566,585	65.0
1983 Christian Democratic party	12,145,800	32.9	37,071,018	65.2
1987 Christian Democratic party	13,132,000	34.1	38,473,000	67.0

1979: IPU 1978–79; Mackie and Rose 1980, 352. *1983:* IPU 1982–83. *1987:* IPU 1986–87; *Keesing's,* 35586–88; Hine 1987.

68. Ivory Coast				
Executive dominance, 1980–88				
1980 Félix Houphouet-Boigny	2,795,150	100.0	2,795,150	34.2
1985 Félix Houphouet-Boigny	3,584,000	100.0	3,584,000	36.5

1980: Keesing's, 30667. *1985: Keesing's,* 33963.

APPENDIX 1 (*continued*)

State/Election year/Largest party or elected presidential candidate	Votes for the largest party		Total votes	
	Number	% of total votes	Number	% of total population

69. Jamaica
Parliamentary dominance, 1980–88

1980 Jamaica Labour party	432,766	57.6	750,416	34.5
1983 Jamaica Labour party	—	(57.6)	—	(34.5)

1980: IPU 1980–81. *1983:* IPU 1983–84; *Keesing's,* 32724. The main opposition party (PNP) boycotted the election of 1983. Consequently, the JLP was opposed only by minor parties and independents in six of the 60 constituencies, and the JLP secured all seats, most of them without voting. However, because Jamaica's political system did not lose its democratic nature, I decided to keep the degree of competition and that of participation the same in the period 1983–88 as they were in the period 1980–82.

70. Japan
Parliamentary dominance, 1980–88

1980 Liberal Democratic party	24,084,140	44.6	54,010,121	50.5
1983 Liberal Democratic party	25,982,785	45.8	56,779,701	47.6
1986 Liberal Democratic party	29,875,501	49.4	60,448,610	49.7

1980: IPU 1979–80. *1983:* IPU 1983–84. *1986:* IPU 1986–87.

71. Jordan
Executive dominance, 1980–88
Executive power is vested in the king, who shares legislative power with a bicameral National Assembly. Political parties have been outlawed since 1963. Parliamentary elections were not held in the period 1980–88. See Delury 1987; Kurian 1987; Banks 1988.

72. Kampuchea
Parliamentary dominance, 1980–88
Kampuchea was invaded by Vietnamese troops in 1979 and was ruled by a People's Revolutionary Council in 1979–80.

1981 National Unity Front	—	100.0	3,389,000	49.6

See Delury 1987; Banks 1988, *Keesing's,* 31414. In 1986 the Assembly postponed the next general election until 1991.

APPENDIX 1 (*continued*)

State/Election year/Largest party or elected presidential candidate	Votes for the largest party		Total votes	
	Number	% of total votes	Number	% of total population

73. Kenya
Parliamentary dominance, 1980–88

1979	KANU	3,733,537	100.0	3,733,537	24.4
1983	KANU	3,331,047	100.0	3,331,047	17.7
1988	KANU	2,231,229	100.0	2,231,229	9.9

1979: IPU 1979–80. *1983:* IPU 1983–84; cf. *Keesing's,* 32544–46. *1988:* Africa South of the Sahara 1989.

74. Korea, People's Democratic Republic of
Parliamentary dominance, 1980–88

1977	Korean Workers' party	—	100.0	—	(50.0)
1982	Korean Workers' party	—	100.0	—	(50.0)
1986	Korean Workers' party	—	100.0	—	(50.0)

1977: IPU 1977–78; *Keesing's,* 31516. In the 1948 election, 49% of the population voted (Blaustein and Flantz 1973, Korean People's Democratic Republic, 9). It is assumed that the degree of participation has remained the same. *1982:* IPU 1981–82. Data on the number of votes cast are not available. *1986:* IPU 1986–87. Data on the number of votes are not available.

75. Korea, Republic of
Concurrent powers, 1980–88 (25–75%)
Parliamentary elections:

1978	New Democratic party	4,861,204	32.8	14,812,443	40.1
1981	Democratic Justice party	5,776,624	35.6	16,207,325	41.9
1985	Democratic Justice party	7,040,811	35.2	19,974,643	48.5
1988	Democratic Justice party	6,670,494	34.0	19,642,040	46.1

Presidential elections:

1980	Chun Doo Hwan	2,525	99.4	2,540	0.0
1981	Chun Doo Hwan (DJP)	4,755	90.2	5,271	0.0
1987	Roh Tae Woo (DJP)	8,282,738	35.9	23,070,748	54.8

1978: IPU 1978–79. *1980: Korea Annual* 1983, 42–43; Banks and Overstreet 1983, 277. Chun was elected president by the National Conference for

APPENDIX 1 (*continued*)

State/Election year/Largest party or elected presidential candidate	Votes for the largest party		Total votes	
	Number	% of total votes	Number	% of total population

Unification on August 27, 1980. *1981:* IPU 1980–81; *Korea Annual* 1983, 42–43; *Keesing's:* 30997–98. *1985:* IPU 1984–85. *1987: Keesing's,* 35768–69. *1988:* IPU 1987–88.

76. *Kuwait*
Concurrent powers, 1980–88 (25–75%)
Parliamentary elections:

1981	Independents	37,500	100.0	37,500	2.6
1985	Independents	47,745	100.0	47,745	2.8

According to the 1962 constitution, executive power is vested in the emir. See Delury 1987; Banks 1988. *1981:* IPU 1980–81. The previous National Assembly was dissolved in 1976. *1985:* IPU 1984–85.

77. *Laos*
Executive dominance, 1980–88
Laos was ruled by the Lao People's Revolutionary party 1980–88.
See Delury 1987; Kurian 1987; Banks 1988.

78. *Lebanon*
Parliamentary dominance, 1980–88

1972	Christians	—	54.5	(515,000)	(17.4)

See IPU 1971–72; 1987–88; McDowall 1984; Delury 1987; Banks 1988. The data on the largest party's share refer to the distribution of the seats in the National Assembly between Muslims and Christians. "Christians" are regarded as the largest "party" because the cleavage between Muslims and Christians has been the most important political cleavage in Lebanese politics since the 1920s. Because of the civil war that started in 1975, it was not possible to elect a new parliament in 1976. Since then the term of the legislature has been extended.

79. *Lesotho*
Parliamentary dominance, 1980–88
Prime Minister Jonathan (BNP) usurped power in January 1970 and ruled without an elected legislature in 1970–84.

1985	Basotho National party	—	100.0	—	0.0

A military coup d'état on January 20, 1986, and military governments in 1986–88.
1970: See Banks and Overstreet 1983. *1985:* IPU 1985–86. Opposition groups refused to run against the ruling BNP. Consequently, the 60 BNP candidates

APPENDIX 1 (*continued*)

State/Election year/Largest party or elected presidential candidate	Votes for the largest party		Total votes	
	Number	% of total votes	Number	% of total population

were declared elected on the nomination day (Aug. 14). *1986:* See IPU 1985–86; *Africa Contemporary Record* 1986–87, B 657–662; Banks 1988.

80. Liberia
Executive dominance, 1980–84
A military coup d'état on April 12, 1980, and Doe's military government in 1980–84.
Concurrent powers, 1985–88 (50–50%)
Parliamentary elections:

1985	Nat. Dem. Party of Liberia	—	(80.0)	—	(23.7)
1986	Nat. Dem. Party of Liberia	—	(86.0)	—	(23.7)

Presidential elections:

1985	Gen. S.K. Doe (NDPL)	264,362	50.9	519,040	23.7

See Delury 1987; IPU 1985–86; Banks 1988; *Keesing's,* 34146–47, 34979–80. In fact, Liberia's governmental system is presidential, but because the NDPL's high percentage of the seats in the House of Representatives indicates President Doe's dominant position in Liberia much better than the results of the 1985 presidential election, the results of parliamentary elections are taken into account, too. The data of 1986 refer to the composition of the House of Representatives after the by-elections in Dec. 1986.

81. Libya
Executive dominance, 1980–88
Col. Gaddafy's government ruled Libya 1980–88.
See Delury 1987; Banks 1988.

82. Luxemburg
Parliamentary dominance, 1980–88

1979	Christian Social party	1,049,393	34.5	175,808	48.4
1984	Christian Social party	1,149,310	34.9	177,300	48.4

1979: IPU 1978–79. Each elector has a multiple number of votes. *1984: Keesing's,* 33298; *Electoral Studies* 1984, 3:319; cf. IPU 1983–84.

83. Madagascar
Executive dominance, 1980–88

1975	Didier Ratsiraka	3,213,146	94.7	3,394,400	44.2

APPENDIX 1 (*continued*)

State/Election year/Largest party or elected presidential candidate	Votes for the largest party		Total votes	
	Number	% of total votes	Number	% of total population
1982 Didier Ratsiraka	3,112,156	80.0	3,890,000	42.3

1975: Keesing's, 27558. 1982: Keesing's, 32060–61.

84. Malawi
Executive dominance, 1980–88

1971 Hastings K. Banda (MCP)	—	100.0	—	0.0

1971: Banks and Overstreet 1983. On July 6, 1971, President Banda, originally elected for a five-year term by the National Assembly, was sworn in as president for life.

85. Malaysia
Parliamentary dominance, 1980–88

1978 National Front	1,987,907	57.2	3,473,430	26.9
1982 National Front	2,522,079	60.5	4,165,697	28.7
1986 National Front	2,649,238	57.3	4,625,272	28.7

1978: IPU 1978–79. *1982:* IPU 1981–82. *1986:* IPU 1986–87; see also Khai Leong Ho 1988.

86. Mali
Executive dominance, 1980–88

1979 Gen. Moussa Traoré	3,298,477	100.0	3,298,477	47.8
1985 Gen. Moussa Traoré	—	100.0	(3,500,000)	42.6

1979: Keesing's, 29789. 1985: Delury 1987; *Africa Research Bulletin,* July 15, 1985; *Europa Year Book* 1987. The number of voters was 3,620,474 in the 1988 parliamentary election (IPU 1987–88).

87. Malta
Parliamentary dominance, 1980–88

1976 Labour party	105,854	51.5	205,440	62.3
1981 Labour party	109,990	49.1	224,151	61.6
1987 Nationalist party	119,721	50.9	235,168	61.0

1976: IPU 1976–77. *1981:* IPU 1981–82. *1987:* IPU 1986–87; Hove 1987.

88. Mauritania
Executive dominance, 1980–88
A military coup in 1978, and military governments 1978–88.
See Delury 1987; Banks 1988; *Keesing's,* 33449–50.

APPENDIX 1 (continued)

State/Election year/Largest party or elected presidential candidate	Votes for the largest party		Total votes	
	Number	% of total votes	Number	% of total population
89. Mauritius				
Parliamentary dominance, 1980–88				
1976 MMM	471,401	40.1	(393,000)	43.7
1982 MMM/PSM	907,087	62.0	(488,000)	49.5
1983 MSM/Labour/PMSD alliance	—	51.5	464,465	46.8
1987 MSM/Labour/PMSD alliance	—	49.8	543,500	54.3

1976, 1982: Africa Contemporary Record 1982–83, B 228; cf. Africa Contemporary Record 1976–77, B 280; IPU 1976–77, 1981–82; Simmons 1982, 196; Keesing's, 28189, 31763; Nohlen and Nuscheler 1982 Vol. 5, 276. 1983: Delury 1987; Keesing's, 32542–43; IPU 1983–84. 1988: Africa Research Bulletin, Oct. 15, 1987; Europa Year Book 1988; IPU 1987–88.

90. Mexico				
Executive dominance, 1980–88				
1976 Lopes Portillo (PRI)	17,695,043	94.4	18,750,000	30.2
1982 Madrid Hurtado (PRI)	16,700,000	74.4	22,446,000	30.7
1988 Carlos Salinas (PRI)	—	50.7	—	(30.0)

1976: Keesing's, 27915. 1982: Keesing's, 31730. 1988: Keesing's, 36368– 69. Salinas secured 50.7% of the votes cast.

91. Mongolia				
Parliamentary dominance, 1980–88				
1977 MPRP	694,000	100.0	694,000	45.9
1981 MPRP	792,000	100.0	792,000	46.3
1986 MPRP	929,393	100.0	929,400	47.9

1977: IPU 1976–77; Keesing's, 28606. 1981: IPU 1980–81; Keesing's, 31026. 1986: IPU 1985–86; Keesing's, 34678.

92. Morocco				
Concurrent powers, 1980–88 (25–75%)				
Parliamentary elections:				
1977 Independents	2,254,297	44.7	5,045,363	27.5
1984 Union constitutionelle (UC)	1,101,502	24.8	4,443,004	20.8

Executive and many other powers are highly concentrated in the hands of the king, although legislative power is nominally vested in the Chamber of Representatives.

APPENDIX 1 (*continued*)

State/Election year/Largest party or elected presidential candidate	Votes for the largest party		Total votes	
	Number	% of total votes	Number	% of total population

See Delury 1987; Banks 1988. *1977:* IPU 1976–77; *Keesing's,* 28477. *1984:* IPU 1984–85; *Keesing's,* 33247.

93. Mosambique
Parliamentary dominance, 1980–88

1977	Frelimo	—	100.0	—	0.0
1986	Frelimo	—	100.0	—	0.0

1977: IPU 1977–78; *Africa Reserach Bulletin* 1977, 4669; Delury 1987. Indirect elections. *1986:* IPU 1986–87; *Africa Contemporary Record* 1986–87, B 682–683.

94. Nepal
Concurrent powers, 1980–88 (25–75%)
Parliamentary elections:

1981	Independents	—	100.0	3,885,723	25.9
1986	Independents	—	100.0	5,197,953	30.3

Executive power is vested in the king.
See Jha 1981; Kurian 1987; Delury 1987; Banks 1988. *1981:* Jha 1981, 16; cf. IPU 1980–81. *1986:* IPU 1985–86; *Keesing's,* 34423.

95. Netherlands
Parliamentary dominance, 1980–88

1977	Labour party	2,813,793	33.8	8,317,612	60.0
1981	CDA	2,677,259	30.8	8,689,263	61.0
1982	Labour party	2,501,665	30.3	8,228,582	57.5
1986	CDA	3,170,081	34.6	9,127,335	62.7

1977: Mackie and Rose 1978, 324. *1981:* IPU 1980–81. *1982:* IPU 1982–83. *1986:* IPU 1985–86.

96. New Zealand
Parliamentary dominance, 1980–88

1978	Labour party	691,076	40.4	1,710,173	54.8
1981	Labour party	702,630	39.0	1,801,303	57.6
1984	Labour party	829,154	43.0	1,929,201	59.7
1987	Labour party	878,526	48.0	1,831,902	56.3

1978: IPU 1978–79. *1981:* IPU 1981–82. *1984:* IPU 1984–85. *1987:* IPU 1987–88.

APPENDIX 1 (*continued*)

State/Election year/Largest party or elected presidential candidate	Votes for the largest party		Total votes	
	Number	% of total votes	Number	% of total population

97. Nicaragua
Executive dominance, 1980–88
The Sandinista National Liberation Front's (FSLN) provisional government in
  1979–83.
1984   Daniel Ortega (FSLN)   735,967   67.0   1,098,933   34.7
See Banks 1988. *1984:* Delury 1987; cf. IPU 1984–85; *Keesing's,* 33269–70.

98. Niger
Executive dominance, 1980–88
A military coup in 1974, and military governments 1974–88.
See Delury 1987; Kurian 1987; Banks 1988.

99. Nigeria
Executive dominance, 1980–88
1979   Shehu Shagari (NPN)   5,688,857   33.8   16,846,633   21.6
A military coup on December 31, 1983, and military governments 1984–88.
1979: Keesing's, 30621–27. *1983:* See *Keesing's,* 32841–42; Banks 1988;
  Diamond 1988b.

100. Norway
Parliamentary dominance, 1980–88
1977   Labour party   972,434   42.3   2,301,110   56.9
1981   Labour party   914,749   36.7   2,495,076   60.9
1985   Labour party   1,061,712   40.8   2,601,817   62.6
1977: Mackie and Rose 1978, 325. *1981:* IPU 1981–82. *1985:* IPU 1985–86.

101. Oman
Executive dominance, 1980–88
Legislative and executive powers are vested in the sultan, who rules with the
  assistance of a cabinet of personal aids and a nominated assembly. See Delury
  1987; Kurian 1987; Banks 1988.

102. Pakistan
Executive dominance, 1980–87
A military coup d'état in 1977, and Gen. Zia ul-Haq's military government
  1977–87.
Parliamentary dominance, 1988
1988   Pakistan People's party   —   (39.0)   —   (20.0)

APPENDIX 1 (*continued*)

State/Election year/Largest party or elected presidential candidate	Votes for the largest party		Total votes	
	Number	% of total votes	Number	% of total population

See Delury 1987; Banks 1988; *Keesing's*, 33339–40. *1988:* Rahman 1988. The percentage of the seats in the National Assembly. Turnout was only 40%.

103. Panama
Executive dominance, 1980–88

1978	Aristides Royo	452	89.5	505	0.0
1984	Artido Barletta (PRD)	300,748	48.8	615,759	28.9

General Noriega usurped power in 1988.
1978: Keesing's, 29327–28. The National Assembly elected Aristides Royo president for a six-year term. *1984: Keesing's*, 33150–51, 33975; Delury 1987. *1988: Keesing's*, 35815–19; Banks 1988.

104. Papua New Guinea
Parliamentary dominance, 1980–88

1977	Pangu Pati	—	(36.0)	(928,000)	33.0
1982	Pangu Pati	—	34.0	1,184,500	38.3
1987	Pangu Pati	—	14.7	1,354,468	38.4

1977: Papua New Guinea Newsletter, Week ending 24 June, 1977; Premdas 1978; Chronicle 1977–78; *Keesing's*, 28651. Pangu Pati won 39 out of 109 seats. *1982:* IPU 1982–83; *Keesing's*, 32373–75. Each voter had to cast two votes. Therefore, it is assumed that the number of electors was 50% of the number of valid votes (2,369,116). *1987: Europa Year Book* 1988; IPU 1987–88. The number of valid votes was 2,708,937.

105. Paraguay
Executive dominance, 1980–88

1978	Gen. A. Stroessner (Colorado)	890,361	89.6	993,547	33.4
1983	Gen. A. Stroessner (Colorado)	919,533	90.0	1,021,597	29.4
1988	Gen. A. Stroessner (Colorado)	1,186,693	89.6	1,324,956	33.5

1978: Keesing's, 28974. *1983: Keesing's*, 32189. *1988: Keesing's*, 35887.

106. Peru
Executive dominance, 1980–88

1980	Belaunde Terry (AP)	—	45.4	4,030,000	23.3
1985	Alan Garcia (APRA)	3,457,030	53.4	6,469,200	32.8

1980: Keesing's, 30545–46. *1985: Keesing's*, 33836.

APPENDIX 1 (*continued*)

State/Election year/Largest party or elected presidential candidate	Votes for the largest party		Total votes	
	Number	% of total votes	Number	% of total population

107. Philippines

Executive dominance, 1980–88

President Marcos declared martial law throughout the Philippines on September 23, 1972, and remained in power without elections until the 1981 election.

1981 F.E. Marcos (NSM)	18,309,360	88.0	20,806,000	42.0
1986 Cory Aquino (UNIDO)	—	(53.0)	(20,098,000)	36.2

See Banks and Overstreet 1983. *1981: Keesing's*, 31139. *1986: Keesing's*, 34299–02; Jackson 1989. Exact results of the 1986 presidential election are not known. Mrs. Aquino was sworn in as president on Feb. 25, three weeks after the election, and Marcos fled the country.

108. Poland

Parliamentary dominance, 1980–88

1980 National Unity Front	24,683,056	99.5	24,802,612	69.7
1985 Patriotic Front	—	(99.5)	20,489,086	55.1

1980: IPU 1979–80. *1985:* IPU 1985–86. Local lists; cf. *Keesing's*, 33954.

109. Portugal

Concurrent powers, 1980–88 (50–50%)

Parliamentary elections:

1980 Democratic Alliance	2,706,667	46.0	5,888,733	59.6
1983 Socialist party	2,061,305	37.1	5,560,925	55.5
1985 Social Democrats (PSD)	1,732,288	30.6	5,653,600	55.2
1987 Social Democrats (PSD)	2,850,84	51.3	5,552,690	53.4

Presidential elections:

1980 Gen. Eanes	3,248,837	56.4	5,756,988	58.2
1986 Mario Soares (PS)	3,015,350	50.8	5,935,294	

1980: IPU 1980–81; Mackie and Rose 1981, 323. *1983:* Mackie and Rose 1984, 340. *1985:* IPU 1985–86. *1986: Keesing's*, 34311–12; *Europa Year Book* 1988. *1987:* IPU 1987–88.

110. Qatar

Executive dominance, 1980–88

Legislative and executive powers are in the hands of the emir and his relatives. See Delury 1987; Banks 1988.

APPENDIX 1 (*continued*)

State/Election year/Largest party or elected presidential candidate	Votes for the largest party		Total votes	
	Number	% of total votes	Number	% of total population

111. Romania
Parliamentary dominance, 1980–88

1980	Front of Democracy	15,398,443	98.5	15,629,054	70.4
1985	Front of Democracy	15,375,522	97.7	15,732,095	68.3

1980: IPU 1979–80. *1985:* IPU 1984–85.

112. Rwanda
Executive dominance, 1980–88

1978	Gen. J. Habyarimana	—	99.0	(2,054,813)	42.8
1983	Gen. J. Habyarimana (MRND)	—	(100.0)	(3,364,592)	58.4
1988	Gen. J. Habyarimana	2,701,682	100.0	2,701,756	40.3

1978: Keesing's, 29487; *Africa Contemporary Record* 1978–79, B 353–354; *Année Africaine* 1978, 225. The number of voters was 2,054,813 in the 1978 referendum. *1983: Africa Research Bulletin,* Dec. 1–31, 1983; IPU 1983–84. The number of valid votes was 3,364,592 in the 1983 legislative election. *1988: Africa Research Bulletin,* Jan. 15, 1989; cf. *Keesing's,* 36482.

113. Saudi Arabia
Executive dominance, 1980–88
Legislative and executive powers are in the hands of the king and the ruling dynasty. See Delury 1987; Banks 1988.

114. Senegal
Executive dominance, 1980–88

1978	Leopold Senghor (PS)	800,882	81.8	978,876	18.2
1983	Abdou Diouf (PS)	908,879	83.4	1,089,075	17.2
1988	Abdou Diouf (PS)	828,301	73.2	1,131,468	16.6

1978: Africa Contemporary Record 1978–79, B 758. *1983: Keesing's,* 32179; IPU 1982–83. *1988: Africa Research Bulletin,* April 15, 1988; *Europa Year Book* 1988.

115. Sierra Leone
Executive dominance, 1980–88

1978	Siaka Stevens (APC)	—	100.0	—	0.0
1985	Maj.-Gen. J.S. Momoh (APC)	2,784,591	99.9	2,788,687	77.4

1978: Banks and Overstreet 1983; *Keesing's,* 29124. After the adoption of the new constitution in 1978, Siaka Stevens was formally sworn in for a seven-

APPENDIX 1 (*continued*)

State/Election year/Largest party or elected presidential candidate	Votes for the largest party		Total votes	
	Number	% of total votes	Number	% of total population

year term as the first president under the new constitution. Originally he was elected president by the House of Representatives in 1971. *1985: Africa Contemporary Record* 1985–86, B 162.

116. Singapore
Parliamentary dominance, 1980–88

1980 People's Action Party	494,268	77.7	636,452	26.3
1984 People's Action Party	568,310	64.8	876,596	34.6
1988 People's Action Party	848,029	61.8	1,372,200	52.0

1980: IPU 1980–81. *1984:* IPU 1984–85. *1988: The Far East* and *Australasia* 1989; *Keesing's,* 36352.

117. Solomon Islands
Parliamentary dominance, 1980–88

1980 United party	—	(42.0)	58,136	25.8
1984 People's Alliance party	—	23.0	—	
1988 People's Action party	—	(37.0)	—	(25.0)

1980: IPU 1980–81. The largest party won 16 out of 38 seats (42%). *1984:* IPU 1984–85; *Keesing's,* 33336–37. Data on the number of valid votes were not available. *1988: Keesing's,* 36465. The largest party won 14 out of 38 seats (37%). Data on the number of valid votes were not available.

118. Somalia
Executive dominance, 1980–88

1980 Gen. Siad Barre	—	100.0	—	0.0
1986 Gen. Siad Barre	4,865,200	99.9	4,869,120	(40.0)

1980: Banks 1988. Gen. Barre was acclaimed president for a six-year term by the People's Assembly. *1986: Keesing's,* 35042. According to this source, the number of voters was higher than the population of Somalia in 1986 (4,760,000). Therefore, the reported number of voters cannot be correct. I estimate that the number of voters was hardly higher than 40% of the population.

119. South Africa
Parliamentary dominance, 1980–88

1977 National party	689,108	66.1	1,042,501	3.9
1981 National party	777,558	57.0	1,364,967	4.7
1987 National party	1,075,642	52.7	2,042,254	6.0

1977: IPU 1977–78. *1981:* IPU 1980–81. *1987:* IPU 1986–87; cf. Du Toit 1987.

APPENDIX 1 (continued)

State/Election year/Largest party or elected presidential candidate	Votes for the largest party		Total votes	
	Number	% of total votes	Number	% of total population

120. Spain
Parliamentary dominance, 1980–88

1979	UCD	6,268,593	35.0	17,929,011	48.2
1982	PSC-PSOE	10,127,392	48.7	20,807,181	54.8
1986	PSOE	8,887,345	44.3	20,057,740	51.9

1979: IPU 1978–79. *1982:* IPU 1982–83. *1986:* IPU 1986–87.

121. Sri Lanka
Concurrent powers, 1980–88 (50–50%)
Parliamentary elections:

1977	United National party	3,148,651	51.5	6,111,579	43.8
1982	United National party	3,141,223	54.7	5,747,206	37.8

Presidential elections:

1978	Junius Jayewardene (UNP)	128	100.0	128	0.0
1982	Junius Jayewardene (UNP)	3,436,317	52.9	6,495,874	42.7
1988	R. Premadasa (UNP)	2,569,199	50.4	5,094,778	30.9

1977: Jupp 1978, 371; cf. Phadnis 1989. *1978: Far Eastern Economic Review.*
Asia 1979 Yearbook, 1979, 294; *Keesing's,* 28981. Jayewardene was elected president on Feb. 4, 1978, through an amendment to the 1972 constitution. It was adopted by the Assembly on Oct. 4, 1977, by 128 votes to 0. *1982: Keesing's,* 32077–78; *World Elections on File* 1987. Parliament voted on Nov. 5, 1982, by 142 votes to 4 to prolong the parliamentary term until Aug. 1989, subject to confirmation in a national referendum. In the referendum 54.7% voted yes. See also Delury 1987. *1988: Keesing's,* 36394.

122. Sudan
Executive dominance, 1980–85

1977	J.M. Numayri (SSU)	—	99.1	5,700,000	33.6
1983	J.M. Numayri (SSU)	—	99.6	—	(33.0)

Military coup in April 1985.
Parliamentary dominance, 1986–88

1986	Umma party	—	(38.0)	(4,200,000)	18.9

1977: Keesing's, 28427; *Facts on File 1977,* 417. Numayri was reelected by a referendum. *1983: Keesing's,* 32292. Data on the number of votes are not available. It is assumed that the degree of participation was the same as in 1977. *1985:* Delury 1987; *Keesing's,* 33700. *1986:* IPU 1985–86; *Keesing's,* 34530–31; *Africa Research Bulletin,* May 15, 1986; Banks 1988. The Umma party secured 100 out of 260 seats (38%).

APPENDIX 1 (*continued*)

State/Election year/Largest party or elected presidential candidate	Votes for the largest party		Total votes	
	Number	% of total votes	Number	% of total population

123. Suriname
Executive dominance, 1980–86
A military coup in 1980, and Lt.-Col. Bouterse's government in 1980–86.
Parliamentary dominance, 1987–88

1987	Front for Democracy and Development	—	85.0	181,000	47.0

See Kurian 1987; Banks 1988. *1987: Keesing's,* 35758–59; IPU 1987–88.

124. Swaziland
Executive dominance, 1980–88
Executive and legislative powers are in the hands of the king and his relatives.
See *Commonwealth Fact Sheet.* Swaziland, 1979; *Keesing's,* 32485–86, 32664; Delury 1987; Banks 1988.

125. Sweden
Parliamentary dominance, 1980–88

1979	SDP	2,356,234	43.2	5,448,638	65.7
1982	SDP	2,533,250	45.6	5, 554,394	66.7
1985	SDP	2,491,551	44.7	5,571,022	66.7
1988	SDP	2,321,826	43.2	5,373,719	64.0

1979: IPU 1979–80. *1982:* IPU 1982–83. *1985:* IPU 1985–86. *1988:* Sveriges officiella statistik. Allmänna valen 1988, 8.

126. Switzerland
Parliamentary dominance, 1980–88

1979	Social Democratic Party	—	24.9	1,833,205	28.8
1983	Radical-Democratic Party	454,268	23.2	1,959,895	30.1
1987	Radical-Democratic Party	440,384	22.8	1,934,457	29.6

1979: IPU 1979–80; *Keesing's,* 32642. *1983:* IPU 1983–84; *Keesing's,* 32642. *1987:* IPU 1987–88.

127. Syria
Executive dominance, 1980–88

1978	Hafez al-Assad	3,975,729	99.6	3,991,695	49.0
1985	Hafez al-Assad	6,520,000	100.0	6,520,428	63.5

1978: Keesing's, 28864. *1985: Keesing's,* 33614.

APPENDIX 1 (*continued*)

State/Election year/Largest party or elected presidential candidate	Votes for the largest party		Total votes	
	Number	% of total votes	Number	% of total population

128. Tanzania
Executive dominance, 1980–88

1980 Julius K. Nyerere (CCM)	—	93.0	5,417,099	29.2
1985 Ali Hassan Mwinyi (CCM)	4,778,114	95.7	4,993,740	23.0

1980: IPU 1980–81; *Keesing's,* 30690. The number of valid votes in the National Assembly elections. *1985: Keesing's,* 34148.

129. Thailand
Concurrent powers, 1980–88 (50–50%)
Parliamentary elections:

1979 Social Action party	—	(27.2)	8,936,527	19.4
1983 Social Action party	—	(28.4)	11,797,167	23.8
1986 Democrat party	—	28.9	15,104,000	28.7
1988 Thai Nation	—	24.4	—	(28.0)

Executive power is in the hands of the king and the armed forces.
See Kurian 1987; Banks 1988. *1979:* IPU 1978–79; *Keesing's,* 29818–19. Social Action Party won 82 out of 301 seats (27.2%). The distribution of votes by parties is not known. *1983:* IPU 1982–83; *Keesing's,* 32743–44. SAP won 92 out of 324 seats (28.4%). The distribution of votes by parties is not known. *1986:* IPU 1986–87; *Keesing's,* 36149. *1988: Keesing's,* 36149; *The Far East and Australasia* 1989. Turnout was 63.5% in 1988 and 61.0% in 1986. See also Samudavanija 1989.

130. Togo
Executive dominance, 1980–88

1979 Gen. G. Eyadema (RPT)	1,286,391	100.0	1,286,660	52.1
1986 Gen. G. Eyadema (RPT)	—	100.0	1,720,654	56.4

1979: Keesing's, 30300; Banks 1988. *1986: Africa Contemporary Record* 1986–87, B 155.

131. Trinidad and Tobago
Parliamentary dominance, 1980–88

1976 People's National Movement	176,890	53.0	333,755	30.5
1981 People's National Movement	215,387	53.8	399,964	35.9

APPENDIX 1 (continued)

State/Election year/Largest party or elected presidential candidate	Votes for the largest party		Total votes	
	Number	% of total votes	Number	% of total population
1986 National Alliance for Reconstruction	—	67.3	555,600	46.2

1976: Keesing's, 28097; *Latin America* 1976. A Facts on File Publication, 1977, 198. *1981:* IPU 1981–82. *1986:* IPU 1986–87; *Keesing's*, 35195.

132. Tunisia
Executive dominance, 1980–88

1974 Habib Bourguiba (PSD)	—	100.0	—	0.0

The prime minister, Gen. Ben Ali, deposed President Bourguiba on Nov. 7, 1987.
See Delury 1987; *Keesing's*, 26822–23, 26980, 35801–03; Banks 1988. The National Assembly had elected Bourguiba president for life on Nov. 2, 1974.

133. Turkey
Executive dominance, 1980–82
A military coup on Sept. 12, 1980, and the military government of Gen. Evren 1980–81.

1982 Den. Kenan Evren	—	91.5	—	(36.6)

Concurrent powers, 1983–88 (50–50%)
Parliamentary elections:

1983 Motherland party	7,823,827	45.1	17,328,735	36.6
1987 Motherland party	8,704,335	36.3	23,971,629	46.7

Presidential elections:

1982 Gen. Kenan Evren	—	91.5	—	(36.6)

See Banks and Overstreet 1983. *1982: Keesing's*, 32089–93; Özbudun 1989. The results of the referendum of Nov. 7, 1982, on the new constitution, which made Gen. Evren president of the republic for a period of seven years. It is assumed that the level of participation was about the same as in the 1983 parliamentary elections. *1983:* IPU 1983–84; *Keesing's*, 32581. *1987:* IPU 1987–88; *Keesing's*, 35909; Özbudun 1989.

134. Uganda
Parliamentary dominance, 1980–88

1980 Uganda People's Congress	1,971,779	47.2	4,179,111	31.9

A military coup d'état on July 27, 1985, and military governments 1985–88.
1980: IPU 1980–81; *Keesing's*, 30711–13. *1985: Keesing's*, 34023, 34535–39, 36419; Kokole and Mazrui 1988.

APPENDIX 1 (*continued*)

State/Election year/Largest party or elected presidential candidate	Votes for the largest party		Total votes	
	Number	% of total votes	Number	% of total population

135. USSR
Parliamentary dominance, 1980–88

1979	Communist party and allies	174,734,459	99.9	174,920,221	66.4
1984	Communist party and allies	183,897,279	99.9	184,005,736	66.9

1979: IPU 1978–79. *1984: Helsingin Sanomat,* March 7, 1984; IPU 1983–84.

136. *United Arab Emirates*
Executive dominance, 1980–88
Legislative and executive powers are vested in the Supreme Council, which is composed of the rulers of the seven Emirates. See Delury 1987; Banks 1988.

137. *United Kingdom*
Parliamentary dominance, 1980–88

1979	Conservative party	13,697,753	43.9	31,220,790	55.9
1983	Conservative party	13,012,602	42.4	30,670,895	54.4
1987	Conservative party	13,763,134	42.3	32,536,205	57.6

1979: IPU 1978–78. *1983:* IPU 1982–83. *1987:* IPU 1986–87.

138. *United States*
Executive dominance, 1980–88

1980	Ronald Reagan (Rep.)	43,904,000	50.7	86,515,000	38.0
1984	Ronald Reagan (Rep.)	54,455,000	58.8	92,653,000	39.1
1988	George Bush (Rep.)	47,946,422	53.9	88,962,851	36.2

1980, 1984: U.S. Bureau of the Census, *Statistical Abstract of the United States* 1987, Table 397. *1988: Congressional Quarterly Weekly Report,* Vol. 46, No 46, Nov. 12, 1988.

139. *Uruguay*
Executive dominance, 1980–88
Military governments in 1980–83.

1984	J.M. Sanguinetti (Colorado)	744,701	39.5	1,886,362	63.1

See Banks and Overstreet 1983; Delury 1987. *1984:* Panizza 1985, 270; cf. *Keesing's,* 33515.

140. *Venezuela*
Executive dominance, 1980–88

APPENDIX 1 (continued)

State/Election year/Largest party or elected presidential candidate	Votes for the largest party		Total votes	
	Number	% of total votes	Number	% of total population
1978 Herrera Campins (COPEI)	2,469,042	46.6	5,294,925	37.6
1983 Jaime Lusinchi (AD)	3,733,220	56.8	6,571,400	40.1
1988 Andres Perez (AD)	3,879,024	52.9	7,331,387	39.6

1978: Statistical Abstract of Latin America 1981, 546; *Europa Year Book* 1982 Vol. II, 1777.
1983: Keesing's, 32733. *1988: Keesing's,* 36423; cf. *Europa Year Book* 1988.

141. Vietnam
Parliamentary dominance, 1980–88

1976	National United Front	—	100.0	22,895,611	46.5
1981	Vietnam Fatherland Front	—	100.0	—	(46.0)
1987	Vietnam Fatherland Front	—	100.0	—	(46.0)

1976: Chronicle 1976–77; *The Statesman's Year Book* 1980–81, 1586. *1981:* IPU 1980–81; *Keesing's,* 31589. Data on the number of voters are not available. *1987:* IPU 1986–87; *Europa Year Book* 1988. Data on the number of voters are not available.

142. Yemen Arab Republic
Executive dominance, 1980–88

1978	Col. Ali Abdullah Salih	—	100.0	—	0.0
1983	Col. Ali Abdullah Salih	—	100.0	—	0.0
1988	Col. Ali Abdullah Salih	—	100.0	—	0.0

1978: Banks and Overstreet 1983. On July 17, 1978, the Constituent People's Assembly elected Col. Salih president of the Republic. *1983: Keesing's,* 32535. President Salih was reelected unopposed for a second five-year term by the Constituent People's Assembly. *1988: Keesing's,* 36176. Salih was reelected by the Consultative Council for a third five-year term.

143. Yemen, People's Democratic Republic of
Parliamentary dominance, 1980–88

1978	Yemen Socialist party	596,787	100.0	596,787	32.2
1986	Yemen Socialist party	725,568	100.0	725,568	31.0

1978: IPU 1978–79. *1986:* IPU 1986–87; Delury 1987.

APPENDIX 1 (*continued*)

State/Election year/Largest party or elected presidential candidate	Votes for the largest party Number	Votes for the largest party % of total votes	Total votes Number	Total votes % of total population
144. Yugoslavia				
Parliamentary dominance, 1980–88				
1978 Socialist Alliance	—	100.0	13,112,262	59.7
1982 Socialist Alliance	—	100.0	—	(59.0)
1986 Socialist Alliance	—	100.0	—	(59.0)

1978: IPU 1977–78. The number of registered voters who took part in the process of elections. The members of the Assembly of the Socialist Federal Republic of Yugoslavia are elected by indirect elections. *1982:* IPU 1981–82. It is assumed that the level of participation was the same as in 1978. *1986:* IPU 1985–86. It is assumed that the level of participation was the same as in 1978.

145. Zaire				
Executive dominance, 1980–88				
1977 Mobutu (MRP)	10,692,737	100.0	10,692,737	44.5
1984 Mobutu (MRP)	—	99.2	15,000,000	50.5

1977: Keesing's, 28825. *1984: Keesing's,* 33268.

146. Zambia				
Executive dominance, 1980–88				
1978 Kenneth Kaunda (UNIP)	875,000	80.0	1,093,000	20.0
1983 Kenneth Kaunda (UNIP)	1,424,700	95.2	1,497,000	24.0
1988 Kenneth Kaunda (UNIP)	1,450,672	95.6	1,517,323	20.8

1978: Africa Contemporary Record 1978–79, B 452. *1983: Keesing's,* 32551; cf. IPU 1983–84; *Africa Research Bulletin* 1983, 7005–06. *1988: Africa Research Bulletin,* Nov. 15, and Dec. 15, 1988.

147. Zimbabwe				
Parliamentary dominance, 1980–88				
1980 ZANU	1,668,992	62.6	2,665,931	37.6
1985 ZANU	2,233,320	76.3	2,927,308	34.9

1980: IPU 1979–80. *1985:* IPU 1986–87.

APPENDIX 2

Statistical Data on Urban Population, Nonagricultural Population, Students, and Literates for 147 States in or Around 1980

State	Urban Population %	Nonagricul. Population %	Students per 100,000 inhabitants	Literates 15+ %
1 Afghanistan	15	22	80	20
2 Albania	37	40	533	70
3 Algeria	44	50	425	45
4 Angola	21	42	28	30
5 Argentina	82	87	1741	95
6 Australia	89	94	2203	99
7 Austria	54	91	1822	99
8 Bahamas	54	93	560	93
9 Bahrain	78	97	550	79
10 Bangladesh	11	16	272	30
11 Barbados	42	84	1620	97
12 Belgium	72	97	2111	99
13 Benin	14	54	138	28
14 Bhutan	4	7	25	22
15 Bolivia	33	50	1436	68
16 Botswana	16	20	101	60
17 Brazil	68	62	1162	76
18 Bulgaria	64	67	1144	95
19 Burkina Faso	10	19	27	11
20 Burma	27	48	184	66
21 Burundi	2	17	46	27
22 Cameroon	35	19	136	48
23 Canada	80	95	3688	99
24 Cape Verde Islands	20	44	129	43
25 Central African Republic	41	13	75	33
26 Chad	18	16	47	20
27 Chile	80	82	1308	92
28 China	13	40	117	65
29 Colombia	70	73	1053	85
30 Comoros	11	36	25	59
31 Congo, People's Republic of	45	66	475	50
32 Costa Rica	43	65	2440	92
33 Cuba	65	77	1559	96
34 Cyprus	42	66	308	89
35 Czechoslovakia	63	90	1287	99

APPENDIX 2 (*continued*)

State	Urban Population %	Nonagricul. Population %	Students per 100,000 inhabitants	Literates 15+ %
36 Denmark	84	93	2074	99
37 Djibuti	50	50	0	20
38 Dominican Republic	51	44	900	73
39 Ecuador	45	55	3321	79
40 Egypt	45	50	1724	42
41 El Salvador	41	50	351	68
42 Equatorial Guinea	51	25	0	37
43 Ethiopia	14	21	37	30
44 Fiji	42	60	288	82
45 Finland	62	87	2577	100
46 France	78	91	2005	99
47 Gabon	36	24	273	50
48 Gambia	18	22	37	20
49 German Democratic Republic	77	90	2395	99
50 Germany, Federal Republic of	85	96	1987	99
51 Ghana	36	49	138	45
52 Greece	62	63	1256	92
53 Guatemala	39	45	736	50
54 Guinea	19	20	338	25
55 Guinea-Bissau	24	18	36	19
56 Guyana	38	78	285	94
57 Haiti	28	33	80	30
58 Honduras	36	37	700	60
59 Hungary	54	84	944	99
60 Iceland	88	88	2287	100
61 India	22	37	776	36
62 Indonesia	20	41	367	67
63 Iran	50	61	331	43
64 Iraq	72	60	803	47
65 Ireland	58	79	1610	98
66 Israel	89	93	2504	95
67 Italy	69	89	1959	97
68 Ivory Coast	40	21	238	35
69 Jamaica	41	79	644	96
70 Japan	78	89	2065	99

APPENDIX 2 (*continued*)

State	Urban Population %	Nonagricul. Population %	Students per 100,000 inhabitants	Literates 15+ %
71 Jordan	56	74	1250	65
72 Kampuchea	16	26	9	48
73 Kenya	14	22	77	47
74 Korea, Dem. People's Republic	60	54	1785	95
75 Korea, Republic of	55	61	1614	93
76 Kuwait	88	98	991	68
77 Lao People's Dem. Republic	14	26	38	44
78 Lebanon	76	90	2962	77
79 Lesotho	12	16	141	70
80 Liberia	33	30	203	30
81 Libya	52	84	678	55
82 Luxemburg	78	97	205	100
83 Madagascar	20	17	260	50
84 Malawi	10	16	58	35
85 Malaysia	29	52	419	68
86 Mali	20	13	23	14
87 Malta	60	95	257	84
88 Mauritania	23	17	58	17
89 Mauritius	43	72	109	79
90 Mexico	67	64	1294	83
91 Mongolia	51	51	683	80
92 Morocco	41	49	580	29
93 Mosambique	9	36	8	26
94 Nepal	5	7	262	23
95 Netherlands	76	95	2544	99
96 New Zealand	85	91	2419	99
97 Nicaragua	53	57	1273	75
98 Niger	13	12	27	10
99 Nigeria	20	47	186	34
100 Norway	53	92	1936	99
101 Oman	7	38	60	20
102 Pakistan	28	47	182	26
103 Panama	54	65	2063	87
104 Papua New Guinea	18	18	163	40
105 Paraguay	39	51	850	85
106 Peru	67	63	1771	80

APPENDIX 2 (*continued*)

State	Urban Population %	Nonagricul. Population %	Students per 100,000 inhabitants	Literates 15+ %
107 Philippines	36	54	2641	85
108 Poland	57	70	1656	98
109 Portugal	31	74	932	84
110 Qatar	88	70	1011	51
111 Romania	50	53	868	98
112 Rwanda	4	10	24	50
113 Saudi Arabia	67	40	662	25
114 Senegal	25	26	239	25
115 Sierra Leone	22	35	55	25
116 Singapore	100	98	963	83
117 Solomon Islands	14	10	110	54
118 Somalia	30	20	72	6
119 South Africa	50	71	505	50
120 Spain	74	83	1819	94
121 Sri Lanka	27	47	288	86
122 Sudan	25	23	154	20
123 Suriname	50	82	669	65
124 Swaziland	14	27	336	62
125 Sweden	87	95	2451	99
126 Switzerland	58	95	1346	99
127 Syrian Arab Republic	50	52	1535	53
128 Tanzania	12	19	32	66
129 Thailand	14	25	1290	88
130 Togo	20	32	186	32
131 Trinidad & Tobago	21	84	516	96
132 Tunisia	52	59	498	47
133 Turkey	47	46	554	69
134 Uganda	9	19	45	52
135 U.S.S.R.	62	84	1972	100
136 United Arab Emirates	72	85	279	56
137 United Kingdom	91	98	1478	99
138 United States	77	98	5313	99
139 Uruguay	84	88	1248	94
140 Venezuela	83	82	2044	84
141 Vietnam	19	29	212	84
142 Yemen Arab Republic	10	25	76	9

APPENDIX 2 (*continued*)

State	Urban Population %	Nonagricul. Population %	Students per 100,000 inhabitants	Literates 15+ %
143 Ymen, People's Dem. Rep.	37	41	177	40
144 Yugoslavia	42	63	1848	91
145 Zaire	34	26	110	55
146 Zambia	43	33	133	68
147 Zimbabwe	23	41	113	69

Notes:

Urban Population
Source, if not otherwise noted, *World Development Report* 1982, Table 20. Urbanization. Urban population as percentage of the total population in 1980.
Bahamas: Kurian 1987.
Bahrain: Kurian 1982.
Barbados: Kurian 1987.
Botswana: United Nations, *Demographic Yearbook* 1981, Table 6.
Cape Verde: United Nations, *Demographic Yearbook* 1979, Table 9. cf. Nohlen and Nuscheler 1982 Vol. 4, 218; Kurian 1987.
Comoros: Kurian 1982; cf. Nohlen and Nuscheler 1982 Vol. 5, 208.
Cyprus: United Nations, *Demographic Yearbook* 1981, Table 6.
Djibouti: Nohlen and Nuscheler 1982 Vol. 5, 68; cf. Kurian 1987.
Equatorial Guinea: Kurian 1982; cf. Nohlen and Nuscheler 1982 Vol. 4, 390.
Fiji: Kurian 1982. Cf. United Nations, Demographic Yearbook 1981, Table 6.
Gabon: Kurian 1982; cf. Nohlen and Nuscheler 1982, Vol. 4, 399.
Gambia: United Nations, *Demographic Yearbook* 1981, Table 6.
Guinea-Bissau: Kurian 1982.
Guyana: Kurian 1982.
Iceland: United Nations, *Demographic Yearbook* 1981, Table 6.
Kampuchea: Kurian 1987; cf. *Countries of the World* 1983, 670.
Luxemburg: United Nations, *Demographic Yearbook* 1981, Table 6.
Madagascar: Pryor 1988a, 9.
Malta: Estimation. See Commonwealth Fact Sheet. Malta, 1976, 6. According to this source, the majority of the people live in towns, and over two-thirds of the whole population live in and around Valletta.
Mauritius: United Nations, *Demographic Yearbook* 1981, Table 6.
Oman: Kurian 1982; cf. Nohlen and Nuscheler 1983 Vol. 6, 420.
Qatar: Kurian 1982; cf. Nohlen and Nuscheler 1983 Vol. 6, 379.
Solomon Islands: Kurian 1982; cf. United Nations, *Demographic Yearbook* 1981, Table 6.
Suriname: Kurian 1982; cf. Nohlen and Nuscheler 1982 Vol. 3, 413–14.

Notes (*continued*)

Swaziland: Kurian 1982; cf. Nohlen and Nuscheler 1982 Vol. 5, 381; United Nations, *Demographic Yearbook* 1981, Table 6.

Nonagricultural Population
Source, if not otherwise noted, FAO, *Production Yearbook* 1981, Table 3.
Bahamas: Kurian 1982; cf. Nohlen and Nuscheler 1982 Vol. 3, 244–45.
Bahrain: Kurian 1982.
Djibouti: Kurian 1982.
Luxemburg: *The Statesman's Year Book* 1982–83, 808–10.
Qatar: Kurian 1982; cf. *Countries of the World* 1983, 942.
Solomon Islands: *Europa Yearbook* 1983; cf. *Countries of the World* 1983; Nohlen and Nuscheler 1983 Vol. 8, 306; Kurian 1982.
United Arab Emirates: Kurian 1982; cf. *Countries of the World* 1983.

Students
Sources, if not otherwise noted, Unesco, *Statistical Yearbooks* 1985, 1986, Table 3.10.
Bahamas: Kurian 1987. Students enrolled in institutions of higher learning abroad.
Burma: Year 1975.
Cape Verde: Kurian 1987. Students enrolled in institutions of higher learning abroad.
Chad: Kurian 1987. Including students enrolled in institutions of higher learning abroad.
Comoros: Kurian 1987. Students enrolled in institutions of higher learning abroad.
Djibouti: See *South*, Aug. 1985, 46; Kurian 1987.
Dominican Republic: Year 1975.
Equatorial Guinea: See Kurian 1987.
Gabon: Year 1975.
Gambia: Kurian 1987. Students enrolled in institutions of higher learning abroad.
Guinea-Bissau: Kurian 1987. Students enrolled in institutions of higher learning abroad.
Kampuchea: Kurian 1987.
Korea, North: Kurian 1982.
Mali: Kurian 1987. Including students enrolled in institutions of higher learning abroad.
Mongolia: Year 1975.
Oman: Kurian 1987. Students enrolled in institutions of higher learning abroad.
Solomon Islands: *The Statesman's Yearbook 1982–83*, 1070. Students abroad; cf. *South*, Aug. 1985, 53; Kurian 1987. In 1977 the University of Pacific opened a center in Solomon Islands, but the number of students is not known.
South Africa: *Europa Year Book* 1983 Vol. II, 1456.

Literates
Sources, if not otherwise noted, Unesco, *Statistical Yearbooks* 1982–85, Table 1.3; *World Development Report* 1982, Table 23. Data given in this appendix are census data for 1980 or my estimates for 1980 based on previous or later census data

Notes (*continued*)

and Unesco estimates, or estimates for 1977 given in *World Development Report* 1982; cf. Gastil 1988, Table 9.

Albania: *Countries of the World* 1983.

Angola: Estimation. See Kurian 1987 (24%); Unesco 1985 (41%).

Australia: Estimation; cf. *World Development Report* 1982, Table 23 (100%).

Bahamas: Kurian 1982; cf. World Bank, World Tables 1980, Table 4.

Barbados: Kurian 1982; cf. World Bank, World Tables 1980, Table 4.

Bhutan: Nohlen and Nuscheler 1983 Vol. 7, 103.

Bulgaria: *Countries of the World* 1983; World Bank, World Tables 1980, Table 4.

Burma: Kurian 1987.

Comoros: Kurian 1987; cf. World Bank, World Tables 1980, Table 4.

Cyprus: *Countries of the World* 1983.

Czechoslovakia: *Countries of the World* 1983; cf. World Bank, World Tables 1980, Table 4.

Djibouti: Kurian 1987; cf. Nohlen and Nuscheler 1982 Vol. 5, 74.

Ethiopia: Estimation. See *World Development Report* 1982, Table 23 (15%); Unesco, *Statistical Yearbook* 1985, Table 1.3 (55%); Kurian 1987 (15%).

Iceland: Countries of the World 1983.

Iraq: Nohlen and Nuscheler 1983 Vol. 6, 282; cf. Unesco, *Statistical Yearbook* 1985, Table 1.3 (89%); Kurian 1987 (24%).

Kampuchea: Kurian 1987.

Korea, North: *Countries of the World* 1983; Kurian 1987.

Luxemburg: World Bank, World Tables 1980, Table 4.

Mongolia: *Countries of the World* 1983.

Oman: *Countries of the World* 1983; World Bank, World Tables 1980, Table 4; Kurian 1987.

Solomon Islands: Kurian 1987; cf. Nohlen and Nuscheler 1983 Vol. 8, 308–309.

South Africa: Estimation. See *Africa Insight* 11:204.

APPENDIX 3

Percentual Share of Family Farms of the Total Area of Holdings in 147 States in the Period 1960–80

Notes by countries:
The percentage of Family Farms is calculated, if not otherwise noted, from the total area of holdings, and the upper hectare limit of Family Farms refers, if not otherwise noted, to the total area of holding.

Country	Upper hectare limit or other criterion of Family Farms	Year	Family Farms %
1 Afghanistan	6 ha	1970–79	57
2 Albania	Private farms	1970	0
3 Algeria	50 ha	1973	50
4 Angola	60% of de facto indigenous land	1980	43
5 Argentina	Familiares and subfamiliares	1960	48
6 Australia	1,000 ha	1970	51
7 Austria	100 ha	1980	62
8 Bahamas	20 ha	1980	50
9 Bahrain	5 ha	1980	33
10 Bangladesh	3 ha	1977	68
11 Barbados	10 ha	1971	14
12 Belgium	50 ha	1980	80
13 Benin	60% of indigenous land	1980	52
14 Bhutan	Owner-operated holdings	—	70
15 Bolivia	100 ha and Land Reform Beneficiaries	1970	31
16 Botswana	60% of de facto indigenous land	1980	52
17 Brazil	100 ha	1980	20
18 Bulgaria	Private farms	1978	0
19 Burkina Faso	60% of de facto indigenous land	1980	60
20 Burma	60% of the land in holdings of less than 8 ha	1974–75	52
21 Burundi	60% of de facto indigenous land	1980	60
22 Cameroon	60% of de facto indigenous land	1980	43
23 Canada	453 ha	1980	51
24 Cape Verde	Area owned or in ownerlike possession	1980	51
25 Central African Rep.	60% of de facto indigenous land	1980	60
26 Chad	60% of de facto indigenous land	1980	60
27 Chile	10 basic irrigated hectares	1986	20
28 China	Individual farm households	1958	1
29 Colombia	100 ha	1970–71	25
30 Comoros	70% of the villagers' reserves and Comorian-owned land	1968	27
31 Congo	60% of de facto indigenous land	1980	60
32 Costa Rica	100 ha	1973	32
33 Cuba	Private farms	1977	21
34 Cyprus	20 ha	1980	75
35 Czechoslovakia	Private farms	1978	5
36 Denmark	100 ha	1980	85
37 Djibouti	60% all holdings and of collective tribal lands	—	60

240

APPENDIX 3 (*continued*)

Country	Upper hectare limit or other criterion of Family Farms	Year	Family Farms %
38 Dominican Republic	20 ha	1971	30
39 Ecuador	50 ha	1974	35
40 Egypt	4.2 ha	1975	40
41 El Salvador	20 ha	1970–71	25
42 Equatorial Guinea	50% of collective tribal lands	—	30
43 Ethiopia	60% of de facto indigenous land	1980	13
44 Fiji	20 ha	1980	43
45 Finland	50 ha	1980	95
46 France	100 ha	1980	83
47 Gabon	60% of de facto indigenous land	1980	52
48 Gambia	60% of de facto indigenous land	1980	52
49 German Dem. Republic	Private farms	1978	5
50 Germany, West	50 ha	1980	80
51 Ghana	10 ha	1970	67
52 Greece	10 ha	1971	75
53 Guatemala	45 ha	1980	35
54 Guinea	60% of de facto indigenous land	1980	52
55 Guinea-Bissau	60% of de facto indigenous land	1980	52
56 Guyana	Owner-operated enterprises	1957	8
57 Haiti	3 ha	1971	62
58 Honduras	35 ha	1970	40
59 Hungary	Private farms	1978	2
60 Iceland	Owner-operated farms	1967	74
61 India	10 ha	1970	63
62 Indonesia	5 ha	1963	50
63 Iran	10 ha	1974	44
64 Iraq	50 ha	1971	35
65 Ireland	100 ha	1970	87
66 Israel	20 ha	1971	40
67 Italy	50 ha	1980	55
68 Ivory Coast	60% of de facto indigenous land	1980	56
69 Jamaica	10 ha	1980	35
70 Japan	5 ha	1980	79
71 Jordan	20 ha	1975	46
72 Kampuchea	Private farms	—	10
73 Kenya	10 ha	1974	56
74 Korea, North	Private farms	1958	0
75 Korea, South	3 ha	1980	93
76 Kuwait	20 ha	1970	14
77 Laos	50% of the area of peasant farms	1980	35
78 Lebanon	20 ha	1970	48
79 Lesotho	60% of de facto indigenous land	1980	60
80 Liberia	10 ha	1970	43
81 Libya	50 ha	1960	40
82 Luxemburg	50 ha	1980	60
83 Madagascar	60% of the area of indigenous land under traditional land tenure systems	1980	56
84 Malawi	60% of de facto indigenous land	1980	43
85 Malaysia	10 ha	1960	42

APPENDIX 3 *(continued)*

Country	Upper hectare limit or other criterion of Family Farms	Year	Family Farms %
86 Mali	60% of de facto indigenous land	1980	60
87 Malta	5 ha	1980	75
88 Mauritania	60% of de facto indigenous land	1980	60
89 Mauritius	Owner-cultivator operated enterprises	1965	46
90 Mexico	25 ha and 50% of the area of Ejidos and *Comunidades Agrarias*	1970	41
91 Mongolia	Private farms	1978	0
92 Morocco	10 ha	1969	44
93 Mosambique	60% of de facto indigenous land	1980	43
94 Nepal	5 ha	1980	61
95 Netherlands	50 ha	1980	84
96 New Zealand	2,000 ha	1970	64
97 Nicaragua	35 ha	1971	13
98 Niger	60% of de facto indigenous land	1980	60
99 Nigeria	60% of de facto indifenous land	1980	60
100 Norway	20 ha	1969	90
101 Oman	Family-owned farms	—	50
102 Pakistan	20 ha	1980	37
103 Panama	50 ha	1980	34
104 Papua New Guinea	60% of the area of indigenous land under traditional tenure systems	1965	58
105 Paraguay	100 ha	1980	12
106 Peru	100 ha	1972	18
107 Philippines	25 ha	1980	58
108 Poland	Private farms	1978	76
109 Portugal	50 ha	1980	44
110 Qatar	Family-owned farms	—	40
111 Romania	Private farms	1978	9
112 Rwanda	60% of de facto indigenous land	1980	60
113 Saudi Arabia	50 ha	1980	42
114 Senegal	60% of de facto indigenous land	1980	52
115 Sierra Leone	60% of de facto indigenous land	1980	60
116 Singapore	Holdings owned by the holder	1973	7
117 Solomon Islands	60% of native land	1951	57
118 Somalia	60% of de facto indigenous land	1980	60
119 South Africa	85 ha and 70 % of de facto indigenous land	1959–60	10
120 Spain	50 ha	1980	31
121 Sri Lanka	8 ha	1980	73
122 Sudan	60% of de facto indigenous land	1980	52
123 Suriname	20 ha	1969	16
124 Swaziland	60% of de facto indigenous land	1980	34
125 Sweden	50 ha	1980	71
126 Switzerland	50 ha	1980	94
127 Syria	25 ha	1970	40
128 Tanzania	60% of de facto indigenous land	1980	43
129 Thailand	10 ha	1980	65
130 Togo	60% of de facto indigenous land	1980	60
131 Trinidad and Tobago	10 ha	1963	38
132 Tunisia	50 ha	1974	48

APPENDIX 3 (*continued*)

Country	Upper hectare limit or other criterion of Family Farms	Year	Family Farms %
133 Turkey	20 ha	1980	68
134 Uganda	60% of de facto indigenous land	1980	60
135 USSR	Private farms	1978	0
136 United Arab Emirates	Family-owned holdings	—	40
137 United Kingdom	100 ha	1980	37
138 United States	809 ha	1980	55
139 Uruguay	1,000 ha	1980	43
140 Venezuela	200 ha	1971	10
141 Vietnam	Private farms	—	5
142 Yemen Arab Republic	10 ha	1980	46
143 Yemen, South	Private farms	1980	10
144 Yugoslavia	20 ha	1980	75
145 Zaire	60% of de facto indigenous land	1980	52
146 Zambia	60% of de facto indigenous land	1980	52
147 Zimbabwe	60% of de facto indigenous land	1980	30

Notes:

Afghanistan: Lakanwal 1980, 77. The data refer to cultivated land; cf. Klimburg 1966, 169–71, according to whom only 27% of the total area of holdings belonged to farms of less than 10 ha in 1955; *World Atlas of Agriculture* 1973 Vol. 2, 34–35; Kurian 1982, 35, who estimates that 29% of the total cultivated land belongs to holdings of less than 4 ha.

Albania: Shoup 1981, 207; cf. *World Atlas* 1973 Vol. 3, 23–24.

Algeria: Estimation. See Land Tenure Center, Land Concentration in the Third World: Statistics on Number and Area of Farms, 1979 (LTC, Land Concentration 1979), 1; Kurian 1982, 51–52; cf. *World Atlas* 1976 Vol. 4, 39–41; Nohlen and Nuscheler 1983 Vol. 6, 96.

Angola: Estimation. See *World Atlas* 1976 Vol. 4, 55; Riddell and Dickerman 1986. cf. Nohlen and Nuscheler 1982 Vol. 5, 301–02; Kurian 1982, 69.

Argentina: *World Atlas* 1970 Vol. 3, 50–54; cf. LTC, Land Concentration 1979, 124.

Australia: FAO, *1970 World Census of Agriculture*. Analyses and international comparison of the results, 1981 (FAO, *1970 World Census of Agriculture* 1981), 80. Percentage of the total arable land. cf. FAO, *1960 World Census of Agriculture* 1966 Vol. 1/a, 14–15; World Atlas 1973 Vol. 2, 588–589.

Austria: FAO, *Report of the 1980 World Census of Agriculture* (FAO, Report 1980), Census Bulletin No. 20, 1986. Size classification by productive area of holding; cf. FAO, *1970 World Census of Agriculture* 1981, 53.

Bahamas: FAO, *Report 1980*, Census Bulletin No. 8, 1984. Percentage of the total arable area. Size classification by cultivated area of holding; cf. World Atlas 1970 Vol. 3, 11, 65.

Bahrain: FAO, *Report 1980*, Census Bulletin No. 9, 1984; cf. FAO, *1970 World Census of Agriculture* 1981, 93, 102.

Notes (*continued*)

Bangladesh: FAO, *Report 1980,* Census Bulletin No. 5, 1983; cf. LTC, Land Concentration 1979, 67–68; Kurian 1982, 134; Nohlen and Nuscheler 1983 Vol. 7, 85–86.

Barbados: LTC, Land Concentration 1979, 126; cf. World Atlas 1970 Vol. 3, 67; Nohlen and Nuscheler 1982 Vol. 3, 259–60; Beckles and Russell 1982, 1.

Belgium: FAO, *Report 1980,* Census Bulletin No. 11, 1984; cf. FAO, *1970 World Census of Agriculture* 1981, 53.

Benin: Estimation. See *World Atlas* 1976 Vol. 4, 148–49; Riddell and Dickerman 1986; cf. Kurian 1982, 163–64; Nohlen and Nuscheler 1982 Vol. 4, 136–37.

Bhutan: Estimation. See *World Atlas* 1973 Vol. 2, 38–40; Shah 1984, 50; Haaland 1986.

Bolivia: Eckstein et al. 1978, 21–23; LTC, Land Concentration 1979, 128–29; cf. *World Atlas* 1970 Vol. 3, 76–79.

Botswana: Estimation. See *World Atlas* 1976 Vol. 4, 72–73; Riddell and Dickerman 1986; cf. FAO, *Report on the 1970 World Census of Agriculture* (FAO, *Report 1970*), Census Bulletin 1, 1973; LTC, Land Concentration 1979, 2; Kurian 1982, 209.

Brazil: FAO, *Report 1980,* Census Bulletin No. 22, 1986; cf. FAO, *1970 World Census of Agriculture* 1981, 100–02; LTC, Land Concentration 1979, 131–32; Ortega 1982.

Bulgaria: Council for Mutual Assistance (CMEA) 1979, 42.

Burkina Faso: Estimation. See *World Atlas* 1976 Vol. 4, 736–37; Riddell and Dickerman 1986.

Burma: Report to the Pyithu Hluttaw . . . 1978–79, 40; Kurian 1982, 258. The government holds title to all land, but land is cultivated by private peasants.

Burundi: Estimation. See *World Atlas* 1976 Vol. 4, 82–84; Riddell and Dickerman 1986; cf. Nohlen and Nuscheler 1982 Vol. 5, 127.

Cameroon: Estimation. See *World Atlas* 1976 Vol. 4, 93–95; Riddell and Dickerman 1986; cf. FAO, *Report 1970,* Census Bulletin 22, 1978; FAO, *1970 World Census of Agriculture* 1981, 100–01.

Canada: FAO, *Report 1980,* Census Bulletin No. 18, 1985; cf. FAO, *Report 1970,* Census Bulletin 4, 1973.

Cape Verde Islands: FAO, Report 1980, Census Bulletin No. 23, 1986; cf. *World Atlas* 1976 Vol. 4, 112.

Central African Republic: Estimation. See *World Atlas* 1976 Vol. 4, 116–17; Riddell and Dickerman 1986; cf. LTC, Land Concentration 1979, 4; FAO, *1970 World Census of Agriculture* 1981, 100–01.

Chad: Estimation. See *World Atlas* 1976 Vol. 4, 125–26; Riddell and Dickerman 1986; cf. LTC, Land Concentration 1979, 5.

Chile: Estimation. William Thiesenhusen, Land Tenure Center, Madison, estimated (Feb. 14, 1986) that the share of family farms might be about 20 percent; cf. Eckstein et al. 1978, 29–34; LTC, Land Concentration 1979, 135–36.

China: *World Atlas* 1973 Vol. 2, 105–06.

Colombia: FAO, *1970 World Census of Agriculture* 1981, 100–03. Area owned by the holder or in ownerlike possession; cf. LTC, Land Concentration 1979, 137.

Comoros: *World Atlas* 1976 Vol. 4, 134.

Notes (*continued*)

Congo: Estimation. See *World Atlas* 1976 Vol. 4, 140; Riddell and Dickerman 1986; cf. FAO, Report 1970, Census Bulletin 21, 1978.

Costa Rica: FAO, *1970 World Census of Agriculture* 1981, 100–03. Area owned by the holder or in ownerlike possession; cf. *World Atlas* 1970 Vol. 3, 213–14.

Cuba: Nohlen and Nuscheler 1982 Vol. 3, 366; cf. *World Atlas* 1970 Vol. 3, 224–25; Kurian 1982, 468–69.

Cyprus: FAO, *Report 1980,* Census Bulletin No. 12, 1984; cf. *World Atlas* 1969 Vol. 1, 71–72.

Czechoslovakia: CMEA *Statistical Yearbook* 1979, 42; cf. *World Atlas* 1969 Vol. 1, 80–81; FAO, *Report 1980,* Census Bulletin No. 6, 1983.

Denmark: FAO, *Report 1980,* Census Bulletin No. 11, 1985. Size classification by agricultural area of holding; cf. FAO, *1970 World Census of Agriculture* 1981, 53.

Djibuti: Estimation. See *World Atlas* 1976 Vol. 4, 197.

Dominican Republic: FAO, *1970 World Census of Agriculture* 1981, 52, 100–01; cf. *World Atlas* 1970 Vol. 3, 234–35; LTC, Land Concentration 1979, 143.

Ecuador: FAO, *1970 World Census of Agriculture* 1981, 53; cf. *World Atlas* 1970 Vol. 3, 247–48; LTC, Land Concentration 1979, 144.

Egypt: Mittwally 1980, 204; Kurian 1987. Holdings of less than 4.2 ha cover 83% of the agricultural area, but, according to Kurian 1987, sharecropping was the system in 62% of the farms in the early 1980s and it covered 57.2% of the farmland; cf. *World Atlas* 1976 Vol. 4, 163–64; LTC, Land Concentration 1979, 7; Nohlen and Nuscheler 1983 Vol. 6, 58–60.

El Salvador: FAO, *1970 World Census of Agriculture* 1981, 100–02. Area owned by the holder or in ownerlike possession; cf. *World Atlas* 1970 Vol. 3, 257–58; LTC, Land Concentration 1979, 147–48; Kurian 1987.

Equatorial Guinea: Estimation. See *World Atlas* 1976 Vol. 4, 172–76.

Ethiopia: Estimation. See Cohen and Koehn 1978; *World Atlas* 1976 Vol. 4, 183–85; Riddell and Dickerman 1986.

Fiji: FAO, *Report 1980,* Census Bulletin No. 11, 1984; cf. FAO, *1970 World Census of Agriculture* 1981, 54; *World Atlas* 1973 Vol. 2, 611–12; LTC, Land Concentration 1979, 71; Kurian 1982, 617.

Finland: FAO, *Report 1980,* Census Bulletin No. 16, 1985. Size classification by areable area of holding; cf. FAO, *1970 World Census of Agriculture* 1981, 102.

France: FAO, *Report 1980,* Census Bulletin No. 7, 1984. Size classification by agricultural area of holding; cf. FAO, Census Bulletin 9, 1975.

Gabon: Estimation. See *World Atlas* 1976 Vol. 4, 202; Riddell and Dickerman 1986; cf. Kurian 1982, 629–30.

Gambia: Estimation. See *World Atlas* 1976 Vol. 4, 208–09; Riddell and Dickerman 1986.

German Democratic Republic: CMEA, *Statistical Yearbook* 1979, 42; cf. *World Atlas* 1969 Vol. 1, 146–50.

Germany, Federal Republic of: FAO, *Report 1980,* Census Bulletin No. 22, 1986; cf. FAO, *l970 World Census of Agriculture* 1981, 53; *World Atlas* 1969 Vol. 1, 172–73.

Ghana: FAO, *Report 1970,* Census Bulletin No. 8, 1975; FAO, *1970 World Census*

Notes (*continued*)

of Agriculture 1981: 52; cf. *World Atlas* 1976 Vol. 4, 215–16; LTC, Land Concentration 1979, 14; Riddell and Dickerman 1986.

Greece: FAO, *1970 World Census of Agriculture* 1981, 53; cf. *World Atlas* 1969 Vol. 1, 198.

Guatemala: FAO, *Report 1980,* Census Bulletin No. 17, 1985; cf. LTC, Land Concentration 1979, 152; *World Atlas* 1970 Vol. 3, 276–77.

Guinea: Estimation. See *World Atlas* 1976 Vol. 4, 227–28; Riddell and Dickerman 1986.

Guinea-Bissau: Estimation. See *World Atlas* 1976 Vol. 4, 232–33; Riddell and Dickerman 1986.; cf. LTC, Land Concentration 1979, 15; Nohlen and Nuscheler 1982 Vol. 4, 213–14.

Guyana: *World Atlas* 1970 Vol. 3, 286; cf. Kurian 1982, 735.

Haiti: LTC, Land Concentration 1979, 154; Kurian 1982, 750; Nohlen and Nuscheler 1982 Vol. 3, 334–36.

Honduras: LTC, Land Concentration 1979, 155; cf. *World Atlas* 1970 Vol. 3, 301; Nohlen and Nuscheler 1982 Vol. 3, 106–08; Kurian 1987, 855.

Hungary: CMEA, *Statistical Yearbook* 1979, 42; cf. *World Atlas* 1969 Vol. 1, 213.

Iceland: *Statistical Abstract of Iceland* 1967, 90. Freeholders; cf. *World Atlas* 1969 Vol. 1, 224–25.

India: *All India Report on Agricultural Census* 1970–71, 114. Area of owner-operated holdings of less than 10 ha; cf. *World Atlas* 1973 Vol. 2, 187–200; LTC, Land Concentration 1979, 73–94; FAO, *Report 1980,* Census Bulletin No. 22, 1986.

Indonesia: FAO, *1960 World Census of Agriculture* 1970 Vol. 1/c, 72–73. Area owned by the holder or in ownerlike possession; cf. LTC, Land Concentration 1979, 95–105.

Iran: Ajami 1978, 146. Estimated area of owner-operated holdings of less than 10 ha; cf. *World Atlas* 1973 Vol. 2, 260; Nohlen and Nuscheler 1983 Vol. 6, 289–94.

Iraq: FAO, *1970 World Census of Agriculture* 1981, 100–02. Area owned or in ownerlike possession; cf. *World Atlas* 1973 Vol. 2, 274–75.

Ireland: FAO, *1970 World Census of Agriculture* 1981, 53; cf. *World Atlas* 1969 Vol. 1, 231–32.

Israel: FAO, *1970 World Census of Agriculture* 1981, 53. Size classification by crop land; cf. *World Atlas* 1973 Vol. 2, 286–88; FAO, Report 1980, Census Bulletin No. 24, 1986.

Italy: FAO, *Report 1980,* Census Bulletin No. 23, 1986; cf. FAO, *1970 World Census of Agriculture* 1981, 54; *World Atlas* 1969 Vol. 1, 249–52.

Ivory Coast: Estimation. See *World Atlas* 1976 Vol. 4, 239–41; Riddell and Dickerman 1986; cf. LTC, Land Concentration 1979, 16; FAO, *1970 World Census of Agriculture* 1981, 52.

Jamaica: FAO, *Report 1980,* Census Bulletin No. 15, 1985;' cf. LTC, Land Concentration 1979, 157; FAO, *1970 World Census of Agriculture* 1981, 52.

Japan: FAO, Report 1980, Census Bulletin No. 12, 1984. Percentage of the total agricultural area of holdings. Size classification by arable area of holding; cf.

Notes (*continued*)

FAO, *Report 1970,* Census Bulletin No. 2, 1973; *World Atlas* 1973 Vol. 2, 300–03.

Jordan: LTC, Land Concentration 1979, 196; cf. *World Atlas* 1973 Vol. 2, 313–14; Jordan. A Country Study 1980, 126–27.

Kampuchea: Estimation. See Kurian 1987; Nohlen and Nuscheler 1983 Vol. 7, 349–58. In 1975 the Khmer Rouge government abolished private ownership of land, and all landholdings were transferred to the state; cf. *World Atlas* 1973 Vol. 2, 59–60.

Kenya: FAO, *1970 World Census of Agriculture* 1981, 52; cf. LTC, Land Concentration 1979, 17–22; Riddell and Dickerman 1986; FAO, *Report 1980,* Census Bulletin No. 25, 1986.

Korea, Democratic People's Republic of: *World Atlas* 1973 Vol. 2, 33; Länder der Erde 1981, 357.

Korea, Republic of: FAO, *Report 1980,* Census Bulletin No. 15, 1985. Percentage of the agricultural area of holdings. Size classification by cropland area of holding; cf. FAO, *1970 World Census of Agriculture* 1981, 100–02; LTC, Land Concentration 1979, 108.

Kuwait: FAO, *Report 1970,* Census Bulletin No. 12, 1975. Area in holdings operated by the holder; cf. LTC, Land Concentration 1979, 197.

Laos: Estimation. See Stuart-Fox 1980; Zasloff 1981; Nohlen and Nuscheler 1983 Vol. 7, 369–84; cf. *World Atlas* 1973 Vol. 2, 345–46.

Lebanon: FAO, *1970 World Census of Agriculture* 1981, 53; cf. *World Atlas* 1973 Vol. 2, 253–54.

Lesotho: Estimation. See *World Atlas* 1976 Vol. 4, 271–76; Riddell and Dickerman 1986; cf. FAO, Census Bulletin 9, 1975; LTC, Land Concentration 1979, 23; Eckert 1980.

Liberia: FAO, *Report 1970,* Census Bulletin No. 29, 1980; cf. *World Atlas* 1976 Vol. 4, 290–91; LTC, Land Concentration 1979, 24; Riddell and Dickerman 1986.

Libya: FAO, *1960 World Census of Agriculture* 1969 Vol. 1/a, 118–119. Area owned by the holder or in ownerlike possession and 50% of the area under tribal form of tenure; cf. *World Atlas* 1976 Vol. 4, 301–03; LTC, Land Concentration 1979, 25–27.

Luxemburg: FAO, *Report 1980,* Census Bulletin No. 16, 1985. Percentage of the agricultural area of holdings. Size classification by agricultural area of holding; cf. FAO, *Report 1970,* Census Bulletin No. 3, 1973.

Madagascar: FAO, *Report 1980,* Census Bulletin No. 25, 1986; cf. *World Atlas* 1976 Vol. 4, 315–18; Kurian 1982, 1116–17; Riddell and Dickerman 1986; Pryor 1988a, 3–4.

Malawi: Estimation. See *World Atlas* 1976 Vol. 4, 339–40; Riddell and Dickerman 1986; cf. FAO, *Report 1970,* Census Bulletin No. 9, 1975; LTC, Land Concentration 1979, 28; FAO, *Report 1980,* Census Bulletin No. 25, 1986; Pryor 1988b, 1–5.

Malaysia: FAO, *1960 World Census of Agriculture* 1967 Vol. 1/b, 110–11, 130–31; cf. *World Atlas* 1973 Vol. 2, 371–72; LTC, Land Concentration 1979, 109.

Mali: *World Atlas* 1976 Vol. 4, 348–49; Riddell and Dickerman 1986; cf. FAO,

Notes (*continued*)

1960 World Census of Agriculture 1967 Vol. 1/b, 145–47.

Malta: FAO, *Report 1980*, Census Bulletin No. 6, 1983. Size classification by agricultural area of holding; cf. FAO, *Report 1970*, Census Bulletin No. 2, 1973; *World Atlas* 1969 Vol. 1, 271.

Mauritania: Estimation. See *World Atlas* 1976 Vol. 4, 359–60; Riddell and Dickerman 1986.

Mauritius: *World Atlas* 1976 Vol. 4, 370–71; cf. Nohlen and Nuscheler 1982 Vol. 5, 263–65.

Mexico: LTC, Land Concentration 1979, 159–61. Cultivated area; cf. *World Atlas* 1970 Vol. 3, 331–33; FAO, *1970 World Census of Agriculture* 1981, 52, 100; Nohlen and Nuscheler 1982 Vol. 3, 126–30.

Mongolia: CMEA, 1979, 42; cf. *World Atlas* 1973 Vol. 2, 387–89; Sugarragtschaa 1980.

Morocco: LTC, Land Concentration 1979, 30; cf. *World Atlas* 1976 Vol. 4, 380–81.

Mosambique: Estimation. See *World Atlas* 1976 Vol. 4, 394–95; Riddell and Dickerman 1986; cf. LTC, Land Concentration 1979, 32–33; Binkert 1983, 16–19; Caballero et al. 1984, 84–87.

Nepal: FAO, *Report 1980*, Census Bulletin No. 20, 1986. Area owned or held in ownerlike possession; cf. *Agricultural Statistics of Nepal* 1972, 8–9; Zaman 1973, 6–13; Regmi 1976, 179–211; LTC, Land Concentration 1979, 112.

Netherlands: FAO, *Report 1980*, Census Bulletin No. 19, 1985.

New Zealand: FAO, *Report 1970*, Census Bulletin No. 11, 1975, 6–7.

Nicaragua: LTC, Land Concentration 1979, 168; cf. *World Atlas* 1970 Vol. 3, 349–50; Kaimowitz and Thome 1980; Hodgson 1984; Thome and Kaimowitz 1985.

Niger: Estimation. See *World Atlas* 1976 Vol. 4, 405; Riddell and Dickerman 1986; cf. LTC, Land Concentration 1979, 37.

Nigeria: Estimation. See *World Atlas* 1976 Vol. 4, 412–14; Riddell and Dickerman 1986; cf. LTC, Land Concentration 1979, 38–41; Olayide 1980, 254.

Norway: FAO, *1970 World Census of Agriculture* 1981, 54. Size classification by agricultural area; cf. FAO, *Report 1980*, Census Bulletin No. 19, 1985.

Oman: Estimation. See *World Atlas* 1973 Vol. 2, 395; Birks 1976, 9–12; Peterson 1978, 24; Graz 1982, 75; Kurian 1982, 1354.

Pakistan: FAO, *Report 1980*, Census Bulletin No. 9, 1984. Area owned by the holder or held in ownerlike possession; cf. FAO, *1970 World Census of Agriculture* 1981, 100–02; *World Atlas* 1973 Vol. 2, 416–18; LTC, Land Concentration 1979, 115.

Panama: FAO, *Report 1980*, Census Bulletin No. 11, 1984; cf. FAO, *1970 World Census of Agriculture* 1981, 55, 100–03.

Papua New Guinea: Estimation. See *World Atlas* 1973 Vol. 2, 657–58; cf. Papua New Guinea 1978, 45; *Pacific Islands Yearbook* 1981, 336–37; Kurian 1982, 1406.

Paraguay: FAO, *Report 1980*, Census Bulletin No. 24, 1986; cf. *World Atlas* 1970 Vol. 3, 367–68; LTC, Land Concentration 1979, 173–75.

Peru: FAO, *1970 World Census of Agriculture* 1981, 100–02. Area owned or in

Notes (*continued*)

ownerlike possession; cf. *World Atlas* 1970 Vol. 3, 379–80; Eckstein et al. 1978, 27–30; LTC, Land Concentration 1979, 177.

Philippines: FAO, *Report 1980*, Census Bulletin No. 23, 1986. Area owned or in ownerlike possession; cf. *World Atlas* 1973 Vol. 2, 434–35; Harkin 1976.

Poland: CMEA, 1979, 42; cf. *World Atlas* 1969 Vol. 1, 314–17; FAO, *Report 1980*, Census Bulletin No. 24, 1986.

Portugal: FAO, *Report 1980*, Census Bulletin No. 18, 1985. Area owned or in ownerlike possession; cf. FAO, *Report 1970*, Census Bulletin No. 5, 1974; *World Atlas* 1969 Vol. 1, 332–34.

Qatar: Estimation; cf. Nyrop et al. 1977, 244; Bowen-Jones 1980, 56–59.

Romania: CMEA 1979, 42; cf. *World Atlas* 1969 Vol. 1, 352–54.

Rwanda: Estimation. See *World Atlas* 1976 Vol. 4, 463; Riddell and Dickerman 1986; cf. Kurian 1982, 1493–94.

Saudi Arabia: FAO, *Report 1980*, Census Bulletin No. 17, 1985; cf. *World Atlas* 1973 Vol. 2, 463–64.

Senegal: Estimation. See *World Atlas* 1976 Vol. 4, 478–79; Riddell and Dickerman 1986; cf. FAO, *1960 World Census of Agriculture* 1970 Vol. 1/c, 165–67; LTC, Land Concentration 1979, 47.

Sierra Leone: Estimation. See *World Atlas* 1976 Vol. 4, 502–04; Riddell and Dickerman 1986; cf. LTC, Land Concentration 1979, 49.

Singapore: FAO, *1970 World Census of Agriculture* 1981, 93–94; cf. LTC, Land Concentration 1979, 117. Nearly all land belongs to holdings of less than 10 ha.

Solomon Islands: Estimation. See *World Atlas* 1973 Vol. 2, 664; cf. Kurian 1982, 1610; Shand 1980.

Somalia: Estimation. See *World Atlas* 1976 Vol. 4, 520–22; Riddell and Dickerman 1986; cf. LTC, Land Concentration 1979, 50.

South Africa: See FAO, *1960 World Census of Agriculture* 1967 Vol. 1/b, 232–33; LTC, Land Concentration 1979, 51–53; Riddell and Dickerman 1986; cf. *World Atlas* 1976 Vol. 4, 544–55.

Spain: FAO, *Report 1980*, Census Bulletin No. 21, 1986; cf. *World Atlas* 1969 Vol. 1, 379–82.

Sri Lanka: FAO, *Report 1980*, Census Bulletin No. 14, 1985; cf. *World Atlas* 1973 Vol. 2, 69–70.

Sudan: Estimation. See *World Atlas* 1976 Vol. 4, 633; Riddell and Dickerman 1986; cf. LTC, Land Concentration 1979, 54.

Suriname: FAO, *Report 1970*, Census Bulletin No. 1, 1973. Area owned by the holder or in ownerlike possession; cf. *World Atlas* 1970 Vol. 3, 399–400; LTC, Land Concentration 1979, 182; FAO, *Report 1980*, Census Bulletin No. 20, 1986.

Swaziland: Estimation. See *World Atlas* 1976 Vol. 4, 655–56; Riddell and Dickerman 1986; cf. LTC, Land Concentration 1979, 55; Nohlen and Nuscheler 1982 Vol. 5, 384–85.

Sweden: FAO, *Report 1980*, Census Bulletin No. 21, 1986. Size classification by arable area of holding.

Switzerland: FAO, *Report 1980*, Census Bulletin No. 21, 1986.

Syria: FAO, *1970 World Census of Agriculture* 1981, 53; cf. *World Atlas* 1973 Vol.

Notes (*continued*)

2, 482–84; *Syria. A Country Study* 1979, 118–20; Al-Ashram 1980, 139; Kaimowitz 1980; Kurian 1982, 1701.

Tanzania: Estimation. See Kurian 1982, 1721; Riddell and Dickerman 1986; cf. *World Atlas* 1976 Vol. 4, 673–76; *Tanzania. A Country Study* 1978, 190–201.

Thailand: FAO, *Report 1980,* Census Bulletin No. 10, 1984; cf. FAO, *1960 World Census of Agriculture* 1967 Vol. 1/b, 255; *World Atlas* 1973 Vol. 2, 517–18; LTC, Land Concentration 1979, 120–21.

Togo: Estimation. See *World Atlas* 1976 Vol. 4, 696–97; Riddell and Dickerman 1986; cf. LTC, Land Concentration 1979, 57; FAO, *1970 World Census of Agriculture* 1981, 52.

Trinidad and Tobago: LTC, Land Concentration 1979, 183; cf. *World Atlas* 1970 Vol. 3, 405; FAO, *Report 1980,* Census Bulletin No. 16, 1985.

Tunisia: LTC, Land Concentration 1979, 58. The data cover five Northern Provinces; cf. FAO, *1960 World Census of Agriculture* 1970 Vol. 1/c, 199; *World Atlas* 1976 Vol. 4, 707–10; Van Dooren 1977; Kurian 1982, 1798–99.

Turkey: FAO, *Report 1980,* Census Bulletin No. 13, 1985; cf. Agricultural Policy in Turkey 1974, 26; *World Atlas* 1969 Vol. 1, 427–28; LTC, Land Concentration 1979, 200–03.

Uganda: Estimation. See *World Atlas* 1976 Vol. 4, 724–25; Riddell and Dickerman 1986; cf. Kurian 1982, 1844–45.

USSR: Comecon, *Statistical Yearbook* 1979, 42.

United Arab Emirates: Estimation; cf. *World Atlas* 1973 Vol. 2, 143; Nyrop et al. 1977, 312; Bowen-Jones 1980, 59–62.

United Kingdom: FAO, *Report 1980,* Census Bulletin No. 17, 1985; cf. FAO, *1970 World Census of Agriculture* 1981, 54–57.

USA: FAO, *Report 1980,* Census Bulletin No. 14, 1985; cf. FAO, Census Bulletin 7, 1974.

Uruguay: FAO, *Report 1980,* Census Bulletin No. 8, 1984; cf. FAO, *1970 World Census of Agriculture* 1981, 100–02; *World Atlas* 1970 Vol. 3, 470; LTC, Land Concentration 1979, 184.

Venezuela: FAO, *1970 World Census of Agriculture* 1981, 100–02. Area owned or in ownerlike possession; cf. *World Atlas* 1970 Vol. 1970, 485–87; LTC, Land Concentration 1979, 185–87.

Vietnam: Kurian 1982, 1931. The data refer to North Vietnam; cf. *World Atlas* 1973 Vol. 2, 531.

Yemen Arab Republic: FAO, *Report 1980,* Census Bulletin No. 10, 1984. Estimated area owned or held in ownerlike possession; cf. *World Atlas* 1973 Vol. 2, 554–55; Kurian 1982, 1955; *Worldmark* 1984 Vol. 4, 424, according to which more than 80% of farm families work as tenants under a sharecropping system.

Yemen, People's Democratic Republic of: See *Economic Handbook of the World* 1981, 508; cf. Länder der Erde 1981, 311; Kurian 1982, 1969; Nohlen and Nuscheler 1983 Vol. 6, 349–50.

Yugoslavia: FAO, *Report 1980,* Census Bulletin No. 24, 1986; cf. FAO, *1970 World Census of Agriculture* 1981, 54; *World Atlas* 1969 Vol. 1, 518–20.

Notes *(continued)*

Zaire: Estimation. See *World Atlas* 1976 Vol. 4, 745; Riddell and Dickerman 1986; cf. FAO, Census Bulletin 20, 1978; LTC, Land Concentration 1979, 62–63.
Zambia: Estimation. See *World Atlas* 1976 Vol. 4, 753–55; Riddell and Dickerman 1986; cf. FAO, *Report 1970,* Census Bulletin No. 11, 1975; LTC, Land Concentration 1979, 64–65; FAO, *1970 World Census of Agriculture* 1981, 52.
Zimbabwe: Estimation. See *World Atlas* 1976 Vol. 4, 452–55; Riddell and Dickerman 1986; cf. LTC, Land Concentration 1979, 43–46.

APPENDIX 4

Estimated Degree of the Concentration of Nonagricultural Economic Resources

State	Public Sector	Public and foreign sectors	Concentrated private and foreign sectors	Concentrated private sector	Combined degree of concentration
1 Afghanistan	95				95
2 Albania	100				100
3 Algeria	90				90
4 Angola		90			90
5 Argentina	20		50		70
6 Australia				30	30
7 Austria				30	30
8 Bahamas	30		30		60
9 Bahrain		90			90
10 Bangladesh	75			10	85
11 Barbados			60		60
12 Belgium				30	30
13 Benin		90			90
14 Bhutan		30	30		60
15 Bolivia	40		30		70
16 Botswana		80			80
17 Brazil	35	15		20	70
18 Bulgaria	100				100
19 Burkina Faso		80		10	90
20 Burma	60			20	80
21 Burundi		90			90
22 Cameroon	40		50		90
23 Canada				40	40
24 Cape Verde	50		30		80
25 Central Af. Republic		90			90
26 Chad		90			90
27 Chile	20		40		60
28 China	98				98
29 Colombia		70		70	
30 Comoros		90			90
31 Congo, People's Rep. of		80			80
32 Costa Rica	20		30		50
33 Cuba	100				100
34 Cyprus				30	30
35 Czechoslovakia	100				100
36 Denmark				30	30
37 Djibouti	40		40		80
38 Dominican Republic			70		70
39 Ecuador	30		40		70
40 Egypt	80				80
41 El Salvador			70		70
42 Equatorial Guinea		95			95
43 Ethiopia	90				90
44 Fiji		70			70
45 Finland			30	30	
46 France				30	30

APPENDIX 4 (*continued*)

State	Public Sector	Public and foreign sectors	Concentrated private and foreign sectors	Concentrated private sector	Combined degree of concentration
47 Gabon		80			80
48 Gambia	40		40		80
49 German Dem. Republic	98				98
50 Germany, West				30	30
51 Ghana	40		30		70
52 Greece	20			30	50
53 Guatemala			80		80
54 Guinea		95			95
55 Guinea-Bissau		90			90
56 Guyana	80				80
57 Haiti			80		80
58 Honduras			70		70
59 Hungary	99				99
60 Iceland				20	20
61 India	30			20	50
62 Indonesia		80			80
63 Iran	60				60
64 Iraq	70			10	80
65 Ireland				30	30
66 Israel			40		40
67 Italy				30	30
68 Ivory Coast	40		40		80
69 Jamaica	30		40		70
70 Japan				40	40
71 Jordan	20		50		70
72 Kampuchea	100				100
73 Kenya	20		60		80
74 Korea, North	100				100
75 Korea, South	20		40		60
76 Kuwait		90			90
77 Laos	95				
78 Lebanon			40		40
79 Lesotho		90			90
80 Liberia			80		80
81 Libya		90			90
82 Luxemburg				30	30
83 Madagascar		80			80
84 Malawi		90			90
85 Malaysia			60		60
86 Mali		90			90
87 Malta	20		20		40
88 Mauritania		90			90
89 Mauritius				60	60
90 Mexico	30		40		70
91 Mongolia	100				100
92 Morocco		30		40	70
93 Mosambique	60		30		90
94 Nepal			80		80
95 Netherlands				30	30
96 New Zealand				30	30

APPENDIX 4 *(continued)*

State	Public Sector	Public and foreign sectors	Concentrated private and foreign sectors	Concentrated private sector	Combined degree of concentration
97 Nicaragua	40		40		80
98 Niger		90			90
99 Nigeria		80			80
100 Norway				30	30
101 Oman		90			90
102 Pakistan	40			30	70
103 Panama	30		50		80
104 Papua New Guinea		70			70
105 Paraguay		80			80
106 Peru	20		50		70
107 Philippines			70		70
108 Poland	98				98
109 Portugal	30		30		60
110 Qatar		95			95
111 Romania	100				100
112 Rwanda		80			80
113 Saudi Arabia		90			90
114 Senegal		90			90
115 Sierra Leone		50		20	70
116 Singapore			70		70
117 Solomon Islands		40			40
118 Somalia	90				90
119 South Africa	20		60		80
120 Spain				30	30
121 Sri Lanka	40			20	60
122 Sudan	50		30		80
123 Suriname	40		50		90
124 Swaziland		90			90
125 Sweden				35	35
126 Switzerland				30	30
127 Syria	80				80
128 Tanzania	50		30		80
129 Thailand		20	50		70
130 Togo		80			80
131 Trinidad and Tobago		30	40		70
132 Tunisia		50		30	80
133 Turkey	40			30	70
134 Uganda		80			80
135 USSR	100				100
136 United Arab Emirates		95			95
137 United Kingdom				30	30
138 United States				40	40
139 Uruguay	20		40		60
140 Venezuela	40		30		70
141 Vietnam	95				95
142 Yemen Arab Republic	60		30		90
143 Yemen, South	90				90
144 Yugoslavia	70				70
145 Zaire		90			90
146 Zambia		80			80
147 Zimbabwe			80		80

Notes:

Afghanistan: Since the 1978 revolution, the dominant sector has been public. The government controls virtually all of the country's utilities and the bulk of its investment capital. Population in absolute poverty 63% (see Banks et al. 1981; Nohlen and Nuscheler 1983 Vol. 7, 56; Kurian 1987).

Albania: All of the major means of production are owned by the state or cooperatives (see Länder der Erde 1981, 24–25; EIU, *Quarterly Economic Review of Rumania, Bulgaria, Albania.* Annual Supplement 1985, 49).

Algeria: Economy is basically Socialist; the government dominates all the key sectors. The state controls about 90% of Algerian industry (see *Algeria. A country study* 1979, 132–51; Banks et al. 1981; Länder der Erde 1981, 29; EIU, Algeria. Annual 1985; Kurian 1987). Public enterprises accounted for 68% of gross fixed capital formation in 1978–81 (Short 1984).

Angola: A centrally planned Socialist economy in which the dominant sector is public (see *Angola. A country study* 1979, 226–31; Banks et al. 1981; Länder der Erde 1981, 37; Kurian 1987). Nationalized industries accounted for 58% of total production in 1982, the private sector 29%, and joint ventures 13% (*Africa South of the Sahara* 1982–83, 197).

Argentina: A market economy in which the dominant sector is private, but the government also plays a significant role in the economy. Foreign sector provides about 40% of the production of manufacturing enterprises. On the other hand, about 40% of the industrial workers are employed by small enterprises (see Banks et al. 1981; Länder der Erde 1981, 45; Kurian 1987). Public enterprises accounted for 20% of gross fixed capital formation in 1978–80 (Short 1984).

Australia: See notes for Canada, Finland, and Sweden. Public enterprises accounted for 19% of gross fixed capital formation in 1978–79. In nearly all industrially developed countries this percentage was between 10 and 20 in 1978–80, which means that the private sector is dominant in these countries (see Short 1984, 116–29; Gardner 1988, 465).

Austria: See notes for Australia, Canada, Finland, and Sweden.

Bahamas: The private sector is dominant, but the public sector is also significant. Tourism is the major industry, and many hotels are owned by foreign companies (see Banks et al. 1981; Nohlen and Nuscheler 1982 Vol. 3, 244–46; Graham and Edwards 1984, 25–26; Kurian 1987). Public enterprises accounted for 32% of gross fixed capital formation in 1975–77 (Short 1984).

Bahrain: The Bahrain economy is based on oil (80%). The petroleum sector is completely owned and controlled by the government and foreign companies (see Banks et al. 1981; EIU, Bahrain, Qatar, Oman, The Yemens. Annual 1984; Kurian 1987).

Bangladesh: By 1975 about 80% of the manufacturing enterprises had been nationalized as well as foreign trade and most banks, but in the early 1980s private companies and new investments were being encouraged. In its first five-year plan (1973–78), about 80% of the plan's total outlay was allocated to the public sector (see Banks et al. 1981; Länder der Erde 1981, 64; Nohlen and Nuscheler 1983 Vol. 7, 77–84; Short 1984; Kurian 1987). Population below absolute poverty income level was 86% in 1975 (*Social Indicators of Development* 1988).

Barbados: A market economy in which the dominant sector is private (see Banks et al. 1981; Nohlen and Nuscheler 1982 Vol. 3, 258–63; Kurian 1987). Public en-

Notes (*continued*)

terprises accounted for 11% of gross fixed capital formation in 1978–80 (Short 1984). Population below absolute poverty income level was 23% in 1975 (*Social Indicators of Development* 1988).

Belgium: See notes for Australia, Canada, Finland, and Sweden.

Benin: The key sectors of nonagricultural economy were nationalized in 1972–74. The bulk of the manufacturing sector is controlled by the government. Population in absolute poverty 65% (see Banks et al. 1981; Länder der Erde 1981: 75; Nellis 1986, 5–11; Kurian 1987). According to *Worldmark* (1984 Vol. 2, 21), the government's share of industrial investments is nearly 50%, foreign investors' share 40%, and the private sector's share only 10%. Public enterprises accounted for 57% of gross domestic fixed capital formation in manufacturing in 1978–79 (Short 1984).

Bhutan: A market economy in which the predominant sector is private, but only 2% of the workforce is employed in industry. Most development plans have been financed through Indian grants. All industrial enterprises are small (Banks et al. 1981; Nohlen and Nuscheler 1983 Vol. 7, 101; Kurian 1987).

Bolivia: Since the 1952 popular revolution, the state has played a significant role in directing the economy, particularly in mining, which contributes 75–90% of the nation's export earnings (see Banks et al. 1981; Nohlen and Nuscheler 1982 Vol. 2, 116–29; Kurian 1987). Public enterprises accounted for 41% of gross fixed capital formation in 1974–77 and 85% of gross domestic product at factor cost in mining and quarring in 1973–75, but only 6% in manufacturing (Short 1984). Rural population below absolute poverty income level was 85% in 1975 (*Social Indicators of Development* 1988). However, according to Kurian (1987), only 20% of the population was living in absolute poverty.

Botswana: Mining and quarrying are the most important nonagricultural industries. Mining enterprises are nearly completely owned and controlled by the state and private foreign interests (see Banks et al. 1981; Nohlen and Nuscheler 1982 Vol. 5, 323–26; Kurian 1987). Public enterprises accounted for only 8% of gross fixed capital formation in 1978–79 (Short 1984; Nellis 1986). Population in absolute poverty 30–50% (Kurian 1984, Table 69; Kurian 1987).

Brazil: The government plays a central role in the economy. The state accounts for 37% of the total capital in 5000 largest enterprises, foreign investors 15%, and the private domestic sector 48% (Banks et al. 1981; Nohlen and Nuscheler 1982 Vol. 2, 150–59; Kurian 1987). Public enterprises accounted for 23% of gross fixed capital formation in 1980 (Short 1984). According to Kurian (1987), 8% of the population lives in absolute poverty.

Bulgaria: The share of the Socialist sector of gross industrial production was 99.8% in 1978 (CMEA 1979, 41; cf. Gardner 1988, 466).

Burkina Faso: Manufacturing is the most important nonagricultural industry. The state controls some large enterprises, but most industrial firms are wholly or partly foreign-owned. France continues to be the principal source of investment capital (see Banks et al. 1981; Nohlen and Nuscheler 1982 Vol. 4, 322–26; Nellis 1986, 5–11; Kurian 1987). Population in absolute poverty 75% (Kurian 1984, Table 69).

Notes (*continued*)

Burma: The key sectors of industry were nationalized in 1963. The public sector contributes nearly 3/4 of the value of industrial production (Länder der Erde 1981, 117; see also Worldmark 1984; Banks et al. 1981; EIU, Thailand, Burma. Annual 1985; Kurian 1987). Public enterprises accounted for 60% of gross fixed capital formation in 1978–80 and 56% of gross domestic product in manufacturing in 1980 (Short 1984). Population below absolute poverty income level was 40% in 1975 (*Social Indicators of Development* 1988).

Burundi: There is little industry apart from the processing of agricultural products. Europeans own about 40% of the manufacturing enterprises, which account for 96% of industrial employment (Banks et al. 1981; Kurian 1982, 273; *Africa South of the Sahara* 1982–83, 213–14; Nellis 1986, 8). Population below absolute poverty income level was 75% (urban 55 and rural 85) in 1975 (*Social Indicators of Development* 1988; cf. Kurian 1984, Table 69; Kurian 1987).

Cameroon: All industries are nearly completely owned or controlled by the government and foreign participants. The public sector accounted for 39% and the foreign sector 57% of the total capital in all industries in 1976 (see L'economie Camerounaise. Numéro spécial du bulletin de l'Afrique noire, 1977; Banks et al. 1981, 79–80; Nohlen and Nuscheler 1982 Vol. 4, 418–19; Kurian 1987). Population below absolute poverty income level was 15% in urban and 40% in rural areas in 1975 (*Social Indicators of Development* 1988; Kurian 1987).

Canada: Time (October 6, 1986, 40) refers to Diane Francis' book *Controlling Interest: Who Owns Canada?*, according to which 32 families and five conglomerates control a third of Canadian nonfinancial assets. The private sector's share of gross fixed capital formation was 87% in 1979 (United Nations, 1982; cf. Short 1984).

Cape Verde: Many industrial enterprises are joint ventures with foreign interests. The public and parastatal sectors accounted for nearly 50% of GDP in 1980 (see Banks et al. 1981; Kurian 1982, 324–27; EIU, The Economist Intelligence Review of Senegal, The Gambia, Guinea-Bissau, Cape Verde. Annual Supplement 1985, 79).

Central African Republic: Most large enterprises, whether in agriculture or industry, are partly owned by the state. On the other hand, there is a substantial private sector, but it is dominated by foreign capital (see Banks et al. 1981; Nohlen and Nuscheler 1982 Vol. 4, 528–29; EIU, Cameroon, CAR, Chad. Annual 1985, 38). Population in absolute poverty is 53% (Kurian 1984, Table 69; Kurian 1987).

Chad: Most of the industrial enterprises are owned by the state or are joint ventures by the state and foreign participants (see Banks et al. 1981; *Africa South of the Sahara* 1982–83, 297–99). Population below absolute poverty income level was 30% in urban and 56% in rural areas in 1975 (*Social Indicators of Development* 1988).

Chile: A market economy in which the dominant sector is private. The bulk of Chile's industries consists of relatively small manufacturing facilities that employ 50 or fewer workers. However, the private sector remains dominated by six major conglomerates: of over 95,000 firms, about 2% control nearly 2/3 of fixed assets. Participation by foreign firms in the Chilean economy has expanded markedly,

Notes (*continued*)

and some nationalized properties have been resold to foreign interests. Over 500 state-owned companies nationalized during the Allende years have been resold to private investors (see Banks et al. 1981; Kurian 1982 and 1987; Nohlen and Nuscheler 1982 Vol. 2, 205–06). Public enterprises accounted for 13% of gross fixed capital formation in 1978–80 (Short 1984). Population in absolute poverty is 8% (Kurian 1984, Table 69; Kurian 1987).

China: According to *Far East* and *Australasia* 1983–84 (1984, 271–76), only 1.5 million of the 115 million urban workers were in private enterprises (less than 2%).

Colombia: A market economy in which the dominant sector is private. Ten monopolies control 67% of the production capital (Länder der Erde 1981, 346. See also Banks et al. 1981; Nohlen and Nuscheler 1982 Vol. 2, 261–64; Kurian 1987). Public enterprises accounted for 9% of gross fixed capital formation in 1978–80 (Short 1984). Urban population below absolute poverty income level was 34% in 1975 (*Social Indicators of Development* 1988).

Comoros: The government is virtually the only employer of nonagricultural labor (EIU, Madagascar, Mauritius, Seychelles, Comoros. Annual 1985, 78. cf. Banks et al. 1981; Kurian 1987).

Congo: A centralized economic system in which the dominant sector is public (see Banks et al. 1981; EIU, Congo, Gabon, Equatorial Guinea. Annual 1985; Kurian 1987). Population in absolute poverty 23% (Kurian 1984, Table 69).

Costa Rica: As a consequence of the 1948 revolution, the state became a significant economic unit and took control of the major financial institutions by nationalizing the banking system. Most industrial enterprises are small; 18,000 out of the 29,000 enterprises employ fewer than 20 workers (see Banks et al. 1981; Nohlen and Nuscheler 1982 Vol. 3, 48–54; Kurian 1987). Public enterprises accounted for 20% of gross fixed capital formation in 1978–79 (Short 1984). Population in absolute poverty is 8% (Kurian 1984, Table 69; Kurian 1987).

Cuba: The share of the Socialist sector of gross industrial production was 100% in 1978 (CMEA 1979, 41; see also Nohlen and Nuscheler 1982 Vol. 3, 365; Kurian 1987; Gardner 1988, 466).

Cyprus: At independence, the manufacturing sector consisted almost entirely of small, family-owned enterprises having fewer than five workers. According to a census conducted in 1972, over 4/5 of the 7,612 plants in manufacturing still had from one to four employees; only about 30 establishments had more than 100 (*Cyprus. A Country Study* 1980, 126–30. See also Banks et al. 1981). Population in absolute poverty is 7% (Kurian 1984, Table 69).

Czechoslovakia: The public sector's share of gross industrial production was 100% in 1978 (CMEA 1979, 41; cf. Gardner 1988, 466).

Denmark: See notes for Australia, Canada, Finland, and Sweden.

Djibouti: Traditionally dependent on the activities of the port and railway and official capital flows from France. The public sector, which consists mostly of salaries paid by France to French civilian and military personnel, provides about 40% of the total GDP. There are no significant productive industries. Services and commerce generate virtually all the national income (see IMF Survey, Feb. 19, 1979, Banks et al. 1981; Kurian 1982; Nohlen and Nuscheler 1982 Vol. 5, 69–74).

Notes *(continued)*

Dominican Republic: The dominant sector is private (see Banks et al. 1981; Nohlen and Nuscheler 1982 Vol. 3, 289–94; *Latin America & Caribbean Review* 1986, 175–77; Kurian 1987). Public enterprises accounted for 8% of gross fixed capital formation in 1978–79 (Short 1984). Population below absolute income level was 43–45% in 1975 (*Social Indicators of Development* 1988).

Ecuador: The petroleum industry accounts for over half of national export earnings and most of the foreign capital invested in the country. This sector is completely owned and controlled by the state and foreign companies. The manufacturing industry is dominated by private domestic and foreign enterprises. Fewer than 100 factories account 70% of the total value of manufacturing (see Banks et al. 1981; *Latin America & Caribbean Review* 1986, 69–73; Kurian 1987). The public sector's share of gross fixed investments was 34% in 1979 (United Nations, 1982). Population below absolute poverty income level was 40% in urban and 65% in rural areas in 1975 (*Social Indicators of Development* 1988).

Egypt: The share of the public sector of the total industrial output was about 70% in the mid-1970s (see Banks et al. 1981; Nohlen and Nuscheler 1983 Vol. 6, 48–68) According to Kurian (1987), by 1971 the public industrial sector employed more than 80% of the work force and accounted for 90% of the value added. Public enterprises accounted for 48% of gross fixed capital formation and 80% of gross domestic fixed capital formation in mining, quarring, and manufacturing in 1979 (Short 1984). Population below absolute poverty income level was 21–25% in 1975 (*Social Indicators of Development* 1988).

El Salvador: The nonagricultural economy is dominated by private enterprises. Traditionally the so called 14 families have dominated the agricultural sector and played a significant role in El Salvador's industry, which centers on processing the country's principal farm commodities (see Banks et al. 1981; Nohlen and Nuscheler 1982 Vol. 3, 70–75; *Latin America & Caribbean Review* 1986, 75–77). Population below absolute poverty income level was 20–32% in 1975 (*Social Indicators of Development* 1988).

Equatorial Guinea: The nonagricultural sector of economy is very small. There are only few industrial and mining enterprises, and they are owned by the state or foreign companies (EIU, Congo, Gabon, Equatorial Guinea. Annual 1985. See also Banks et al. 1981; Nohlen and Nuscheler 1982 Vol. 4, 394–96; Kurian 1987).

Ethiopia: A centrally planned socialist economy. During the 1974–75 revolution 1/3 of industrial enterprises were nationalized. They employ about 90% of industrial workers. Handicrafts and cottage industries were left to the private sector. The financial sector was completely nationalized (see Länder der Erde 1981, 51; *Ethiopia. A Country Study* 1981, 166–70, 181–83; Nohlen and Nuscheler 1982 Vol. 5, 61–62; *Africa South of the Sahara* 1982–83, 377–81; Kurian 1987). Public enterprises accounted for 61% of gross domestic fixed capital formation in manufacturing in 1979–80 (Short 1984; see also Nellis 1986, 7–8; Marsden and Bélot 1988, 10–11). Population below absolute poverty income level was 60–65% in 1975 (*Social Indicators of Development* 1988).

Fiji: A market-oriented private enterprise system. Manufacturing employs about 15% of the labor force. Most of the industrial enterprises are owned and controlled by foreign investors (see Banks et al. 1981; Nohlen and Nuscheler 1983 Vol. 8, 258–

Notes *(continued)*

62; Kurian 1987). According to Ward (1971, 261), the share of foreign companies is almost 4/5 in overall (see also Browne 1989, 34–47). Population in absolute poverty is nine percent (Kurian 1984, Table 69; Kurian 1987).

Finland: According to Koste (1969, 64–83), large enterprises controlled by the so-called 10 families produced 25% of the total industrial production and paid 28% of the wages. It seems reasonable to assume that the level of nonagricultural economic resource concentration is approximately the same in most other industrially developed Western countries (cf. notes for Canada and Sweden).

France: See notes for Australia, Canada, Finland, and Sweden; cf. Gardner 1988, 173–84.

Gabon: Mining and oil are the largest sectors in Gabon's economy. They are dominated by foreign companies. In 1978 the oil sector accounted for 40% of the GDP, 70% of export receipts, and 55% of government revenue. The state holds 25% interests in all oil companies. Most manufacturing establishments are owned by French private interests. The government has pursued a policy of encouraging private foreign investment. However, more recently it has acquired from 10 to 60% of the equity in most of the major companies operating in Gabon (see Banks et al. 1981; *Worldmark* 1984 Vol. 2, 104–05; EIU, Congo, Gabon, Equatorial Guinea. Annual 1985, 37; Kurian 1987). Population in absolute poverty is 7% (Kurian 1984, Table 69; Kurian 1987).

Gambia: Tourism is the most dynamic sector of the economy. It remains almost exclusively under foreign control. Manufacturing contributes 7% to the GDP and employs 8% of the labor force. The major industry is peanut processing, which was nationalized with the acquisition of two crushing mills in 1975 (see *The Gambia*. 1977, 4–7; Banks et al. 1981; Nohlen and Nuscheler 1982 Vol. 4, 165–67; Kurian 1987). Public enterprises accounted for 38% of gross fixed capital formation in 1978–80 (Short 1984. See also Nellis 1986, 9–11). Population in absolute poverty 45% (Kurian 1984, Table 69).

German Democratic Republic: The share of the socialist sector of gross industrial production was 97.8% in 1978 (CMEA 1979, 41; cf. Gardner 1988, 466).

Germany, Federal Republic of: See notes for Australia, Canada, Finland, and Sweden; cf. Gardner 1988, 131–46.

Ghana: A mixed economy has evolved, in which the government and various state enterprises play key roles in major sectors. Much of the country's heavy industry is run by the government's Ghana Industrial Holding Company. Many manufacturing, mining, and oil enterprises are still partly or completely foreign-owned. On the other hand, most industrial enterprises (85%) are small establishments, which employ less than six persons (see Banks et al. 1981; Nohlen and Nuscheler 1982 Vol. 4, 185–86; *Worldmark* 1984 Vol. 2, 117; EIU, Quarterly Economic Review of Ghana, Sierra Leone, Liberia 1985, 25; Kurian 1987). In manufacturing, the percentage share of public enterprises was 33% of the gross value of product in 1970 (Short 1984). According to Marsden and Blot (1988, 12), by 1977 an estimated 49% of manufacturing value added came from the state sector. Population in absolute poverty 25% (Kurian 1984: Table 69; Kurian 1987).

Greece: About 40 % of the manufacturing sector is owned by the state (Länder der

Notes (*continued*)

Erde 1981, 209). Public enterprises accounted for 9% of gross fixed capital formation in 1979 (Short 1984).

Guatemala: A market economy in which the dominant sector is private. Most of the large enterprises are owned and run by the richest two percent of Guatemalans and foreigners who dominate not only agriculture but commerce and finance (see Banks et al. 1981; Nohlen and Nuscheler 1982 Vol. 3, 92–97; Kurian 1987). Public enterprises accounted for 13% of gross fixed capital formation in 1978–80 (Short 1984). Population below absolute poverty income level was 21–25% in 1975 (*Social Indicators of Development* 1988).

Guinea: Mining, which accounts for nearly 1/4 of GDP and 95% of export earnings, is completely dominated by the state and foreign companies. Almost all manufacturing enterprises are owned by the state. The public sector's share of industrial production is nearly 90% (see Banks et al. 1981; Länder der Erde 1981, 235; Kurian 1982; Nohlen and Nuscheler 1982 Vol. 4, 200–03; Nellis 1986, 7–11; Marsden and Bélot 1988, 11). Population in absolute poverty 70% (Kurian 1984, Table 69; Kurian 1987).

Guinea-Bissau: A centrally planned Socialist economy in which the dominant sector is public. The modern sector of economy is dominated by state enterprises, although mixed and joint ventures also participate in industry. In 1980 about 80% of the work force were employed in the public sector (see Banks et al. 1981; EIU, The Economist Intelligence Review of Senegal, The Gambia, Guinea-Bissau, Cape Verde. Annual Supplement 1985, 58; Kurian 1987).

Guyana: Economy is dominated by the public sector, which, as a consequence of a nationalization program carried out in the mid 1970s, controls about 80% of the total productive capacity (see Banks et al. 1981; Länder der Erde 1981, 238–39; Nohlen and Nuscheler 1982 Vol. 3, 320–21; Kurian 1987). Public enterprises accounted for 35% of gross fixed capital formation in 1978–80 (Short 1984). Population in absolute poverty 17% (Kurian 1984, Table 69).

Haiti: A market economy in which the dominant sector is private. Most of the largest industrial enterprises are wholly or partly foreign-owned. According to Länder der Erde (1981, 242), U.S. investments represent about 70% of the total investments in Haiti (see also Banks et al. 1981; Kurian 1987). Public enterprises accounted for 12% of gross fixed capital formation in 1978–80 (Short 1984). Population below absolute poverty income level was 55–78% in 1975 (*Social Indicators of Development* 1988).

Honduras: A market economy in which the dominant sector is private. According to one estimate, 60% of industry is owned by foreign companies (see Banks et al. 1981; Nohlen and Nuscheler 1982 Vol. 3, 109; Kurian 1987). Public enterprises accounted for 15% of gross fixed capital formation in 1978–80 (Short 1984). Population below absolute poverty income level was 14% in urban and 55% in rural areas in 1975 (*Social Indicators of Development* 1988).

Hungary: The share of the Socialist sector of gross industrial production was 99.4% in 1978 (CMEA 1979, 41; cf. Gardner 1988, 466).

Iceland: See notes for Australia, Canada, Finland, and Sweden.

India: A mixed economy in which a sizable public sector exists side-by-side with a

Notes (*continued*)

vigorous private sector. In 1977–78 there were 84,924 factories employing 10 or more workers. The public sector's share of these factories was 4.6%, of employment 24%, of fixed capital 65.3%, and of gross output 29.9% (*Statistical Outline of India* 1982, 77; see also India 1979, 286–28; Banks et al. 1981; Länder der Erde 1981, 263; Kurian 1987). According to Länder der Erde (1981, 263), the public sector controls 30% of the industrial production. In the private sector, the 10 largest monopol groups control over 50% of the capital investments. However, most industrial workers (70–80%) are employed by village and small industries. Therefore, nonagricultural economic resources seem to be relatively widely distributed. Public enterprises accounted for 34% of gross fixed capital formation in 1978 and 16% of gross domestic product at factor cost in manufacturing in 1978 (Short 1984). Population in absolute poverty is 40% in urban and 51% in rural areas (Kurian 1987).

Indonesia: Most large industries are owned by the state or partly foreign-owned. According to one estimate, as much as 90% of the economy may fall under government (largely Malay) control (see Banks et al. 1981; Nohlen and Nuscheler 1983 Vol. 7, 323–28; Kurian 1987). According to EIU, Indonesia. Annual (1985, 38), cottage industries (less than five workers) employ about 80% of the industrial work force, although they produce only 13% of the value of production. Medium-size and large enterprises (more than 20 workers) employ 13% of the industrial work force, but produce 80% of the value of production. Population below absolute poverty income level was 28% in urban and 51% in rural areas in 1975 (*Social Indicators of Development* 1988).

Iran: After the 1979 revolution, the rest of the foreign oil companies, banks and insurance companies, and foreign trade were nationalized. A considerable part of manufacturing industries were also nationalized. As a consequence, the public sector is by far the most exhaustive, including large industries, mines, and irrigation networks; banking, insurance, transportation, communications, and foreign trade (see Banks et al. 1981; EIU, *Quarterly Economic Review of Iran*. Annual Supplement 1984; Kurian 1987). Population in absolute poverty 5% (Kurian 1984, Table 69; Kurian 1987).

Iraq: In the 1960s and 1970s a nationalization program was carried out. In addition to the oil industry, major manufacturing firms and large companies performing banking, insurance, and commercial services were nationalized. A small number of state-owned establishments generates more than half the value and employs more than half of the workers in the manufacturing sector, although numerous small and middle-size firms exist in the private sector. According to one estimate, the public sector generates 75% of the value of industrial production (see Banks et al. 1981; Länder der Erde 1981, 263; see also *Iraq. A Country Study* 1979, 138–53; Kurian 1987). Public enterprises accounted for 97% of gross domestic fixed capital formation in manufacturing in 1975 (Short 1984). Population in absolute poverty 11% (Kurian 1984, Table 69).

Ireland: See notes for Australia, Canada, Finland, and Sweden.

Israel: In 1976 private owners operated 96% of industrial establishments and employed 70% of the industrial workers. About 70% of the 12,000 industrial estab-

Notes (*continued*)

lishments had fewer than ten workers. 100 of the largest plants, employing more than 300 workers, accounted for about 40% of industrial output and over 80% of industrial exports in 1977. The nearly 5,000 medium-size plants, employing 25 to 300 workers, accounted for nearly 45% of industrial production (see *Israel. A Country Study* 1979, 206).

Italy: See notes for Australia, Canada, Finland, and Sweden. Of all the industrial enterprises, 99.6% had less than 200 workers and they employed 59.4% of all industrial workers (see *Annuario Statistico Italiano* 1980, 162).

Ivory Coast: In 1979, 32% of the industry was owned by the state, 55% by foreign interests, and 13 % by domestic participants (*Worldmark* 1984 Vol. 2, 137). According to EIU, *Quarterly Economic Review of Ivory Coast* (1985, 31), in 1982, the share of the state was 51%, the share of foreign interests 35%, and the share of domestic participants 13% (see also Banks et al. 1981; *Africa South of the Sahara* 1982–83, 507–08). Public enterprises accounted for 39% of gross fixed capital formation in 1979 (Short 1984; Nellis 1986, 5–11). Population in absolute poverty 26–30% (Kurian 1987).

Jamaica: A mixed economy in which the dominant sector is private. About 80% of industry is in the hands of the private sector, a considerable part in the hands of foreign interests (see Banks et al. 1981; *Latin America & Caribbean Review* 1986, 185–87). According to Nohlen and Nuscheler (1982 Vol. 3, 351–52), 21 families control the large enterprises and banks. Public enterprises accounted for 27% of gross fixed capital formation in 1978–81 (Short 1984). Population below absolute poverty income level was 80 % in rural areas in 1975 (Social Indicators of Development 1988).

Japan: Of the industrial enterprises, 99% are small (fewer than 100 employees), and they employ 75% of industrial workers (Gardner 1988, 195), but the three largest monopol groups (Mitsui, Mitsubishi, and Sumitomo) control over 40% of industrial production (Länder der Erde 1981, 301; see also *Japan Statistical Yearbook* 1982, 188–89; Short 1984).

Jordan: In 1976 only 15 out of nearly 5,000 industrial establishments employed 100 or more workers, but they accounted for a substantial part of industrial employment and fixed assets. Large-scale plants are owned by the state or foreign companies, whereas most of the medium-size and small enterprises are domestically owned (see *Jordan. A Country Study* 1980, 134–35; Nohlen and Nuscheler 1983 Vol. 6, 371–72). Population in absolute poverty 14–17% (Kurian 1987).

Kampuchea: A centrally planned Socialist economy in which the entire economic sector is public. The Pol Pot government nationalized all businesses in 1975 (see Banks et al. 1981; Länder der Erde 1981, 329; EIU, Indochina: Vietnam, Laos, Cambodia. Annual 1985, 44–45; Kurian 1987).

Kenya: A market-oriented economy with a sizable private sector and substantial foreign investments. In 1976 it was estimated that the share of foreign investments in large industrial and service establishments was over 40%. According to one estimate (Länder der Erde), about 80% of industrial production is controlled by the British monopol capital (see Banks et al. 1981; Länder der Erde 1981, 343; Nohlen and Nuscheler 1982 Vol. 5, 139–40; EIU, Kenya. Annual 1985, 17).

Notes (*continued*)

Public enterprises accounted for 17% of gross fixed capital formation in 1978–79 (Short 1984; Nellis 1986, 9). Population below absolute poverty income level was 10% in urban areas and 55% in rural areas in 1975 (*Social Indicators of Development* 1988).

Korea, Democratic People's Republic of: A centrally planned Socialist economy with virtually no market sector. About 90% of all industry is owned by the state and 10% by cooperatives (see Banks et al. 1981; Länder der Erde 1981, 355–56; Kurian 1987).

Korea, Republic of: A market-oriented economy in which the dominant sector is private, but the government plays an important role in the economic system, too. The state-owned enterprises contribute about 10% to the GDP (see Banks et al. 1981; Nohlen and Nuscheler 1983 Vol. 8, 122–28). Privately owned small- and medium-scale manufacturing establishments, having under 200 regular employees, constitute 98% of all industrial units, provide 54% of employment, and account for 36% of value added in manufacturing (Kurian 1987). Public enterprises accounted for 23% of gross fixed capital formation in 1978 and 15% of gross domestic product at factor cost in manufacturing in 1974–77 (Short 1984).

Kuwait: Oil accounts for about 3/4 of the GNP and 9/10 of export earnings. The petroleum industry is completely owned and controlled by the state and foreign companies. Manufacturing accounts for about 7% of the GDP. There are some large state-owned enterprises alongside numerous small and medium private concerns (see Banks et al. 1981; Länder der Erde 1981; Nohlen and Nuscheler 1983 Vol. 6, 392–93; Kurian 1987).

Laos: A centrally planned economy dominated by the public sector. In 1977 the government nationalized all the major sectors of the economy. Manufacturing and mining contributed less than 15% of the GDP in 1977. Small enterprises have remained in the hands of the private sector (see Banks et al. 1981; EIU, Indochina: Vietnam, Laos, Cambodia. Annual 1985, 30; Kurian 1987).

Lebanon: A market economy in which the dominant sector is private. The services sector is the largest one. It employs about 60% of the work force and contributes 70% of the GDP. Manufacturing has played a smaller role. State participation has been limited to equity in number of concerns. Most enterprises are small or medium-size, and they employ most of the workers (see Banks et al. 1981; Kurian 1987).

Lesotho: The country is economically dependent on South Africa, which is its major trading partner and the source of employment for a very large part of its labor force. There are only few mining and manufacturing enterprises, they are mostly owned by foreign companies or they are joint ventures with the state (see Banks et al. 1981; Kurian 1987). Population in absolute poverty 50–55% (Kurian 1987).

Liberia: A market economy in which the dominant private sector consists mainly of foreign companies. The rubber and mining industries, the banking system, construction, and the railways are almost entirely in the hands of foreign investors, particularly American businesses (see Banks et al. 1981; Länder der Erde 1981, 380; Kurian 1987). According to Nohlen and Nuscheler (1982 Vol. 4, 230–31), about 3/4 of all the enterprises are foreign owned. Public enterprises accounted

Notes (*continued*)

for 14% of gross fixed capital formation in 1974–76 (Short 1984; Nellis 1986, 5–9). Population below absolute poverty income level was 23% in urban areas in 1975 (*Social Indicators of Development* 1988).

Libya: The economy is dominated by the petroleum industry, which employs only 10% of the labor force but contributes over half of the country's GDP and more than 99% of export earnings. The petroleum industry is completely owned and controlled by the government and foreign oil companies (see Libya. A country study 1979, 152–53; Banks et al. 1981; Kurian 1987). Most manufacturing enterprises are still privately owned, but, according to one estimate (Länder der Erde 1981, 329), the share of public sector is about 70% of industrial production.

Luxemburg: See notes for Australia, Canada, Finland, and Sweden.

Madagascar: As a consequence of comprehensive nationalization that encompassed banking, insurance, most trade, petroleum refining, a number of other industries, and plantations, the government controlled over 70% of the national economy in 1979. Before nationalization foreign investors controlled approximately 85% of the industrial sector, whereas now direct foreign investment is limited to minority participation (see Banks et al. 1981; Länder der Erde 1981, 390; Nohlen and Nuscheler 1982 Vol. 5, 236–40; Kurian 1987). The state sector and public enterprises employed 72% of the labor force in the modern sector in 1980 (Pryor 1988a, 48, 70). Population below absolute poverty income level 50% (Social Indicators of Development 1988). Malawi: A nonagricultural economy that is nearly completely dominated by foreign companies and the Press (Holding) Ltd., which is 99% owned by President Banda. Through this company economic power is also concentrated in the hands of the president (see Länder der Erde 1981, 394; Nohlen and Nuscheler 1982 Vol. 5, 344–48, 353–54; Nellis 1986, 5–9; Kurian 1987; Pryor 1988b). Population below absolute poverty income level was 25% in urban areas and 85% in rural areas in 1975 (*Social Indicators of Development* 1988).

Malaysia: A market economy in which the government plays an active role and in which the private sector is still dominated by foreign investors. In 1970 foreigners owned 60% of publicly listed corporations. Since then the share of the state and domestic investors has increased (see Banks et al. 1981; Nohlen and Nuscheler 1983 Vol. 7, 392–96; Kurian 1987). According to Länder der Erde (1981), foreign capital controls about 50% of the Malaysian economy. Population below absolute poverty income level was 21% in urban areas and 59% in rural areas in 1975 (*Social Indicators of Development* 1988).

Mali: All large enterprises, as well as virtually all communications, transportation, and power facilities, are owned by the state. Private firms tend to be either small or medium-size. Over 85% of the industrial output is accounted for by state companies. The present structure of industry is characterized by the dominance of few large public enterprises, mostly processing local raw materials for domestic and export markets, and by a smaller private sector consisting of number of small and mainly foreign-owned firms in miscellaneous activities (see Banks et al. 1981; Länder der Erde 1981, 400; Nohlen and Nuscheler 1982 Vol. 4, 254; Kurian 1987). Population below absolute poverty income level was 27% in urban areas and 48% in rural areas in 1975 (*Social Indicators of Development* 1988).

Notes (*continued*)

Malta: The economy is dominated by the private sector, but the government employs 25% of the labour force. Most industrial enterprises are small or medium-size (see Banks et al. 1981; *Commonwealth Fact Sheet*. Malta 1976). Public enterprises accounted for 6% of gross fixed capital formation in 1978–80 (Short 1984).

Mauritania: Mining is the most important nonagricultural sector of the economy. Mining enterprises are completely owned by the state and foreign companies (see Banks et al. 1981; Nohlen and Nuscheler 1982 Vol. 4, 268–70; Kurian 1987). Public enterprises accounted for 37% of gross fixed capital formation in 1978–79 (Short 1984). Population in absolute poverty 34% (Kurian 1984, Table 69).

Mauritius: A market economy in which the dominant sector is private. Manufacturing is the largest nonagricultural sector. Industrial enterprises are partly locally owned and partly foreign owned. In the Export Processing Zone, which was established in 1971 and which produced 4/5 of all manufacturing exports in 1976, about half of the firms are locally owned (see *Mauritius. Commonwealth Fact Sheet* 1978; Banks et al. 1981; Kurian 1987). Public enterprises accounted for 14% of gross fixed capital formation in 1977–79 (Short 1984; Nellis 1986). Population in absolute poverty 19% (Kurian 1984, Table 69).

Mexico: A mixed economy with a substantial public sector. The state controls about 50% of industrial capital investments (Länder der Erde 1981, 413). According to a *Time's* story (Aug. 25, 1986), the Institutional Revolutionary Party (P.R.I.) employs 3 million bureaucrats and controls about half of the economy. However, according to Aspe and Sigmund (1984, 360–67), the state enterprises employed only 8% of the industrial workers in 1975 (see also Nohlen and Nuscheler 1982 Vol. 3, 131–37; Kurian 1987). Public enterprises accounted for 29% of gross fixed capital formation in 1978 (Short 1984). Population in absolute poverty 10% (Kurian 1984, Table 69).

Mongolia: The share of the socialist sector of gross industrial production was 100% in 1978 (CMEA 1979, 41; cf. Gardner 1988, 466).

Morocco: A mixed economy in which both public and private sectors play important roles. Small-scale industry, employing between 10 and 50 persons, accounts for 3/4 of industrial employment and 40% of the value of industrial production. Mining is controlled by the public sector and foreign companies, whereas almost all textile mills are privately owned (see *Morocco. A Country Study* 1978, 184–86; Banks et al. 1981; Kurian 1987). Public enterprises accounted for 26% of gross domestic fixed capital formation in manufacturing in 1974–76 (Short 1984). Population below absolute poverty income level was 38–45% in 1975 (*Social Indicators of Development* 1988).

Mosambique: A centrally planned economy in which the dominant sector is public. Before independence 85 % of industry was privately owned. In 1982 the government controlled 62% of industry, the private sector 27%, and the rest 11% were mixed state/private enterprises (see Banks et al. 1981; EIU, Tanzania, Mozambique. Annual 1985, 38; Kurian 1987).

Nepal: The private sector predominates Nepal's market economy (Kurian 1987; see also Banks et al. 1981; Shrestha 1982: 15–20). According to one estimate (Länder der Erde 1981, 432), about 80% of industrial enterprises are controlled by Indian

Notes (*continued*)

investors. Public enterprises accounted for 13% of gross fixed capital formation in 1971–73 but only 4% of gross domestic product at factor cost in manufacturing in 1974–75 (Short 1984). Population below absolute poverty income level was 55–61% in 1975 (*Social Indicators of Development* 1988).

Netherlands: See notes for Australia, Canada, Finland, and Sweden.

New Zealand: See notes for Australia, Canada, Finland, and Sweden.

Nicaragua: A mixed economy in which the dominant sector is public. By 1980 over 200 companies had been nationalized, but more than half of the industry remained privately owned (see Banks et al. 1981; Nohlen and Nuscheler 1982 Vol. 3, 155–58; Kurian 1987). According to one estimate (*Countries* 1983 Supplement, 294), about 40% of industry is controlled by the government. The rest is in the hands of domestic and foreign private companies. Population below absolute poverty income level was 19–21% in 1975 (*Social Indicators of Development* 1988).

Niger: Mining serves as the economy's principal engine of growth. Uranium production accounts for approximately 2/3 of the country's trade receipts and is the major single source of national income. Mining is completely controlled by the state and foreign companies. In manufacturing the pattern of ownership is mixed. Most industrial enterprises are owned by French companies (see Banks et al. 1981; Nohlen and Nuscheler 1982 Vol. 4, 286–88; Nellis 1986, 5–11; Kurian 1987). Population below absolute poverty income level was 35% in rural areas in 1975 (*Social Indicators of Development* 1988).

Nigeria: The economy is dependent on petroleum exports. In 1980 the petroleum industry's share of export earnings was 96% and of the state's budget revenue 84%. The petroleum sector is completely controlled by the state and foreign companies. Manufacturing, which employs only 1% of the labor force, is dominated by low-technology light industries. Most of the industrial enterprises are privately owned (see Banks et al. 1981; Nohlen and Nuscheler 1982 Vol. 4, 305–07; *Worldmark* 1984 Vol. 2, 240–41; Kurian 1987; Marsden and Bélot 1988, 12). According to Schatz (1977, 122), in the modern sector of manufacturing, the share of foreign companies was 85% and the share of domestic entrepreneurs 15% in 1965. Population in absolute poverty 30% (Kurian 1984, Table 69).

Norway: See notes for Australia, Canada, Finland, and Sweden.

Oman: All sectors of economy are overshadowed by oil, which contributes 99% of Oman's exports. The oil industry is completely owned by the state and foreign companies. Most manufacturing enterprises are privately owned (see Banks et al. 1981; Nohlen and Nuscheler 1983 Vol. 6, 429–33; Kurian 1987).

Pakistan: Before the nationalizations in 1972–74, the so called 22 families controlled the major part of the nonagricultural economy. Prime Minister Bhutto nationalized insurance firms in 1972 and banks in 1974, as well as numerous large factories (see Banks et al. 1981; Nohlen and Nuscheler 1983 Vol. 7, 207–17; Kurian 1987). Public enterprises accounted for 44% of gross fixed capital formation in 1978–81 (Short 1984). Population below absolute poverty income level was 42–43% in 1975 (*Social Indicators of Development* 1988).

Panama: A market economy in which the dominant sector is private. Large enterprises (50 or more workers) employ 55% of industrial workers and generate about

Notes (*continued*)

75% of industrial production. Most of them are privately (foreign and domestic) owned (see Banks et al. 1981; Nohlen and Nuscheler 1982 Vol. 3, 180–85; Kurian 1987). Public enterprises accounted for 28% of gross fixed capital formation in 1978–79 (Short 1984). Population below absolute poverty income level was 21% in urban areas and 30% in rural areas in 1975 (*Social Indicators of Development* 1988).

Papua New Guinea: Most industrial enterprises are foreign-owned. However, in mining, which provides about 55% of export earnings, the ownership is shared by the state and foreign companies (see *Papua New Guinea. Commonwealth Fact Sheet* 1976; Banks et al. 1981; Nohlen and Nuscheler 1983 Vol. 8, 289–94; Kurian 1987; Browne 1989, 84–88). Public enterprises accounted for 19% of gross fixed capital formation in 1977 (Short 1984). Population below absolute poverty income level is 10% in urban areas and 75% in rural areas (*Social Indicators of Development* 1988).

Paraguay: Foreign capital controls about 80% of the industrial production in Paraguay (see Länder der Erde 1981, 478; Kurian 1987). Public enterprises accounted for only 5% of gross fixed capital formation in 1978–80 (Short 1984). Population below absolute poverty income level was 19% in urban areas and 50% in rural areas in 1975 (*Social Indicators of Development* 1988).

Peru: In the 1960s foreign corporations accounted for 40% of the fixed assets and 44% of the value of production in manufacturing. Since then nationalizations have reduced the share of foreign ownership, but foreign-owned companies still play a significant role in Peru's economy. Mining is dominated by large establishments owned by the state and foreign companies (see Stepan 1978; *Peru. A Country Study* 1981, 149–51; Banks et al. 1981; Nohlen and Nuscheler 1982 Vol. 2, 305–24; Kurian 1987). The share of large public sector enterprises is about 25% of industrial production (Länder der Erde 1981, 483). Public enterprises accounted for 11% of gross fixed capital formation in 1978 (Short 1984). Population below absolute poverty income level was 49% in urban areas in 1975 (*Social Indicators of Development* 1988).

Philippines: A market-oriented economic system in which the dominant sector is private. Manufacturing is dominated by the private sector and is generally concentrated in large-scale capital-intensive units. Firms employing over 100 workers contribute 70% of the value of manufacturing (see Banks et al. 1981; Nohlen and Nuscheler 1983 Vol. 7, 412–16). According to one estimate (Länder der Erde 1981, 486), U.S. companies control about 40% of manufacturing industries. Public enterprises accounted for 11% of gross fixed capital formation in 1978 (Short 1984). Population in absolute poverty is 32% in urban and 41% in rural areas (Kurian 1987).

Poland: The share of the socialist sector of gross industrial production was 98.2% in 1978 (Comecon Statistical Yearbook 1979, 41; cf. Gardner 1988, 466).

Portugal: In 1974–75 many sectors of nonagricultural economy were nationalized completely or partly (see *Countries* 1983, 940). Public enterprises accounted for 33% of gross fixed capital formation in 1978–80 (Short 1984). Population in absolute poverty is 6% (Kurian 1984, Table 69).

Notes (*continued*)

Qatar: The economy is dominated by petroleum, which accounts for 50% of the GNP, over 90% of government revenue, and 95% of exports. The oil sector is wholly owned by the state and foreign companies. The private sector has played a limited role in industrial development (see Banks et al. 1981; Nohlen and Nuscheler 1983 Vol. 6, 381–83; Kurian 1987).

Romania: The share of the Socialist sector of gross industrial production was 100% in 1978 (CMEA 1979, 41).

Rwanda: Manufacturing employs less than 2% of the labor force and contributes 15% to the GDP. Most manufacturing firms are owned by Europeans or Asians. The mining sector is controlled by four Belgian companies (see Banks et al. 1981; Nohlen and Nuscheler 1982 Vol. 5, 156–60; *Africa South of the Sahara* 1982–83, 822–23; *Worldmark* 1984 Vol. 2, 250–52). Percentage of population in absolute poverty is 30% in urban and 90% in rural areas (Kurian 1987).

Saudi Arabia: Petroleum dominates the economy. Oil accounts for almost all national exports and approximately 90% of government revenue. The petroleum sector is wholly controlled by the state and foreign companies (see Banks et al. 1981; Länder der Erde 1981, 530; Nohlen and Nuscheler 1983 Vol. 6, 451–59; Kurian 1987). Population in absolute poverty 10% (Kurian 1984, Table 69).

Senegal: Industry and mining together account for about 20% of the country's GDP. Much of the industry is foreign-owned, especially by French firms, but the state plays an active role in the economy, too. In the mining, energy, manufacturing, and banking sectors French firms controlled 82% of the capital in the end of the 1970s (see Banks et al. 1981; Nohlen and Nuscheler 1982 Vol. 4, 336–37; *Worldmark* 1984 Vol. 2, 261; Kurian 1987). Public enterprises accounted for 18% of gross fixed capital formation in 1974 (Nellis 1986, 9). Population in absolute poverty 36% (Kurian 1987).

Sierra Leone: Mining and manufacturing are the most important nonagricultural sectors of the economy. In both areas mining the large enterprises are owned by the state and foreign companies, whereas many small enterprises are locally owned. The sector of small manufacturing and cottage enterprises employs 95% of the labor force and generates 50% of the value of industrial production (see Banks et al. 1981; Nohlen and Nuscheler 1982 Vol. 4, 351–58; EIU, *Quarterly Economic Review of Ghana*, Sierra Leone, Liberia 1985, 47). Public enterprises accounted for 20% of gross fixed capital formation in 1979 (Short 1984; Nellis 1986, 9). Percentage of population in absolute poverty is 39 (Kurian 1984, Table 69; Kurian 1987).

Singapore: A market-oriented economic system in which the private sector is predominant. Services and manufacturing are the most important sectors of the economy. The Census of Industrial Production in 1980 listed 451 foreign firms accounting for 26% of manufacturing establishments, contributing 66% to the value added in manufacturing, 69% to the gross value of output, and employing 55% of the work force (see Banks et al. 1981; Nohlen and Nuscheler 1983 Vol. 7, 436–63; Kurian 1987). Public enterprises accounted for 14% of gross domestic product at factor cost in manufacturing in 1972 (Short 1984). Population in absolute poverty 6% (Kurian 1987).

Notes (*continued*)

Solomon Islands: About 5% of the labor force was employed in manufacturing in 1977. Manufacturing activities are rudimentary and mainly intended for local use. There are light industries, located at Honiara, such as boatmaking, furniture assembly, soapmaking, garment production, and the manufacturing of nails (see Banks et al. 1981; Nohlen and Nuscheler 1983 Vol. 8, 304–08; Kurian 1987; Browne 1989, 9–17, 109–13).

Somalia: Substantial nationalization of the Somali economy in 1975 eliminated most private foreign investment (see Banks et al. 1981; Nohlen and Nuscheler 1982 Vol. 5, 81–83). According to one estimate (Länder der Erde 1981, 556), the public sector controls about 70% of industrial production. Kurian (1987) estimates that 89% of the value added in manufacturing is accounted for by the public sector. According to Short (1984), the percentage share of public enterprises was 59% of gross domestic product at factor cost in manufacturing in 1974–77. Population below absolute poverty income level was 40% in urban and 70% in rural areas in 1975 (*Social Indicators of Development* 1988).

South Africa: The concentration of the means of production in the hands of a few large firms is characteristic of many of South Africa's industries. Government participation is extensive, particularly in heavy industry and energy. The white minority controls practically all the means of production (see Banks et al. 1981; *Africa South of the Sahara* 1982–83, 944–51).

Spain: See notes for Australia, Canada, Finland, and Sweden.

Sri Lanka: A mixed economy in which the public and private sectors are roughly in balance. The state intervenes in most areas of economic life. Manufacturing is dominated by the public sector. Its corporations account for 40–50% of the total industrial output, but a large number of small private enterprises contribute the other half of industrial production and employ considerably more industrial workers than the public sector (see Lakshman 1980, 18–20; Banks et al. 1981; *Worldmark* 1984 Vol. 4, 327; EIU, Sri Lanka (Ceylon). Annual 1985, 14). According to Kurian (1987), the public sector accounts for 40% of the industrial output. Public enterprises accounted for 28% of gross fixed capital formation in 1978 and 33% of gross domestic product at factor cost in manufacturing in 1974 (Short 1984). Population in absolute poverty 22% (Kurian 1984, Table 69).

Sudan: At independence in 1956, the "commanding heights" of the economy were owned and/or controlled by foreign firms. The private sector was dominated by foreign companies. In 1969–71 the government nationalized numerous private enterprises, which reduced the share of foreign ownership and retarded private domestic and foreign investment (see Banks et al. 1981; Nohlen and Nuscheler 1982 Vol. 5, 100–02; Oesterdiekhoff and Wahlmuth 1983, 260; Kurian 1987; Marsden and Bélot 1988, 11–12). The percentage share of public enterprises of gross domestic product at factor cost was 40% in 1975 (Nellis 1986, 7). Population below absolute poverty income level was 85% in rural areas in 1975 (*Social Indicators of Development* 1988).

Suriname: A mixed public-private economy which is dominated by private foreign companies. Mining (bauxite) is the most important nonagricultural sector of the economy. It accounts for about 85% of export earnings, 40% of government rev-

Notes (*continued*)

enue, and 30% of gross domestic product. Mining is controlled by foreign companies. Manufacturing is also dominated by foreign companies. They employ about 15% of the total labor force. The government is the largest employer. It employs about 40% of the labor force (see Banks et al. 1981; Nohlen and Nuscheler 1982 Vol. 3, 415–22; Kurian 1987) .

Swaziland: A market-oriented economic system dominated by foreign companies. Manufacturing and mining are the most important nonagricultural economic sectors. The economy is almost completely dominated by foreign companies, which contribute about 80% to the GDP and employ about 1/3 of the labor force. The government has many joint ventures with foreign companies. South Africans are believed to hold about 2/3 of all equity investment in the country, with the United Kingdom being the next largest source of direct participation (see Banks et al. 1981; Nohlen and Nuscheler 1982 Vol. 5, 383–89; Kurian 1987). Population below absolute poverty income level is 45% in urban and 50% in rural areas (*Social Indicators of Development* 1988).

Sweden: According to a Swedish study, 17 large industrial groups generate 36% of the value of industrial production (Bruun 1969, 15–20). Manufacturing enterprises in the size-class of less than 200 workers employed 40% of all workers in 1980 (Statistisk rsbok fr Sverige 1982/83, 132–33).

Switzerland: See notes for Australia, Canada, Finland, and Sweden. Manufacturing enterprises in the size-class of less than 200 workers employed 64% of all workers in 1975 (Statistisches Jahrbuch 1982, 150–151).

Syria: A centrally planned economic system in which the public sector is dominant. By the mid-1960s most of the country's larger establishments had been nationalized. The public sector accounts for 60% of GDP (see *Syria. A Country Study* 1979, 132–33; Banks et al. 1981; Nohlen and Nuscheler 1983 Vol. 6: 471–75). The public sector's share of investments is more than 80% and 65–75% of industrial production capacity (Länder der Erde 1981, 614). According to Kurian (1987), the state-owned sector provides 75% of the value of industrial production. Public enterprises accounted for 96% of gross domestic fixed capital formation in manufacturing in 1975 (Short 1984). Population in absolute poverty 10% (Kurian 1984, Table 69).

Tanzania: Until the 1967 Arusha Declaration, the nonagricultural economy was dominated by the private sector (mostly foreign), which accounted for 90% of value added in industry. Since then nationalizations have reduced the share of private and foreign sectors. In 1975 the public sector was responsible for over 50% of industrial production. The remaining private sector is almost entirely in the hands of Europeans and Asians; 25% of companies are foreign-owned (see *Tanzania. A Country Study* 1978, 212–13; Banks et al. 1981; Länder der Erde 1981, 618; Nohlen and Nuscheler 1982 Vol. 5, 162–72; Kurian 1987). Public enterprises accounted for 33% of gross fixed capital formation in 1970–80 (Nellis 1986, 9. See also Short 1984). Population below absolute poverty income level was 10% in urban and 60% in rural areas in 1975 (*Social Indicators of development* 1988).

Thailand: A market-oriented economic system in which the dominant sector is private. Previously the country's Chinese minority controlled over 90% of manu-

Notes (*continued*)

facturing. Now the government owns a variety of manufacturing plants, and some are joint Thai-foreign ventures. About 10% of the manufacturing output is produced by government-owned enterprises (see *Thailand. A Country Study* 1981, 148–49; Banks et al. 1981; Nohlen and Nuscheler 1983 Vol. 7, 479–85; Kurian 1987). Public enterprises accounted for 13% of gross fixed capital formation in 1978–79 (Short 1984). Population below absolute poverty income level was 15% in urban and 34% in rural areas in 1975 (*Social Indicators of Development* 1988).

Togo: The industry sector, which contributes less than 30% of GDP, is dominated by several large establishments (100 or more workers). They are owned by the state and foreign companies and employ 80–85% of industrial workers (see Banks et al. 1981; Nohlen and Nuscheler 1982 Vol. 4, 376–78; *Worldmark* 1984 Vol. 2, 325). Population below absolute poverty income level was 42% in urban areas in 1975 (*Social Indicators of Development* 1988).

Trinidad and Tobago: The Trinidad and Tobago economy is dominated by the private sector. The public sector's share of total investment was 19% in 1971. Oil and natural gas are central to the country's economic vitality, with the petroleum industry accounting for about 40% of GDP, although it employs only 4–5% of the labor force. The petroleum industry is owned by the state and foreign companies. The manufacturing sector consists of more than 600 establishments. Many of them are owned by foreign companies (see Chernick 1978, 6–7; Banks et al. 1981; Nohlen and Nuscheler 1982 Vol. 3, 432–40; Kurian 1987). Population below absolute poverty income level was 39% in rural areas in 1975 (*Social Indicators of Development* 1988).

Tunisia: The public sector is restricted to heavy industry. The mining sector, including petroleum and natural gas, is controlled by the state and foreign companies, whereas most of the more than 1,000 manufacturing establishments are owned by private Tunisian firms. Enterprises employing more than 100 workers employ more than 70 % of the industrial workers (see *Tunisia. A Country Study* 1979, 150–51; *Middle East Annual Review* 1980, 373; Banks et al. 1981; Nohlen and Nuscheler 1983 Vol. 6, 166–73; Kurian 1987). Public enterprises accounted for 36% of gross fixed capital formation in 1980–81 and 59% of gross domestic fixed capital formation in manufacturing in 1978–81 (Short 1984). Population below absolute poverty income level was 20% in urban and 15% in rural areas in 1975 (*Social Indicators of Development* 1988).

Turkey: A public-private mixed economy. The bulk of heavy industries and almost all utilities are concentrated in the public sector, but the private sector dominates the production of consumer goods. In 1977 the public sector produced about 40% of industrial output (Banks et al. 1981). According to another estimate (Länder der Erde 1981, 647), its share of industrial production is 50%. *Worldmark* (1984 Vol. 4, 372) informs that the public sector produced 37% of industrial production and the private sector 63% in 1981. The dozen largest state enterprises and the 100 largest private enterprises produced 50% of the net output of the manufacturing sector in 1982 (Kurian 1987). Public enterprises accounted for 29% of gross fixed capital formation in 1978–81 and 42% of gross domestic fixed capital for-

Notes (*continued*)

mation in industries (Short 1984). Population in absolute poverty 11% (Kurian 1984, Table 69).

Uganga: Idi Amin nationalized almost all foreign-owned enterprises in 1972–73. In 1983, however, property expropriated by Amin was restored to the former owners (see Banks et al. 1981; Nohlen and Nuscheler 1982 Vol. 5, 194–96; *Worldmark* 1984 Vol. 2, 340–41; Kurian 1987). Population in absolute poverty 64% (Kurian 1984, Table 69; Kurian 1987).

USSR: The share of the socialist sector of the gross industrial production was 100% in 1978 (CMEA 1979, 41; cf. Gardner 1988, 466).

United Arab Emirates: The economy is almost totally dominated by the petroleum industry, which is completely owned by the state and foreign companies (see Banks et al. 1981; Nohlen and Nuscheler 1983 Vol. 6, 523–29; Kurian 1987).

United Kingdom: See notes for Australia, Canada, Finland, and Sweden. Enterprises of less than 200 workers employ 36% of all the workers (*Annual Abstract of Statistics* 1983, 131; see also Gardner 1988, 106–121).

United States: See notes for Australia, Canada, Finland, and Sweden. According to Hurst (1979, 24–29), the top 10% of U.S. adults in the United States held 50% of the personal wealth and the top 1% about 21% in 1962. The largest 100 corporations controlled 48% of the corporate assets in 1972 (cf. Gardner 1988, 79–83).

Uruguay: A market-oriented economic system in which the dominant sector is private (see Banks et al. 1981; Nohlen and Nuscheler 1982 Vol. 2, 344–50; Kurian 1987). Public enterprises accounted for 18% of gross fixed capital formation in 1978–80 (Short 1984); with 6% of the population in absolute poverty (Kurian 1984, Table 69).

Venezuela: Venezuela has a mixed economy, approximately 60% of which remains in private hands. The oil sector is the most important one. Petroleum accounts for about 1/3 of gross domestic product, two-thirds of government revenue, and over 90% of export earnings. The petroleum and iron industries are controlled by the state (see Banks et al. 1981; Nohlen and Nuscheler 1982 Vol. 2, 376–77; *Countries* 1983, 1183–84; Kurian 1987). Public enterprises accounted for 36% of gross fixed capital formation in 1978–80 (Short 1984). Small and medium-size enterprises (less than 100 workers) employed 43% of the workers and produced 25% of the value of production in 1976 (*Anuario Estadistico* 1977, 329). Absolute poverty level includes 5% of the population (Kurian 1984, Table 69).

Vietnam: Centrally directed Socialist economy. Nearly all means of production are in the hands of the Socialist sector (see Banks et al. 1981; Nohlen and Nusheler 1983 Vol. 7, 499–504; *The Far East and Australasia* 1983, 896; EIU, Indochina: Vietnam, Laos, Cambodia. Annual 1985). According to Kurian (1987), there exists a very small private industrial sector, although all large industries have been brought under state control.

Yemen Arab Republic: A public-private mixed economy. The public sector owns most large enterprises, while the private sector consists primarily of smaller enterprises producing, for example, soft drinks, aluminum pots and pans, furniture,

Notes (*continued*)

ceramic tiles, and foodstuffs (see Banks et al. 1981; Nohlen and Nuscheler 1983 Vol. 6, 333–39; *The Middle East and North Africa* 1983–84, 694–97; Kurian 1987). Public enterprises accounted for 59% of gross domestic fixed capital formation in manufacturing in 1975–76 (Short 1984).

Yemen, People's Democratic Republic of: South Yemen has a centrally planned economic system dominated by the public sector (see Banks et al. 1981; Länder der Erde 1981, 311; The Middle East and North Africa 1983–84, 710–14). In 1977 the share of state-owned enterprises was 66% of industrial production and 82% of employment, the share of mixed state/private enterprises was 23% of production and 6% of employment, and the share of private enterprises only 10% of production and employment (Nohlen and Nuscheler 1983 Vol. 6, 348–52; cf. Kurian 1987).

Yugoslavia: Yugoslavia has a centrally planned Socialist economy, which is, to some degree, decentralized by its unique workers' social self-management system (see Banks et al. 1981; Länder der Erde 1981, 318; *Countries* 1983, 1212; Dahl 1985, 144–47; Gardner 1988, 320–33, 466).

Zaire: Mining and manufacturing are the most important nonagricultural sectors of the economy. The mining sector is controlled by the state and foreign companies. Mineral products constitute nearly 90% of the export. Manufacturing is dominated by foreign companies (see Banks et al. 1981; Nohlen and Nuscheler 1982 Vol. 4, 473–87; Kurian 1987; Marsden and Blot 1988, 13–14). Population below absolute poverty income level was 80% in rural areas in 1975 (*Social Indicators of Development* 1988).

Zambia: A mixed economy with substantial government participation in the industrial and marketing sectors through the parastatal system. Since independence over 60 foreign corporations have been nationalized under a Zambianization program, and the government has acquired a commanding position in manufacturing through the Industrial Development Corporation. About 80% of the country's industrial output originates in parastatal enterprises. Foreign investments in Zambia have been progressively reduced through nationalization (see Banks et al. 1981; Nohlen and Nuscheler 1982 Vol. 5, 397–403; Worldmark 1984 Vol. 2, 367–68; Kurian 1987). Public enterprises accounted for 61% of gross fixed capital formation in 1979–80 (Short 1984). Population below absolute poverty income level was 25% in urban areas in 1975 (*Social Indicators of Development* 1988).

Zimbabwe: A mixed public-private economic system in which the private sector is dominant. Manufacturing (26% of GDP in 1980) and mining (8% of GDP in 1980) are the most important nonagricultural sectors of the economy. Mining is entirely dominated by subsidiaries of British, South African and U.S. firms, whereas most manufacturing enterprises are owned by local white entrepreneurs and foreign companies. The role of the public sector has been growing during the Mugabe government since 1980 (see Banks et al. 1981; Nohlen and Nuscheler 1982 Vol. 5, 424–32; Kurian 1987).

APPENDIX 5

GNP per Capita in US Dollars in 147 Countries in 1983

Country	GNP per capita in 1983	Country	GNP per capita in 1983
1 Afghanistan	190	76 Kuwait	17,880
2 Albania	900	77 Laos	144
3 Algeria	2,320	78 Lebanon	1,150
4 Angola	470	79 Lesotho	460
5 Argentina	2,070	80 Liberia	480
6 Australia	11,490	81 Libya	8,480
7 Austria	9,250	82 Luxemburg	9,838
8 Bahamas	3,793	83 Mdagascar	310
9 Bahrain	10,360	84 Malawi	210
10 Bangladesh	130	85 Malaysia	1,860
11 Barbados	3,930	86 Mali	160
12 Belgium	9,150	87 Malta	3,710
13 Benin	290	88 Mauritania	480
14 Bhutan	110	89 Mauritius	1,150
15 Bolivia	510	90 Mexico	2,240
16 Botswana	920	91 Mongolia	830
17 Brazil	1,880	92 Morocco	760
18 Bulgaria	4,150	93 Mosambique	150
19 Burkina Faso	180	94 Nepal	160
20 Burma	180	95 Netherlands	9,890
21 Burundi	240	96 New Zealand	7,730
22 Cameroon	820	97 Nicaragua	880
23 Canada	12,310	98 Niger	240
24 Cape Verde	360	99 Nigeria	770
25 Central African Republic	280	100 Norway	14,020
26 Chad	80	101 Oman	6,250
27 Chile	1,870	102 Pakistan	390
28 China	300	103 Panama	2,120
29 Colombia	1,430	104 Papua New Guinea	760
30 Comoros	340	105 Paraguay	1,410
31 Congo	1,230	106 Peru	1,040
32 Costa Rica	1,020	107 Philippines	760
33 Cuba	1,534	108 Poland	3,900
34 Cyprus	3,720	109 Portugal	2,230
35 Czechoslovakia	5,820	110 Qatar	21,060
36 Denmark	11,570	111 Romania	2,560
37 Djibouti	480	112 Rwanda	270
38 Dominican Republic	1,370	113 Saudi Arabia	12,230

APPENDIX 5 (*continued*)

Country	GNP per capita in 1983	Country	GNP per capita in 1983
39 Ecuador	1,420	114 Senegal	440
40 Egypt	700	115 Sierra Leone	330
41 El Salvador	710	116 Singapore	6,620
42 Equatorial Guinea	417	117 Solomon Islands	640
43 Ethiopia	120	118 Somalia	250
44 Fiji	1,790	119 South Africa	2,490
45 Finland	10,740	120 Spain	4,780
46 France	10,500	121 Sri Lanka	330
47 Gabon	4,250	122 Sudan	400
48 Gambia	290	123 Suriname	3,520
49 German Democratic		124 Swaziland	890
Republic	7,180		
50 Germany, Federal		125 Sweden	12,470
Republic of	11,430		
51 Ghana	310	126 Switzerland	16,290
52 Greece	3,920	127 Syria	1,760
53 Guatemala	1,120	128 Tanzania	240
54 Guinea	300	129 Thailand	820
55 Guinea-Bissau	180	130 Togo	280
56 Guyana	520	131 Trinidad and Tobago	6,850
57 Haiti	300	132 Tunisia	1,290
58 Honduras	670	133 Turkey	1,240
59 Hungary	4,180	134 Uganda	220
60 Iceland	11,083	135 U.S.S.R.	4,550
61 India	260	136 United Arab Emirates	22,870
62 Indonesia	560	137 United Kingdom	9,200
63 Iran	2,590	138 United States	14,110
64 Iraq	3,020	139 Uruguay	2,490
65 Ireland	5,000	140 Venezuela	3,840
66 Israel	5,370	141 Vietnam	245
67 Italy	6,400	142 Yemen Arab Republic	550
68 Ivory Coast	710	143 Yemen, People's Dem.	
		Rep.	520
69 Jamaica	1,300	144 Yugoslavia	2,570
70 Japan	10,120	145 Zaire	170
71 Jordan	1,640	146 Zambia	580
72 Kampuchea	100	147 Zimbabwe	740
73 Kenya	340		
74 Korea, Democratic			
Republic of	1,079		
75 Korea, Republic of	2,010		

Notes:
Source, if not otherwise noted, *World Development Report* 1985, Table 1.

Afghanistan: Kurian 1987; cf. *Statistical Abstract of the United States* 1987 ($269); Dye and Zeigler 1988 ($225 in 1980).

Albania: Dye and Zeigler 1988 (in 1980).

Angola: Kurian 1987.

Bahamas: Kurian 1987.

Bahrain: Kurian 1987; *World Resources* 1986.

Barbados: Kurian 1987; *World Resources* 1986; cf. *World Development Report* 1982 ($2,080 in 1980).

Bhutan: Kurian 1987.

Botswana: Kurian 1987; *World Resources* 1986.

Bulgaria: *World Development Report* 1982 (in 1980); cf. Dye and Zeigler 1988 ($5,492); *Statistical Abstract of the United States* 1987 ($5,684).

Cape Verde: Kurian 1987; *World Resources* 1986.

Chad: Kurian 1987; Dye and Zeigler 1988 (in 1980).

Comoros: Kurian 1987.

Costa Rica: cf. *World Development Report* 1982 ($1,730 in 1980).

Cuba: Kurian 1987; cf. *World Development Report* 1982 ($1,270 in 1980); Dye and Zeigler 1988 ($1,579 in 1980).

Cyprus: *World Resources* 1986.

Czechoslovakia: World Development Report 1982 (in 1980); cf. Dye and Zeigler 1988 ($7,430 in 1980); *Statistical Abstract of the United States* 1987 ($7,511 in 1983).

Djibouti: Kurian 1987.

Equatorial Guinea: Kurian 1987.

Fiji: Kurian 1987; *World Development Report* 1986.

Gabon: Kurian 1987; *World Resources* 1986.

Gambia: Kurian 1987; *World Resources* 1986.

German Democratic Republic: *World Development Report* 1982 (in 1980); cf. Dye and Zeigler 1988 ($8,576 in 1980); *Statistical Abstract of the United States* 1987 ($8,800 in 1983).

Guinea-Bissau: Kurian 1987; *World Resources* 1986.

Guyana: Kurian 1987; *World Resources* 1986.

Hungary: *World Development Report* 1982 (in 1980); cf. Dye and Zeigler 1988 ($6,405 in 1980); *World Development Report* 1985 ($2,150 in 1983); *World Resources* 1986 ($2,150 in 1983); *Statistical Abstract of the United States* 1987 ($6,570 in 1983).

Iceland: *Statistical Abstract of the United States* 1987.

Iran: Kurian 1987.

Iraq: *World Development Report* 1982 (in 1980); cf. Dye and Zeigler 1988 ($3,533 in 1980); Kurian 1987 ($1,800 in 1984); *Statistical Abstract of the United* States 1987 ($3,533 in 1980 and $1,667 in 1983).

Kampuchea: Dye and Zeigler 1988 (in 1980).

Korea, Democratic Republic of: *Statistical Abstract of the United States* 1987; cf. Kurian 1987 ($998 in 1984); Dye and Zeigler 1988 ($1,008 in 1980).

Laos: Kurian 1987.

Notes (*continued*)

Lebanon: Dye and Zeigler 1988 (in 1980).
Luxemburg: *Statistical Abstract of the United States* 1987; cf. *World Resources* 1986
(12,190 dollars).
Malta: *World Resources* 1986.
Mauritius: Kurian 1987; *World Resources* 1986.
Mongolia: Wolf-Phillips 1980 (in 1977).
Mosambique: Kurian 1987; cf. *Statistical Abstract of the United States* 1987 (360).
Poland: *World Development Report* 1982 (in 1980); cf. Dye and Zeigler 1988 ($5,884
in 1980); *Statistical Abstract of the United States* 1987 ($5,580 in 1983).
Qatar: Kurian 1987; cf. *World Resources* 1986 ($21,170); *World Development Report* 1982 ($15,050 in 1980).
Romania: cf. Dye and Zeigler 1988 ($4,576 in 1980).
Solomon Islands: Kurian 1987; *World Resources* 1986.
Suriname: Kurian 1987; *World Resources* 1986.
Swaziland: Kurian 1987; *World Resources* 1986.
U.S.S.R.: *World Development Report* 1982 (in 1980); cf. Dye and Zeigler 1988
($7,640 in 1980); *Statistical Abstract of the United States* 1987 ($6,490 in 1983).
Vietnam: Kurian 1987; cf. Dye and Zeigler 1988 ($170 in 1980).

APPENDIX 6

Largest Ethnic Group and Its Percentage of the Total Population in the Comparison Group of 147 States in and Around 1980

State	Largest ethnic group	% of the population
1 Afghanistan	Pashtun or Pathan	50
2 Albania	Albanian	93
3 Algeria	Arab	83
4 Angola	Ovinbundu (tribe)	37
5 Argentina	European	97
6 Australia	European	96
7 Austria	Austrian	96
8 Bahamas	African	70
9 Bahrain	Bahraini	70
10 Bangladesh	Muslim	85
11 Barbados	African	92
12 Belgium	Dutch-Flemish (language)	58
13 Benin	Fon (tribe)	59
14 Bhutan	Bhutia	61
15 Bolivia	American Indian	45
16 Botswana	Bamankwato (tribe)	34
17 Brazil	European	53
18 Bulgaria	Bulgarian	87
19 Burkina Faso	Mossi	54
20 Burma	Burman	68
21 Burundi	Hutu (tribe)	83
22 Cameroon	Bamileke (tribe)	21
23 Canada	English (language)	61
24 Cape Verde	Mixed	70
25 Central African Reopublic	Banda (tribe)	32
26 Chad	Sudanese Arab	30
27 Chile	Mestizo	90
28 China	Han	94
29 Colombia	Mestizo	50
30 Comoros	Muslim	99
31 Congo	Kongo	52
32 Costa Rica	European	85
33 Cuba	European	72
34 Cyprus	Greek	81
35 Chechoslovakia	Czech	64
36 Denmark	Danish	99
37 Djibouti	Issa and Somali	47
38 Dominican Republic	Mulatto	75

APPENDIX 6 *(continued)*

State	Largest ethnic group	% of the population
39 Ecuador	American Indian	50
40 Egypt	Muslim	94
41 El Salvador	Mestizo	94
42 Equatorial Guinea	Fang (tribe)	71
43 Ethiopia	Amhara	30
44 Fiji	Indian	50
45 Finland	Finnish (language)	94
46 France	French	93
47 Gabon	Fang (tribe)	34
48 Gambia	Malinke (tribe)	43
49 German Democratic Republic	German	99
50 Germany, Federal Republic of	German	93
51 Ghana	Akan	44
52 Greece	Greek	95
53 Guatemala	American Indian	50
54 Guinea	Fulani (tribe)	41
55 Guinea-Bissau	Balante (tribe)	27
56 Guyana	Asian Indian	51
57 Haiti	African	95
58 Honduras	Mestizo	90
59 Hungary	Magyar	99
60 Iceland	Icelanders	97
61 India	Hindi (language)	40
62 Indonesia	Jawanese (language)	40
63 Iran	Persian (language)	45
64 Iraq	Arab	77
65 Ireland	Irish	96
66 Israel	Jewish	83
67 Italy	Italian	98
68 Ivory Coast	Bete (tribe)	20
69 Jamaica	African	76
70 Japan	Japanese (language)	99
71 Jordan	Arab	98
72 Kampuchea	Khmer	93
73 Kenya	Kikuya (tribe)	21
74 Korea, North	Korean	100
75 Korea, South	Korean	100
76 Kuwait	Kuwaiti	42
77 Laos	Lao-Lum	56
78 Lebanon	Muslim	65
79 Lesotho	Basotho	90

APPENDIX 6 (*continued*)

State	Largest ethnic group	% of the population
80 Liberia	Bakwe (tribe)	27
81 Libya	Arab-Berber	82
82 Luxemburg	Luxemburger	74
83 Madagascar	Hova/Merina	26
84 Malawi	Malawi	59
85 Malaysia	Malay Muslims	44
86 Mali	Bambara (tribe)	33
87 Malta	Maltese	94
88 Mauritania	Moor	80
89 Mauritius	Indo-Mauritian	68
90 Mexico	Mestizo	55
91 Mongolia	Khalkha	84
92 Morocco	Arab-Berber	99
93 Mosambique	Makua (tribe)	52
94 Nepal	Nepali	54
95 Netherlands	Roman Catholic	36
96 New Zealand	European (White)	90
97 Nicaragua	Mestizo	69
98 Niger	Hausa (tribe)	52
99 Nigeria	Hausa-Fulani	29
100 Norway	Norwegian	98
101 Oman	Arab	87
102 Pakistan	Punjabi	66
103 Panama	Mestizo	70
104 Papua New Guinea	Papuan	83
105 Paraguay	Mestizo	90
106 Peru	American Indian	54
107 Philippines	Christian	93
108 Poland	Polish	99
109 Portugal	Portuguese	99
110 Qatar	Arab	70
111 Romania	Romanian	89
112 Rwanda	Hutu (tribe)	88
113 Saudi Arabia	Arab	90
114 Senegal	Wolof (tribe)	35
115 Sierra Leone	Mende (tribe)	34
116 Singapore	Chinese	77
117 Solomon Islands	Melanesian	93
118 Somalia	Somali	95
119 South Africa	African	72
120 Spain	Spanish	73

APPENDIX 6 (*continued*)

State	Largest ethnic group	% of the population
121 Sri Lanka	Sinhalese	74
122 Sudan	Arab	46
123 Suriname	Asian Indian	35
124 Swaziland	Swazi	95
125 Sweden	Swedish	95
126 Switzerland	German (language)	65
127 Syria	Arab	89
128 Tanzania	Nyamwezi and Sukuma (tribe)	21
129 Thailand	Thai	54
130 Togo	Ewe (tribe)	46
131 Trinidad and Tobago	African	41
132 Tunisia	Arab	98
133 Turkey	Turkish	87
134 Uganda	Baganda (tribe)	18
135 USSR	Russian	52
136 United Arab Emirates	Arab	42
137 United Kingdom	White	94
138 USA	European (White)	83
139 Uruguay	European	90
140 Venezuela	Mestizo	69
141 Vietnam	Vietnamese	88
142 Yemen Arab Republic	Arab	98
143 Yemen, People's Dem. Rep.	Arab	93
144 Yugoslavia	Serbian	36
145 Zaire	Luba (tribe)	18
146 Zambia	Bemba	34
147 Zimbabwe	Shona (group of tribes)	80

Notes:

Afghanistan: Kurian 1987; *World in Figures* 1987. Editorial information compiled by the Economist 1987.

Albania: *World in Figures* 1987.

Algeria: *World in Figures* 1987; cf. Kurian 1987 (80%); Rustow 1967 (Arabic 87%).

Angola: *Countries of the World and Their Leaders Yearbook* 1989; cf. Kurian 1987 (33%); Rustow 1967 (36%).

Argentina: *Countries* 1989; cf. *World in Figures* 1987 (98%); Kurian 1987 (85%); Rustow 1967 (Spanish 84%).

Australia: *Countries* 1989; *World in Figures* 1987.

Austria: *World in Figures* 1987; cf. *Countries* 1989 (German 98%); Rustow 1967 (99%).

Notes (*continued*)

Bahamas: *World in Figures* 1987; cf. *Countries* 1989 (Blacks 85%); Kurian 1987 (Negroes 80%).

Bahrain: *World in Figures* 1987; cf. *Countries* 1989 (Arabs 73%); Kurian 1987 (Indigeneous Arabs 75%).

Bangladesh: *World in Figures* 1987; cf. *Countries* 1989 (83%); Kurian 1987 (90%).

Barbados: *World in Figures* 1987; Kurian 1987; cf. *Countries* 1989 (80%).

Belgium: *World in Figures* 1987; cf. *Countries* 1989 (Dutch 57%).

Benin: *World in Figures* 1987; cf. Kurian 1987 (20%); Rustow 1967 (Ewe-Fon 58%).

Bhutan: *World in Figures* 1987; cf. *Countries* 1989 (Ngalops and Sharchos 75%); Kurian 1987 (Bhote 54%); Worldmark Encyclopedia of the Nations, Vol. 4, 1984 (Worldmark 1984) (Bhutanese 60%).

Bolivia: *World in Figures* 1987; cf. *Countries* 1989 (Aymara and Quechua 55%); Kurian 1987 Indians 52%).

Botswana: *World in Figures* 1987; cf. Kurian 1987 (Tswana tribes 71%).

Brazil: *World in Figures* 1987; cf. Kurian 1987 (Caucasians 60%).

Bulgaria: *World in Figures* 1987; cf. *Countries* 1989 (85%); Rustow 1967 (86%).

Burkina Faso: *World in Figures* 1987; cf. *Worldmark*, Vol. 2, 1984 (55%).

Burma: *World in Figures* 1987; cf. Kurian 1987 (70%); Rustow 1967 (Burmese 71%).

Burundi: *World in Figures* 1987; Kurian 1987; cf. *Countries* 1989 (85%).

Cameroon: Kurian 1987; cf. *World in Figures* 1987 (Bantu 52%); Rustow 1967 (Fang 19%).

Canada: *World in Figures* 1987; cf. *Countries* 1989 (British 40%); Rustow 1967 (English 58%).

Cape Verde: *World in Figures* 1987; cf. *Countries* 1989 (Creoles 71%); Kurian 1987 (Mestizos or Creoles 60%); *Worldmark*, Vol. 2, 1984 (mixed 70%).

Central African Republic: *World in Figures* 1987; Kurian 1987; cf. *Countries* 1989 (Baya 34%).

Chad: *World in Figures* 1987; cf. Kurian 1987 (Sara 24%).

Chile: *World in Figures* 1987; cf. Kurian 1987 (65%).

China: *Countries* 1989; cf. *World in Figures* (93%); *Worldmark*, Vol. 4, 1984. 93%).

Colombia: *Countries* 1989; *World in Figures* 1987; cf. Kurian 1987 (58%).

Comoros: *World in Figures* 1987.

Congo: *World in Figures* 1987; cf. Kurian 1987 (45%); Rustow 1967 (50%).

Costa Rica: *World in Figures* 1987; cf. *Countries* (96%); Kurian 1987 (Whites and Mestizos 97%).

Cuba: *World in Figures* 1987; cf. *Countries* 1989 (Whites 66%); Kurian 1987 (Mulattoes 51%); cf. Kurian 1984 (96%).

Cyprus: *World in Figures* 1987; cf. *Countries* 1989 (Greek 77%); Kyle 1984 (undivided Cyprus 80%); Rustow 1967 (Greek 77%).

Czechoslovakia: *World in Figures* 1987; *Countries* 1989.

Denmark: *World in Figures* 1987.

Djibouti: *World in Figures* 1987.

Dominican Republic: *World in Figures* 1987; cf. *Countries* 1989 (Mixed 73%); Kurian 1987 (Mulattoes 73%).

Notes (*continued*)

Ecuador: *World in Figures* 1987; cf. *Countries* 1989 (Mixed 55%); Kurian 1987 (Mestizos 40%).

Egypt: *World in Figures* 1987; cf. Kurian 1987 (Native Egyptians 93%).

El Salvador: *World in Figures* 1987; cf. *Countries* 1989 (Mestizos 89%); Kurian 1987 (92%).

Equatorial Guinea: *World in Figures* 1987; cf. *Countries* 1989 (Fang 80%).

Ethiopia: World in Figures 1987; cf. Kurian 1987 (Galla 40%); *Worldmark,* Vol. 2, 1984 (Amhara-Tigrey 45%).

Fiji: *Countries* 1989; *World in Figures* 1987; cf. Kurian 1987 (51%).

Finland: *Countries* 1989; *World in Figures* 1987.

France: *World in Figures* 1987; cf. *Countries* 1989 (French 86%).

Gabon: *World in Figures* 1987; cf. *Worldmark,* Vol. 2, 1984 (29%); Rustow 1967 (Fang 30%).

Gambia: *World in Figures* 1987; cf. *Countries* 1989 (Mandinga 41%); Kurian 1987 (Mandigo 41%).

German Democratic Republic: *Countries* 1989; *World in Figures* 1987.

Germany, Federal Republic of: *Countries* 1989; *World in Figures* 1987.

Ghana: *World in Figures* 1987; cf. *Worldmark,* Vol. 2, 1984 (40%); Rustow 1967 (Akan 44%).

Greece: *World in Figures* 1987; cf. *Countries* 1989 (97%).

Guatemala: *World in Figures* 1987; cf. Kurian 1987 (44%).

Guinea: *World in Figures* 1987; cf. Kurian 1987 (Malinke 30%).

Guinea-Bissau: *World in Figures* 1987; cf. Kurian 1987 (Balante 30%).

Guyana: *Countries* 1989; *World in Figures* 1987.; cf. Kurian 1987 (50%).

Haiti: *World in Figures* 1987; cf. *Countries* 1989 (Black African descent 95%); Kurian 1987 (Negroes 90%).

Honduras: *Countries* 1989; *World in Figures* 1987; Kurian 1987.

Hungary: *Countries* 1989; *World in Figures* 1987.

Iceland: *World in Figures* 1987.

India: Census of India 1981.

Indonesia: *World in Figures* 1987; cf. Kurian 1987 (50%).

Iran: *World in Figures* 1987; cf. Kurian 1987 (Farsi 54%).

Iraq: *World in Figures* 1987.; cf. Kurian 1987 (80%).

Ireland: *World in Figures* 1987.

Israel: *World in Figures* 1987; Arian 1984.

Italy: *World in Figures* 1987.

Ivory Coast: *World in Figures* 1987; cf. Kurian 1987 (Akan 25%); Rustow 1967 (Anyi-Baule 24%); *Worldmark,* Vol. 2, 1984 (Baule 15%).

Jamaica: *World in Figures* 1987; Kurian 1987.

Japan: *Countries* 1989; *World in Figures* 1987; Rustow 1967.

Jordan: *World in Figures* 1987; cf. Kurian 1987 (Palestinian Arabs 40%); Rustow 1967 (Arabic 98%).

Kampuchea: *World in Figures* 1987; cf. *Countries* 1989 (90%); Kurian 1987 (85%).

Kenya: *Countries* 1989; *World in Figures* 1987; cf. Kurian 1987 (20%).

Korea, North: Kurian 1987.

Notes (*continued*)

Korea, South: Kurian 1987.

Kuwait: *World in Figures* 1987; cf. *Countries* 1989 (Arabs 84%); Kurian 1987 (Native Arabs 40%).

Laos: *World in Figures* 1987; cf. *Countries* 1989 (Lao 48%).

Lebanon: *World in Figures* 1987; cf. *Countries* 1989 (Arabs 93%); McDowall 1984 (Shiites 31%); Kurian 1987 (Shiites 27%, Maronites 23%).

Lesotho: *World in Figures* 1987; cf. Kurian 1987 (85%); *Worldmark*, Vol. 2, 1984 (Basotho 93%).

Liberia: *World in Figures* 1987; cf. Kurian 1987 (Kpelle 21%).

Libya: *World in Figures* 1987; cf. *Countries* 1989 (80%); Kurian 1987 (90%).

Luxemburg: *World in Figures* 1987; cf. Rustow 1967 (Letzeburgesh 93%).

Madagascar: *World in Figures* 1987; cf. Kurian 1987 (Merina 26%); *Worldmark*, Vol. 2, 1984 (Merina 25%).

Malawi: *World in Figures* 1987; cf. Kurian 1987 (Chewan and Nyanja 50%); Rustow 1967 (Nyanja 36%).

Malaysia: *Countries* 1989; Kurian 1987; cf. *World in Figures* 1987 (Malay and other indigeneous peoples 60%).

Mali: *World in Figures* 1987; cf. *Countries* 1989 (Mande 50%); Kurian 1987 (Bambara 30%).

Malta: *Commonwealth Fact Sheet*. Malta 1976; cf. Rustow 1967 (Maltese 95%).

Mauritania: *World in Figures* 1987; cf. Kurian 1987 (81%).

Mauritius: *Countries* 1989; *World in Figures* 1987; cf. *Mauritius. Commonwealth Fact Sheet* 1978 (Hindus 52%).

Mexico: *World in Figures* 1987; cf. *Countries* 1989 (60%); Kurian 1987 (60%).

Mongolia: *World in Figures* 1987; cf. *Countries* 1989 (77%); Rustow 1967 (Mongolian-Khalkha 78%).

Morocco: *Countries* 1989; *World in Figures* 1987; Kurian 1987.

Mosambique: *World in Figures* 1987; cf. Kurian 1987 (Makua-Lomue 38%); *Worldmark*, Vol. 2, 1984 (Makua-Lomue 38%).

Nepal: *World in Figures* 1987; cf. Kurian 1987 (49%); *Countries* 1989 (Nepali 90%).

Netherlands: *World in Figures* 1987.

New Zealand: *World in Figures* 1987; cf. *Countries* 1989 (Europeans 87%).

Nicaragua: *World in Figures* 1987; Kurian 1987.

Niger: *World in Figures* 1987; cf. Kurian 1987 (Hausa 50%); *Countries* 1989 (Hausa 56%).

Nigeria: Diamond 1988b, 35; cf. *World in Figures* 1987 (Hausa 21%); *Worldmark*, Vol. 2, 1984 (Hausa 21%).

Norway: *World in Figures* 1987.

Oman: *World in Figures* 1987; cf. Kurian 1987 (Arabs 88%).

Pakistan: *World in Figures* 1987; cf. Kurian 1987 (Punjabi 63%).

Panama: *World in Figures* 1987; Kurian 1987.

Papua New Guinea: *World in Figures* 1987; cf. Rustow 1967 (Papuan 69%).

Paraguay: *World in Figures* 1987; cf. Kurian 1987 (95%).

Peru: *World in Figures* 1987; cf. Kurian 1987 (Indian 46%); Rustow 1967 (Quechua 47%).

Notes (*continued*)

Philippines: *World in Figures* 1987; cf. Kurian 1987 (Christian Filipinos 91%).

Poland: *World in Figures* 1987.

Portugal: *World in Figures* 1987.

Qatar: Kurian 1987; cf. *Countries* 1989 (Arabs 45%); *World in Figures* 1987 (Muslim 92%).

Romania: *World in Figures* 1987; cf. Rustow 1967 (Romanian 86%).

Rwanda: *World in Figures* 1987; cf. *Countries* 1989 (Hutu 85%); Kurian 1987 (Hutu 80%).

Saudi Arabia: *Countries* 1989; Kurian 1987; cf. *World in Figures* (Muslim 99%); Rustow 1967 (Arabic 96%).

Senegal: *World in Figures* 198; cf. Kurian 1987 (Wolof 36%).

Sierra Leone: *World in Figures* 1987; cf. *Countries* 1989 (Temne 30%); Kurian 1987 (Mende 31%).

Singapore: *World in Figures* 1987.

Solomon Islands: *World in Figures* 1987; Kurian 1987.

Somalia: *World in Figures* 1987; cf. Kurian 1987 (Somali 98%).

South Africa: *Countries* 1989; cf. *World in Figures* 1987 (Bantu 68%); Rustow 1967 (Zulu-Xhosa 40%).

Spain: *World in Figures* 1987; Rustow 1967.

Sri Lanka: *Countries* 1989; *World in Figures* 1987; cf. Kurian 1987 (Sinhalese 72%).

Sudan: *World in Figures* 1987; *Worldmark,* Vol. 2, 1984; cf. Rustow 1967 (Arabic 48%).

Suriname: *World in Figures* 1987. Kurian 1987 (East Indians 37%).

Swaziland: *World in Figures* 1987; cf. Kurian 1987 (Swazi 50%).

Sweden: *World in Figures* 1987; cf. Rustow 1967 (Swedish 98%).

Switzerland: *World in Figures* 1987.

Syria: *World in Figures* 1987; cf. Kurian 1987 (Arabs 90%).

Tanzania: *World in Figures* 1987.

Thailand: *World in Figures* 1987; cf. *Countries* 1989 (Thai 84%); Kurian 1987 (Thai stock 75%); Rustow 1967 (Thai-Lao 91%).

Togo: *World in Figures* 1987; cf. *Countries* (Ewe 25%); Kurian 1987 (Ewe 21%); Rustow 1967 (Ewe-Fon 41%).

Trinidad and Tobago: *Countries* 1989; *World in Figures* 1987; cf. Kurian 1987 (Negroes 46%).

Tunisia: *Countries* 1989; *World in Figures* 1987.

Turkey: *World in Figures* 1987; cf. Kurian 1987 (Turks 92%).

Uganda: *World in Figures* 1987; cf. Kurian 1987 (Baganda 16%).

USSR: *Countries* 1989.

United Arab Emirates: *World in Figures* 1987; cf. Kurian 1987 (Arabs 25%).

United Kingdom: *World in Figures* 1987.

United States: *World in Figures* 1987.

Uruguay: *World in Figures* 1987; cf. Rustow 1967 (Spanish 94%).

Venezuela: *World in Figures* 1987; cf. Kurian 1987 (Mestizos 67%).

Vietnam: *World in Figures* 1987; cf. Kurian 1987 (Vietnamese 85%).

Notes (*continued*)

Yemen Arab Republic: *World in Figures* 1987; cf. Rustow 1967 (Arabic 98%).
Yemen, People's Democratic Republic: *World in Figures* 1987; cf. Kurian 1987 (Arabs 99%); Rustow 1967 (Arabic 97%).
Yugoslavia: *World in Figures* 1987; cf. *Countries* 1989 (Serbs 36%).
Zaire: *World in Figures* 1987.
Zambia: *World in Figures* 1987; cf. Kurian 1987 (35%); *Worldmark*, Vol. 2, 1984 (Bemba 37%).
Zimbabwe: *Countries* 1989; cf. World in figures (African 96%); Kurian 1987 (Shona 71%).

Bibliography

Africa Contemporary Record. Years 1974–1987. 1975–88. London: Rex Collings, and New York: Africana Publishing Co.

Africa at a glance, 1982. *Africa Insight,* 1981. 11 (3). Pretoria: The Africa Institute of South Africa.

Africa Research Bulletin. Political Series. 1977–89. Exeter and Woolfardisworthy, England: Africa Research Limited.

Africa South of the Sahara 1982–83. 1982. London: Europa Publications Limited.

Africa South of the Sahara 1989. 1989. London: Europa Publications Limited.

Africa Today. 1981.

Agricultural Policy in Turkey. 1974. Paris: Organization for Economic Co-operation and Development.

Agricultural Statistics of Nepal. 1972. Compiled and edited by His Majesty's Government of Nepal. Kathmandu: Ministry of Food and Agriculture.

Ajami, I. 1978. *Agricultural Development in Iran. Three articles,* LTC Reprint 134. Madison: Land Tenure Center, University of Wisconsin.

Al-Ashram, M. 1980. Auswirkungen der Agrarreform auf die Entwicklung der syrischen Landwirtschaft. In *Agrarreformen und Agraraufbau in den Ländern Asiens, Afrikas und Lateinamerikas.* Leipzig: V. Internationales Sommerseminar des Institutes für Tropische Landwirtschaft der Karl-Marx-Universität, DDR, 23. Juni– 2. Juli.

Alexander, R.D. 1980. *Darwinism and Human Affairs.* London: Pitman Publishing Limited.

Algeria. A Country Study. 1979. Washington, DC: U.S. Government Printing Office.

All India Report on Agricultural Census 1970–71. 1975. New Delhi: Government of India, Ministry of Agriculture and Irrigation.

Almond, G.A. 1960/1964. Introduction: A Functional Approach to Comparative Politics. In *The Politics of the Developing Areas,* eds. G.A. Almond and J.S. Coleman. Princeton, NJ: Princeton University Press.

Almond, G.A., and J.S. Coleman, eds. 1960/1964. *The Politics of the Developing Areas.* Princeton, NJ: Princeton University Press.

Angola. A Country Study. 1979. Washington, DC: U.S. Government Printing Office.

Année Africaine 1978. 1979. Paris: Editions A. Pedone.

Annual Abstract of Statistics. No. 119. 1983 edition. 1983. London: Her Majesty's Stationery Office.

Annuario Statistico Italiano 1980. 1980. Roma: Instituto Centrale di Statistica.

Anuario Estadistico 1977. 1979. Caracas: Republica de Venezuela, Oficina Central de Estadistica e Informatica.

Apter, D.E. 1963. *Ghana in Transition.* New York: Atheneum.

Arian, A. 1984. Israeli Democracy 1984. *Journal of International Affairs* 38(2):259–76.

Aristotle. 1952. *The Politics of Aristotle* or *A Treatise on Government,* trans. W. Ellis. London: J.M. Dent.

————. 1983. *The Politics.* Trans. Carnes Lord. Chicago: University of Chicago Press.

————. 1961. *The Politics of Aristotle,* trans. E. Barker. Oxford: Clarendon.

Aspe, P., and P.E. Sigmund, eds. 1984. *The Political Economy of Income Distribution in Mexico.* New York: Holmes & Meier.

Austin, D. 1964. *Politics in Ghana 1946–1960.* London: Oxford University Press.

Babiy, B., and V. Zabigailo. 1979. Popular Participation in Government as a Criterion of Democracy. In *Political Systems: Development Trends,* Soviet Political Sciences Association. Moscow: USSR Academy of Sciences.

Badie, B. 1984. *Le développement politique.* Paris: Economica.

Baechler, J. 1985. *Démocraties.* Paris: Calmann-Lévy.

Banks, A.S. 1970. Modernization and political change: The Latin American and Amer-European nations. *Comparative Political Studies* 2 (4):405–18.

————. 1972. Correlates of democratic performance. *Comparative Politics* 4 (2): 217–30.

————. 1981. An index of socio-economic development 1869–1975. *The Journal of Politics* 43: 390–411.

————, ed. 1988. *Political Handbook of the World 1988.* New York: CSA Publications.

Banks, A.S., et al., eds. 1981. *Economic Handbook of the World: 1981.* New York: McGraw-Hill.

Banks, A.S., and W. Overstreet, eds. 1983. *Political Handbook of the World 1982–83.* New York: McGraw-Hill.

Banks, A.S., and R.B. Textor. 1963. *A Cross-Polity Survey.* Cambridge: MA: Institute of Technology Press.

Banta, K.W. 1989. Rumania. Life in the saint's nightmare. As conditions worsen, opposition to Ceausescu's despotism grows, even at home. *Time* 133 (14):26–27.

Barash, D.P. 1982. *Sociobiology and Behavior.* 2nd ed.. London: Hodder and Stoughton.

Barkan, J.D. 1987. The Electoral Process and Peasant-State Relations in Kenya. In *Elections in Independent Africa*, ed. F.M. Hayward. Boulder: Westview Press.

Barraclough, S.L., and A. Domike. 1970. Agrarian Structure in Seven Latin American Countries. In *Agrarian Problems and Peasant Movements in Latin America*, ed. R. Stavenhagen. New York: Anchor Books.

Bauder, I. 1985. Migrationen till Latinamerica, unpublished paper. Göteborg.

Beckett, P.A. 1987. Elections and Democracy in Nigeria. In *Elections in Independent Africa*, ed. F.M. Hayward. Boulder: Westview Press.

Beckles, E.L., and N.P. Russell. 1982. A Programming Analysis of Small-Holder Barbadian Agriculture (paper). Madison, Wisconsin; Land Tenure Center.

Bedeski, R.E. 1985. Electoral Reform in China. Paper presented at the IPSA XIIIth World Congress, Paris, July 15–20.

Belal, A.A. 1980. *Developpement et facteurs non-economiques*. Rabat: Société Marocaine des Editeurs Réunis.

Berg-Schlosser, D. 1985. On the Conditions of Democracy in Third World Countries. Paper presented at the IPSA World Congress, Paris, July 15–20.

———. 1987. Three Paths to Democracy in Third World Countries. Paper presented at the ECPR Joint Sessions of Workshops, Amsterdam, April 10–15.

Bertrand, T.F.M., and R.A.G. van Puijenbroek. 1987. The Measurement of Democracy in Cross-National Reserach: The Construction of a Scale. Paper presented at the ECPR Joint Sessions of Workshops, Amsterdam, April 10–15.

Binkert, G.H. 1983. *Agricultural Production and Economic Incentives: Food Policy in Mosambique*. Development Discussion Paper No. 154. Harvard University, Harvard Institute for International Development.

Birks, J.S. 1976. The Shawani population of northern Oman: A pastoral society in transition. *The Journal of Oman Studies* 2:9–16.

Björkman, J.W. 1987. The Social Ecology of Democracy in South Asia: Ethno-Politics within and between India and Sri Lanka. Paper presented at the ECPR Joint Sessions of Workshops, Amsterdam, April 10–15.

Blaustein, A.P., and G.H. Flanz, eds. 1973. *Constitutions of the Countries of the World*. Dobbs Ferry, NY: Oceana Publications.

Blitzer, C. 1960. *An Immortal Commonwealth. The Political Thought of James Harington*. New Haven: Yale University Press.

Blondel, J. 1969. *An Introduction to Comparative Government*. London: Weidenfeld and Nicolson.

Bogdanor, V. 1983. Introduction. In *Democracy and Elections*, eds. V. Bogdanor and D. Butler. Cambridge: Cambridge University Press.

———. *What is Proportional Representation?* Oxford: Martin Robertson.

Bogdanor, V., and D. Butler, eds. 1983. *Democracy and Elections. Electoral systems and their political consequences*. Cambridge: Cambridge University Press.

Bollen, K.A. 1979. Political democracy and the timing of development. *American Sociological Review* 44 (4):572–87.

————. 1980. Issues in the comparative measurement of political democracy. *American Sociological Review* 45 (3):370–90.

————. 1983. World system position, dependency, and democracy: The cross-national evidence. *American Sociological Review* 48:468–79.

Bollen, K.A., and B.D. Grandjean. 1981. The dimension(s) of democracy: Further issues in the measurement and effects of political democracy. *American Sociological Review* 46:651–59.

Booth, J.A. 1985. Costa Rican Democracy. Paper presented at the Conference on Democracy in Developing Nations, Hoover Institution, Stanford University.

Borrell, J. 1989a. Poland: History is made. Government and opposition reach a dramatic reform agreement. *Time* 133 (16):12–14.

————. 1989b. Postmortems on a victory. Solidarity's big win opens a fierce debate over the precidency. *Time* 134 (1):14.

Borrell, J. 1989c. Hungary. At Long Last, Hail and Farewell. *Time* 133 (26):9–10.

Borrell, J. 1989d. Inconceivable! Poland gives the bloc its first non-communist leader since 1948. *Time* 134 (9): 8–13.

Bowdler, G.A., and P. Cotter. 1982. *Voter Participation in Central America, 1954–1981. An Exploration*. Washington, DC: University Press of America.

Bowen-Jones, H. 1980. Agriculture in Bahrain, Kuwait, Qatar, and UAE. In *Issues in Development: The Arab Gulf States*, ed. M. Ziwar-Daftari. London: MD Research and Sciences Ltd.

Browne, C. 1989. *Economic Development in Seven Pacific Island Countries*. Washington, DC: International Monetary Fund.

Bruce, J.W. 1985. *Land Tenure Issues in Project Design and Strategies for Agricultural Development in Sub-Saharan Africa*. Madison: Land Tenure Center, University of Wisconsin.

Bruneau, T.C. 1985. Consolidating civilian Brazil. *Third World Quarterly* 7 (4):973–87.

Bruun, K. 1969. Taloudellisen vallan ongelma. In *Taloudellinen valta Suomessa*, eds. K. Bruun and A. Eskola. Helsinki: Tammi.

Bryce, J. 1921. *Modern Democracies*. London: Macmillan.

Buchmann, J. 1962. *L'Afrique Noire Indépendente*. Paris: R. Pichon.

Bulletin de l'Afrique noire. 1980.

Burlatski, F. 1978. *Nykyajan valtio ja politiikka*. Moskova: Kustannusliike Edistys.

Burnham, W.D. 1980. The Appearance and Disappearance of the American Voter. In *Electoral Participation. A Comparative Analysis*, ed. R.Rose. Beverly Hills: Sage Publications.

Busia, K.A. 1967. *Africa in Search of Democracy*. London: Routledge and Kegan Paul.

Caballero, L., et al. 1984. *Mosambique—Food and Agriculture Sector*. Uppsala: Swedish University of Agricultural Sciences, International Rural Development Centre.

Canadian News Facts. 1988.

Card. E, and B. Callaway. 1970. Ghanaian politics: The elections and after. *Africa Report* 15 (3):10–15.

Carson, R.L. 1973. *Comparative Economic Systems*. New York: Macmillan.

Casanova, P.G. 1972. *La democracia en México*. Mexico: Ediciones Era.

————. 1985. The State and Political Parties in Mexico. Paper presented at the Conference on Democracy in Developing Nations, Hoover Institution, Stanford University.

Census of India 1981. Series 1 India. Paper of 1987. Households and Household Population by Language spoken in the Household. 1987. Delhi: The Controller of Publications.

Central Statistical Office of Finland. 1988. *Presidential Election 1988*. Helsinki: Valtion painatuskeskus.

Cerdas, R. 1986. The Costa Rican Elections of 1986. *Electoral Studies* 5 (3): 311–12.

Chazan, N. 1988. Ghana: Problems of Governance and the Emergence of Civil Society. In *Democracy in Developing Societies. Vol. 2. Africa, eds*. L. Diamond et al. Boulder: Lynne Rienner.

Chekharin, E. 1977. *The Soviet Political System Under Developed Socialism*. Moscow: Progress Publishers.

Chernick, S.E. 1978. *The Commonwealth Caribbean. The Integration Experience*. Baltimore: The John Hopkins University Press.

Chitnis. P.C. 1984. Observing El Salvador: The 1984 elections. *Third World Quarterly* 6 (4):963–80.

Chkhikvadze, V.M., ed. 1969. *The Soviet State and Law*. Moscow: Progress Publishers.

Chua-Eoan, H.G. 1989. China. The Wrath of Deng. *Time* 133 (25):16–19.

Clubb, Flanigan, and Zingale, eds. 1981. *Analyzing Electoral History*. Beverly Hills: Sage Publications.

Cohen, J.M., and P.H. Koehn. 1978. *Rural and Urban Land Reform in Ethiopia*. LTC Reprint No. 135. Madison: Land Tenure Center, University of Wisconsin.

Coleman, J.S. 1960/1964. Conclusion: The Political Systems of the Developing Areas. In *The Politics of the Developing Areas*, ed. G.A. Almond and J.S. Coleman. Princeton, NJ: Princeton University Press.

Coleman, J.S., and C.R. Rosberg, eds. 1964. *Political Parties and National Integration in Tropical Africa*. Berkeley: University of California Press.

Collier, D. 1978a. Industrialization and authoritarianism in Latin America. *Social Science Research Council Items* 31/32 (4/1).

————. 1978b. Industrial modernization and political change: A Latin American perspective. *World Politics* 30 (4):593–614.

Commonwealth Fact Sheet. Malta. 1976. London: Commonwealth Institute.

Commonwealth Fact Sheet. Swaziland. 1979. London: Commonwealth Institute.

Congressional Quarterly Weekly Report. 1988.

Coppedge, M., and W. Reinicke. 1988. A Scale of Polyarchy. In *Freedom in the*

World. Political Rights & Civil Liberties 1987–1988, ed. R.D. Gastil. New York: Freedom House.

Corning, P.A. 1971. *The Theory of Evolution as a Paradigm for the Analysis of Political Phenomena*. Ann Arbor: University Microfilm International.

Coulon, C. 1988. Senegal: The Development and Fragility of Semidemocracy. In *Democracy in Developing Societies. Vol. 2. Africa,* eds. L. Diamond et al. Boulder: Lynne Rienner.

Coulter, P. 1975. *Social Mobilization and Liberal Democracy. A Macroquantitative Analysis of Global and Regional Models*. Lexington, MA: Lexington Press.

Council for Mutual Economic Assistance (CMEA). Secretariat. 1979. *Statistical Yearbook of Member States of the Council for Mutual Economic Assistance*. London: IPC Industrial Press Ltd.

Countries of the World and Their Leaders Yearbook 1983. 1983. Detroit: Gale Research.

Countries of the World and Their Leaders Yearboolk 1989. 1989. Detroit: Gale Research Inc., Book Towers.

Cutright, P. 1963. National political development: Measurement and analysis. *American Sociological Review* 28 (2):253–264.

Cutright, P., and J.A. Wiley. 1970. *Modernization and Political Representation: 1927–1966*. New Brunswick, NJ: Rutgers University.

Cyprus. A Country Study. 1980. Washington, DC: U.S. Government Printing Office.

The Cyprus Problem. 1977. Nicosia: Printing Office of the Republic of Cyprus.

Dahl, R.A. 1956/1968. *A Preface to Democratic Theory*. Chicago: The University of Chicago Press.

———. 1971. *Polyarchy. Participation and Opposition*. New Haven and London: Yale University Press.

———. 1976. *Modern Political Analysis*. 3rd ed. Englewood Cliffs, NJ: Prentice-Hall.

———. 1982. *Dilemmas of Pluralist Democracy. Autonomy vs. Control*. New Haven: Yale University Press.

———. 1984. *Modern Political Analysis*. 4th ed. Englewood Cliffs, NJ: Prentice-Hall.

———. 1985. *A Preface to Economic Democracy*. Berkeley: University of California Press.

Delury, G.E., ed. 1987. *World Encyclopedia of Political Systems & Parties,* 2nd ed.. New York: Facts on File.

Deutsch, K.W. 1961. Social mobilization and political development. *The American Political Science Review* 60 (3):493–514.

Diamond, L. 1987. Sub-Saharan Africa. In *Democracy. A Worldwide Survey,* ed. R. Wesson New York: Praeger.

———. 1988a. Introduction: Roots of Failure, Seeds of Hope. In *Democracy in Developing Countries. Vol. 2 Africa,* eds. L. Diamond et al. Boulder: Lynne Rienner.

————. 1988b. Nigeria: Pluralism, Statism, and the Struggle for Democracy. In *Democracy in Developing Societies. Vol. 2. Africa,* eds. L. Diamond et al. Boulder: Lynne Rienner.

Diamond, L., J.J. Linz, and S.M. Lipset.1986. Developing and Sustaining Democratic Government in the Third World. Prepared for delivery at the 1986 Annual Meeting of the American Political Science Association, August 28–31, Washington, DC.

————, eds. 1988a. *Democracy in Developing Countries. Africa. Vol. 2; Asia. Vol. 3.* Boulder: Lynne Rienner.

————, eds. 1988b. Democracy in Developing Countries: Facilitating and Obstructing Factors. In *Freedom in the World. Political Rights & Civil Liberties 1987–1988,* ed. D. Gastil. New York: Freedom House.

Diamond, L., and D. Galvan. 1988. Sub-Saharan Africa. In *Democracy. World Survey 1987,* ed. R. Wesson. Boulder: Lynne Rienner.

Diskin, A. 1989. The Israeli general election of 1988. *Electoral Studies* 8 (1):75–85.

Dobzhansky, T., et al. 1977. *Evolution.* San Francisco: W.H. Freeman.

Doerner, W.R. 1989. USSR. Presiding over a new Soviet Congress, Gorbachev gets a glamorous lesson in democracy. *Time* 133 (23):18–19.

Dogan, M., and D. Pelassy. 1984. *How to Compare Nations. Strategies in Comparative Politics.* Chatham, NJ: Chatham House.

Dorner, P. 1972. *Land Reform and Economic Development.* Harmondsworth: Penguin.

Dror, Y. 1988. Visionary political leadership: On improving a risky. *International Political Science Review* 9 (1):7–22.

Du Toit, A. 1987. The South African House of Assembly election of 1987. *Electoral Studies* 6 (3):273–79.

Duverger, M. 1954. *Political Parties.* Trans. Barbara and Robert North. London: Methuen.

Dye, T.R., and H. Zeigler. 1988. Socialism and equality in cross-national perspective. *PS: Political Science & Politics* 21 (1):45–56.

Eckert, J. 1980. Lesotho's Land Tenure: An Analysis and Annotated Bibliography. Madison, WI: Land Tenure Center.

Eckstein, S., et al. 1978. *Land Reform in Latin America: Bolivia, Chile, Mexico, Peru and Venezuela.* Staff Working Paper No. 275. Washington, DC: The World Bank.

L'economie Camerounaise. 1977. Numéro spécial du bulletin de l'Afrique noire. Paris: Ediafric la documentation africaine.

The Economist Intelligence Unit (EIU). 1984–85. *Quarterly Review of Bahrain, Qatar, Oman, The Yemens.* Annual Supplement 1984; *Quarterly Economic Review of Algeria.* Annual Supplement 1985; *Quarterly Economic Review of Cameroon, CAR, Chad.* Annual Supplement 1985; *Quarterly Economic Review of Ghana, Sierra Leone, Liberia.* Annual Supplement 1985; *Quarterly Economic Review of Congo, Gabon, Equatorial Guinea.* Annual Supplement 1985; *Quarterly Eco-*

nomic Review of Indochina: Vietnam, Laos, Cambodia. Annual Supplement 1985; Quarterly Economic Review of Indonesia. Annual Supplement 1985; Quarterly Economic Review of Iran. Annual Suppelement 1984; Quarterly Economic Review of Ivory Coast. Annual Supplement 1985; Quarterly Economic Review of Kenya. Annual Supplement 1985; Quarterly Economic Review of Madagascar, Mauritius, Seychelles, Comoros. Annual Supplement 1985; Quarterly Economic Review of Rumania, Bulgaria, Albania. Annual Supplement 1985; The Economist Intelligence Review of Senegal, The Gambia, Guinea-Bissau, Cape Verde. Annual Supplement 1985; Quarterly Economic Review of Sri Lanka (Ceylon). Annual Supplement 1985; Quarterly Economic Review of Tanzania, Mosambique. Annual Supplement 1985; Quarterly Review of Thailand, Burma. Annual Supplement 1985. London: The Economist Publications.

Eibl-Eibesfeldt, I. 1984. Die Biologie des menschlichen Verhaltens. Grundriss der Humanethologie. München: Piper.

Electoral Studies. 1984–89.

Elson, J. 1989. China. Backed by the army and Deng Xiaoping, Beijing's hardliners win the edge over moderates in a closed-door struggle for power. Time 133 (23):12–16.

Ethiopia. A Country Study. 1981. Washington, DC: U.S. Government Printing Office.

The Europa Year Book. Years 1982–1988. London: Europa Publications Ltd.

Facts on File. Weekly World News Digest With Cumulative Index. 1977–89. New York: Facts on File.

FAO. 1953. Agricultural Studies No. 17. Communal Land Tenure. Prepared by Sir Gerard Clauson. Rome: FAO.

―――. 1966–1970. Report on the 1960 world census of agriculture; Vol 1: a-c. Rome: Food and Agriculture Organization of the United Nations.

―――. 1970a. Progress in Land Reform. Fifth Report. New York: United Nations.

―――. 1970b. Provisional Indicative World Plan for Agricultural Development. Rome: FAO.

―――. 1973–80. Report on the 1970 World Census of Agriculture. Census bulletins numbers 1–29. Rome: FAO.

―――. 1981. 1970 World Census of Agriculture. Analyses and international comparison of the results. Rome: FAO.

―――. 1981. Production Yearbook, 1981. Vol. 35. 1982. Rome: FAO.

―――. 1983–1986. Report on the 1980 World Census of Agriculture. Results by countries. Census bulletins numbers 3–26. Rome: FAO.

The Far East and Australasia. 1983–84, 1989. London: Europa Publications Ltd.

Far Eastern Economic Review. 1979. Asia 1979 Yearbook. Hong Kong: Far Eastern Economic Review Ltd.

Farrell, D.M. 1987. The Irish election of 1987. Electoral Studies 6 (2):160–63.

Fishel, J., ed. 1978. Parties and Elections in an Anti-Party Age. Bloomington: Indiana University Press.

Fitzgibbon, R.H. 1951. Measurement of Latin-American political phenomena: A statistical experiment. *The American Political Science Review* 45 (2):517–23.

———. 1956. A Statistical evaluation of Latin-American democracy. *The Western Political Quarterly* 9 (3):607–19.

Fitzgibbon, R., and K.F. Johnson. 1961. Measurement of Latin American political change. *The American Political Science Review* 55 (3):515–26.

Flanigan, W., and E. Fogelman. 1971. Patterns of Political Development and Democratization: A Quantitative Analysis. In *Macro-Quantitative Analysis. Conflict, Development, and Democratization,* eds. J.V. Gillespie and B.A. Nesvold. Beverly Hills: Sage Publications.

Flora, P. 1973. Historical Processes of Social Mobilization: Urbanization and Literacy, 1850–1965. In *Building States and Nations. Models and Data Resources, Vol. I,* eds. S.N. Eisenstadt and S. Rokkan. Beverly Hills: Sage Publications.

Fossedal, G. A. 1989. *The Democratic Imperative. Exporting the American Revolution.* New York: Basic Books.

Frank, A.D. 1970. *Kapitalism och underutveckling i Latinamerika.* Translation. DDR: Paul Dünnhaupt KG.

Friedrich, C.J. 1950. *Constitutional Government and Democracy,* Rev. ed.. Boston: Ginn.

The Gambia. Commonwealth Fact Sheet. 1977. London: Commonwealth Institute.

Gardner, H.S. 1988. *Comparative Economic Systems.* Chicago: Dreyden Press.

Garreton, M.A. 1986. The Political Evolution of the Chilean Military Regime and Problems in the Transition to Democracy. In *Transitions from Authoritarian Rule. Latin America,* eds. G. O'Donnell et al. Baltimore: John Hopkins University Press.

Gastil, R.D. 1985. The past, present, and future of democracy. *Journal of International Affairs* 38 (2):161–79.

———. 1988. *Freedom in the World. Political Rights & Civil Liberties 1987–1988.* New York: Freedom House.

Gebethner, S. 1986. Perception of the Electoral System and Democracy in Public Opinion according to the 1985 Survey in Poland. First draft. Paper presented at the Polish-Finnish Colloquim in political science, Cracow, Mogilany, September 8–14.

Gonidec, P.-F. 1971. *Les systems politiques Africains.* Paris: R. Pichon et R. Durand-Auzias.

Graham, N.A., and K.L. Edwards.1984. *The Caribbean Basin to the Year 2000. Demographic, Economic, and Resource-Use Trends in Seventeen Countries. A Compendium of Statistics and Projections.* Boulder: Westview Press.

Grawitz, M, and J. Leca, eds. 1985. *Traité de science politique. 2. Les régimes politiques contemporains.* Paris. Presses Universitaires de France.

Graz, L. 1982. *The Omanis. Sentinels of the Gulf.* London: Longman.

Greenwald, J. 1988. Chile. Fall of the Patriarch. Pinochet loses at the polls, but democracy is not the victor yet. *Time* 132 (16):16–17.

Grigulevich, I.R., and S.Ya. Kozlov, eds. 1979. *Ethnocultural Processes and National Problems in the Modern World.* Moscow: Progress Publishers.

Grofman, B., and A. Lijphart, eds. 1986. *Electoral Laws and their Political Consequences*. New York: Agathon Press.

Gupta, J.D. 1989. India: Democratic Becoming and Combined Development. In *Democracy in Developing Countries. Vol. 3. Asia*, eds. L. Diamond et al. Boulder: Lynne Rienner.

Gutterridge, W.F. 1975. *Military Regimes in Africa*. London: Methuen.

Haaland, G. 1986. Farming systems, land tenure and ecological balance in Bhutan. Paper presented at the Ninth European Conference on Modern South Asian Studies, July 9–12, Heidelberg.

Haberler, G. 1981. Capitalism, Socialism, and Democracy after 40 Years. In *Schumpeter's Vision. Capitalism, Socialism, and Democracy after 40 Years*, ed. A. Heertje. New York: Praeger.

Hadenius, A. 1987. Democracy and Capitalism. Collective Action Theory and Structural Analysis. Paper presented at the ECPR Joint Sessions of Workshops, Amsterdam.

Hamilton, W.D. 1964/1978. The Genetic Evolution of Social Behavior. In *The Sociobiology Debate*, ed. A.L. Caplan. New York: Harper & Row.

Hammond, T.T., ed. 1975. *The Anatomy of Communist Takeovers*. New Haven and London: Yale University Press.

Hannan, M.T., and G.R. Carroll. 1981. Dynamics of Formal Political Structure: An event-history analysis. *American Sociological Review* 46 (1):19–35.

Harkin, D.A. 1976. *Philippine Agrarian Reform in the Perspective of Three Years of Martial Law*. A Research Paper, No. 68. Madison: Land Tenure Center, University of Wisconsin.

Harrington, James. (1656) 1924. *James Harrington's Oceana*, ed. S.B. Liljegren. Heidelberg: Carl Winters Universitätsbuchandlung.

Hayward, F.M., ed. 1987. *Elections in Independent Africa*. Boulder: Westview Press.

Hayward, F.M., and S.N. Grovogui. 1987. Persistence and Change in Senegalese Electoral Processes. In *Elections in Independent Africa*, ed. F.M. Hayward. Boulder: Westview Press.

Hayward, F.M., and J.D. Kandeh. 1987. Perspectives on Twenty-Five Years of Elections in Sierra Leone. In *Elections in Independent Africa*, ed. F.M. Hayward. Boulder: Westview Press.

Heilbroner, R.L. 1981. Was Schumpeter Right? In *Schumpeter's Vision*, ed. A. Heertje. New York: Praeger.

Heine, J. 1989. Countdown for Pinochet: A Chilean diary. *PS: Political Science & Politics* 21 (2):242–47.

Helsingin Sanomat. 1984. Helsinki.

Herodotus. 1984. *The Histories*. Trans. A. de Sélincourt. Revised, with an introduction and notes by A.R. Burn. Harmondsworth: Penguin.

Hewitt, C. 1977. The Effect of political democracy and social democracy on equality in industrial societies: A cross-national comparison. *American Sociological Review* 42 (2):450–64.

Hine, D. 1987. The Italian General Election of 1987. *Electoral Studies* 6 (3):267–70.

Hobbes, T. 1651/1962. *Leviathan,* ed. Michael Oakeshott. New York: Collier.

Hodgson, O.C. 1984. *Collectivizacion de la organizacion cooperativa CCS.* Managua: Universidad Nacional Autonoma de Nicaragua, Facultad de sciencias economicas, Departemento de economia agricola. Paper.

Holm, J.D. 1988. Botswana: A Paternalistic Democracy. In *Democracy in Developing Countries. Vol. 2. Africa,* eds. L. Diamond et al. Boulder: Lynne Rienner.

Holt, R.T., and J.E. Turner, eds. 1970. *The Methodology of Comparative Research.* New York: Free Press.

Horowitz, Donald L. 1985. *Ethnic Groups in Conflict.* Berkeley: University of California Press.

Hove, S. 1987. The Maltese general election of 1987. *Electoral Studies* 6 (3):235–47.

Hung-Chao Thai. 1974. *Land Reform and Politics: A Comparative Analysis.* Berkeley: University of California Press.

Huntington, S.P. 1984. Will more countries become democratic? *Political Science Quarterly* 99 (2):193–218.

Hurst, C. E. 1979. *The Anatomy of Social Inequality.* St. Louis: The C.V. Mosby Company.

Ike, D.N. 1977. A comparison of communal, freehold and leasehold land tenure: A preliminary study in Ibadan and Ife, Western Nigeria. *American Journal of Economics and Sociology* 68 (2):187–95.

IMF Survey, February 19, 1979. Newly Independent Djibouti Handles Ethiopian Trade Through Railway, Port Facilities.

India. A Reference Annual 1979. 1979. New Delhi: Publications Division, Ministry of Information and Broadcasting, Government of India.

Inter-Parliamentary Union. 1977–88. *Chronicle of Parliamentary Elections and Developments.* Years 1976–88. Geneva: International Centre for Parliamentary Documentation.

Iraq. A Country Study. 1979. Washington, DC: U.S. Government Printing Office.

Isaacson, W. 1989. Eastern Europe. A freer, but messier, order. *Time* 134 (2):12–14.

Israel. A Country Study. 1978. Washington, DC: U.S. Government Printing Office.

Jackman, R.W. 1974. Political Democracy and Social Equality: A Comparative Analysis. *American Sociological Review* 39 (1):29–45.

Jackson, K.D. 1989. The Philippines: The Search for a Suitable Democratic Solution, 1946–1986. In *Democracy in Developing Countries,* eds. Diamond et al. Boulder: Lynne Rienner.

Japan Statistical Yearbook 1982. 1982. Japan: Statistics Bureau, Prime Minister's Office.

Jha, S.K. 1981. Some Reflections on the 1981 National Panchayat Elections in Nepal. In *Election for the National Panchayat in Nepal (1981).* Varanasi: Centre for the Study of Nepal, Department of Political Science, Banaras Hindu University.

Johnson, K.H. 1982. The 1980 Image-Index Survey of Latin American political democracy. *Latin American Research Review* 17 (3):193–201.

Jordan. A Country Study. 1980. Washington, D.C.: U.S. Government Printing Office.

Jupp, J. 1978. *Sri Lanka: Third World Democracy.* London: Frank Cass and Company Ltd.

Kaimowitz, D. 1980. The organization of agricultural production in the Syrian Arab Republic. *Land Tenure Center Newsletter.* Number 60:3–6.

Kaimowitz, D., and J.R. Thome. 1980. *Nicaragua's Agrarian Reform: The First Year (1979–80).* LTC No. 122. Madison: Land Tenure Center, University of Wisconsin.

Kamarck, A.M. 1971. *The Economics of African Development.* Rev. ed. New York: Praeger.

———. 1976. *The Tropics and Economic Development. A Provocative Inquiry into the Poverty of Nations.* A World Bank Publication. Baltimore: The World Bank, Johns Hopkins University Press.

Kanel, D. 1971. Land Tenure Reform As a Policy Issue in the Modernization of Traditional Societies. In *Land Reform in Latin America: Issues and Cases,* ed. P. Dorner. Madison: Land Tenure Center, University of Wisconsin.

Kaufman, R.R. 1986. Liberalization and Democratization in South America: Perspectives from the 1970s. In *Transitions from Authoritarian Rule. Comparative Perspectives,* eds. G. O'Donnell et al. Baltimore: Johns Hopkins University Press.

Kavanagh, D.A. 1987. Western Europe. In *Democracy. A Worldwide Survey,* ed. R. Wesson. New York: Praeger.

Keesing's Contemporary Archives (Keesing's Record of World Events). 1975–89. Bristols: Keesing's Publications.

Keesing's Research Report 6. Africa Independent. 1972. New York: Charles Scribner's.

Kelle, V., and M. Kovalson. 1973. *Historical Materialism. An Outline of Marxist Theory of Society.* Moscow: Progress Publishers.

Keren, M. 1988. Moses as a Visionary Realist. *International Political Science Review* 9 (1):71–84.

Khai Leong Ho. 1988. The 1986 Malaysia general election: An analysis of the campaign and results. *Asian Profile* 16 (3):209–23.

Khan, M.M., and H.M. Zafarullah. 1979. The 1979 parliamentary elections in Bangladesh. *Asian Survey* 19 (10):1023–36.

Kim, Chong Lim. 1971. Socio-economic development and political democracy in Japanese prefectures. *American Political Science Review* 65 (1):184–86.

Kirkpatrick, J.J. 1981. Democratic Elections, Democratic Government, and Democratic Theory. In *Democracy at the Polls. A Comparative Study of Competitive National Elections,* eds. D. Butler et al. Washington, DC: American Enterprise Institute for Public Policy Research.

Kitromilides, P.M. 1985. The Model of Athenian Democracy as a Political Ideal in the post-Classical Era. In *Democracy and Classical Culture*. Athens: Ministry of Culture and Sciences.

Klimburg, Max. 1966. *Afghanistan: Das Land im historischen Spannungsfeld Mittelasiens*. Wien und München: Austria Edition.

Kling, M. 1962. Towards a Theory of Power and Political Instability in Latin America. In *Political Change in Underdeveloped Countries. Nationalism and Communism*, ed. J.H. Kautsky. New York: John Wiley.

Kokole, O.H., and A.A. Mazrui. 1988. Uganda: The Dual Polity and the Plural Society. In *Democracy in Developing Societies. Vol. 2. Africa*, eds. L. Diamond et al. Boulder: Lynne Rienner.

Korea Annual 1983. 1983. 20th Annual Edition. Seoul: Yonhop.

Kornhauser, W. (1959)1965. *Politics of Mass Society*. London: Routledge & Kegan Paul.

Koste, T. 1969. "20 perhettä." In *Taloudellinen valta Suomessa*, eds. K. Bruun and A. Eskola. Helsinki: Tammi.

Kristensen, T. 1974. *Development in Rich and Poor Countries. A General Theory with Statistical Analyses*. New York: Praeger.

Kurian, G.T. 1982. *Encyclopedia of the Third World*. Rev. ed. London: Mansell Publishing Ltd.

―――. 1984. *The New Book of World Rankings*. New York: Facts On File Publications.

―――. 1987. *Encyclopedia of the Third World*, 3rd ed. New York: Facts on File.

Kyle, K. 1984. *Cyprus*. London: Minority Rights Group Ltd.

Lakanwal, A.G. 1980. Implementation of a democratic land reform in the democratic republic of Afghanistan. In *Agrarreformen und Agraraufbau in den Ländern Asiens, Afrikas und Lateinamerikas*. Leipzig: Institut für tropische Landwirtschaft, Karl-Marx-Universität, DDR.

Lakshman, W.D. 1980. *Income and Wealth Distribution in Sri Lanka: An Examination of Evidence Pertaining to Post-1960 Experience*. Tokyo: International Development Center of Japan.

Land Tenure Center. 1979. *Land Concentration in the Third World: Statistics on Number and Area of Farms Classified by Size of Farms*. Number 28. Training & Methods Series. Madison: University of Wisconsin.

LaPalombara, J., and M. Weiner. 1966. The Origin and Development of Political Parties. In. *Political Parties and Political Development*, eds. J. LaPalombara and M. Weiner. Princeton, NJ: Princeton University Press.

Latin America 1976. A Facts on File Publication. 1977. New York: Facts on File.

Latin American & Caribbean Review, 7th ed. 1986. Essex: World of Information.

Lavau, G. 1985. La démocratie. In Traité de science politique. 2. Les régimes politiques contemporaines, eds. M. Grawitz and J. Leca. Paris: Presses Universitaires de France.

Leduc, L. 1987. Performance of the Electoral System in Recent Canadian and British Elections: Advancing the Case for Electoral Reform. In *The Logic of Multiparty Systems*, ed. M.J. Holler. Dordrecht: Kluwer Academic Publishers.

Lerner, D. (1958)1968. *The Passing of Traditional Society. Modernizing the Middle East.* New York: Free Press.

Letterie, J.W., and A.F.M. Bertrand. 1982. Social Welfare, its economic and political determinants: A comparison of 115 countries. Paper presented at the IPSA World Congress, Rio de Janeiro.

Letterie, J.W., and R.A.G. van Puijenbroek. 1987. Determinants of Democracy: A cross-sectional analysis. Paper presented at the ECPR Joint Sessions of Workshops, Amsterdam, April 10–15.

Lewis, W.A. 1965. *Politics in West Africa.* London: Allen & Unwin.

Libya. A Country Study. 1979. Washington, DC: U.S. Government Printing Office.

Lijphart, A. 1968. *The Politics of Accommodation: Pluralism and Democracy in the Netherlands.* Berkley: University of California Press.

———. 1971. Comparative politics and the comparative method. *American Political Science Review* 65 (3):682–93.

———. 1975. The comparable-cases strategy in comparative research. *Comparative Political Studies* 8 (2):158–77.

———. 1980/1977. *Democracy in Plural Societies. A Comparative Exploration.* New Haven: Yale University Press.

———. 1984. *Democracies. Patterns of Majoritarian and Consensus Government in Twenty-One Countries.* New Haven: Yale University Press.

Lindblom, Charles E. 1977. *Politics and Markets. The World's Political-Economic Systems.* New York: Basic Books.

Linz, J.J. 1978. Crisis, Breakdown, and Reequilibration. In *The Breakdown of Democratic Regimes,* eds. J.J. Linz and A. Stephan. Baltimore: John Hopkins University Press.

———. 1982. The Transition from Authoritarian Regimes to Democratic Political Systems and the Problems of Consolidation of Political Democracy. IPSA Tokyo Round Table, March 29–April 1.

———. 1984. Democracy: Presidential or Parliamentary. Does it make a difference? First unfinished draft. Prepared for the Workshop on "Political Parties in the Southern Cone," sponsored by the World Peace Foundation at the Woodrow Wilson International Center for Scholars, Washington, D.C.

———. 1985. From Primordialism to Nationalism. In *New Nationalisms of the Developed West,* eds. E.A. Tiryakian and R. Rogowski. London: Allen & Unwin.

———. 1986. Political Crafting of Democratic Consolidation or Destruction: European and South American Comparisons. Paper prepared for "A Consultation: Reinforcing Democracy in the Americas", The Carter Center of Emory University with The Institute of the Americas, November 17–18, Atlanta.

Lipset, D. 1989. Papua New Guinea: The Melanesian Ethic and the Spirit of Capitalism. In *Democracy in Developing Countries,* eds. L. Diamond et al. Boulder: Lynne Rienner.

Lipset, S.M. 1959. Some social requisites of democracy: Economic development and political legitimacy. *The American Political Science Review* 53 (1):69–105.

————. 1960. *Political Man. The Social Bases of Politics.* New York: Doubleday; 1983, expanded and updated. London: Heinemann.

Lorenz, K. (1973)1977. *Peilin kääntöpuoli.* Trans. A. Leikola. Helsinki: Kustan- nusosakeyhtiö Tammi.

Lorenz, K.Z. 1982. *The Foundations of Ethology. The Principal Ideas and Dis- coveries in Animal Behavior.* Trans. K. Z. Lorenz and R.W. Kickert. New York: Simon and Schuster.

Lusignan, G. de. 1970. *L'Afrique Noire depuis l'Independence.* Paris: Fayard.

Länder der Erde. Politisch-ökonomisches Handbuch. 1981. 7. Auflage. Autoren- kollektiv. Köln: Pahl-Rugenstein Verlag.

Mabileau, A., and J. Meyriat, eds. 1967. *Decolonisation et regimes politiques en Afrique noire.* Paris: Armand Colin.

MacDougall, T.E. 1988. Yoshida Shigeru and the Japanese transition to liberal de- mocracy. *International Political Science Review* 9, (1):55–69.

McDowell, D. 1984. *Lebanon: A Conflict of Minorities.* Report No. 61. London: Minority Rights Group Ltd.

Machiavelli, Niccolo. (1513)1985. The Prince. In *The Portable Machiavelli.* ed. and trans. P. Bondanella and M. Musa. Harmondsworth: Penguin.

Mackie, T.T. 1983. General elections in Western nations during 1982. *European Journal of Political Research* 11:345–49.

————. 1984. General elections during 1983. *European Journal of Political Re- search* 12:335–42.

Mackie, T.T., and R. Rose. 1975. General elections in Western nations during 1974. *European Journal of Political Research,* Vol. 3, pp. 319–28.

————. 1978. General elections in Western nations during 1977. *European Journal of Political Research* 6:319–26.

————. 1979. General elections in Western nations during 1978. *European Journal of Political Research* 7:305–09.

————. 1980. General elections in Western nations during 1979. *European Journal of Political Research* 8:349–57.

————. 1981. General elections in Western nations during 1980. *European Journal of Political Research* 9:319–24.

————. 1982. General elections in Western nations during 1981. *European Journal of Political Research* 10:333–39.

————. General elections in Western nations during 1982. *European Journal of Political Research* 11:345–49.

————. 1984. General elections in Western nations during 1983. *European Journal of Political Research* 12:335–42.

Macridis, R.C. 1963. A Survey of the Field of Comparative Government. In *Com- parative Politics. A Reader,* eds. H. Eckstein and D. Apter. London: Free Press of Glencoe.

Makeig, D.C. 1987. South Asia. In *Democracy. A Worldwide Survey,* ed. R. Wes- son. New York: Praeger.

————. 1988. South Asia. In Democracy. *World Survey 1987,* ed. R. Wesson. Boulder: Lynne Rienner.

Marquette, J.F. 1974. Social change and political mobilization in the United States: 1870–1960. *American Political Science Review* 68 (3):1058–74.

Marsden, K., and T. Bélot. 1988. *Private Enterprise in Africa. Creating a Better Environment.* World Bank Discussion Papers. Washington, DC: The World Bank.

Martz, J.D. 1987. Latin America and the Caribbean. In *Democracy. A Worldwide Survey,* ed. R. Wesson. New York: Praeger.

Marxilais-leniniläinen valtio- ja oikeusoppi. 1980. Moskova: Kustannusliike Progress.

Mauritius. Commonwealth Fact Sheet. 1978. London: Commonwealth Institute.

May, J.D. 1973. *Of the Conditions and Measures of Democracy.* Morristown, NJ: General Learning Press.

Maynard Smith, J. 1964. Group selection and kin selection. *Nature* 201: 1145–47.

Mayr, E. 1982. *The Growth of Biological Thought. Diversity, Evolution, and Inheritance.* Cambridge, Massachusetts: Harvard University Press.

————. 1988. *Toward a New Philosophy of Biology. Observations of an Evolutionist.* Cambridge: Harvard University Press.

Merle, M., et al. 1968. *L'Afrique noire contemporaine.* Paris: Armand Colin.

Meyer, P. 1981. *Evolution und Gewalt. Ansätze zu einer biosoziologischen Synthese.* Berlin: Verlag Paul Parey.

Michels, R. 1962. *Political Parties.* Trans. Eden and Cedar Paul. New York: Collier Books.

The Middle East and North Africa 1983–84. 1983. London: Europa Publications Ltd.

Middle East Annual Review 1980. 1979. London: World of Information.

Milbrath, L.W., and M.L. Goel. 1977. *Political Participation,* 2nd ed. Chicago: Rand McNally College Publishing Co.

Mittwally, S.H. 1980. Sozialökonomische Aspekte der Nahrungsmittelproduktion in Ägypten. In *Agrarreformen und Agraraufbau in den Ländern Asien, Afrikas und Lateinamerikas.* Leipzig: V. Internationales Sommerseminar des Institutes für Tropische Landwirtschaft der Karl-Marx-Universität, DDR.

Mohnot, S.R. 1962. *Concentration of Economic Power in India.* Allahabad: Chaitanya Publishing House.

Montesquieu. (1748)1961. *De l'Esprit des lois.* Vols. I–II. Paris: Garnier Freres.

Morlino, L. 1986. Democratic Establishments: A Dimensional Analysis. In *Comparing New Democracies,* ed. E.A. Baloyra. Boulder: Westview Press.

Morocco. A Country Study. 1978. Washington, DC: U.S. Government Printing Office.

Morrison, D.G., et al. 1972. *Black Africa. A Comparative Handbook.* New York: Free Press.

Mulford, D.C. Some observations on the 1964 elections. *Asian Survey* 9 (2):13–17.

Muller, E.N. 1985. Dependent economic development, aid dependence on the United States, and democratic breakdown in the Third World. *International Studies Quarterly* 29 (4): 445–69.

Muller, E.N., et al. 1989. Land inequality and political violence. *American Political Science Review* 83 (2):577–95.

Needler, M.C. 1967. Political development and socioeconomic development: The Case of Latin America. *The American Political Science Review* 62 (3):889–97.

Nellis, J.R. 1986. *Public Enterprises in Sub-Saharan Africa*. World Bank Discussion Papers. Washington, DC: The World Bank.

Neubauer, D.E. 1967. Some conditions of democracy. *The American Political Science Review* 61 (4):1002–9.

Nie, N.H., S. Verba, and J.R. Petrocik, eds. 1976. *The Changing American Voter*. Cambridge: Harvard University Press.

Nohlen, D. 1978. *Wahlsysteme der Welt. Daten und Analysen. Ein Handbuch.* München: R. Piper.

———. 1984. Electoral Systems Between Science and Fiction. Historical and Theoretical Prerequisites for a Rational Debate, unpublished paper.

Nohlen, D., and F. Nuscheler, eds. 1982–83. *Handbuch der Dritten Welt*, Vols. 2–8. Hamburg: Hoffmann und Campe.

Nyrop, R.F., et al. 1977. *Area Handbook for the Persian Gulf States*. DAPam 550–185. Washington, DC: U.S. Government Printing Office.

O'Donnell, G. A. 1973. *Modernization and Bureaucratic-Authoritarianism. Studies in South American Politics*. Berkeley: Institute of International Studies, University of California.

O'Donnell, G., and P.C. Schmitter. 1986. *Transitions from Authoritarian Rule. Tentative Conclusions about Uncertain Democracies*. Baltimore: The John Hopkins University Press.

Oesterdiekhoff, P., and K. Wohlmuth, eds. 1983. *The Development Perspective of the Democratic Republic of Sudan*. München: Weltforum Verlag.

Olayide, S.O. 1980. Economics of agrarian reforms and rural development in Nigeria. In *Agrarreformen und Agraraufbau in den Ländern Asiens, Afrikas und Lateinamerikas*. Leipzig: V. Internationales Sommerseminar des Institutes für Tropische Landwirtschaft der Karl-Marx-Universität, DDR.

Olsen, E.A. 1987. Far East and Pacific. In *Democracy. A Worldwide Survey*, ed. R. Wesson. New York: Praeger.

Olsen, M.E. 1968. Multivariate Analysis of National Political Development. *American Sociological Review* 33 (5):699–712.

Ortega, E. 1982. Peasant Agriculture in Latin America. In *Cepal Review* Number 16:77–114. Santiago de Chili: United Nations, Economic Commission for Latin America.

Özbudun, E. 1989. Turkey: Crisis, Interruptions, and Reequilibrations. In *Democracy in Developing Countries. Volume Three. Asia*, eds. L. Diamond et al. Boulder: Lynne Rienner.

Pacific Islands Yearbook, 14th ed. 1981. Sydney: Pacific Publications.

Panizza, F.E. 1985. The Uruguayn Election of 1984. *Electoral Studies* 4:265–71.

Papua New Guinea. *Commonwealth Fact sheet.* 1976. London: Commonwealth Institute.

Papua New Guinea. *Its Economic Situation and Prospects for Development.* 1978. A World Bank Country Economic Report. Washington, D.C.: The World Bank.

Papua New Guinea Newsletter. 1977.

Pennock, J.R. 1979. *Democratic Political Theory.* Princeton, NJ: Princeton University Press.

Perry, C.S. 1980. Political Contestation in Nations: 1960, 1963, 1967, and 1970. *Journal of Political & Military Sociology* 8 (2):161–74.

Perry, G.E. 1987. North Africa and the Middle East. In *Democracy. A Worldwide Survey,* ed. R. Wesson. New York: Praeger.

Peru. *A Country Study.* 1981. Washington, DC: U.S. Government Printing Office.

Peterson, J.E. 1978. *Oman in the Twentieth Century. Political Foundations of an Emerging State.* London: Croom Helms.

Phadnis, U. 1989. Sri Lanka: Crises of Legitimacy and Integration. In *Democracy in Developing Countries. Volume Three. Asia, eds. L.* Diamond et al. Boulder: Lynne Rienner.

Plamenatz, J. 1978. *Democracy and Illusion.* London: Longman.

Polonsky, A. 1975. *The Little Dictators. The History of Eastern Europe since 1918.* London: Routledge.

Popper, K.R. (1945)1977. *The Open Society and its Enemies.* Vols. I–II. London: Routledge and Kegan Paul.

———. 1983. See *A Pocket Popper,* ed. David Miller. Oxford: Fontana.

Popper, K.R. (1957)1984. *The Poverty of Historicism.* London: Routledge & Kegan Paul.

Post, K.W.J. 1964. *The Nigerian Federal Election of 1959.* London: Oxford University Press.

Powell, D.E. 1987. Soviet Union and Eastern Europe. In *Democracy. A Worldwide Survey,* ed. R. Wesson. New York: Praeger.

———. 1988. The Soviet Sphere and Eastern Europe. In *Democracy. World Survey 1988,* ed. R. Wesson. Boulder: Lynne Rienner.

Powell, G.B.1982. *Contemporary Democracies. Participation, Stability, and Violence.* Cambridge: Harvard University Press.

Premdas, R.R. 1978. Papua New Guinea in 1977: Elections and relations with Indonesia. *Asian Survey* 18 (1):58–67.

Pride, R.A. 1970. *Origins of Democracy: A Cross-National Study of Mobilization, Party Systems, and Democratic Stability.* Beverly Hills: Sage Publications.

Pryor, F.L. 1988a. *Income Distribution and Economic Development in Masagascar. Some Historical Statistics.* World Bank Discussion Papers. Washington, DC: The World Bank.

———. 1988b. *Income Distribution and Economic Development in Malawi. Some*

Historical Statistics. World Bank Discussion Papers. Washington, DC: The World Bank.

Przeworski, A. 1986. Some Problems in the Study of Transition to Democracy. In *Transitions from Authoritarian Rule. Comparative Perspectives,* eds. G. O'Donnell et al. Baltimore: John Hopkins University Press.

Rabushka, A., and K.A. Shepsle. 1972. *Politics in Plural Societies. A Theory of Democratic Instability.* Columbus: Charles E. Merrill.

Rae, D.W. 1967. *The Political Consequences of Electoral Laws.* New Haven: Yale University Press. Rahman, M. 1988. Benazir Bhutto. The new challenge. *India Today* 13 (23):42–49.

Rajasekharaiah, A.M. 1987. Centre-State Relations in India: The Demand for State Autonomy. In *Parliamentary Democracy in India,* eds. V.B. Rao and B. Venkateswarlu. Delhi: Mittal Publications.

Regmi, M.C. 1976. *Landownership in Nepal.* Berkeley: University of California Press.

Report to the Pyithu Hluttaw on the Financial, Economic and Social Conditions of the Socialist Republic of the Union of Burma for 1978–79. 1978. Rangoon: Ministry of Planning and Finance.

Riddell, J.C., and C. Dickerman. 1986. *Country Profiles of Land Tenure: Africa 1986.* Madison: Land Tenure Center, University of Wisconsin.

Riggs, F.W. 1970. The Comparison of Whole Political Systems. In *The Methodology of Comparative Research,* eds. R.T. Holt and J.E. Turner. New York: Free Press.

Roberts, G. 1987. 'Representation of the People': Aspects of the Relationship between Electoral Systems and Party Systems in the Federal Republic of Germany and the United Kingdom. In *The Logic of Multiparty Systems,* ed. M.J. Holler. Dordrecht: Kluwer Academic Publishers.

Rose, L.E. 1989. Pakistan: Experiments with Democracy. In *Democracy in Developing Countries. Volume Three. Asia,* eds. L. Diamond et al. Boulder: Lynne Rienner.

Rousseau, J.-J. 1971. *The Social Contract and Discourse on the Origin and Foundation of Inequality among Mankind,* ed. L.G. Crocker. New York: Washington Square Press.

Rubinson, R., and D. Quinlan. 1977. Democracy and social inequality: A reanalysis. *American Sociological Review* 42 (4):611–23.

Ruse, M. 1987. *Taking Darwin Seriously.* Oxford: Basil Blackwell.

Russell, B. (1938)1975. *Power. A New Social Analysis.* London: George Allen.

Russett, B.M., et al. 1964. *World Handbook of Political and Social Indicators.* New Haven: Yale University Press.

Russett, B.M. 1968. Inequality and Instability. The Relation of Land Tenure to Politics. In *Readings in Modern Political Analysis,* eds. R.A. Dahl and D.E. Neubauer. Englewood Cliffs, NJ: Prentice-Hall.

———. (1965)1969. *Trends in World Politics.* London: Macmillan.

Rustow, D.A. 1963. New Horizons for Comparative Politics. In *Comparative Politics. A Reader*, eds. H. Eckstein and D. Apter. London: Free Press of Glencoe.

Rustow, D.A. 1967. *A World of Nations*. Washington: The Brookings Institution.

Sabine, G.H. 1966. *A History of Political Theory*, 3rd ed. London: George G. Harrap.

Sahnazarov, G. 1974. *Sosialistinen demokratia*. Translation. Moskova: Kustannusliike Edistys.

Samoff, J. 1987. Single-Party Competitive Elections in Tanzania. In *Elections in Independent Africa*, ed. F.M. Hayward. Boulder: Westview Press.

Samudavanija, C.-A. 1989. Thailand: A Stable Semi-Democracy. In *Democracy in Developing Countries. Volume Three. Asia*, eds. L. Diamond et al. Boulder: Lynne Rienner.

Sancton, T.A. 1987. Democracy's fragile flower spreads its roots. *Time* 130 (2):10–11.

Sancton, T.A. 1989. Poland. A humiliation for the party. *Time* 133 (25):21–23.

Sartori, G. 1969. What Democracy Is Not. In *Empirical Democratic Theory*, eds. C.F. Cnudde and D.E. Neubauer. Chicago: Markham.

———. 1976. *Parties and Party Systems. A Framework for Analysis. Vol. I*. London: Cambridge University Press.

———. 1987. *The Theory of Democracy Revised*. Chatham, NJ: Chatham House Publishers.

Schatz, S.P. 1977. *Nigerian Capitalism*. Berkeley: University of California Press.

Schlesinger, A. 1988. Leadership and Democracy. *Dialogue* Number 79:20–25.

Schumpeter, J.A. 1947. *Capitalism, Socialism, and Democracy*, 2nd ed. New York: Harper.

Schwartz, F.A.O. 1965. *Nigeria: The Tribes, the Nation, or the Race. The Politics of Independence*. Cambridge: M.I.T. Press.

Schweinitz, K. de. 1964. *Industrialization and Democracy*. New York: Free Press of Glencoe.

Scott, I., and R. Molteno. 1969. The Zambia general elections. *Africa* Report 14 (1):42–47.

Seligson, M.A. 1987. Development, Democratization, and Decay: Central America at the Crossroads. In *Authoritarians and Democrats. Regime Transition in Latin America*, eds. J. H. Malloy and M.A. Seligson. Pittsburgh: University of Pittsburgh Press.

Seligson, M.A. 1988. Political Culture and Democratization in Latin America. Paper presented at the IPSA World Congress, Washington.

Seton-Watson, H. 1956. *The East European Revolution*. New York: Praeger.

Shah, S. 1984. Bhutan economy has been slow to modernize, but development plan envisages rapid growth. *IMF Survey*, February 20.

Shand, R.T. 1980. *The Island States of the Pacific and Indian Oceans: Anatomy of Development*. Development Studies Centre Monograph no. 23. Canberra: The Australian National University.

Short, R.P. 1984. The Role of Public Enterprises: An International Statistical Comparison. In *Public Enterprise in Mixed Economies. Some Macroeconomic Aspects.* eds. R.H. Floyd et al., Washington, DC: International Monetary Fund.

Shoup, P.S. 1981. *The East European and Soviet Data Handbook: Political, Social, and Developmental Indicators, 1945–1975.* New York: Columbia University Press.

Shrestha, J.B. 1982. Industrial Development of Nepal. In *Occasional Papers. Series Four.* Varanasi: Centre for the Study of Nepal, Department of Political Science, Banaras Hindu University.

Siegfried, A. 1913. *Table politique de la France de l'ouest sous la troisieme republique.* Paris: Librairie Armand Colin.

Simmons, A.S. 1982. *Modern Mauritius. The Politics of Decolonization.* Bloomington: Indiana University Press.

Singh, U. 1986. Ethnic Conflicts in Pakistan: Sind as A Factor in Pakistani Politics. In *Domestic Conflicts in South Asia. Volume 2,* eds. U. Phadnis et al. New Delhi: South Asian Publishers.

Sithole, M. 1988. Zimbabwe: In Search of a Stable Democracy. In *Democracy in Developing Societies. Vol. 2. Africa,* eds. L. Diamond et al. Boulder: Lynne Rienner.

Sklar, R.L., and C.S. Whitaker. 1964. Nigeria. In *Political Parties and National Integration in Tropical Africa,* eds. J.S. Coleman and C.R. Rosberg. Berkley: University of California Press.

Slack, W.H. 1981. *The Grim Science. The Struggle for Power.* Port Washington, NY: Kennikot Press.

Smith, A.K. 1969. Socio-economic development and political democracy: A causal analysis. *Midwest Journal of Political Science* 30 (1):95–125.

Smith, T.L. 1968. Introduction: A General View of Agrarian Reform Proposals and Programs in Latin America. In *Agrarian Reform in Latin America,* ed. T.L. Smith. New York: Knopf.

Smolowe, Jill. 1989. Trading Places. *Time* 134 (18): 32–34.

Soares, G.A.D. 1985. Economic Development and Democracy: A Specification Effect. University of Florida, manuscript.

————. 1987. Economic Development and Democracy in Latin America. Revised version of a paper presented to the Conference on Liberty, Democracy and Political Change. Philadelphia, Nov. 30–Dec. 2.

————. 1988. Economic Development and Democracy in Latin America. Paper presented at the IPSA World Congress, Washington.

Social Indicators of Development 1988. 1988. A World Bank Publication. Baltimore: Johns Hopkins University Press.

South. 1985. South Special Project, Education.

The Soviet Political Sciences Association. 1979. *Political Theory and Political Practice.* Moscow: USSR Academy of Sciences.

————. 1985. *The Present-Day State: Theory and Practice.* Moscow: USSR Academy of Sciences.

Spoormans, Huub. 1987. Pluralism or Class Struggle? On the paradoxes of socio-economic development and democratization. Paper presented at the ECPR Joint Sessions of Workshops, Amsterdam, April 10–15.

The Statesman's Year Book. Years 1980–81 and 1982–83. London: Macmillan.

Statistical Abstract of Iceland. 1967. Statistics of Iceland. II, 40. Reykjavik.

Statistical Abstract of Latin America. Vol. 21. 1981. ed. James W. Wilkie. Los Angeles: UCLA Latin American Center.

Statistical Abstract of Latin America. Vol. 23. 1984. ed. James W. Wilkie. Los Angeles: UCLA Latin American Center.

Statistical Abstract of the United States 1987. 1986. Washington, D.C.: U.S. Bureau of Census.

Statistical Outline of India 1982. 1982. Bombay: Tata Services Ltd.

Statistisches Jahrbuch der Schweiz 1982. 1982. Herausgegeben vom Bundesamt für Statistik. Basel: Birkhuser Verlag.

Statistisk årsbok för Sverige 1982/83. 1982. Stockholm: Sveriges officiella statistik, Statistiska centralbureau.

Stepan, A. 1978. *The State and Society. Peru in Comparative Perspective.* Princeton, NJ: Princeton University Press.

———. 1986. Paths toward Redemocratization: Theoretical and Comparative Considerations. In *Transitions from Authoritarian Rule. Comparative Perspectives*, eds. G. O'Donnell et al. Baltimore: John Hopkins University Press.

Stevens, R.P. 1966. The New Republic of Botswana. *Africa Report* 11 (7):15–20.

Stuart-Fox, M. 1980. The initial failure of agricultural cooperativization in Laos. *Asia Quarterly a Journal from Europe* 1980/4:273–298.

Sugarragtschaa, Z. 1980. Die sozialistische Umgestaltung der Landwirtschaft in der Mongolischen Volksrepublik. In *Agrarreformen und Agraraufbau in den Ländern Asiens, Afrikas und Lateinamerikas*. Leipzig: V. Internationales Sommerseminar des Institutes für Tropische Landwirtschaft der Karl-Marx-Universitt, DDR.

Sukhwal, B.L. 1985. *Modern Political Geography of India.* New Delhi: Sterling Publishers Private Ltd.

Sung-Joo Han. 1989. South Korea: Politics in Transition. In *Democracy in Developing Countries*, eds. L. Diamond et al. Boulder: Lynne Rienner.

Suryanarayan, V. 1986. Ethnic Conflict in Sri Lanka. In *Domestic Conflicts in South Asia. Volume 2. Economic and Ethnic Dimensions*, eds. U. Phadnis et al. New Delhi: South Asian Publishers.

Sveriges officiella statistik. Allmänna valen 1988. Del 1. Riksdagsvalet den 18 september 1988. 1989. Stockholm: Statistiska centralbyrån.

Syria. A Country Study. 1979. Washington, DC: U.S. Government Printing Office.

Taagepera, R., and M.S. Shugart. 1989. Designing Electoral Systems. *Electoral Studies* 8 (1):49–58.

Tanzania. A Country Study. 1978. Washington, DC: U.S. Government Printing Office.

Thailand. A Country Study. 1981. Washington, DC: U.S. Government Printing Office.

Thome, J.R., and D. Kaimowitz. 1985. *A Half-Decade of Agrarian Reform in Nicaragua*. Madison: Land Tenure Center, University of Wisconsin.

Time. 1986–89. New York.

Tocqueville, Alexis de. 1963. *Democracy in America*, Vols. I–II. New York: Knopf.

Topornin, B., and E. Machulsky. 1974. *Socialism and Democracy. A Reply to Opportunists*. Moscow: Progress Publishers.

Tornaritis, C.G. 1977. *Cyprus and its Constitutional and Other Legal Problems*. Nicosia: Proodos Ltd.

Tunisia. A Country Study. 1979. Washington, DC: U.S. Government Printing Office.

Unesco. 1982–85. *Statistical Yearbook*. Years 1982–86. Paris: Unesco.

Ungar, S.J. 1989. *Africa. People and Politics of an Emerging Continent*. New York: Simon & Schuster.

United Nations. 1980–88. *Demographic Yearbook*. 1979–86. New York: United Nations.

United Nations. 1982. *Yearbook of National Accounts Statistics 1980*. New York: United Nations.

U.S. Bureau of the Census. 1987. *Statistical Abstract of the United States 1988*. Washington, DC

Van den Berghe, P.L. 1981. *The Ethnic Phenomenon*. New York: Elsevier

Van Dooren, P.J. 1977. *The Cooperative Approach in Implementing Land Reform Programs: The Tunisian and Egyptian Experiences*. LTC No. 113. Madison: Land Tenure Center, University of Wisconsin.

Vanhanen, T. 1968. *Puolueet ja pluralismi*. With English Summary *Parties and Pluralism*. Porvoo: Werner Söderström Osakeyhtiö.

————. 1971. *Dependence of Power on Resources. A Comparative Study of 114 States in the 1960's*. Institute of Social Science Publications. Jyväskylä: University of Jyväskylä.

————. 1975. *Political and Social Structures. Part 1: American Countries 1850–1973*. Institute of Political Science, Research Reports No. 38. Tampere: University of Tampere,

————. 1977. *Political and Social Structures. Asian and Australasian Countries 1850–1975*. Ann Arbor: Published for Centre for the Study of Developing Societies, Delhi, by University Microfilms International.

————. 1979. *Power and the Means of Power. A Study of 119 Asian, European, American, and African States, 1850–1975*. Ann Arbor: Published for Centre for the Study of Developing Societies, Delhi, by University Microfilms International.

————. 1981. *Military Rule and Defense Expenditures: A Study of 119 States, 1850–1975*. Hong Kong: Asian Research Service.

————. 1982. *The Roots of Democracy: India Compared with its Neighbours*. Hong Kong: Asian Research Service.

————. 1984. *The Emergence of Democracy. A Comparative Study of 119 States, 1850–1979*. Commentationes Scientiarum Socialium 24 1984. Helsinki: The Finnish Society of Sciences and Letters.

————. 1985. The State and Prospects of Democracy in the 1980s. Paper presented at the IPSA World Congress, Paris.

————. 1987. What Kind of Electoral System for Plural Societies? India as an Example. In *The Logic of Multiparty Systems,* ed. M.J. Holler. Dordrecht: Martinus Nijhoff Publishers.

Von der Mehden, F.R. 1969. *Politics of the Developing Nations.* Englewood Cliffs, NJ: Prentice.-Hall

Die Wahl der Parlamente und anderer Staatsorgane. Ein Handbuch. Band II: Afrika. Politische Organisation und Repräsentation in Afrika. 1978. Von Franz Nuscheler und Klaus Ziemer. Berlin: Walter de Gruyter.

Wallerstein, I. 1982. The Rise and Future Demise of the World Capitalist System: Concepts for Comparative Analysis. In *Toward a Just World Order, Volume 1,* eds. R. Falk et al. Boulder: Westview Press.

Ward, M. 1971. *The Role of Investment in the Development of Fiji.* Cambridge: University Press.

Warnapala, W.A.W. 1980. Sri Lanka's New Constitution. *Asian Survey* 20 (9):914–30.

Wattenberg, M.P. 1987. North America. In *Democracy. A Worldwide Survey,* ed. R. Wesson. New York: Praeger.

Weiner, M. 1983. *India at the Polls, 1980. A Study of the Parliamentary Elections.* Washington, DC: American Enterprise Institute for Public Policy Research.

Wesson, R., ed. 1987. *Democracy. A Worldwide Survey.* New York: Praeger.

———— ed. 1988. *Democracy. World Survey 1987.* Boulder: Lynne Rienner.

West, D. 1988. Ethnic Strife in Paradise - Fiji 1987. *Conflict* 8:217–35.

Whitehead, L. 1986. International Aspects of Democratization. In *Transitions from Authoritarian Rule. Comparative Perspectives,* eds. G. O'Donnell et al. Baltimore: John Hopkins University Press.

Wiarda, H.J. 1985. Democratic Development in the Dominican Republic: The Difficult Legacy. Paper presented at the Conference on Democracy in Developing Nations, Hoover Institution, Stanford University, December.

Wilson, E.O. 1975. *Sociobiology. The New Synthesis.* Cambridge: Belknap Press of Harvard University Press.

————. 1978. *On Human Nature.* Cambridge: Harvard University Press.

Wilson, J.Q. 1987. *American Government.* Brief edition. Lexington: D.C. Heath.

Wilson, R.K., and C.S. Woods. 1982. *Patterns of World Economic Development.* Melbourne: Longman Sorrett.

Wind, J. 1984. Sociobiology and the Human Sciences. An Introduction. In *Essays in Human Sociobiology,* ed. J. Wind. London: Academic Press.

Winham, G.R. 1970. Political development and Lerner's theory: Further test of a causal model. *American Political Science Review* 64 (3):810–18.

Wittfogel, K.A. 1963/1957. *Oriental Despotism. A Comparative Study of Total Power.* New Haven: Yale University Press.

Wolf-Phillips, L., et al. 1980. Why 'Third World'? Third World Foundation Monograph 7. London: Third World Foundation.

World Atlas of Agriculture. Volume 1. Europe, U.S.S.R., Asia Minor. 1969. Volume 2. Asia and Oceania. 1973. Volume 3. Americas. 1970. Volume 4. Africa. 1976. ed. Committee for the World Atlas of Agriculture. Novara: Instituto Geografico De Agostini.

World Bank. 1980. *World Tables. The Second Edition (1980) from the Data Files of the World Bank.* Baltimore: John Hopkins University Press.

World Development Report. Years 1982–86. New York: Published for the World Bank Oxford University Press.

World Elections on File. Vols. 1–2. 1987. New York: Facts on File.

World in Figures. 1987. Editorial information compiled by the Economist. London: Holder and Stoughton.

World Resources 1986. 1986. A Report by The World Resources Institute and The International Institute for Environment and Development. New York: Basic Books.

Worldmark Encyclopedia of the Nations. Vols. 1–4, 6th ed. 1984. New York: Worldmark Press.

Zaman, M.A. 1973. *Evaluation of Land Reform in Nepal.* Kathmandu: Ministry of Land Reforms, His Majesty's Government of Nepal.

Zasloff, J.J. 1981. *The Economy of the New Laos. Part II: Plans and Performance.* American Universities Field Staff, Reports. 1981/No. 45. Asia. Hanover, NH.

Zollberg, A.R. 1985. L'influence des facteurs "externes" sur l'ordre politique interne. In *Traité de science politique. Vol. 1,* eds. M. Grawitz and J. Leca. Paris: Presses Universitaires de France.

Index

315

About the Author

Tatu Vanhanen, doctor of social sciences from the University of Tampere (1968), is an associate professor of political science at the University of Tampere, Finland. Among his earlier works are *Power and the Means of Power. A Study of 119 Asian, European, American, and African States, 1850–1975* (1979), *The Roots of Democracy: India Compared with its Neighbours* (1982), and *The Emergence of Democracy. A Comparative Study of 119 States, 1850–1979* (1984).